Think *First Certificate*

Jon Naunton

C000150225

We are grateful to the following for permission to reproduce copyright material:

Authors' Agents for an adapted version of 'Cinderella Re-examined' by Maeve Binchy from *Repunzel's Revenge - Fairytales for Feminists* pubd. Attic Press, Dublin and a slightly adapted extract from an article by Maeve Binchy from *Cosmopolitan* Magazine; British Airways Holidays for extracts from their *Florida Brochure 1995*; BBC Worldwide Ltd for extracts from *Lingo - How to Learn a Language* by Terry Doyle and Paul Meara; Authors' Agents on behalf of the Chichester Partnership for an extract from *Rebecca* by Daphne du Maurier (Longman Fiction 1993). Reproduced with permission of Curtis Brown Ltd. Copyright © 1938 by Daphne du Maurier Browning; Victor Gollancz Ltd/Viking Penguin, a division of Penguin Books USA Inc for an extract from *The Outsiders* by S E Hinton. Copyright © 1967 by S E Hinton; Greenpeace for extracts from their leaflet pubd. 1992; Guerba Expeditions Ltd for a slightly adapted extract from 'West African Train Holiday' in *Guerba Expeditions 1987/8 Travel Brochure* pp11-12; Hodder Headline plc/Ballantine (Div. of Random House Inc) for 'Call me Arnold' by Studs Terkel from *American Dreams: Lost and Found* (1980); Independent Television Publications Ltd for the article 'Letters of Love' by Doris Stokes in Chat Magazine 24.1.87; News Group Newspapers Ltd for extracts from the article 'The Long and Wounding Road' from *News of the World* Magazine 21.11.93; Random House UK Ltd on behalf of Mrs Laura Huxley for an extract from *Brave New World* by Aldous Huxley (abridged and simplified by H A Cartledge pubd. Longman 1973); The Society of Authors on behalf of the Bernard Shaw Estate for extracts from *Pygmalion*; W H Smith Retail for adapted extracts from the article 'Courage Beyond the Call' from *Bookcase* September/October 1994 p7; Solo Syndication & Literary Agency Ltd for adapted articles 'Blind Man who tried to rob Bank' from the *Evening Standard* 14.11.85 and 'A Life of Crime' from *Mail on Sunday*; the Author, Polly Toynbee for an adaptation of her article 'Jungle Warefare' in *The Guardian* 19.12.87.

We are grateful to the following for permission to reproduce copyright material:

Ace Photo agency for 72,99,108,129t,168,169, Action Plus for 23tr,24tm,167l,167r, All Action/Suzan Moore for 196bl, All Sport/Pascal Rondeau for 26bl/Alain Patrice for 26br /Stephen Dunn for 27, Art Directors for 80,168,169, Aspect Picture library for 64, Bantam Press for 29t, Barnaby's Picture Library for 35, Bridgeman Art Library/Birmingham City Museum and Art for 136/Giraudon for 137/Guildhall Library for 36/37/Nasjonal Galleriet,Oslo for 103, Bruce Coleman Ltd for 40l, Colorific/Enrico Ferorelli for 23tl/Penny Tweedie for 23br, Comstock for 23bl, The Enviromental Picture library for 82, Format/Brenda Prince for 72/Pam Isherwood for 72/Sarita Sharma for 106bl, Impact Visuals for 170l, Greenpeace for 83, Greg Evans for 40r, Hulton Deutsch for 26t,126l, Hutchison Library for 11bl,99, Image bank for 11tl, J Allan Cash Ltd for 60,65,133,140bl, Kobal Collection for 106b,166r, Liam White Photography for 74r, London Features/Steve Rapport for 150, Longman/Alan Spain for 178/Gareth Boden for 18,34,73, Mansell Collection for 160, Magnum for 170r, Mary Evans Picture Library for 140tr,160, Mirror Syndication/Bulls Press for 69, Penguin for 28mb,28b, National Motor Museum for 26l,86r, Network/Laurie Sparham for 106tl, Pictor for 196tr, Popperfoto for 106cl,172r, Punch for 110,144,145, Range/Bettman archive for 160, Rex Features for 41,86m, 94,161,172b,173/Images for 172l/Clive Dixon for 162t, Robert Harding Picture Library for 72,80,128,129b,165,166, 169, Ronald Grant Archive for 140br, 166l, Royal Geographical Society for 68, Telegraph Colour Library for 60,80,92,126r,127m,196l, The Press Association for 162b, Tony Stone Images for 24mr,24tl,24br,24ml, 24bm,24m,80, 99,127b,132,168, 169, 196r, Topham Picturepoint for 82, Viewfinder for 106cr, Warner books for 28t, Wet N' Wild for 168, Zefa for 10, 86l,106tr.

We have been unable to trace the copyright holder of the photograph on page 122 and 134 and would be grateful for any information that would enable us to do so.

Picture Researcher: Veena Holkar.

Commissioned photography by Jaqui Rivers.

Designed by Sue Dorrington.

Illustrated by Gary Benfield, David Browne, Gino D'Achille, Jo Dennis, Colin Elgie, 1-11 Line Art, Barbara Lofthouse, Pantelis, Tony Richards, Julie Scott, Sally Taylor, Andy Walker, Celia Witchard.

Addison Wesley Longman Limited
Edinburgh Gate, Harlow,
Essex CM20 2JE England
and Associated Companies throughout the world.

© Longman Group Limited 1989, 1993
This edition © Addison Wesley Longman Limited 1996
All rights reserved; no part of this publication may be reproduced, stored in a retrieval system, or transmitted in any form or by any means electronic, mechanical, photocopying, recording or otherwise, without the prior written permission of the Publishers.

First published 1989
Second impression 1996
New edition (with Reviser Guide) first published 1993
This edition first published 1996

Set in 10/12pt New Century Schoolbook

Printed in Spain by Graficas Estella

ISBN 0 582 27628 4

Author Acknowledgements

The author would like to express thanks and appreciation to:

- the editorial, design and production team, especially Judith King, Dave Francis, Jennifer Coles, John Newton, Donna Wright and Yolanda Durham.
- L.G. Alexander, Michael Swan, J.B. Heaton, N.D. Turton, Stuart Redman, Rob Ellis and Richard Acklam, whose works informed and helped in the preparation of this material.
- the readers and reporters whose comments and criticisms proved invaluable in the development of this new edition, in particular Heather Buchanan, Jain Cook, Mark Foley, Bob Obee, Tim Oswald, Gina Pagoulatou-Vlachou, Neide Silve and David Vaughan.

Reviser Guide p186   Grammar Reference p202

About the Examination

The *First Certificate* examination tests all aspects of your English through five "papers". Papers have equal importance.

Paper 1 Reading   1 hour 15 minutes
Paper 2 Writing   1 hour 30 minutes
Paper 3 Use of English   1 hour 15 minutes
Paper 4 Listening   about 40 minutes
Paper 5 Speaking   about 15 minutes.

Paper 1 READING

This tests your reading and how well you can
- understand gist (general meaning).
- guess meaning and make intelligent assumptions
- find specific information
- identify the main points, style or purpose of a text.

The paper is divided into four parts.

Part 1 MATCHING

You match headings to paragraphs. See page 36-37.

Part 2 MULTIPLE CHOICE

You choose the best answer to a question from four choices A,B,C or D. See page 50-51.

Part 3 GAPPED TEXT

You match sentences to gaps within a text. See page 27.

Part 4 MULTIPLE MATCHING

You search for information in a number of short texts. See page 28.

Paper 2 WRITING

You answer two questions each between 120 and 180 words . Part 1 consists of one compulsory question, i.e. you <u>must</u> answer it. Part 2 gives you a choice of four questions from which you must choose one.

Question 1: A letter based around a situation which is presented through one or more short texts. See page 67.

Part 1

For all other questions you are given two or three lines of instructions.

Part 2

Question 2: An article, report or a letter. See pages 25,45,91.
Question 3: a discursive (discussion), descriptive or narrative composition (i.e. a story.) See pages 123,129,155.
Question 4: As question 2 or 3.
Question 5: A composition, article, report or letter based around a book you have read. See pages 59,125.

Paper 3 USE OF ENGLISH

This tests grammar and vocabulary. It is divided into five parts.

Part 1 MULTIPLE CHOICE CLOZE (GAP FILLING)

A text containing 15 gaps is followed by 15 multiple choice questions (i.e. choose A,B,C or D). This focuses on vocabulary. See page 15.

Part 2 OPEN CLOZE

A passage with 15 gaps to be completed. This focuses on grammar and vocabulary. See page 25.

Part 3 KEY WORD TRANSFORMATION

You are given a sentence which you have to re-write using a "key word" and other words. See page 13.

Part 4 ERROR CORRECTION. 15 QUESTIONS

You decide which lines of a text are correct. Other lines contain an extra and unnecessary word which you identify. See page 61.

Part 5 WORD FORMATION. 10 QUESTIONS

You are given a text with ten gaps. Each gap has the base form of a word which you change into an appropriate form to provide the missing word. See page 38.

Paper 4 LISTENING

This paper is divided into four parts.

PART 1 UNRELATED EXTRACTS

Eight short unrelated extracts with multiple choice questions. See page 8.

Part 2 NOTE-TAKING OR BLANK FILLING

You listen to a text and complete a set of notes. See page 35.

Part 3 RELATED EXTRACTS

Five short extracts related to a topic accompanied by a matching exercise. See page 20.

Part 4 EXTENDED TEXT

A longer text, either a monologue or text involving interacting speakers. You answer questions where there are two or three possible choices, e.g. True/False, three option multiple choice (A,B,C), which speaker said what. See page 54.

Paper 5 SPEAKING

For this part of the examination candidates are usuallly tested in pairs, in other words, two candidates take the examination together. (Of course they are assessed individually!)

There are two examiners: the interlocutor who conducts the test and asks questions, and the assessor who also gives marks but does not join in the conversation. Candidates are marked on grammar and vocabulary, fluency and pronunciation. The assessor will take into account how well candidates interact e.g. take turns to speak, negotiate etc.

The test is divided into four parts. Look at the cartoons and notes.

Part ONE: PERSONAL INFORMATION

The interlocutor asks you a few personal questions to help you relax.

Part TWO: TALKING ABOUT PHOTOGRAPHS

Each candidate is given two photographs around the same theme to talk about and compare.
Each candidate has a different theme. For example candidate A's photographs could show two different kinds of concerts, pop and classical; candidate B's photographs show two different jobs.

Candidates take it in turn to speak but there will usually be an opportunity to comment on the other candidate's photographs.

Part THREE: INTERACTIVE TASK

Together, candidates carry out a task based around pictures or other prompts e.g. a diagram, plan, pictures of objects, photographs. This could involve planning, prioritising, problem solving, speculating etc.

Part FOUR: EXTENSION

The interlocutor joins in and asks questions to develop the discussion from part three.

For a full example of the interview see page 195 in the Reviser Guide.

BREAKING THE ICE

FIRST THOUGHTS

1 When we first meet new people it is important to "break the ice". What do you think this means?

2 Break the ice by finding out about your classmates.

Find someone in your class who:

- lives near you.
- is going to have a birthday soon.
- plays a musical instrument.
- is good at sport.
- watched the same TV programmes as you last night.
- has an interesting hobby.
- has the same taste in music.
- has travelled a lot.

LISTENING

English overheard

In **Part 1** of **Paper 4 (Listening)** you will hear a number of short unrelated pieces and be asked to answer a multiple-choice question based around each one. Listen to the situations and choose the best answer: **A**, **B** or **C**.

> **Examination advice:** Always make sure that you read the questions first so that you know what you have to listen out for. This will help you to listen selectively. Don't worry if you can't understand everything that is said.

1 You are outside a hotel room where some businessmen are listening to a seminar. The speaker is talking about
  A how to be a successful salesman.
  B how to impress strangers.
  C self-confidence.

2 Two examiners are discussing a candidate. They decide to
  A pass the candidate.
  B fail the candidate.
  C discuss him again.

3 The principal of a language school is talking to a student. From what the principal says it is clear that the student
  A is ill.
  B can't change her course.
  C has to pay an extra fee.

4 You overhear this exchange in a travel agent's. The two women
  A are old colleagues.
  B are a teacher and old student.
  C are friends who have lost touch.

5 You are waiting to use the phone in a students' residence when you hear a young woman talking to her mother. The young woman
  A is working hard.
  B wants to end the conversation.
  C is having problems at the college.

6 Listen to this landlady talking to a lodger. She says that lodgers
  A can't use the kitchen.
  B are allowed to make outside phone calls.
  C can't prepare complicated meals.

SPEAKING

In **Part 1** of **Paper 5 (Speaking)** an examiner will ask you questions to encourage you to speak about yourself. This will help you to "warm up" and feel more comfortable.

1 🔲 Listen to the conversation between Adriana, a candidate from Italy, and an examiner and find out

- where she comes from exactly.
- her occupation.
- her plans.

- how she spends her free time.
- why English is important for her.

2 🔲 Listen again, and complete the conversation with the examiner's questions.

EXAMINER: OK Jean-Luc. I'll come back to you in a minute. Now it's Adriana, isn't it?
ADRIANA: That's right.
EXAMINER: So, **(1)** ....?
ADRIANA: From Italy.
EXAMINER: I see. **(2)** ....?
ADRIANA: From near Florence.
EXAMINER: Mm, lovely and **(3)** ....?
ADRIANA: I'm a student. I'm finishing high school.
EXAMINER: Huh, huh. And **(4)** ....?
ADRIANA: Well, I'd like to study archaeology.
EXAMINER: Really? **(5)** ....?
ADRIANA: Well, we live quite near some, erm ancient ruins and ... I have always been fascinated by them.
EXAMINER: I see... And erm... tell me **(6)**

............?
ADRIANA: Studying and meeting friends. Oh, and playing basketball.
EXAMINER: **(7)** ....?
ADRIANA: Just for fun.. Nothing serious.
EXAMINER: Oh really. **(8)** ....?
ADRIANA: For four years now.
EXAMINER: Right... And **(9)** ....?
ADRIANA: Well, it's a Mediterranean climate so it's hot and sunny most of the year.
EXAMINER: Lucky you, and erm **(10)** ....?
ADRIANA: It's an important qualification to have and also because in summer my city is full of foreigners. It's important to know English.
EXAMINER: Huh huh. Right, right.

3 Managing conversations
Study the completed conversation.

What **words** does the examiner use to show that:
- he understands?
- he is interested?
- he going to move to another topic?

What **sounds** does he make to show interest and hesitation?

4 In pairs, practise reading the dialogue. Make sure that you sound lively and interested!

SPEAKING

Imagine that you are at a reception or a party. Choose five of the examiner's questions and make small talk with as many people as you can. Remember to be interested and to make your conversations lively. Try to use some of the expressions we have just looked at.

THERE'S NO STOPPING IT!

FIRST THOUGHTS

Look at these reasons for studying English and number them in order of importance for you. Afterwards, compare your answers with a partner.

To get a good job. ☐
To pass an examination. ☐
For travel. ☐
To speak to foreign visitors. ☐
To understand the culture of a
   foreign country better. ☐
To study abroad. ☐
To please someone else. ☐

READING

1 In **Paper 1 (Reading)** you are given a text in which you have to match headings to paragraphs. Study this question:

"You are going to read an article about why different people around the world use English. Choose the most suitable heading **A-H** for each parts of the article (**1-6**). There is one extra heading which you do not have to use. There is an example at the beginning (**0**)."

> **A** There's no stopping it.
> **B** Foreigners are clearer.
> **C** We are victims of necessity.
> **D** It was all so different.
> **E** Ashamed of my mother.
> **F** You'll need it at conferences.
> **G** Songs are best!
> **H** English around the world.

2 Let's take the headings **A**, **B** and **C** as examples. We need to interpret each heading and then find evidence which supports its use.

A There's no stopping it!
Interpretation: This shows that the person seems to have a negative attitude towards English. They believe that nothing can be done to stop its growth.
Evidence: Véronique Arnaud says: "I don't like the way English seems to be taking over." So this heading fits best with paragraph 2.

0	**H**

A few centuries ago, English was hardly spoken by anybody outside the British Isles. Yet nowadays, millions of people around the world use it in their everyday lives. In many countries it has become a political issue. In some places, laws discourage people from using English instead of the mother tongue. However, it is the behaviour of individuals which mostly concerns us here. Today, we are going to look at some of those people and find out who they are, why they use it, and how they *feel* about it.

1	

I'm Kurt Thommen from Zurich in Switzerland. I'm a photographer for a wildlife magazine. I need English because lots of handbooks are written in it and I travel a lot. Next month I'm going to visit South East Asia. I hope I'll be able to make myself understood. I've found it is often easier to speak English to other foreigners than to native speakers! One American colleague doesn't speak slowly enough for me to understand him. It is useful to know English, but I don't approve of foreigners using English expressions in their own language.

B Foreigners are clearer.
Interpretation: The paragraph this heads is obviously going to mention that it is easier to understand other foreigners than native speakers.
Evidence: Kurt Thommen says the same thing but in a different way: "I've found it is often easier to speak English to other foreigners than to native speakers."

C We are victims of necessity.
Interpretation: This seems to say that the person uses English because they have been forced to. It suggests that it is an unwelcome choice.
Evidence: These ideas seem to summarise best what Adebayo Omere has to say in the whole of his paragraph.

2

Hi! My name's Véronique Arnaud and I come from Quebec, which is in the French-speaking part of Canada. I'm an accountant in a big paper mill. I take care of foreign customers, so most of the time I have to use English. In Canada everything's supposed to be bilingual but I don't like the way English seems to be taking over. We had a real fight here, you know, to keep hold of our French past and identity. This is why I voted for independence.

3

I'm Cathy Wong and I'm from Singapore. I've been studying business administration in London for the past two years. I felt really homesick to begin with because I'd never been away from home. It took me time to get used to living on my own and I still miss my parents. They brought me up to speak English and I was sent to an English-speaking school. When I got here, though, I still had a few problems with people's accents and the slang that lots of the other students used. Some of the lecturers were hard to understand at first, and there was lots of business jargon to pick up too. Living in London is expensive and I almost ran out of money but luckily I got a part-time job and now I get by.

3 Do the rest of the exercise. Remember: first **interpret** the heading then find **evidence**.

WRITING

Using the texts as a guide, write a paragraph about yourself. Explain:

- who you are and where you come from.
- what you do.
- why you are studying English.
- what your biggest problems are with the language.
- how you feel about English.
- what your ambitions are.

4

I'm Adebayo Omere from Nigeria and I'm an agricultural engineer. English is the official language because there are so many different languages and dialects spoken in Nigeria. I have to travel all round the country and often English is the only way to communicate. This is a pity because it used to be the colonial language. I'd rather not use English all the time. However, if we had chosen a tribal language, it would have caused political problems. So we will just have to put up with it!

5

Good day. My name is Rob Giuliani. I'm fifteen years old and I come from Melbourne, in Australia. I'm second generation Italian. My parents came over about twenty years ago. I'm bilingual because we still speak Italian at home. Dad speaks much better than Mum. Sometimes her mistakes are really embarrassing and her accent is so strong that some people find it impossible to understand her. I'm still studying but I always spend my spare time out on the tennis court. I've won a few local tournaments and I'd really like to turn professional.

6

I'm Ana Gonzales from São Paulo in Brazil. It is eight years since I started to learn English. My biggest problem is pronunciation. I love listening to English pop music which is a great way of learning new vocabulary. My dad's a businessman and he uses English all the time. He speaks it fluently. He managed to pick it up while he was working in the States. That's no surprise because living in the country is supposed to be the best way to learn. Perhaps I'll study there. He wants me to speak English well enough so that I can join his company. I'd rather work in advertising.

VOCABULARY

Language

Complete the sentences with these words or expressions:

> pick up jargon mother tongue slang
> bilingual languages accent dialects

1 Although she was speaking English, her .... was so strong we could hardly understand her.
2 I went to a computer expert, but when he started using all the technical ...., I got lost.
3 Young people use a lot of .... For instance, they say *copper* instead of policeman.
4 She never studied English but she managed to .... it .... by living in America.
5 Even though the language is basically the same, there are several different .... In the south, some of the words and structures are different from those in the north.
6 COBOL and PASCAL are two computer ....
7 English is Nick's first language. In other words it's his ....
8 A person who speaks two languages is ....

Phrasal verbs

1 Look at these two sentences:

A They **brought** the wine **up** from the cellar.
B They **brought** me **up** to speak English.

The meaning of sentence **A** is clear and literal. It tells us about the movement of the wine. **Bring** and **up** each have their usual and separate meanings.

In sentence **B**, **bring** and **up** combine to create a new, non-literal meaning: to **raise/educate**. In this book, verbs which combine with adverbs and prepositions in this non-literal way are called **phrasal verbs**.

2 Look at these sentences and decide when the verbs and prepositions/adverbs are being used as phrasal verbs, i.e. in a non-literal way.

1 She picked up the pen from the floor.
2 Can you move your bicycle so that we can get by?
3 We changed hotel because we couldn't put up with the noise.
4 We have run out of cigarettes.
5 She picked up Spanish by visiting South America.
6 The girl ran out of the room.
7 They put the picture up with a nail.
8 I don't know how she gets by on her pension.

3 Which phrasal verbs mean:

1 to endure/tolerate?
2 to learn?
3 to finish?
4 to manage?

4 Complete each sentence with one of the four phrasal verbs. Remember to use the right tense.

1 I don't know how they .... They have six children and he doesn't earn very much.
2 She is very clever. She .... how to use the computer without any training.
3 We had to come back from holiday early because we .... money.
4 Passengers are having to .... long waits at airports because of a strike.

LANGUAGE STUDY

Identifying basic constructions

Match constructions **1-15** with sentences **A-O** taken from the texts.

A **I've been studying** business administration in London for the past two years.
B He managed to pick it up while **he was working** in the States.
C **...if we had chosen** a tribal language, **it would have caused** political problems.
D **I'm still studying** but I...
E **...he uses** English all the time.
F My parents **came over** about 20 years ago.
G **I love listening** to English pop music..
H He **managed to pick** it up.
I **I've won** a few local tournaments.
J My **biggest problem** is pronunciation.
K I hope **I'll be able** to make myself understood.
L Dad speaks **much better English than** Mum.
M **I'd never been** away from home.
N ...**I was sent** to an English-speaking school.
O Next month **I'm going to visit** South East Asia.

1 present simple	**2** past perfect
3 past simple	**4** verb+gerund
5 future simple	**6** present perfect
7 third conditional	**8** passive
9 superlative	**10** past continuous.
11 verb+infinitive	**12** comparative
13 *going to* future	**14** present continuous
15 present perfect continuous	

Adverbs of frequency

Rob Giuliani said *"I **always** spend my spare time out on the tennis court."* **Always** is an adverb of frequency. It tells us how often someone does something.

1 Place these adverbs of frequency on the scale.

> often   seldom   occasionally
> sometimes   rarely   usually

never <..........................> always

2 The position of adverbs varies. Study sentences 1-14 and decide if the position of the adverb is **right** or **wrong**.

1 **Seldom** she uses a monolingual dictionary.
2 **Occasionally**, we read English magazines.
3 He **seldom** watches films in English.
4 **Always** she comes to class late.
5 He **sometimes** is late.
6 He checks his spelling **never.**
7 He gives us **often** homework.
8 We **rarely** write in English.
9 We study **usually** English in the evening.
10 They go **always** to the cinema on Fridays.
11 Do you speak **often** English?
12 They are **never** on time.
13 We **always** should help.
14 They can **sometimes** watch English films.

3 Now decide:

1 where the **safest** place to put these adverbs is.
2 where you put the adverb with the verb **to be**.
3 where you put the adverb with modals like **can**, **will** and **should**.

4 Practice
Find out from your partner how often he/she:

- speaks English outside the classroom.
- uses an English-English dictionary.
- listens to English on the radio or watches films in English.
- reads and/or writes in English outside the classroom.

USE OF ENGLISH

1 In **Part 3** of **Paper 3 (Use of English)** you have to complete a sentence so that it has a similar meaning to the one above it. You must use between two and five words including the word given. You must not change the word you are given.

Example: Mr Clark still hasn't put his signature on these documents.
need
These documents still ...*need to be signed*... by Mr Clark.

1 Laws encourage people to use the mother tongue instead of English.
discourage
Laws .... English instead of the mother tongue.

2 A few centuries ago almost nobody spoke English.
hardly
A few centuries ago English was .... anybody.

3 I hope people will understand me.
make
I hope I'll be .... understood.

4 I don't like it when foreigners use English expressions in their own language
approve
I do not .... English expressions in their own language.

5 It was hard to live on my own but I eventually became accustomed to it.
used
It took me a long time to .... on my own.

6 I don't want to use English all the time.
rather
I .... use English all the time.

7 Some people can't understand her at all.
impossible
Some people find .... her.

8 People say the best way to learn a language is by living in the country.
supposed
Living in the country .... the best way to learn a language.

9 He speaks too quickly for me to understand him.
enough
He .... for me to understand him.

10 Knowing English is useful.
know
It .... English.

2 Now check your answers by searching for the second sentences in the texts on pages 10-11.

CHOOSE YOUR WORDS CAREFULLY

FIRST THOUGHTS

A good way of learning a language is to spend a year working abroad. What kind of job do you think you could get?

USE OF ENGLISH

1 In **Part 1** of **Paper 3 (Use of English)** you have to complete a text by deciding which word **A**, **B**, **C** or **D** best fits each space. Study this example, and the explanations which follow.

My mother-in-law first came to England as an au pair **(1) in** a doctor's family. She was **(2) keen**... to improve her English and realised that this would be an excellent way of doing so. **(3) Although**... forty years have passed, her memories of this time have hardly **(4) faded**... . Her job was to look **(5) after**... three energetic youngsters. However, her employers **(6) allowed**... her to spend some time studying and to visit the friends she had managed to **(7) make**. For her, however, the biggest treat of all was to have a **(8) quick**... sleep after lunch, as her main memory is of being exhausted by the children!

1 A by   **B** at   **C** in   **D** from
Choice C is correct because it is the only preposition from the choices available that has the correct meaning. We can **work for** or **in** a doctor's family.

2 A interested   **B** bored   **C** keen   **D** excited
Choice C is correct because **interested** is usually followed by **in** and **bored** by **with**. **Excited** can be followed by **to** but has a different meaning.

3 A Although   **B** Despite   **C** However   **D** Yet
Choice A is correct. **Yet** and **however** *could* be used between the two clauses but *not* at the beginning of the sentence. **Despite** has to be followed by a noun, gerund or **the fact that**.

4 A melted   **B** faded   **C** dissolved   **D** vanished
Choice B is correct because it is the only verb which has the correct concept. Snow **melts** in the sun; an aspirin **dissolves** in water. **Vanish** means **to disappear completely and without trace**.

5 A for   **B** into   **C** down on   **D** after
Choice D is correct because even though **look** can be followed by three other choices, their meaning would not make sense in this context. All four choices produce possible phrasal verbs. **Look into** means to **investigate**; **look for** means to **search for**; and if we **look down** on someone it means we consider ourselves to be superior to them!

6 A let   **B** made   **C** stopped   **D** allowed
Choice D is correct because it is the only verb which is grammatically correct. You **make/let someone do something** (infinitive without **to**). You **stop someone from doing something**.

7 A make   **B** have   **C** take   **D** do
Choice A is correct because in this context it is the only verb that combine with **friends**. In English, many common nouns and verbs combine in this way. When you are studying vocabulary, always make a note of these relationships.

8 A rapid   **B** speedy   **C** quick   **D** fast
Choice C is correct. Although all the choices have the idea of speed, we can only talk about **a quick sleep**. It is a kind of idiom which means **to have a short sleep**.

A quick sleep

2 Now look at the rest of the text and complete it by using one of the choices **A**, **B**, **C** or **D**. If you find it useful, refer to a good monolingual dictionary such as the *Longman Active Study Dictionary*.

"I'd like some bloody oranges."

Now, this was in Cambridge, which is, as you (**1**)........., famous throughout the world (**2**)......... its university. Young women were very popular as there were (**3**)......... any women students and females were in (**4**)......... supply! She soon met and married an Englishman from the university and they settled (**5**)......... in London. In the (**6**)......... days my mother-in-law had some language problems. One day at the local greengrocer's she noticed, quite by (**7**)........., some beautiful oranges half hidden under a newspaper. They were known as "blood oranges" on (**8**)......... of their bright red flesh and distinctive (**9**)......... . In those days, fresh fruit other than apples was (**10**)......... in winter. Perhaps the shopkeeper had reserved this delicacy for favoured customers or (**11**)......... friends. Plucking up her courage my mother-in-law asked "Can I have some of those bloody oranges?" (*Bloody*, of course, is a (**12**)......... swearword.) He laughed and said: "Certainly madam, and you can have some bloody apples too!" Everyone in the shop laughed and she felt rather (**13**)......... . As you can imagine, it took her time to (**14**)......... this incident down.

1 **A** understand **B** know **C** recognise **D** believe
2 **A** from **B** for **C** because **D** of
3 **A** just **B** rarely **C** hardly **D** only
4 **A** small **B** low **C** scarce **D** short
5 **A** down **B** into **C** up **D** for
6 **A** first **B** early **C** beginning **D** primary
7 **A** mistake **B** luck **C** fortune **D** chance
8 **A** view **B** account **C** regard **D** reason
9 **A** skin **B** peel **C** shell **D** rind
10 **A** sparse **B** rare **C** few **D** scarce
11 **A** closed **B** nearby **C** next **D** close
12 **A** light **B** mild **C** soft **D** weak
13 **A** shy **B** shameful **C** ashamed **D** embarrassing
14 **A** live **B** talk **C** put **D** turn

Examination advice: **Always** read the entire text through before attempting to answer any of the questions. This way, you'll get a general idea of what it is about and will be able to make more informed choices. **Remember:** study the words before and after the gaps.

Study advice

As we have seen, this question tests a wide variety of grammatical and lexical relationships. In preparing for the examination, develop your knowledge and awareness of vocabulary. Make lists of the following:

1 verbs and the patterns they follow
e.g. • *you tell someone **to do** something.*
  • *you risk **doing** something*
  • *you make someone **do** something*

2 adjectives which are commonly followed by prepositions
e.g. • *interested **in**, aware **of***

3 preposition+noun+preposition combinations
e.g. • *by means of, in order to*

4 phrasal verbs and their common meanings
e.g. • *look after:* take care of; *settle down:* make a permanent home (and start a family)

5 words of similar meaning and their important differences
e.g. • **skin, peel, shell, rind** all deal with the concept of a layer covering something else. Reference books can give you extra information. Look at this entry from *Right Word Wrong Word* by L.G. Alexander published by Longman.

skin• rind• peel• shell

-The **rind** of parmesan cheese is like rock.
(Not *skin *peel)
(=the inedible, often hard, outside layer of food such as cheese or a thick-skinned fruit)

-*It's not very funny to slip on a banana **skin**.*
(Not *rind *peel)
(=the soft, often thin, outer layer of a fruit which may be edible or inedible)

-*The top of the mountain is littered with orange **peel** and rubbish.* (Not *peels)
(=the outer layer removed - *peeled* - from a fruit or vegetable before it is eaten; uncountable)

-*My hands are black because I've been **shelling** fresh walnuts.* (Not *peeling)
(a *shell* is the outer covering of nuts and shellfish.)

ROOTS

FIRST THOUGHTS

All the following words are used in everyday English. Match each word with its origin.

Words: bistro, algebra, kiosk, pagoda, safari, tycoon, ketchup, swastika, cannibal, anorak.
Origins: Eskimo, Portuguese, Sanskrit (Ancient Indian language), Japanese, Spanish, Turkish, Swahili, Hungarian, Arabic.

READING

1 Quickly read the text and find out why Louise found learning Greek easier than she had at first imagined.

2 Earlier in the unit we looked at **Part 1** of **Paper 1 (Reading)** where you have to match headings to paragraphs.
We are now going to look at **Part 3** where you match missing sentences or paragraphs to gaps in a text. Study this example, and the explanations that follow:
"*You are going to read an article about an English person studying Greek*. Seven sentences have been removed from the article. Choose from sentences **A-H** the one which fits each gap **(1-6)**. There is one extra sentence which you do not need to use. There is an example at the beginning **(0)**."

A	They fell into two sets.
B	She had no idea that it would be such an enjoyable experience.
C	It wasn't so much a question of learning new words, more a question of finding out how many I already knew.
D	These were things like *amphi* (both), *endo* (inside), *hem* (half), *hyper* (above), *hypo* (below), *iso* (equal), *neo* (new), *peri* (around), *proto* (first), etc.
E	But in Greek, these bits crop up all over the place in everyday talk.
F	"Scope" is a good example of this kind of word.
G	My little boy is really interested in dinosaurs. I could never remember their names.
H	English has many words composed of Greek parts, and it was easy to recognise these parts in the words she was learning.

Part A
Louise found that Greek vocabulary was surprisingly easy. [0] [H] "You use words like *telephone* and *polygon* in English without thinking that they've been borrowed from other languages. And you think of words like *polygamy* or *dipsomania* as being unusually difficult words in English - words you might find written down, but you perhaps wouldn't use yourself. [1] *Poly* is just "very", "much" or "many", and *dipso* is "I drink" in Greek."
Louise came across so many connections between Greek and English that she thought it would be useful to make a list of them. [2] There was a list of about 30 words that often appeared at the beginning of English words, and often corresponded to adjectives or prepositions in Greek. [3] Louise could easily think of English words that contained these bits, and so they were easy to learn. The other set was Greek words that usually appeared at the end of English words. [4] You get it in *telescope* and *periscope* and *bioscope* but *scopo* is just Greek for "view". *Sphere* is another Greek word that works in the same way. Louise says: "Learning Greek was completely different from learning any other language. Most of the time I've found it hard to learn vocabulary, but this time I felt I already knew a lot of the vocabulary before I started. [5] It meant that I could often guess how to say something in Greek, even if I wasn't sure what the words were."
The extra bonus from learning Greek was that it made Louise think a lot about English. "[6] But once you find out that the Greek word for "lizard" is *sauros*, *brontis* is "thunder", *ankylos* is "crooked" or "bent" and *stegis* is "roof" or "home", words like *brontosaurus*, *ankylosaurus* and *stegosaurus* stop being difficult, and start to become very funny instead!"

0-H is the example sentence. If fits logically because it explains why Louise found the vocabulary easy.
1-E Sentence E begins with "But" which shows there is a contrast with what went before. "These bits" refer back to *poly-* and *tele-*, two prefixes of Greek origin. The contrast is that words that may seem special in English have a simple everyday use in Greek. The sentence after the gap tells us that "poly" is just "very", "much' or "many", and "dipso" is "I drink" in Greek.
2-A The plural pronoun "they" refers back to the "many connections" of the previous line. The next sentence gives details of one of the "sets" Louise made. Details of the other set come later.

3-D   The pronoun "these" refers back to "adjectives and prepositions". It reinforces the previous sentence with a list of examples of the prepositions and adjectives commonly used in English.

4-F   The sentence after the gap tells us that "scope" appears in *telescope*. This is an excellent clue. In the sentence before, the writer discusses a set of words which are usually put at the end of English words.

5-C   This sentence uses "I" so is an example of where Louise is speaking. We should look for speech marks (In the missing sentence Louise expands the explanation she began in the one before.) Also "new words" is a synonym for "vocabulary".

6-G   "saurus" in the missing sentence is an excellent clue. The missing sentence states what her problem was; the sentence which follows tells us how she was able to solve it. A problem turns into something which is, in fact, "very funny" instead.

Sentence B is the dummy sentence.

3   Read a continuation of the article. Choose from the sentences **A-H** the one which fits each gap **(1-6)**. There is one extra sentence you do not need to use. There is an example at the beginning (**0**).

A   She might say something on those lines when she quarrelled with him later, of course, but that was another matter.
B   Almost all her guesses were partly correct.
C   "It really put me off."
D   These were romantic novels.
E   This was quite a challenge.
F   Things that the people in the story picked up or did something with were the easiest.
G   After about six months learning Greek, she found that she highlighted about 20 words on each page of her novel.
H   Fortunately, the same words kept coming up again and again, and each time she met one, she got a few more clues to what they really meant.

Part B

Because such a lot of basic Greek vocabulary is related to English, it's fairly easy for native English speakers to develop a good passive vocabulary very quickly. Louise wanted to see if this made it easier for her to read Greek.

"When I learned French at school," she says, " I tried to read novels with a dictionary, but I always found so many words I couldn't understand that I never managed to read more than a few pages. | 0 | C | With Greek she tried a different strategy.

"I bought some Greek books from a second-hand bookshop," she says. "Not Homer or anything like that. | 1 | All the stories were really easy, and even with my basic vocabulary I could make a good stab at reading them."

Louise used a marker pen to highlight all the words she wasn't sure about. | 2 | This wasn't a lot, but it was still too many to look them up in the dictionary. Each time she stopped to look a word up, it broke the flow of the story. So, instead of stopping each time she found a new word, she'd make a guess at what it meant, but not stop reading. Then, when she'd got to the end of the chapter - usually four or five pages - she'd look up all the highlighted words in her dictionary, and check how close her guesses were.

She was surprised at how good she was. | 3 | Sometimes she was wrong, but quite often the story made it obvious that she'd made a mistake, and she'd be able to backtrack and get it right. Some words were easier than others, of course. | 4 | For instance, if someone picked up an object and drank out of it, it had to be a cup, or a glass, or a bottle, or a wineskin - the details probably didn't matter. Or if the heroine was describing the man she had just fallen in love with, she'd be unlikely to say he was stupid, ugly and bad-tempered. | 5 | Verbs were the hardest to guess; Louise could guess the general area easily enough, but often needed to be more accurate than that to understand the story properly. | 6 |

Study advice

Texts are not a random collection of sentences. Writers use a variety of techniques to hold the text together:

- They make logical connections between ideas. Causes are linked with results; explanations with examples; a statement may be followed by a contrasting idea.

- They use forward and backward references to connect the text together. Reference words and pronouns also provide us with useful clues.
- They use different vocabulary to say the same thing in a varied and interesting way. E.g. "new words" = "vocabulary".

MAKING CONTACT

1 Two good ways of improving your performance in a foreign language are to have a pen friend or to arrange an exchange visit. Has anyone in the class ever done either of these things?

2 If you were responsible for matching people from different countries, how would you do it? What problems might there be?

LISTENING

1 Andrew Williams and his wife run "Linguapal", an agency which organises international exchanges for young people. Listen to the interview and complete the notes with a word or short phrase.

Mr Williams depends on people replying to (**1**)............
People are asked to write a letter and (**2**)............
The letter helps him to (**3**)............
There are (**4**)............ questions on the form. The questions deal with everything from religious persuasion to (**5**)............
Mr Williams thinks it is a good idea if people come from similar family backgrounds because otherwise it can cause (**6**)........... if people come from different backgrounds.
For example someone from a rich family might expect their own (**7a**)............ and (**7b**)............
A person from a poor family might feel (**8**)............ about the return visit.
Mr Williams doesn't believe he should get involved in social (**9**)............
He gives two examples of mistakes he has made. Once he sent a vegetarian to (**10a**)............ , and on another occasion he sent (**10b**)............ to a family which was keen on riding.

2 **Vocabulary in context** ..... Join these split sentences.

1 If you **take advantage of** a situation.
2 If you are **well off** .....
3 If you can't **see the poin**t of something .....
4 If you **take something for granted** .....
5 If you **don't bother** to do something .....
6 If you have a poor **attitude** towards studying .....

a you don't want to spend your time or take the trouble to do it.
b the way you think is likely to affect your performance.
c you can't see its reason or purpose.
d you exploit it for your benefit.
e you have a lot of money.
f you always expect it to be there.

3 Listen again and note how the words and expressions are used.

WRITING

The compulsory letter

Question 1 of **Paper 2 (Writing)** involves writing a transactional letter, i.e. a letter in which you try to get something done or find out or give information. This question is compulsory, in other words everybody has to answer it.

It is based around a situation and one or more short texts and notes.

1 Study the question below and then look at the two answers (A and B) which follow.

You are interested in organising an exchange visit but only have the advertisement on the right. Read the advertisement from an international magazine and the notes which you have made below. Write a letter to the Linguapal Agency covering the points in your notes and adding any relevant information about yourself. Write a letter to the agency in **120–180** words in an appropriate style. Do not include addresses.

Notes

cost of service?
length of stay? minimum time?
time of year – summer holidays best.
personal details, studies and family background.

> To really understand a foreign language and culture there is no substitute for a stay in the country concerned. Linguapal is a non-profit making organisation with more than twenty years experience of arranging language exchange visits. For further information write to us in English saying why you are interested in Linguapal and which country you would like an exchange with. Include any relevant information about your studies and background. Serious applicants only, please.
>
> Mr and Mrs A. Williams, Linguapal, Box 4000

2 Which of the two answers: • is written in a more appropriate style? • answers the question more fully? • covers the points in the notes? • is better organised? • looks better?

A

Dear Mr and Mrs Williams,
With regard to your advertisement in Polyglot magazine, I would be very interested in receiving further information about your service.

I am a seventeen-year-old secondary school student who will be taking my "A" level examinations next year. My family lives on the outskirts of Bristol. My parents are both teachers and I have one brother and a sister. I would like to have an exchange with a Spanish boy from Madrid or the area around Madrid.

I would be grateful if you could send me further information including details of the cost of the service.
Yours sincerely,
Anthony Clancy

B

Dear Mr and Mrs Williams,
I saw your advertisement in Polyglot magazine. It is just what I have been looking for.
Let me tell you a bit about myself. I am 18 years old and am studying languages: French, German and Spanish. I want to go on to university next year. I am interested in meeting a Spanish boy – or girl!! There are a few extra things I would like to know. Is there a minimum time for an exchange or can it last as long as you like? Also, I would like to have an exchange for the month of August, during the summer holidays. This year we're renting a house near the sea in Wales and I'm really keen on sailing so it would be great if you could find someone with the same hobby. By the way, my mum's a professional musician and dad manages a garage. It would be great if you could send me some more stuff about your service.
All the best,
Raymond West

3 Take letter B and rewrite and organise it in a more appropriate style. Make sure that it is laid out in a way that makes it clear to read.

4 Write your own answer to the question.

LISTENING

Now listen to these five young people who have all been on exchange visits. They were all asked to talk about something that was unfamiliar or difficult. Choose from the list **A–F** the problem each of them experienced. There is one extra letter you do not need to use.

A Waiting in line	Speaker 1 ☐
B Using the bathroom	Speaker 2 ☐
C Different traffic rules	Speaker 3 ☐
D Understanding people	Speaker 4 ☐
E Greetings	Speaker 5 ☐
F Unfamiliar food	

What were the "clues" which helped you to match the speakers to the sentences?

VOCABULARY

Collocations

It is important to know how verbs combine with nouns and adjectives to form set phrases. These relationships are tested in the multiple choice vocabulary questions and sentence transformations of the **Use of English paper** (**Questions 1 and 3**).

1 Combine the verbs in box A with the words and phrases in box B. Some of the words in box B can be used with more than one verb.

A

do   take   give   make   find   have   jump

B

a decision   the queue   oneself understood
advantage of someone/something
something for a living   a description
a good time   a fool of oneself   sure
difficulty in doing something   one's best
someone/something for granted   a mistake
the most of something

2 Extend these questions using the phrases we have studied and then interview a partner.

Example: *Have you ever made a* ..... *fool of yourself* .....*?*
Yes I have. Once I asked a stupid question in class and everybody laughed at me.

1 Have you ever made a .... ?
2 Do you have difficulty .... ?
3 Have you ever been in a situation where you couldn't make .... ?
4 What does your father/mother do .... ?
5 Do members of your family take .... ?

USE OF ENGLISH

Complete the second sentence so that it has a similar meaning to the first sentence. You must use between two and five words including the word given. Do not change the word given.

1 You should make the most of being in Paris and visit the Eiffel Tower.
advantage
You should .... being in Paris and visit the Eiffel Tower.

2 What is your sister's job, Miranda?
for
What does your ...., Miranda?

3 She described the robber to the police.
description
She .... the robber to the police.

4 I hope you enjoy yourselves this evening.
time
I hope you .... this evening.

5 I want you to try as hard as you can, Jenny.
do
I want .... Jenny.

6 You are making yourself look ridiculous.
fool
You .... yourself.

7 We found it difficult to turn the key in the lock.
difficulty
We .... the key in the lock.

8 Paul always expected his mother to be there for him.
granted
Paul always ....

9 Wait your turn like everybody else.
queue
Don't .... like that.

10 I thought people wouldn't be able to understand my Spanish.
myself
I thought I wouldn't be able .... in Spanish.

USE OF ENGLISH

1 In **Part 4** of **Paper 3 (Use of English)** you have to carry out an editing exercise. You are given a text where some lines are correct and others have an extra and unnecessary word. You have to tick any correct lines and write any words which should not be there. Look at this example and the explanations which follow. The extra words are in bold type. In the exam, the first two lines are given as examples:

```
0  |  ✓    |
00 |  will  |
```

  0 I am studying biochemistry and I want to work
00 for a drug company when I **will** graduate.
  1 Perhaps I might **to** continue my studies. After I
  2 finish at university I will do **a** research.
  3 So it is necessary to reach **at** a good level
  4 of English because **of** when I go to international
  5 conferences I'll need to understand **all**.
  6 My mother, who is a professor, **she** says that it is
  7 an important language for all kinds of reason.
  8 Another reason why I **am** study English is that
  9 I like to relax **myself** by listening to music.
10 I hope **that** to learn new expressions and improve
11 my listening too. I can mix learning with the
12 pleasure of music. One other thing **else** is that
13 there are often foreigners for **one** dinner at
14 home who have been invited by my mother, and
15 usually **the** English is our "lingua franca".

Line 00: **When** is not followed by **will** (except in questions).
Line 1: **Might** is followed by the infinitive without **to**.
Line 2: **Research** is an uncountable noun in English.
Line 3: We do not need a preposition after **reach**; **reach** has the idea of **at** or **to** already.
Line 4: **Because** is followed with **of** when we follow it with a noun phrase. *We didn't stay at the beach because of the rain.* If we want to follow **because** with a verb, then we don't use **of**.
Line 5: **All** cannot be used on its own like this. It has to be followed by something else, e.g. *all they say.* (**Everything** would have been correct.)
Line 6: There is already a subject in the sentence: "my mother", so **she** is unnecessary.
Line 8: **Study** is in the present simple, not the continuous.
Line 9: **Relax** is not a reflexive verb in English. (**Enjoy** is.)

Line 10: We can say *I hope that I can learn new expressions* or *I hope to learn new expressions*. We cannot use both **to** and **that**.
Line 12: **Else** is repeating the idea of one other thing.
Line 13: We do not use **one** or articles in front of meals after the preposition **for**: *What's for dinner?* We could, however, say *"It was a wonderful dinner."*
Line 15: We do not usually use the article in front of languages. However, we could say *"**The** English spoken in Aberdeen in Scotland is very clear."*

2 Edit the following text. Identify the correct lines and the extra and unnecessary words in the others.

Dear Mr Williams,

  0 My teacher showed me your advertisement and
00 told to me I should contact you. I would like to
  1 know how much does your service costs. I would
  2 like you to tell me about how to organise an
  3 exchange. I am seventeen years and come from
  4 Bilbao in Spain. I live together with my
  5 parents in Bilbao. We got used to live in Madrid.
  6 I have started to study the English language
  7 for six years ago and now I would like to make
  8 a progress by spending time in England.
  9 I would like an accommodation in a family with a
10 girl my age. My mother she says this would be
11 the best for me. In my free time I like to relax
12 myself by playing the piano. I also like to go
13 to shopping. I enjoy listening to pop music
14 like most of young people.
15 One other thing else: I am allergic to cats and
     dogs.

Yours sincerely,
Marisol Rodriguez

DECISION TIME

FIRST THOUGHTS

1 How do you like to spend your free time? How do you feel about these different kinds of entertainment? Which would you actively participate in?

> boxing   discos   heavy metal music   card games
> horror films   basketball   karate   reading
> eating out

2 Write down your answers and then compare your opinions with a partner. Use the expressions in the box. Example: *I can't stand boxing*

> can't stand   loathe   absolutely detest
> not keen on   don't mind   fond of   really love
> adore

LISTENING

In **Part 4** of **Paper 4 (Listening)** you listen to a group of speakers interacting. One of the tasks is deciding which person said what.
You are going to hear a conversation between three flatmates: John, Eleanor and Richard. They are discussing how to spend the evening. Answer the questions by putting

J (for John)
E (for Eleanor)
R (for Richard)
in the boxes provided.

1 Who makes the most suggestions? ☐
2 Who isn't very keen to go out? ☐
3 Who hates burgers? ☐
4 Who *hasn't* seen Cliffhanger? ☐
5 Who becomes a little bit upset? ☐
6 Who makes the most successful suggestion? ☐
7 Who owns the car? ☐

SPEAKING

Managing conversations

Turn to the tapescript on p.219. Listen again and make a list of expressions the speakers use to:

- ask for suggestions.
- make suggestions.
- express preferences.

LANGUAGE STUDY   25/9/ Start this

It's time.../I'd rather...

1 Look at these two sentences from the Listening.

Eleanor: *I'd rather we did something else.*
John: *It's time we left.*

Which tenses are used?
Are they talking about the past/now/the future?
Study these two groups of sentences and decide which ones are correct.

1 A It's time to leave for the airport.
  B It's time for us to go to the airport.
  C It's time that we go to the airport.
  D It's time we went to the airport.

2 A I'd rather go to the theatre.
  B I'd rather that we go to the theatre.
  C I'd rather we went to the theatre.

In pairs work out a rule for **I'd rather** and **It's time**.

2 What would you say in the following situations?

1 You feel tired. You think you need a holiday.
2 A friend suggests going to a party. You would like to go to a disco.
3 You're looking after a small child. It's 11 o'clock. You think he ought to go to bed.
4 It's raining. Your friend suggests walking home. You want to take a taxi.
5 Your favourite pop singer is coming to your town. Your friend thinks there will be lots of tickets left. You think you should buy them now.
6 You've been to a party with Bill and Simon. Bill is terribly tired. What would you say if he offered to drive?
7 You and your friend are both hungry. Your friend suggests a Chinese meal. You prefer Thai food.
8 This exercise is getting boring!

Short replies

Richard: *I've seen it.*
Eleanor: *I have too.*

1 Match the statements and replies.

A	Carol really liked the film.	**1**	She can't either.
B	She'll love the party.	**2**	I would too.
C	I won't eat there again.	**3**	Neither do we.
D	We can't stand discos.	**4**	So did John.
E	I'd rather go to the cinema.	**5**	They didn't either.
F	She doesn't mind opera.	**6**	So am I.
G	We didn't enjoy the play.	**7**	Daisy will too.
H	Anita is fond of Chinese food.	**8**	Neither shall I.

2 When do we use **so**, **too**, **neither**, and **either**? In pairs, work out a rule. Then move around the class and find someone who shares your opinions about the activities on p22.

SPEAKING

An evening out

1 Work in groups of three or four. Your group has decided to go out for the evening together. You can each spend £20. Look at the options available and decide on an evening's entertainment which everyone will enjoy. You must all agree about what you will do.

KINGSWAY ROLLER RINK
Tonight!!! Roller Disco
Skating to all the rock and roll classics.
Entrance £4.
Ladies free before 7.30 p.m.
Skate hire £3.50 (£10 returnable deposit)

Enjoy the latest pop videos at the
VIDEO CAFÉ
Meals from £6   Entrance £4.50

RANCHEROS TEX-MEX EATERY
Fabulous menus.
Eat all you can for £7.50.

ODEON CINEMA

Screen One
ROCKY XV1

Performances at
7.10, 9.15 £6

Screen Two
Last Snows of Spring
A dying girl finds eternal love.

Performances at
6.45, 8.50 £6

THE WHITE RHINOCEROS
Disco night club
All the latest sounds at your favourite
rendezvous. From 8.00 p.m. till 3 a.m.
Entrance £8 includes one drink.
Drinks £2 before 10 p.m.

---

2 In **Paper 5 (Speaking)** you may have to do an activity like this in pairs. Also you will not have any written information to guide or help you. Your discussion will be based around photographs.

In pairs, choose two photographs each and tell each other which of the activities shown in your pictures looks more attractive to you and why.

USEFUL LANGUAGE

- What would you like to do?
- Why don't we go to the disco?
- Let's have a hamburger instead.
- We could always stay at home.
- How about eating out?
- Do you fancy going to the cinema?

Now look at all four pictures together and discuss:

- which ones you would choose if you were going out for the evening together.
- which ones would be best for a group of tourists.
- which would be the most expensive and difficult to organise.

THE SPORTING LIFE

FIRST THOUGHTS

1 Look at the collage of different sporting activities. Which ones do you recognise? Are there any you have ever done or gone to watch?

2 In pairs or small groups discuss these questions.

1 Do you play any sport?
2 Is there any sport that you hate?
3 What's your national sport?
4 Do you have a national sporting hero?
5 Do you prefer individual or team sports?

LISTENING

1 Listen to these short descriptions. Which three activities are being described?

a ....
b ....
c ....

2 In pairs or small groups make a similar description of your national sport.

VOCABULARY

Do, play or go?

*You **do** aerobics, **play** rugby and **go** skiing (or ski).*

1 Which verbs do we use with the following activities?

> windsurfing   sailing   baseball   motor racing
> athletics   chess   horse riding   volleyball
> tennis   swimming   football   ice hockey
> gymnastics   jogging   cricket   American football

Note: For **wrestling** and **boxing** we say " He wrestles/He's a wrestler " and "He boxes/He's a boxer" without **do**, **play** or **go**.

2 Which of the sports above do you play on/in a: court, track, rink, pool, field, pitch, board, ring?

3 With which of the sports do you associate the following:
a board, gloves, net, racquet, stick, piece, horse, puck, bat?
b a goal, a set, a game, a draw, a round, a half?

4 Which of the following **can't** you do with a ball: throw, bounce, catch, serve, train, tackle, kick, run, bowl, pass, pitch, foul, volley, score, cheat?

5 Where would you find the following people: a referee, a fan, an umpire, a linesman, a spectator, a cheerleader, a quarterback, a hooligan, a forward, a goalkeeper?

6 Where necessary, correct these sentences:
a She won the match.
b She won her opponent.
c She won a prize.
d She beat the other player.

What is the difference between "win" and "beat"?

USE OF ENGLISH

In **Question 2** of **Paper 3 (Use of English)** you have to complete a passage in which there are 15 gaps. Unlike Question 1 which tests vocabulary, the emphasis of Question 2 is on grammar. You should always read the text through first to get a general understanding of what it is about before trying to fill in any of the gaps.

1 Read this passage and answer the questions. Ignore the gaps for now.

1 How was the tournament organised?
2 How did Eva's attitude change?
3 How close was the final match?

In Brazil we take beach volleyball seriously. I am going to tell you **(0)**..*about*. a tournament that took place last summer. It was a beautiful sunny day and **(1)**.......... of families and friends turned **(2)**.......... . There was a great atmosphere with picnics and barbecues. Teams of two girls from up and **(3)**.......... the coast joined in. At first, groups of teams played a set **(4)**.......... each other to see who **(5)**.......... go through to the last sixteen. This first part of the competition was just fun but the knock-out part was **(6)**.......... serious. By the time we got to the semi-finals we realised we **(7)**.......... a chance of winning. We won **(8)**.......... first set easily but lost the second. In the final one the others got a big lead and needed one **(9)**.......... point. Their captain was **(10)**.......... tense she lost control of a smash and the ball was just out. She got really angry with the umpire! **(11)**.......... we fought **(12)**.......... to get level and everyone was shouting encouragement. The others just gave up and we got the points we needed. We **(13)**.......... sorry, but not too sorry, for the other girls, after **(14)**.........., there's only one winner! Also, we were **(15)**.......... exhausted to feel very much else.

2 Now you have understood the text, complete it by using one word only for each of the gaps. To help you with this, the words are in the box below. This will not happen in the exam!

> down   had   afterwards   all   felt   more   back
> against   the   last   about   too   up   lots   would   so

WRITING

In **Paper 2 (Writing)** you may be asked to write a report about something like a film, or a sporting event. Using the Use of English gap filling text as a guide, answer the following question:
*You have been asked to write a report for a local newspaper about a sporting (or other) event you recently attended. Write between **120-180** words.*

Remember, before you begin writing your answer you will need to plan what you are going to say, and make a list of the various words and expressions which you would like to include.

ALL TIME GREATS

FIRST THOUGHTS

1 Who for you are the greatest sportsmen and women in the following sports: football, tennis, basketball and motor racing?

2 What do you think attracts people to compete in dangerous sports like motor racing?

3 Do you know any of the drivers in the pictures?

Left: Moss, Hawthorn, Lewis-Evans, Bhera

Below: Michael Schumacher

Left: Juan Fangio receives his winner's cup from President Péron

Below: Ayrton Senna

READING

You are going to read an article about the great drivers of Formula One motor racing. Choose from **A-H** the sentence or paragraph which fits each gap **(1-6)**. There is one extra letter which you do not need to use. There is an example at the beginning **(0)**.

A This cannot be good for the sport as a whole as it can lead to boredom. In the earlier days races seemed to be as much to do with the driver as the machine.

B Fangio's record of five championship titles were driving for Alfa Romeo, Mercedes and Maserati, Lancia and Ferrari!

C By contrast, a driver like the young German Michael Schumacher fights the car round every corner.

D Before his death at 32 he had won three championships and could have looked forward to another, say, six years of competition.

E There are four who deserve special consideration.

F It was undoubtedly the wise choice.

G Victory seems less to do with the talents of the driver.

H There were few second chances.

Even though Formula One motor racing has only existed since 1950, it is difficult to make a decision about who is the best driver of all. [0 | E] They are the Argentine Juan Fangio who dominated the competition in the 1950s, Britain's Jim Clark who died after winning two world championships, and from the mid 80s France's Alain Prost and the Brazilian Ayrton Senna.

If judgement depended on the number of grand prix wins there would be no contest. Alain Prost scored 51 before his retirement, followed by Ayrton Senna who had 41 to his credit before his tragic death. Even the great Fangio, who won five championships, "only" had 24 victories. Britain's Nigel Mansell won nine times in the 1992 championships. In terms of technical ability too, Prost deserves our admiration. His cool controlled driving and clean lines were the basis of his success. [1 |]

A factor that does make our choice harder is the role of the car in all this. There is a feeling that it is the car that is the real star. [2 |] Over the years the fortunes of different constructors have changed. Ferrari and McLaren have won the constructors' championship nine times. The past fifteen years or so it seems to have been dominated by the McLaren and Williams teams. [3 |]

Prost's decision to quit meant he had to forego the opportunity to equal the Argentine master's record. [4 |] Others have been less fortunate or less wise and Formula One is no stranger to tragedy. The Austrian Jochen Rindt was awarded the 1970 title championship posthumously after being killed at Monza. Jim Clark (who some maintain was the greatest of them all) met his end at Hockenheim at the height of his career when he was just 32. Niki Lauda survived a horrifying crash yet returned to win a second title.

It is certainly true that the risks drivers took in the old days were much higher. [5 |] Nowadays drivers are cocooned in special cockpits and encased in fireproof clothing and sophisticated helmets which mean they can often walk away from the wreckage of a devastated vehicle. Compare this with Fangio who drove in his shirt sleeves with no more than a leather helmet for protection. Englishman Graham Hill – Damon Hill's father – even wore a bow tie. Despite the tragic loss of Senna it is true to say that racing has become a lot safer in recent years.

Yet if we base our final judgement on passion and commitment we must return to Senna. He admitted that winning was like a drug. Before a Formula One career he already had a collection of trophies beginning with those he won as a boy in his karting career. Despite his enormous personal wealth he remained consumed by his thirst for success on the track. Sometimes the risks he took caused great anger among fellow competitors – notably his arch-rival Prost. After Prost's retirement he had seemed the most likely to break Fangio's long standing record. [6 |] Fangio had not begun until he was an "old man" of 38 and continued for eight years. In his case we might ask ourselves what he might have achieved had he started earlier.

USE OF ENGLISH

Complete the text about the basketball player, Michael Jordan, by changing the word in **bold** at the end of each line into a noun.

Michael Jordan's recent (**0**) *decision* to retire from basketball to take up a career in baseball is a (**1**)........... for the sport. Considered the best (**2**).......... of all time, Jordan helped win the college (**3**).......... in 1983, at the age of 20. His impressive medal (**4**).......... includes two Olympic golds. His (**5**).......... as a top scorer and arch-(**6**).......... is legendary.

    Taking every (**7**).......... that presents itself he has the seeming (**8**).......... to fly and win the ball from opponents 30cm more in (**9**).......... . For this he earned his nickname Air Jordan. His personal (**10**).......... is immense and his (**11**).......... at not winning the league title a thing of the past. Perhaps (**12**).......... made him quit after leading the Chicago Bulls to three successive victories.

DECIDE
TRAGIC
PLAY
CHAMPION
COLLECT
SUCCEED
COMPETE
OPPORTUNE
ABLE
HIGH
WEALTHY
DISAPPOINT
BORED

BOOKWORMS!

FIRST THOUGHTS

1 Think of a famous example for each category of the following types of book: science fiction, spy or adventure thrillers, historical novels, detective stories, biography, history, travel, serious literature, war stories, romantic novels, horror, reference books.

2 Which of the categories do you *like* to read and which do you *have* to read?

3 Find out from each other the most boring or interesting books you have read recently.

READING

1 You are going to read some information about books. For questions **1-7** below choose from books **A-H**. Some of the books may be chosen more than once. When more than one answer is required, these may be given in any order. There is an example at the beginning **(0)**.

Which of the books

• is a spy story?	0	G
• is considered to be funny?	1	
• seems to deal with the emotional lives of ordinary people?	2	
• would you recommend to someone who likes war stories?	3	
• has a character who is in danger because of a piece of confidential information?	4	
• continues a story begun by another author?	5	
• was previously published in a different way?	6	
• combines crime and medicine?	7	

Which **three** books contain characters already introduced in previous books?

8		9		10	

A

THE BODY FARM
Patricia D. Cornwell

Dr Kay Scarpetta, investigating the murder of a young girl, needs all her forensic skill to establish how and where she died. At the same time Kay's niece, an FBI trainee, is accused of breaching security, which Kay cannot believe...

B

MRS DE WINTER
The sequel to Daphne du Maurier's Rebecca
Susan Hill

What happened after the fire at Manderley? What became of Max de Winter, his pretty wife, and the evil Mrs Danvers? Find out in this evocative sequel to the ever-popular classic.

C

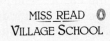

TALES FROM A VILLAGE SCHOOL
Miss Read

Forty short stories about life in a village school, which led to Miss Read's bestselling sequence of books, are brought together and published for the first time in book form.

D

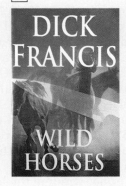

WILD HORSES
Dick Francis

Hot on the heels of *Decider*, which broke all previous records, comes the gripping story of a man who, entrusted with the secrets of the confessional, finds himself in a moral dilemma that could be a matter of life and death. *His.*

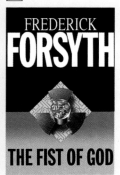

THE FIST OF GOD
Frederick Forsythe

During the dramatic days of the Gulf War, an SAS officer undertakes the most daring assignment of his career - to find "The Fist of God", the deadly supergun capable of firing a nuclear warhead.

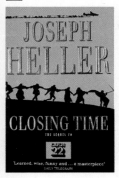

CLOSING TIME
Joseph Heller

Thirty-three years on, this is the long-awaited sequel to *Catch 22*. In a novel of breathtaking comic invention and originality, Joseph Heller revisits the same characters – older but not necessarily wiser – as the twentieth century draws to a close.

LONDON MATCH
Len Deighton

The story should have been over when the KGB major defected, but now some revelations threaten to rock the foundations of British intelligence. The final part of Len Deighton's spy trilogy, which is also available as a gift set.

FAMILY AND FRIENDS
Anita Brookner

Anita Brookner probes deeply behind the veneer to observe the highs and lows of family relationships and friendships.

2 Where has this information come from?

A A brochure.
B The reviews section of a newspaper.
C A magazine.
D A university reading list.

Why would someone read this information?

A To help them select books.
B To find out about the authors.
C To find out where to buy the books.
D For a critical analysis of the books.

3 Assuming you could buy these books in translation, which one would you give your:

• mother   • brother?   • boy/girlfriend?
• teacher?   • father?   • sister?   • best friend?

Which one would you most/least like to get as a present?

LISTENING

1 You will hear five different women talk about the books they have read recently. Choose from the list **A-F** what each person thought about the book she read.

A She felt it wasn't as good as the original.
B She hated the book she read.
C She thought the characters led depressing lives.
D She had to stay up late to finish the book.
E She found the subject of the book unpleasant.
F She strongly recommends the book she has read.

Speaker 1 ☐
Speaker 2 ☐
Speaker 3 ☐
Speaker 4 ☐
Speaker 5 ☐

2 Listen again and decide which of the books **A-H** the women had read.

VOCABULARY

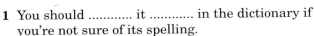

Complete these sentences with a word or expression using **look**.

1 You should .... it .... in the dictionary if you're not sure of its spelling.
2 I can't wait to read that new thriller. I'm really .... to it.
3 What an interesting .... book. Can I borrow it?
4 I'll lend it to you provided you .... it.
5 Would you mind .... this book if you go to a bookshop?

LANGUAGE STUDY

Past simple or present perfect?

1 Read Len Deighton's biography and find out how many occupations Len Deighton has had.

Len Deighton **(0)**..has led.. (*lead*) an interesting life. He **(1)**.......... (*write*) for years but he **(2)**.......... (*be*) also a photographer, waiter and even an advertising man. He **(3)**.......... (*be born*) in London in 1922, and **(4)**.......... (*take*) his first job as a railway clerk. He **(5)**.......... (*do*) his National Service as a photographer, and **(6)**.......... (*be*) stationed in Germany. It was during his time in Berlin that he first **(7)**.......... (*come*) into contact with the shady world of espionage. Afterwards, he **(8)**.......... (*go*) on to be an art student at St. Martin's School of Art in London. He **(9)**.......... (*work*) part-time as a waiter in order to make money. While he **(10)**.......... (*be*) a waiter, he **(11)**.......... (*become*) deeply interested in cookery and **(12)**.......... (*produce*) a regular comic strip on the subject for *The Observer* newspaper. **(13)**.......... (*follow*) on from this, he worked in New York, and **(14)**.......... (*return*) to England to take over as the art director of an advertising firm. At the beginning of the sixties he **(15)**.......... (*go*) to settle in France where he **(16)**.......... (*live*) ever since. In 1962, his first book, *The Ipcress File*, **(17)**.......... (*be*) published. Since then he **(18)**.......... (*write*) over 25 books. Not only **(19)**.......... (*write*) his famous spy novels but he also **(20)**.......... (*write*) a history of the Royal Air Force.

2 Complete the text by changing the verbs in brackets into an appropriate form or tense. You may need to change the word order.

When we use the present perfect

1 Past simple or present perfect?

In pairs, discuss why we can say:

He has been a photographer.
but not
He has been a photographer five years ago.

What did he do when he was in Berlin?
but not
What has he done when he was in Berlin?

Try and work out a rule.
We use the present perfect to ....

2 Different uses of the present perfect

The present perfect can be used in very different ways:
A She has known him for seven years.
B She's been to India.
C Oh! You've had a haircut.
D I've written three letters this morning.

Which of the four sentences **A**, **B**, **C** and **D** decribes something:

1 that happened in the past where you can still see the result now?
2 that started in the past but which is still going on now?
3 that has happened over a period not yet finished?
4 that happened in the past but we do not know when?

3 Present perfect simple or continuous?

We use the present perfect simple when an action is finished and we want to to talk about the result of the action:
Len Deighton has written more than 25 books. ✔
Len Deighton has been writing 25 books. ✗

We use the present perfect continuous when we are talking about an activity which started in the past and is still going on. We are more interested in the activity than the result. For example:
He has been writing for 30 years.

Look through the biography of Len Deighton once more and explain the different uses of the present perfect.

4 Adverbs and word order

Put the following sentences into the right order.
Example: they/ arrived/already/have?
Have they already arrived?

1 for/not/she/spoken/him/to/years/has/ten.
....

2 had/house/decorated/have/just/their/they.
....

3 never/meal/wonderful/a/I/before/have/such/had.
....

4 that/you/have/seen/yet/movie?
....

5 never/she/musical/been/to/a/has.
....

6 are/they/have/waiting/left/or/they/still/already?
....

7 food/this/kind/before/ever/she/eaten/of/has?
....

8 not/ever/the/he/seen/film/has?
....

PRONUNCIATION

Sentence stress

1 Every word in a telegram or telex is expensive so we limit the number of words to those that carry the main meaning.

For example: *I'm coming on Friday. Can you meet me at the airport?* becomes
COMING FRIDAY MEET ME AIRPORT STOP

We do a similar thing when we speak. Of course, we don't leave words out. We just stress the words that carry the most meaning. Sentence stress and meaning are closely connected.

The words in **bold** letters below are strongly stressed. Match the sentences with the speaker's message.

1 **What** have you done with the keys?
2 What have **you** done with the keys?
3 What have you done with the **keys**?

MESSAGE
A I didn't have them last.
B ....not the cheese!
C Surely you didn't do something so stupid!

In pairs practise saying this sentence in different ways: *You might have killed him.*
How can you change the meaning through changing the stress? What effect does this have on the message?

2 Grammar words that are not stressed can become weak. Let's hear how this works with some sentences in the present perfect.

Listen to the sentences and decide which words are **strong** and which are **weak**. Put a line under the strong syllables and a circle around the weak ones.

Example: Len <u>Deigh</u>ton s been a phot<u>og</u>rapher.
A He's been living in France.
B He's been writing books for ages.
C What have you done to my car?
D How long have you been a dancer?
E How long have you been learning English?
F It's late. Where have you been?
G I've been trying to phone.

Listen to the sentences again and try to copy the speaker's pronunciation as closely as you can.

SPEAKING

Role play

You are going to take part in an interview with a famous ballet dancer. Before you begin, practise saying these two sentences:
*How **long** have you been a **dan**cer?*
*I've been a dancer for **twen**ty years.*

STUDENT B: You are the ballet dancer. Go to page 33 for your information.

STUDENT A: You are the interviewer. You are a reporter from *Hi!* magazine. Find out about Lydia/Leonid, why she/he left the former Soviet Union, when she/he started dancing, her/his family and so on. Ask what has changed in the new Russia. Remember that you want an interesting story with as much gossip as possible! So ask her/him lots of questions about her/his private life.

KEEPING IN TOUCH

h/w

1 Look at these opening words for different letters. Which ones will contain good or bad news? Which are formal and which are informal?

a I am pleased to inform you...
b I am writing to enquire about ....
c I was sorry to hear.
d Congratulations....
e With reference to....

2 Think of a continuation for each opening.

3 What kind of letters do you write and receive the most often?

h/w

An informal letter

1 Celia Walker has just moved to a new flat. She is writing to her brother, Andy, to bring him up to date with all her news. Put the letter into the right order. The beginning and end have been done for you.

> 15 Green Road
> London EC3 7HJ
>
> Dear Andy,
>   Thanks a lot for the lovely letter. It was great news about your promotion. You have a great business brain - you take after Uncle Richard. Well done!
>
> 1   Do let me know as I'll have to get tickets.
> 2   Would you like to come too? You can stay at my place.
> 3   What's more, I've just started a new job.
> 4   I've been taken on as a shop assistant in a bookshop. I'm going to be in charge of the foreign section.
> 5   You'll be sad to hear that Mr. Green, our old teacher, passed away last month.
> 6   I'm really sorry for not having written earlier but life has been busy since moving here.
> 7   I've taken to the other staff, they're nice and friendly, and the job is quite well paid.
> 8   Guess what! She has just moved here too.
> 9   Poor Mr. Green. Still, life goes on.
> 10 Incidentally, I've arranged to go to the theatre to see 'Cats' with Anna in a couple of weeks' time.
> 11 She told me some awful news, though.
> 12 By the way, the other day I bumped into Anna Granger in the bookshop.
>
> Anyway, I must sign off as I want to catch the post. Hope to see you soon.
>
>   Lots of love,
>   Celia

h/w

2 **Understanding the organisation of the letter**
Which words and expressions are used to:

1 introduce bad news?
2 move to another subject?
3 apologise?

4 say **and?**
5 make an invitation?
6 introduce a surprise?

3 Changing the subject

Anyway, **by the way** and **incidentally** are all ways of showing that you are going to change the subject. We use them a lot, particularly in informal letters and conversation.

Anyway can mean that you are going to talk about something totally different. **By the way** and **incidentally** show that you are going to move onto something which is less important or which you've just remembered.

homework

4 In pairs, plan and write letters based on one of the following situations.

1 Write to your friends, Paul and Suzanne, congratulating them on the arrival of their new baby. Give a reason why you won't be able to go to the christening.
2 Write to your friends Sarah and Patrick. Congratulate Patrick on finally passing his driving test. Invite them to stay for the weekend. Tell them what you have been doing recently.
3 Imagine you are writing to an English friend. Tell him or her all your good and bad news.

VOCABULARY

Phrasal verbs with **take**

1 Match each definition on the right with a phrasal verb on the left.

A take on	**1**	gain control/responsibility
B take after	**2**	start a new activity/hobby
C take off	**3**	start liking
D take over	**4**	have the same character (or looks) as an older relative
E take to	**5**	copy/imitate someone
F take up	**6**	employ

2 Complete each sentence with one of the phrasal verbs with **take**.

1 He was punished for taking his teacher ....
2 She has just been taken .... at the bank.
3 I am afraid I can't take .... my new boss; he's an extremely unpleasant person.
4 Can you take .... while I go to lunch?
5 You really take .... your grandfather. You're both bad-tempered!
6 She's so tense, she should take .... yoga.

USE OF ENGLISH

Complete the second sentence so that it has a similar meaning to the first sentence. You must use between two and five words including the word given. Do not change the word given.

1 I haven't seen her at this disco before.
 time
 It's the .... her at this disco.

2 This evening I'd prefer us to stay at home.
 we
 I'd .... at home this evening.

3 They employ extra staff in the summer.
 on
 Extra staff .... in the summer.

4 Waters has won the final against Graham.
 been
 Graham .... in the final.

5 Have you thought about learning to sail?
 take
 Why .... sailing?

6 Susan is responsible for student registrations.
 charge
 Susan .... student registrations.

7 She hasn't appeared live for years.
 last
 It's years .... live.

8 Don't throw that dictionary away.
 rid
 Don't .... that dictionary.

9 This terrible weather makes me angry and depressed.
 fed
 I .... this terrible weather.

10 I'm dying for something to drink.
 do
 I .... a drink.

STUDENT B
You are Lydia/Leonid. Answer A's questions. Use this information.
Age: 26. Born in Moscow. Started dancing when you were six. Mother doctor. Father dancer too. Studied music and ballet at conservatory. Like classical music and jazz.
Danced with Bolshoi when 17. Travelled to England and France. Four years ago met Italian ballet dancer. Defected to West. Love not politics the reason. Married dancer. One child. You miss parents and sister. Love Russia. Hope to return one day.

COLD CAN KILL

Your boat has struck rocks on a deserted island and is sinking fast. You only have time to pick up three of the objects above. Which would you take? You know nothing about the island and may have to stay there for years until you are rescued.

1 Read the text to find out who Caitlin and Squib are and what is special about them. Then complete the text by choosing between the words in bold.

Of all the places in Britain, **(1) any/none** is as dangerous as the Scottish Cairngorm mountains. In just **(2) several/some** minutes the weather can change from bright sunshine to bitter cold and snow. Almost **(3) all/every** climbers check the weather before setting off but there are always **(4) few/a few** who go climbing no matter how **(5) much/many** warning they have had. They believe there is **(6) few/little** danger and that somehow the warning does not apply to them.

Sadly a considerable **(7) amount/number** of climbers perish each year, but a great **(8) many/quantity** more survive because of the **(9) many/much** volunteers ready to search for them. The most successful is Caitlin McQuilter, a shy, solitary woman with **(10) few/a few** friends apart from her sheep dog, Squib. **(11) Both/All** make an inseparable team ready to go out in **(12) all/every** weathers on their missions. When there is but **(13) little/some** hope of finding **(14) anyone/none** alive, they often succeed. With patience, determination and **(15) a little/a few** luck they manage to locate **(16) a few/few** lucky climbers each year. Half-frozen after their long searches, Caitlin and Squib refuse **(17) a/any** publicity and retreat to their small stone cottage. Strangely, **(18) almost/hardly** any of the people who are rescued ever accepts responsibility and blames the weather! **(19) No-one/Everyone** who is interviewed seems to forget the great **(20) amount/number** of energy, money and commitment that has gone into saving them.

2 What is the difference between the following?

1 a She has **few** friends.   **b** She has **a few** friends.
Which one suggests fewer than normal?

2 a There is **little** hope.   **b** There is **a little** hope.
Which one has the idea of almost no hope at all?

3 a They spoke to **each** person in turn.   **b** They spoke to **every** person.
Which one has the idea that each person was dealt with as an individual?

3 Which words and expressions can be followed by countable nouns, and which by uncountable nouns?

• all   • every   • a large number of   • a great deal of   • a great amount of

LISTENING

1 Study the situation and, in pairs, discuss your survival plan.

It is two o'clock in the morning. You and a friend are driving along a lonely Canadian mountain road. It has been snowing heavily for the past two hours and you realise there is no possibility of continuing any further because the snow is too deep. You know that last winter two travellers died in similar conditions. You each have a winter coat and a pair of gloves with you. You think there might be a petrol station in another kilometre or so.

2 Now listen to the radio programme on surviving in cold weather and decide if you would have survived!

3 Listen to the interview again and complete these notes.

Your most important piece of survival equipment is **(1)** ....
Rule number one is **(2)** ....
You should make sure you have the following things in the car: blankets, **(3)** .... , **(4)** .... , **(5)** ....
You should make sure your window is open **(6)** .... on the **(7)** .... from the wind.
Car fumes can kill you in **(8)** ....
You should run your car engine for a maximum of **(9)** .... every hour.
Before you leave on your journey, you should **(10)** ....

4 Look at the tapescript on page 220. What ways does the speaker use for giving advice to travellers?

SPEAKING

 Work in pairs. Study the notes and give each other advice about travelling in these two environments. Add/invent any further advice you can think of.

STUDENT A: Give B advice about crossing a desert.
Ring ahead with estimated time of arrival.
Always travel in two vehicles.
Two spare tyres. Double amount of water, e.g. 3 day trip, take 6 days' water. Good maps and a compass.
If anything goes wrong stay near vehicle. Burn tyres to attract attention. Rest in shade to conserve energy. Don't try to walk.

STUDENT B: Give A advice about making a jungle trip.
Take medicine chest and snake serum.
Need water purifying tablets and mosquito nets. Wear boots and long trousers - not shorts. Presents for people we meet! Take a revolver or rifle and maps and compass. If things go wrong find high ground and open space. If you don't have a transceiver radio have rescue flares you can fire into sky.

SCARING OURSELVES TO DEATH

FIRST THOUGHTS

How safe is it to walk alone in your city? What precautions do you take?

READING

1 You are going to read a magazine article about the dangers of modern living. Before you begin, discuss these questions.

- How safe is it to go out in your city at night?
- Is it getting better or worse?

2 Read the article and choose the most suitable heading from the list **A-H** for each part (**1-6**) of the article. There is one extra heading you do not need to use. There is an example at the beginning (**0**). Don't worry if you can't understand the meaning of every word. This should not prevent you from completing the task.

> **A** More to lose.
> **B** Dangers of modern living.
> **C** Self-defence?
> **D** Living in fear.
> **E** Lock your car door.
> **F** Death on a big scale.
> **G** Better over here.
> **H** From A to B.

0	D

Four out of five Londoners are afraid to go out at night **because of** fear of violent crime. Some have given up going out at all! Of course people do get mugged and worse - lightning does have to strike somewhere. Like most large cities there are areas where you don't take an evening stroll. All the same, and despite lurid news reports, the chances against something *really* bad happening to you are remote. So, just what are the risks?

1	

London has been visited regularly by war and disease. Probably the worst time to have been around was in the 1660s. In 1665 the Great Plague claimed thousands of lives, while a great part of the old city was obliterated in the Great Fire of the following year. Two centuries on, in 1849, a cholera epidemic wiped out fourteen thousand Londoners. This was **due to** poor sanitation, and the introduction of clean water and proper sewers eliminated this risk entirely. It is cruelly ironic that more died in the influenza epidemic following the First World War than in the conflict itself. In the Second World War, around thirty thousand perished during the "Blitz" bombing raids. Compared with these statistics, random attacks on individuals pale into insignificance.

2	

Getting around London can be very bad for the health too. Walking is ten times more dangerous than travelling by car, riding a bicycle 15 times, while the worst of all is travelling by motor cycle, where the risks are 33 times higher. As far as travelling by Underground is concerned, you would have to spend eleven entire life-times travelling by Tube before you suffered a serious accident. If from birth you travelled by car continuously, you'd be dead by the age of 40.

3

Returning to the fear of crime, it is certainly true that crime has increased. The time when you could leave your house unlocked has long gone. Burglaries have reached epidemic proportions **so** on go the locks, grills and chains. Perhaps it's **because** nowadays we have more valuables worth stealing. However, it is still a far cry from the lawless days of two hundred years ago when London was in the grip of a crime wave.

4

No rich man would venture out after dark without an armed bodyguard. Strangling was a favoured form of attack. **That's why** unsporting Londoners would wear a reinforced metal collar so that their attackers would be unable to apply the necessary pressure. Some even had spikes set into them! Many gentlemen carried a sword concealed in a walking stick **in case** they ran into an unpleasant situation. Some years ago on the Underground an elderly gentleman enthusiastically "protected" himself from a couple of fellow passengers with a swordstick. Despite a plea of self defence, he was prosecuted by the police!

5

It is undeniable that there are more murders than there used to be. Cases have gone up threefold since the 1960s. Each year around three hundred people in London meet their end this way. However, spare a thought for New York where, **owing to** the ease with which you can buy guns, the number stands at two thousand.

6

The real risks that present-day Londoners face are more mundane. People who go out armed with alarms and tear gas should remember danger lurks indoors. Domestic fires and falls are more deadly than any modern Jack the Ripper or eccentric elderly gentleman. Remember, too, that the biggest killers of all, cancer and heart disease, result from an unhealthy life-style. **Consequently**, if we're not scaring ourselves to death we're stealthily committing suicide by smoking and snacking. So, even though it may be a little dark and menacing outside, don't give up and hide. Go out for a jog or walk the dog – you'll survive longer in the long run. Oh, and fit a smoke alarm just in case!

3 Vocabulary in context

Find the words and expressions which mean:

paragraph **0**	**a** attacked and robbed in the street
	b a casual walk
	c shocking and unpleasant
paragraph **1**	**a** totally destroyed
	b killed in large numbers
	c died
paragraph **3**	**a** a tight hold
paragraph **4**	**b** sharp points
	c a claim
paragraph **6**	**a** waits in hiding threateningly
	b quietly and cautiously

4 Answer these questions by choosing **A**, **B** or **C**. There is one question for each of the paragraphs.

0 What does the writer believe about crime?
  A People should learn to control their fear.
  B There are dangerous spots in most cities.
  C We are all likely to be a victim of crime.

1 Which statement is closest to the writer's opinion?
  A Londoners were safest in the last century.
  B There are events much worse than crime.
  C There is still some risk from cholera.

2 Which is the <u>third</u> most dangerous way of travelling round London?
  A By bicycle
  B On foot
  C By car

3 Why has crime increased?
  A People are wealthier than before.
  B People are less careful than once upon a time.
  C We are in the middle of a crime wave.

4 What does the writer tell us about active self defence?
  A Thieves consider it unfair.
  B People used to take fewer precautions.
  C It can get you into trouble.

5 What was the London murder rate in the 1960s as a percentage of the modern New York rate?
  A 5%
  B 10%
  C 20%

6 What is the greatest danger to Londoners?
  A Fires and falls.
  B Personal habits.
  C Chance attacks by strangers.

LANGUAGE STUDY

Consequences

1 Look at the words in **bold** in the text on pages 36-37. Which ones are followed by reasons, which by precautions and which by results (consequences)?

2 Rephrase the sentences below using the words at the end of each line.

1 You should insure your house because it may catch fire. **in case**
2 He didn't want anyone to recognise him so the film star wore dark glasses. **because**
3 She packed the glasses carefully because she didn't want them to get broken in the post. **so**
4 He always took a map with him. He was afraid of getting lost. **in case**
5 The thief wore gloves because he didn't want to leave any fingerprints. **That's why**
6 The notices are in seven languages because the manager wants foreign guests to feel welcome. **so that**
7 The show was cancelled because she was ill. **due to**
8 The trains didn't operate because there had been a heavy snow fall. **Consequently**
9 He was young. That's why the judge didn't send him to prison. **because of**
10 The exchange rate improved so we got more money. **owing to**

3 What advice would you give to a foreigner about where to go in your city and how to avoid trouble? Use some of the forms we have examined in the previous exercise. Say something about: carrying cash, wearing jewellery, having a map and guide book, people and places to avoid.

USE OF ENGLISH

1 Has anyone in the class shared a room with a brother or sister? Did this ever cause problems? For example, were there arguments about who would sleep where?

2 Read the text below and find out why the sisters were happy to sleep where they did.

3 Now complete the text by changing the word in capital letters at the end of each line into a suitable form. Think carefully what kind of word you will need, e.g. noun, adjective, adverb.

When I was small I shared a room with my sister, Sue. She slept by the window while I was next to the door. I was happy with the **(0)** arrangement .. **ARRANGE**
because I was **(1)**............ that Guy the Gorilla was going to escape from **TERROR**
London Zoo and climb through the window. While he ate up my
(2)............ sister I would get away down the stairs! Even though I knew **FORTUNE**
this was an **(3)**............ fear (why on earth would Guy come to our **RATIONAL**
ordinary house in the suburbs?), knowing it was silly made no **(4)**............ . **DIFFERENT**
Years later when I told Sue my **(5)**............ reasons for sleeping near the **SELF**
door she was able to **(6)**............ . **SYMPATHY**
She confessed **(7)**............ that for years she had a similar **GUILT**
(8)............ that an escaped lion was going to come up the stairs. It would **BELIEVE**
have me for supper while she got away through the window! Sadly, Guy,
the bogeyman of my **(9)**............, passed away many years ago. He was a **CHILD**
(10)............ vegetarian who, had he come to my home, would have only **HARM**
attacked the fruit bowl.

VOCABULARY

Phrasal verbs using *give*

1 Look at these two sentences from the text about surviving in London.
- *Some have given up going out at all!*
- *Don't give up and hide.*

Give up is being used in two different ways. Look at the dictionary entry for **give up** to see which meaning is represented in each case. Note the number of each meaning.

> **give** sbdy./sthg.↔**away** *v adv* [T] **1** to make someone a present or prize of (something): *She gave away all her money to the poor.*/(fig.) *Our team just gave the match away by playing so badly.* **2** to deliver or formally hand over a woman) to the husband at the wedding: *Mary was given away by her father.* **3** to make known (a secret) intentionally or unintentionally: *He tried to pretend that he wasn't worried, but his shaking hands gave him away.* (=showed his real feelings) —see also GIVE AWAY
>
> **give** sbdy. **back** sthg. *v adv* [T] to return (something) to the owner or original possessor: *Give me back my pen.*/*Give me my pen back.* – see Study Notes on page 429
>
> **give in** *v adv* **1** [I *to*] to yield: *The boys fought until one gave in.*/*Don't give in to him.* **2** [T] (**give** sthg.↔**in**) to deliver;hand in: *Give your examination papers in (to the teacher) when you've finished.*
>
> **give off** sthg. *v adv* [T] to send out (esp. a liquid, gas, or smell): *to give off steam.*
>
> **give out** *v adv* **1** [T] (**give** sthg.↔**out**) to give to each of several people: *Give out the examination papers.*/*Give the money out to the children.* **2** [I] also **run out**–*infml* to come to an end: *His strength gave out.*
>
> **give over** *v adv* [I;T (=**give over** sthg.) + *v-ing*; *often in commands*] BrE *infml* to stop
>
> **give up** *v adv* **1** [T + *v-ing*] (**give up** sthg.) to stop having or doing: *The doctor told me to give up smoking.*/*I gave that idea up a long time ago.* **2** [I;T (=*give* sthg.↔**up**] to stop working at or trying to do (something): *to give up ones studies*/ *He tried to swim the English Channel, but had to give up halfway.* **3** [T] (**give** sbdy. **up**) to stop believing that (someone) can be saved, esp. from death: *The boy was given up for lost/dead.* **4** [T (*to*)] (**give** sbdy. **up**) to offer (someone or oneself) as a prisoner: *He gave himself up (to the police).* –compare SURRENDER **5** [T (*to*)] (**give** sthg.↔**up**) to deliver or allow to pass (to someone else): *Give your seat up to the old lady.*

2 Substitute the words in bold with a suitable phrasal verb with **give**. Write down the number of the meaning which is expressed

gave out 2
Example: *The explorer's food ~~finished~~ in the middle of the desert.*

1 Can you **distribute** the books to the class, Claudia?
2 Before she died, she **left** all her money to the dogs' home.
3 When the plastic caught fire, it **produced** a terrible smell.
4 Joanna **offered** her seat to the man with the walking stick.
5 They had to **stop** the climb when it started snowing.
6 Stop! Stop! I **surrender**. Don't hurt me any more!
7 She talked in her sleep and **said** where the money was hidden.
8 If I were you, I'd **stop** drinking whisky.
9 He never **returns** the books he borrows.

3 Work in pairs and ask and answer these questions.

Have you ever...
1 given something away which you regretted afterwards?
2 forgotten to give back a book or record/CD to someone?
3 given up something that you thought was too difficult?
4 given up a bad habit or sporting activity?
5 been forced to give in and do something you didn't want to do, e.g. wear different clothes, visit boring relatives?

DEVIL'S ALTERNATIVES

FIRST THOUGHTS

1 Describe the two photographs to each other in as much detail as you can. Say which of the people in the photographs you would rather be and why.

2 Look at the questionnaire which appeared in a magazine for young people and decide which answers you would choose.

Imagine you have no choice in the matter but have to decide between **a** and **b** in each case. Would you rather...

1 a give a ten minute speech to 5000 people or
  b clean the toilets of your school for a month?

2 a do a bungee jump or
  b sit in a cage with snakes?

3 die **a** young and rich or
  b old and poor?

4 be **a** a tragic genius or
  b a normal average person?

LISTENING

1 Two friends, Lucinda and Damien, are discussing the questionnaire. Listen and find out what choices each of them makes for questions **1** and **2**.

2 Managing conversations

1 In conversations, people often need to create thinking time. One way of doing this is by using the expressions: *You know* and *I mean*. Listen to the conversation again and count how many times *I mean* and *you know* are used.

2 Sometimes we may not know or be able to remember the exact words for describing something. Look at the way Lucinda uses *sort of* and *kind of* in her description of bungee jumping:

Well, it's a **sort of** *.... you know... it's when you tie a* **kind of** *cord around your legs and jump off a bridge or something like that.* **It's kind of** *... you know ... elastic.*

3 Work in pairs and practise describing these objects to each other.

A    B

C 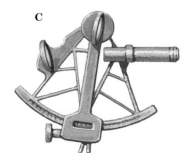   D

USE OF ENGLISH

Complete the text by using each of the words in the box once only. Of course, in the examination you will not have any help like this!

Austin's luck finally ran out on day 92 when a cobra bit him on the arm. He **(1)**............ wanted to break the world record for living in a glass cage with poisonous snakes. **(2)**............ was as part of a publicity stunt to attract visitors to a snake and animal park in South Africa. His companions had been no **(3)**............ than 36 deadly snakes. They included 20 cobras **(4)**............, most dangerous of all, six black mambas **(5)**............ bite can kill in under a minute. He hadn't been **(6)**............ to relax for a moment as **(7)**............ movement which was made excited his "room mates". He fed **(8)**............ on live mice but had to make sure that he didn't touch them in **(9)**............ he was mistaken for food too!
By day 92 he had **(10)**............ been bitten twice, but on both occasions, by a miracle, **(11)**............ venom entered his bloodstream. One day he even fell on top of a black mamba. Fortunately for him, **(12)**............ of striking, the mamba shot across to the other side of the cage. When he **(13)**............ bitten for the third time, Austin could have left the cage but decided to wait for the antidote to arrive. Even though he was in terrible pain, he decided **(14)**............ he might as well die trying to break the record. As it was, he managed to survive and spent **(15)**............ further two weeks in the cage to set a new record of 107 days.

no	and	them	that	it	able	any	instead
was	whose	had	fewer	a	case	already	

VOCABULARY

1 Complete the following sentences with words based on **live**.

Example: *What do you do for a* .....living..... ?
1 They managed to find three miners who were still .... three days after the underground explosion.
2 She was sent to prison for .... for murdering her husband.
3 The rock concert isn't going to be recorded. Instead it's going to be broadcast .... on television.
4 Young children are often very .... They have so much energy they can't sit still for a minute.
5 She was married six times in her ....
6 Cats are supposed to have nine ....

2 Complete the following sentences with a word based on **die**.

1 "Look after your mother" were his .... words.
2 This bottle contains a .... poison.
3 The snake and the alligator fought to the ....
4 I can't get through; the phone seems to be ....
5 There was a .... silence when he mentioned his ex-wife's name.

3 Complete the following sentences with an expression based on **live** or **die**.

1 I'm .... a drink. I'm so thirsty.
2 She had to .... the little food she had in the hut.
3 Whales are .... because people keep hunting them.
4 It took him 20 years to .... the scandal.
5 Come quickly, doctor. It's a matter of .... or ....

A NARROW ESCAPE

FIRST THOUGHTS

Yoshi comes from Kobe in Japan. While he was visiting England an earthquake destroyed his home. He would probably have died if he had been there. Have you or has anyone in your group ever had a narrow escape from an accident or disaster?

LISTENING

You will hear people talking in eight different situations. For questions **1-8** choose the best answer **A**, **B** or **C**.

1 You turn on your radio and hear someone reading an extract from a book. The book is
   A a thriller.
   B a love story.
   C an autobiography.

2 A studio newsreader is reading the evening bulletin. At the end she
   A moves to the next item.
   B announces some good news.
   C hands over to someone else.

3 You are waiting outside the auditorium for the next film to begin. The film that is about to finish is
   A a horror movie.
   B a western.
   C a film about the French foreign legion.

4 You are in a café when you overhear two women talking about a car accident. From what you hear you can understand that
   A one of the women was driving.
   B the car was hit in the side.
   C what saved one of the women was her seat belt.

5 A mathematics teacher is talking to a pupil who has had trouble with her homework. The teacher is
   A understanding.
   B critical.
   C patient.

6 You are on the bus when you overhear this exchange between a father and a teenage son. The father thinks his son
   A has wrong priorities.
   B is an idealist.
   C is selfish like most young people.

7 You are watching a doctor at work in a park. It is
   A a real emergency.
   B a demonstration on a student.
   C a demonstration on a model.

8 Listen to this woman on the TV talking about another woman. She is talking about her because
   A she is an old friend.
   B she is a famous sailor.
   C she is going to interview her.

LANGUAGE STUDY

Ability

1 *Everybody panicked except Blond. She **could** control her fear.*

1 Turn to page 221 and find the first three passages we have just listened to. Underline all the other words and expressions that are used to talk about **ability**.

2 In the first passage why does it say *Blond was **able to** get out* and not *Blond **could** get out*?

3 What are the differences in structure between **manage** and **succeed**?

2 Complete these sentences. In some cases both answers may be correct.

1 When he was a child , he .... swim like a fish.
   A was able to   **B** could

2 We drove into town but we .... find anywhere to park.
   A couldn't   **B** weren't able to

3 They have finally .... in selling their old car.
   A managed   **B** succeeded

4 They .... escape by climbing through the window.
   A were able to   **B** managed

5 She .... sing beautifully as a little girl.
   A was able to   **B** could

6 Good news! I .... buy the last tickets.
   A could   **B** was able to

7 Did you .... to open the tin?
   A succeed   **B** manage

VOCABULARY

Collocations

In Unit 1 we looked at how verbs combine with nouns and adjectives to form fixed phrases. In the passages you have just listened to there are further examples of these.

1 Turn to page 221-222 and study the tapescript of the eight passages you have just heard. Find out which verbs collocate with the words and phrases **a-l**.

Then match **a-l** with the definitions **1-12**.

a .... an effort	**1** to check
b .... charge of	**2** to have a short conversation
c .... one's word	**3** to gradually accept
d .... a promise	**4** to have a significant effect
e .... one's temper	**5** to assume control
f .... a warning	**6** to try hard
g .... attention	**7** not do what you said you would
h .... a word	**8** to become uncontrollably angry
i .... a difference	**9** to discuss angrily
j .... an argument	**10** to watch/listen carefully
k .... sure	**11** to caution
l .... to terms with	**12** to do what you say you will

2 Complete the second sentence so that it has a similar meaning to the first. You must use between two and five words including the word given. Do not change the word given.

1 Listen carefully to what I am about to say.
attention
Please .... what I am about to say.

2 Someone told the boys it was dangerous to play by the lake.
warning
The boys .... about playing by the lake.

3 Jenny and her mother argued over the wedding dress.
argument
Jenny .... her mother over the wedding dress.

4 He finally managed to get over his wife's death.
terms
He succeeded .... his wife's death.

5 I am going to get very angry in a minute.
temper
I am going to .... in a minute.

6 If you don't try hard you won't succeed.
effort
Unless .... you'll fail.

7 What they say doesn't change anything.
difference
It .... what they say.

8 She assumed control of the business when her father retired.
charge
She .... the business when her father retired.

9 I couldn't speak to her.
word
I wasn't .... with her.

10 We should always keep our word.
promise
We should never ....

Study note
A number of important collocations are on page 216 of the Reviser Guide. When you come across new examples, add them to the section.

QUICK THINKING

FIRST THOUGHTS

1 How do you contact the emergency services in your country? Is there ever a problem with hoax (false) calls?

2 Have you ever rescued someone, or been rescued yourself from a difficult situation?

3 Look at the pictures. What do you think happened? What would you do if you came across the scene?

READING

Choose from the sentences **A-I** the one which fits each gap (**1-7**). There is one extra sentence which you do not need to use. There is an example at the beginning (**0**).

A	Such tales of courage defy belief.
B	He simply lets the facts rivet you, then applies his journalistic skills to sketch in the everyday human details that make these stories so vivid.
C	You have no previous flying experience.
D	Take John Gething, saviour of 12-year-old Hayley Rogers.
E	You may have witnessed their acts of courage in the gripping BBC television series of the same name.
F	For instance, Hayley's story is followed by a clear explanation of the ABC of resuscitation – Airway, Breathing and Circulation.
G	Who can forget his moving film reports from the scene of the Ethiopian famine in 1984?
H	A five-year-old girl is trapped beneath the wreckage of a container lorry which is about to crush her to death any second.
I	The swirling water plaited her hair into what was, effectively, a thick rope, pulling her head beneath the pool's surface.

Imagine you are the first on the scene of an horrific road accident. **0** **H** Are you prepared to put your own life at risk just to comfort her?

Now imagine you're the passenger in a two-seater light aircraft at 2,500 feet. **1** Suddenly the pilot has a massive heart attack and dies at the controls. How do you react?

Kathryn Clayton and Alan Anderson, who faced these dilemmas for real, are just two of the everyday heroes celebrated in Michael Buerk's new book, *999: Dramatic Stories of Real-Life Rescues*. **2** But, here in print, the inherent drama and nail-biting suspense of these true stories comes across with even greater impact. For the first time, you find yourself inside the minds of the victims and the rescuers, experiencing their terror, sharing their sense of disbelief.

What soon becomes clear is that when life is on the line, human beings are capable of drawing on amazing qualities deep inside themselves. **3** Hayley was paddling in a children's swimming pool

when her long hair got sucked into one of the intake valves. **4** In a flash of inspiration, John – himself only a teenager – was able to improvise resuscitation techniques that kept her alive under water for well over four minutes.

Given the cautionary nature of so many of these tales, *999* takes the opportunity to pass on a series of simple practical tips which could help you deal with similar life-threatening situations. **5** The author behind this inspiring book is the acclaimed news reporter, Michael Buerk – in his own way a lifesaver.

6 To a large extent, it was Michael who first alerted the world to the scale of that tragedy, triggering massive international relief effort which eventually saved over a million lives.

In *999*, as ever, Michael Buerk resists the temptation to sensationalise. **7** The result is a welcome reminder of the immense capacity for self-sacrifice that can be found inside every one of us.

Let's examine two ways of adding emphasis that can be found in the reading text.

To a large extent, ***it was Michael who*** *first alerted the world to the scale of the tragedy...*
This is almost the same as *Michael first alerted the world to the scale of the tragedy.*
However, by putting **It...** first, we emphasise that Michael, more than anyone else, was responsible.
(We use **It was... that...** for things.)

What soon becomes clear is that *when life is on the line, human beings are capable of drawing on amazing qualities deep inside themselves.*
This is almost the same as *When life is on the line, it becomes clear that human beings...*
Again, by beginning the sentence with **What...**, we are emphasising what comes next.

Rewrite these sentences, beginning with the words in **bold**.

1 He was rescued from the mountain by Caitlin.
  It was
2 I was moved by her act of courage.
  What
3 Her telephone call raised the alarm.
  It was

4 People who ignore weather warnings make me angry.
  What
5 His rescue took us all by surprise.
  What
6 We found the missing sailor by chance.
  It was

1 Look at the illustrations of a remarkable rescue which took place at a sky-diving display in Paris. Tell each other what you think happened then quickly read the text below to see if you were correct.

2 Now correct the text. Some lines are correct and some have an extra or word which should not be there. There are two examples at the beginning (**0** and **00**).

  0 A man knocked unconscious when he jumped ✔
 00 out of **from** a plane was saved by the quick
  1 thinking of another one sky diver. This drama
  2 it took place at a sky-diving festival near
  3 to Paris. It began after Italian Maurizio
  4 Brambilla had to thrown himself from a Hercules
  5 aircraft at 15000 feet. He was knocked himself out
  6 on the edge of the plane. Ex-marine Andy Peckett
  7 acted quickly and set off him in a deadly chase
  8 as the Italian was disappeared from sight.
  9 Very few of divers would have acted so quickly.
 10 Rather than to adopt the flat face to earth position,
 11 he dived headfirst to gain the speed. At 240 kph
 12 he caught at Maurizio in a rugby tackle and
 13 opened his chute. He opened his own a few seconds
 14 before impact. Andy, the hero, couldn't feel too
 15 afraid because of it happened so fast.

Imagine that you were an eyewitness at one of the incidents described in the review of *999*. Write a report in **120-180** words, explaining to your readers what happened.

BEDTIME STORIES

FIRST THOUGHTS

All around the world small children are told stories at bedtime. What stories were you told? What were your favourites?

LANGUAGE STUDY

Past tenses

1 Read the beginning of *The tale of Little Red Riding Hood* and find examples of the following past tenses in the text:

1 the past simple tense, e.g. *She went...*
2 the past continuous tense, e.g. *She was going...*
3 the past perfect tense, e.g. *She had gone...*
4 the past perfect continuous tense, e.g. *She had been going...*

NCE UPON A TIME there was a little girl called Little Red Riding Hood who lived with her mother. Little Red Riding Hood's grandmother had not been feeling very well, so one fine day she decided to visit her. The little girl got ready, waved goodbye to her mother and promised to be careful. On her arm she carried a basket which contained a cake her mother had baked specially. It was a lovely spring morning, the sun was shining and the birds were singing, happy that the winter was over. She had been walking a little way when the basket seemed to become heavier and heavier.

So even though Little Red Riding Hood's mother had told her to follow the path through the fields, the naughty child decided to ignore her advice and take a short cut through a wood. As she went deeper and deeper into it, the cold and darkness frightened her. She was making her way along the narrow path when she heard a noise. All of a sudden a big, fierce-looking wolf jumped out from behind a bush and came towards her...

2 We can use these four past tenses in different ways. Study each of the example sentences and the description of their use.

Past simple
*Once upon a time there **was** a little girl called Little Red Riding Hood who **lived** with her mother.*
Here the past simple is being used to describe simple facts and states.

*The little girl **got** ready, **waved** goodbye to her mother and **promised** to be careful.*
Here the past simple is used on its own because the events follow each other in a clear chronological sequence.

Past continuous
*The sun **was shining** and the birds **were singing.***
Here the past continuous is being used to set the scene.

*She **was making** her way along the narrow path when she heard a noise.*
Here the past continuous is being used together with the past simple to show that one action was going on when it was interrupted by another action.

Past perfect
*...which contained a cake her mother **had baked** specially.*
Here the past perfect is used to show that the cake was baked earlier. In other words it is like the **past in the past**. As well as using the **past perfect** for the "past in the past", we also use it in past narratives with these words:
just/already/yet/recently/once (meaning after) and **since** (for duration); **for** is used with either the past simple or the past perfect.

Past perfect continuous
*She **had been walking** a little way when the basket seemed to become heavier . . .*
Here the past perfect continuous is used to show the duration of an action up to a point in the past.

3 Put the verbs in this continuation of the story of Little Red Riding Hood into the most suitable tense form.

....licking his lips in anticipation of a tasty meal. He **(1)**............ (*have*) fantasies about such a tender and delicious dish all day and suddenly his dream **(2)**............ (*come*) true. He **(3)**............(*not want*) to chase her as he **(4)**............ (*feel*) weak with hunger so instead he **(5)**............ (*smile*) his most friendly smile and **(6)**............ (*ask*) her where she **(7)**............ (*go*). The girl, who **(8)**............ (*never see*) a wolf before, **(9)**............ (*tell*) him all about her grandmother and where she **(10)**............ (*live*). By the time the sweet child **(11)**............ (*finish*) her tale the wolf **(12)**............ (*already eat*) her three times in his imagination, once raw, once roasted and once boiled. Just as he **(13)**............ (*make up*) his mind to attack her he **(14)**............ (*hear*) two woodcutters approaching and **(15)**............ (*hurry*) off. He **(16)**............ (*know*) they **(17)**............ (*look*) for him for some time in connection with some sheep which **(18)**............ (*disappear*)! Suddenly, he **(19)**............ (*think*) of a clever plan! While his supper – Little Red Riding Hood – **(20)**............ (*slowly make*) her way along the path, not realising what a narrow escape she **(21)**............ (*have*), the wolf **(22)**............ (*rush*) through the forest towards the old lady's door. The cottage door **(23)**............ (*be*) locked because the dear old lady **(24)**............ (*forget*) to open it after her mid-morning nap. Using all his skills as an actor, the wolf **(25)**............ (*pretend*) to be the granddaughter by copying her voice. Granny **(26)**............ (*open*) the door to let "her" in and ...

4 Working in pairs or small groups, tell each other the rest of the Little Red Riding Hood story. Pay special attention to your use of past tenses.

VOCABULARY

1 Make as many connections as you can between the various words and expressions in the box. Example: *The wicked witch flew away on her broomstick.*

wicked witch   fairy godmother   hero   heroine to wave a magic wand   villain   monster   to curse handsome prince   enchanted castle   genie sleeping beauty   to grant a wish   curse   dwarf cruel stepmother   flying carpet   to cast a spell to turn someone into something   big bad wolf   frog wizard   evil queen   magic lamp   broomstick giant   beanstalk   to break a spell   dark forest raven   woodcutter

2 Tell each other a traditional story from your own country.

VERSIONS

/d/   /t/   /ɪd/

stayed   asked   waited

FIRST THOUGHTS

Many fairy stories are set in far off times with princesses, knights, witches, wizards, dragons and magic wands, mirrors and carpets. How could these stories be made more up-to-date and modern? Which people and objects would you use in a modern tale?

LISTENING

An alternative Cinderella

Listen to this modern version of the Cinderella story and complete the notes which summarise what the speaker says. In **Part 2** of **Paper 4** **(Listening)** you have a task like this.

1 One of Cinderella's sisters had a beauty parlour and the other had ....
2 She entered the competition because if she won she could ....
3 The newspapers said the Prince was having a party because he wanted to .... and ....
4 Fairy Godmother also called herself ....
5 The main part of the prize was a ....
6 Cinderella had to agree to ....
7 The king had organised the party because ....
8 Cinderella told the king he could improve his finances by ....
9 Cinderella's new job was as ....
10 Cinderella helped the prince by ....

PRONUNCIATION

Past tenses

1 Regular verbs in the past

Put the verbs in columns according to how their **-ed** ending is pronounced.

> stayed   asked   waited   invited   promised
> carried   contained   decided   frightened

2 Was and were

In *The tale of Little Red Riding Hood* it says *It was a lovely spring morning, the sun was shining and the birds were singing...*

1 Which words would normally be stressed in this sentence?
2 How does this affect the pronunciation of **was** and **were**?
3 Listen to this short dialogue which contains **was** and **were**. When are **was** and **were** strong and when are they weak?

> **A:** Where were you last night?
> **B:** I was at the office.
> **A:** Were you?
> **B:** Yes, I was. I was working late.
> **A:** You were with Paul!
> **B:** No, I wasn't!
> **A:** Yes, you were.

4 Practise reading the dialogue in pairs, paying attention to the strong and weak forms.

LANGUAGE STUDY

After and afterwards

We often use **after** when we want to show the order of two or more events. It is all right, particularly in speech, to use it at the beginning of a sentence.

After he killed the dragon he rescued the princess.
It is clear that killing the dragon was the first action and rescuing the princess came second.

However, if we put **after** between the events, we often follow **after** with either the **gerund** or the **past perfect**:
He rescued the princess after killing the dragon.
He rescued the dragon after he had killed/after having killed the dragon.

We can avoid the past perfect or gerund by using **after that** or **afterwards** instead. They always come before the second action:
He killed the dragon. After that/Afterwards he rescued the princess.

WRITING

1 In the writing paper you may have to write a narrative in the past.

Read the story and give it a title.

> This story is set in Wales in the Middle Ages. There was a prince whose name was Llewellyn. He lived in a valley. He had a baby son. He also had a dog called Gelert. One day the prince went hunting. He left the dog to look after the baby. Some wolves came out from a wood. They ran towards the cottage. The dog saw the wolves and hid the baby. The dog ran outside and fought the wolves. He killed two but was wounded. He was tired and lay down to sleep. The prince returned. He saw the dog covered in blood. He saw that his son's cot was empty. He took his sword and killed the dog while it slept. Then he heard the baby cry and found him. Through the window he saw the two dead wolves. Then he understood. He carried the dog to the top of the hill and buried it. He collected a pile of stones to mark the grave. You can still see it today.

2 The tale is told in a basic way. Expand it to make it more interesting. Also, put it in paragraphs and vary the use of past tenses. Make sure that you use **after** and **afterwards** correctly!

Answer these questions in your version.

1 What did the prince/the dog/the wolves/his house/the valley look like?
2 What was the time of day and what was the weather like at each point of the story?
3 How did the prince feel at different times?

USE OF ENGLISH

1 Read the whole of this text so that you have an idea of what it is about. Think of a title for the story.

A lot of people are familiar with the story of *Brave Gelert*, the dog that faithfully defended the prince's son, but which was then killed while it was fast **(1)**............ through a terrible misunderstanding. **(2)**............, only a few people know that the story is really a pack of lies. Let me explain.

About a hundred or so years ago there was a hotel owner in Wales who was **(3)**............ up with business being so bad. His hotel was stuck in the middle of nowhere and hardly **(4)**............ came to stay. Then, one day, he had an idea. A famous prince called Llewellyn had lived in the area **(5)**............ the Middle Ages and had been **(6)**............ of dogs. This is **(7)**............ surprising as hunting was extremely popular at that time. So what he did was to **(8)**............ up the story of the brave and faithful Gelert and how he had been killed by his **(9)**............ master.

Of course, people would be far more **(10)**............ to believe the story if there was something they could see. **(11)**............, one day, the hotel keeper went to the top of a high hill and built a sort of monument from the stones he found **(12)**............ around. A friend of his, who was, **(13)**............, an accountant helped him to construct it. The "legend" soon caught **(14)**............ and developed a life of its own. Afterwards, people came from far and wide to see the spot where the hound was buried. **(15)**............ to say, business became very good for the hotel owner!

2 Read the text and decide which word **A**, **B**, **C** or **D** best fits each space.

1 **A** sleepy **B** sleepless **C** sleeping **D** asleep
2 **A** So **B** However, **C** Just **D** While
3 **A** fed **B** called **C** looked **D** tied
4 **A** no one **B** everyone **C** anyone **D** someone
5 **A** while **B** since **C** at **D** during
6 **A** keen **B** crazy **C** fond **D** interested
7 **A** really **B** barely **C** strangely **D** hardly
8 **A** turn **B** make **C** call **D** do
9 **A** ungrateful **B** disloyal **C** unfaithful
   D disgraceful
10 **A** possibly **B** probably **C** surely **D** likely
11 **A** So **B** Then **C** Actually **D** Since
12 **A** lying **B** laying **C** hanging **D** looking
13 **A** anyway **B** truthfully **C** incidentally
   D mainly
14 **A** up **B** up with **C** on **D** out
15 **A** Without **B** Needless **C** Nothing **D** Going

RAGS TO RICHES, RICHES TO RAGS

FIRST THOUGHTS

Many fairy tales or traditional stories are to do with poor people suddenly becoming rich. Can you think of any tales like this in your culture?

READING

Quickly read the story of Dick Whittington and put the pictures in the right order.
Then answer the questions by choosing **A**, **B**, **C** or **D**.

1 Why did Dick go to London?
 A Because his parents were dead.
 B It was a long way away.
 C Prospects seemed better.
 D He wanted to experience city life.

2 What did Dick discover when he tried to find work?
 A There were plenty of jobs available.
 B Things were no better in London.
 C Market stalls were best.
 D People were interested in what he had to say.

3 Why did Mr Fitzwarren offer Dick a job?
 A It was a response to Dick's story.
 B An apprentice had just left.
 C Dick had managed to take him in.
 D He recognised Dick's great potential.

4 What was his life like at Mr Fitzwarren's house when he first arrived?
 A Comfortable.
 B Completely awful.
 C A mixture of good and bad.
 D Better than he'd known before.

5 Dick decided to leave London because
 A Alice didn't return the love he felt for her.
 B he was unpopular with the other servants.
 C of a number of reasons.
 D he had been dismissed.

6 What happened after he had heard the bells?
 A He and the cook became friends.
 B He was welcomed home.
 C He returned to the house.
 D He decided to get his cat back.

7 When the ship returned, Dick
 A gave up his job.
 B had already become wealthy.
 C felt ashamed of his past.
 D achieved his dreams.

Once upon a time there was a poor orphan called Dick Whittington. The boy had heard stories about the great city of London where the streets were paved with gold. Although London was a long way from his tiny village, this didn't put him off making a bundle of his few possessions and setting off to seek his fortune.

Once Dick had arrived, he soon realised that work and money were no easier to come by than in the country. He stopped at every shop and market stall to ask for work but the answer was always no. Each time he was turned down, his bundle seemed to grow a little heavier. By nightfall, he had grown tired and hungry and was desperate for somewhere to rest. While he was wandering though the streets, he saw a doorway of a fine house which looked like a good place to take shelter. Using his precious bundle as a pillow, he settled down and quickly fell asleep. The owner of the house was a rich merchant called Mr Fitzwarren who came across Dick on his return home. Luckily for Dick, he was a kind-hearted gentleman. He felt sorry for the lad and decided to take him in. He made sure he was fed and, on hearing Dick's tale, offered him a job as an apprentice.

The boy was given a place to sleep in the attic but was greatly disturbed by the rats and mice that lived there too. So, with his last penny, Dick bought

a cat which soon chased the rats and mice away. It became his greatest friend.

Dick was deeply grateful towards his master and became a trusted member of his household. The boy fell for his lovely daughter, Alice, but Dick believed that he would never be rich or worthy enough to win her hand in marriage. Dick got on well with nearly everybody except for the cook, who made his life a misery and told him off for the slightest thing.

Time passed, until one day his master called all the servants together. He solemnly told them he was going to send a ship off on a long trading voyage. He then asked whether anyone had anything they wished to send on the voyage which could be sold or bartered. Young Dick thought about this a lot and eventually, after much heart searching, decided to send his beloved cat.

Afterwards, he felt sad and lonely and the cook's treatment of him became more and more cruel. Alice seemed more and more unobtainable. Finally he couldn't put up with his situation any longer and decided to run away. With a heavy heart, he prepared his bundle and crept out of the house before anyone was awake. As he reached the green fields which marked the edge of the city, he heard the bells of a nearby church which seemed to be telling him to turn back from his journey. What's more, the bells told him that he would become Lord Mayor of London, not just once but three times. He decided to obey their message

and returned home before anyone had noticed he was missing.

In the meantime, Mr Fitzwarren's ship had arrived in a port of a strange country where no European had ever been before. The captain was invited to the royal palace for a feast in his honour When he got there, the king greeted him and he was taken to a dining room where there was a magnificent meal waiting. Yet, the moment they sat down to eat, hundreds of rats rushed in and ate the food in front of their eyes. The royal host was embarrassed and apologised to his guest, who told him that what he needed was a cat. The good man had no idea what a cat was, so the sailor ordered Dick's pet to be sent ashore. It was the first time anyone had ever seen one and the king himself was even a little afraid of the creature. However, as soon as he saw how it dealt with the rats, he was delighted. Within a couple of days, the entire palace had been cleared of them. The king was so pleased that he gave the captain gold and silver in return for the cat.

Finally, on the ship's return to England, the captain handed over the money and jewels he had received and Dick became extremely rich. He continued to work for Mr Fitzwarren and he eventually married Alice. His fortune grew and, as the bells had promised, he became Lord Mayor of London. He never forgot what it had been like to be poor, and he became famous for the good work he did to help the less fortunate and orphans.

WRITING

Understanding style

1 Study this extract from the text and work out what the words in bold refer to. How does the writer avoid repeating the words **captain**, **cat**, **king** and **palace** too often?

....ever been before. The captain was invited to the royal palace for a feast in **his** honour. When **he** got **there**, the king greeted him and he was taken to a dining room **where** there was a magnificent meal waiting. Yet, the moment **they** sat down to eat, hundreds of rats rushed in and ate the food in front of **their** eyes. The **royal host** was embarrassed and apologised to his **guest who** told **him** that what he needed was a cat. The **good man** had no idea what a cat was, so the **sailor** ordered **Dick's pet** to be sent ashore. It was the first time anyone had ever seen **one** and the king himself was even a little afraid of the **creature**.

2 Read the following story and rewrite it so that you don't repeat the words **princess**, **pond**, **frog** and **witch** too often.

THE PRINCESS SAW A FROG. The frog was in a pond. The pond was near a castle. The frog spoke to the princess. The princess was surprised. The princess went to the pond every day to talk to the frog. The princess fell in love with the frog. One day the frog asked the princess for a kiss. The princess gave the frog a kiss. The frog turned into a handsome prince. A witch had cast a spell on the prince. The witch had taken the prince's castle. The witch lived in the castle. The prince went to the castle. The prince killed the witch. The princess married the prince. The princess and the prince lived happily ever after.

VOCABULARY

Time expressions

Complete these sentences using one of the time expressions or words in the box.

1 The phone rang .... he was in the bath.
2 Mary fell very ill and died suddenly .... the night.
3 Everybody got up and left .... of the film.
4 We queued for the tickets .... two hours.
5 She told us she had .... lived in Paris.
6 The bus .... arrived half an hour late.
7 .... I decide to play tennis it always seems to rain.
8 The plane's arriving in half an hour .... let's have a cup of tea.
9 She insisted on staying .... the concert ended, even though it was awful.
10 We can go to the park and then .... we can visit Lucy.
11 We couldn't get a taxi and we had decided to walk, but .... someone gave us a lift.
12 Just .... leaving work, he phoned home to say he'd be late.

> whenever   before   while   until   during
> afterwards   at the end   for   eventually
> in the meantime   in the end   previously

Phrasal verbs

1 Match the phrasal verbs with their definitions.

A	put up with	**1**	find by chance
B	take in	**2**	stop/discourage from doing something
C	find out	**3**	criticise
D	look after	**4**	discover information/facts
E	set off	**5**	have a (good) relationship with someone
F	turn down	**6**	give hospitality/shelter
G	tell off	**7**	endure/tolerate
H	fall for	**8**	take care of
I	come across	**9**	refuse/reject
J	get on with	**10**	fall in love with/be attracted to someone
K	turn up	**11**	leave on a journey
L	put off	**12**	arrive

2 Complete each sentence with one of the twelve phrasal verbs. Remember to use the correct form.

1 They went to the bus station to .... the time of the next bus to Edinburgh.
2 They .... their grandmother's old school books while they were clearing out the attic.
3 The teacher was angry and .... the pupils .... for not doing their homework.
4 A farmer .... the travellers .... during the snow storm and gave them a bed for the night.
5 She did not .... her new boss so she found another job.
6 Please could you make less noise. It's .... me .... my work.
7 While she was studying in England she .... her landlady's son and they later got married.
8 I can't .... your childish behaviour any longer. I'm leaving.
9 He was .... for the job because of his dirty appearance and long hair.
10 A baby-sitter .... the kids while they went to the cinema.
11 They finally .... at the party at twelve o'clock just as everybody else was leaving.
12 After she had finished loading the car, she .... on her holiday.

3 Choose the four phrasal verbs that you find most difficult and write a sentence for each that clearly shows the meaning of the verb. Use a dictionary to help you if you like.

LANGUAGE STUDY

1 Transitive and intransitive verbs

Our intuition often tells us all we need to know about the grammar of phrasal verbs. However, it is useful to know the difference between transitive and intransitive verbs to understand better how phrasal verbs work.

1 Transitive verbs
We can say

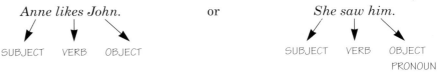

Anne likes John.   or   *She saw him.*

SUBJECT   VERB   OBJECT   SUBJECT   VERB   OBJECT
                                                           PRONOUN

But we can't say ~~Anne likes.~~
Like is a transitive verb. In other words, it must be followed by an object. Without an object it does not makes sense. In the *Longman Active Study Dictionary* transitive verbs are shown like this: [T].

2 Intransitive verbs
We can say

The sun rose.

SUBJECT   VERB

We can't say ~~The sun rose the sky.~~
This is because **rise** does not take an object. It is intransitive. In the *Longman Active Study Dictionary* intransitive verbs are shown like this: [I].

3 Using your dictionary, find out if these verbs are transitive or intransitive or both:
rise, raise, thank, understand, go, see, open, laugh, arrive.

2 Exploring the grammar of phrasal verbs

1 With a partner, look at these groups of sentences and quickly decide if they are correct. Use your intuition in English!

A turn up
  a She turned up.
  b She turned up him.
  c She turns up late for everything.

B tell off
  a She told off.
  b She told off Dick.
  c She told Dick off.
  d She told off him.
  e She told him off.

C look after
  a She looked after.
  b She looked after him.
  c She looked him after.
  d She looked after Bill.
  e She looked Bill after.

D get on with
  a She gets on with.
  b She gets on her with.
  c She gets on with her.
  d She gets on with Ann.

2 In pairs or small groups work out the four types of phrasal verbs. Decide:
  • whether each verb is transitive or intransitive.
  • where we can put the object if it is transitive.
  • what happens to the object if it is a pronoun.

3 Look at the dictionary entry for **turn up**. How many different meanings does it give? Is the grammar of **turn up** always the same?

Note The most important thing you have to discover when you meet a new phrasal verb is whether it is possible to separate the verb and the particle.

> **turn up** *v adv* **1** [T] (**turn** sthg. ↔ **up**) to find: *to turn up new information* **2** [I] to be found: *The missing bag turned up, completely empty, in the river.* **3** [T] (**turn** sthg. ↔ **up**) to shorten (a garment) – compare TURN-UP **4** [I] to arrive: *She turns up late for everything.* | *Don't worry, something will turn up.* (= happen) **5** [T] (**turn** sthg. ↔ **up**) to increase the force, strength, loudness, etc., of (a radio, heating system, etc.) by using controls

LISTENING

Listen to the story of Alexandre Aufredi and decide if the following statements are true (**T**), false (**F**) or not stated (**NS**).

1 Aufredi was a satisfied man.
2 He had made his money from the spice trade.
3 His friends advised him against the venture.
4 His steward took money to buy goods.
5 Aufredi's problems started immediately.
6 There were unpleasant stories about his ships.
7 His ships returned after seven years.
8 Everybody in La Rochelle knew where the Aufredis were.
9 Aufredi's children suffered a great deal.
10 Aufredi became friends again with his old business associates.
11 The good work he began continues to this day.

LANGUAGE STUDY

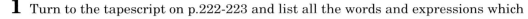

1 Turn to the tapescript on p.222-223 and list all the words and expressions which

- put events in order.
- use a form or expression based around **first** or **last**.

2 Study these sentences. Which word or expression in **bold** is used for instructions, which for reasons and which for first impressions?

a **At first** I didn't think I was going to enjoy the film but surprisingly I did.
b I don't like horror stories for the following reasons: **firstly** they give me nightmares, secondly they're stupid...
c OK now, are you ready? **First of all**, lift the bow with your left hand and draw the string back, then...

3 Now look at these sentences. Which word or expression in **bold** is used • to introduce a last point, • to suggest that something happened after a lot of other actions, • to describe the finish of an event, • to suggest that something happened after a long time?

a We looked everywhere. **In the end** we found the book in the boot of the car.
b It was an extremely moving play; **at the end** everyone applauded the actors.
c **Finally**, I would like to thank everybody for continuing to support the history society.
d The injured mountaineers were losing hope but **at last** they heard the sound of the helicopter.

4 Complete these two situations using one of the forms given.

1 **At first/ First of all,** hold the racquet and ball together. **Then/After** throw the ball, bringing the racquet behind your head. **After/Afterwards**, throw the racquet and your body forward. **After/Afterwards** hitting the ball, follow through. **In the end/Finally**, prepare yourself for the return

2 Last month I went to my first football match. **At first/First of all,** I thought I wasn't going to like it. However, **after/afterwards** ten minutes I started to enjoy it. The other team scored **first/firstly** but **after/afterwards** we scored twice. Unfortunately, **after/afterwards** we had scored, our best player was injured and **in the end/finally** we lost.

5 In pairs or small groups

- list reasons either for or against allowing children to watch TV.
- give instructions to a foreigner about how to make tea or coffee or dance a traditional dance!
- describe a journey where everything went wrong.
- talk about a situation where you had to revise your first impressions. Begin: *At first I thought...*

TALL TALES

FIRST THOUGHTS

In England, a favourite excuse when your teacher asks for your homework is to say: *"I did do it, but the dog ate it"*, or *" My young brother threw it away."* Can you think of any other ridiculous excuses?

LISTENING

A tall story

1 Working in pairs or small groups, try to make the connection between a dead cat, a department store and a thief! Then listen to the story and see if it is similar to the one you invented.

2 Listen to the story again and answer these questions by choosing **A**, **B** or **C**.

1 From what Arthur says we understand that
   A Carol seldom tells stories.
   B Carol has a reputation as a storyteller.
   C Carol knows a lot of jokes.

2 The cat
   A was in the street.
   B was asleep under the car.
   C was near the garage.

3 Why doesn't the woman in Carol's story put the cat in the dustbin?
   A The children could find it.
   B She wants to bury it properly.
   C It's against the law.

4 The woman takes the bag to the department store because
   A she thinks her friend can help.
   B she picked it up by mistake.
   C she intends to leave it there.

5 The middle-aged woman
   A was a customer.
   B had a horrible shock.
   C was trying to escape from the store.

WRITING

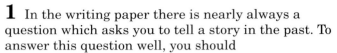

The narrative composition

1 In the writing paper there is nearly always a question which asks you to tell a story in the past. To answer this question well, you should

1 make sure your composition is relevant, i.e. answer the question!
2 show a good command of past tenses.
3 show that you can link sentences and ideas well.
4 use a good range of vocabulary.
5 write in a well organised and logical fashion.
6 keep within the word limit set by the exam.
7 be accurate.

2 Here is an example answer to the exam task. "Write a story ending with the words *We never saw him again.*"
Find out

1 how many past tenses the writer uses.
2 the ways in which the writer puts events in order.
3 how the young man and weather are described.
4 if the writer uses a good range of vocabulary.

When we arrived in London, we were two hours late because our train had been held up by the bad weather. Outside the station it was snowing hard and there was a long queue of people waiting for taxis. As we were about to join it, a young man pulled up in his car and asked us where we wanted to go. Although it was not an official taxi, the car was new and shiny and the young man looked clean and respectable; so we decided to accept his offer. When we told him that we did not have a hotel, he said he could take us to one which was clean and cheap.

He put our luggage in the boot and we drove off to the hotel. On the way, we chatted and he pointed out any interesting sights. We could hardly believe our luck and thought of all the people we had left queuing in the freezing cold. When we got to the hotel, he told us that he would wait while we checked in. After we had found out that the hotel was full, we went down the steps only to find that our driver had disappeared with our luggage. Needless to say we never saw him again.

WRITING

The sixteen pictures make up two stories in the past. Work in groups and decide which pictures belong to which story. Afterwards put them in the right order. Try to use the tenses and ways of linking ideas we have covered in this unit. Then choose the story you liked best and write a composition in **120 -180** words telling the story.

ACCENT AND CLASS

FIRST THOUGHTS

In your country, how easy is it to say where somebody comes from and what their social position is from their accent or dialect?

"Cockney" is a dialect spoken by working class people in London. Speakers of standard English often believe users of Cockney are ignorant and vulgar. How easy do you think it would be for a speaker of Cockney to find a good job?

USE OF ENGLISH

1 Read the summary of the play *Pygmalion* and answer the questions.

1 Who is Eliza Doolittle and what is her ambition?
2 How does she think Professor Higgins can help her?
3 What sort of man is Higgins? Why does he decide to take Eliza on?
4 How does Eliza change in the course of the play?

2 Complete the text by changing the words in capitals into the correct form.

Pygmalion

Pygmalion, by George Bernard Shaw, describes the (1).......... of a Cockney flower girl called Eliza Doolittle into someone who could pass for a duchess. The person who does this is Professor Henry Higgins, a phonetician who is able to place exactly where someone was born and their position in society by their (2).......... . His gifts as a phonetician are matched by his (3).......... as a person. **TRANSFORM** **PRONOUNCE** **ARROGANT**

The play opens in Covent Garden in London where Higgins is noting down accents. There he forms a (4).......... with a fellow linguist, Dr Pickering, and the pair meet Eliza, a simple flower seller. The men forget all about her. However, the unfortunate Eliza is (5)....... of her accent and her (6).......... English which prevent her from getting a job in a proper flower shop. The following day, she goes to Higgins' house to seek his help. Higgins (7).......... says Eliza's English will keep her in the gutter all her life. Pickering bets Higgins that he could not pass her off as a duchess in six months and the professor finds the challenge (8).......... . **FRIEND** **SHAME** **GRAMMAR** **RUDE** **RESIST**

Higgins teaches her to speak standard English, and – with the help of Pickering and Mrs Pearce his housekeeper – trains her in manners and (9).......... introduces her to good society. During this process she emerges as a young woman of (10).......... and sensitivity. She fights against Higgins' (11).......... of her and against his (12).......... rudeness. Pickering is always a gentleman, kind and courteous, but Higgins (13).......... regards Eliza merely as an experiment proving his genius. Yet Eliza achieves her (14).......... and a sense of her worth. The play has had (15).......... versions. The most famous, the (16).......... comedy *My Fair Lady*, has a different ending: Higgins and Eliza come together at the end of the film. **SUCCEED** **BEAUTIFUL** **TREAT** **TOLERATE** **SHAME** **FREE** **VARY** **MUSIC**

You may be (17).......... to know that the play gets its title from the (18).......... legend in which Pygmalion, king of Cyprus, fall in love with his own sculpture. The goddess Aphrodite turns it into flesh and blood as the woman Galatea. **INTEREST** **CLASSIC**

LISTENING

Listen to this extract from *Pygmalion* and
answer these questions by choosing **A**, **B** or **C**.

1 When Mrs Pearce tells Higgins about the visitor it
is clear
  A that she disapproves of her.
  B that she is unused to having strange people in
  the house.
  C that she is sure Higgins will want to see her.

2 How does Higgins feel when Mrs Pearce tells him
about the visitor ?
  A Angry
  B Bored
  C Interested

3 What does Higgins want to do once he recognises
the visitor?
  A Send her away.
  B Record her.
  C Find out the reason for her visit.

4 What does Eliza think about her money?
  A It is a pity to waste it on taxis.
  B That Higgins will want to earn some of it.
  C Higgins will want to teach her for nothing.

5 What does Eliza think when Higgins calls her a
baggage?
  A She is a lady.
  B Her treatment has been unfair.
  C She'll never find a job in a shop.

USE OF ENGLISH

Read the review of a production of *Pygmalion*
and tick (✔) those lines which are correct. Where a
line has an extra word which should not be there,
identify the word and write it down.

 0 The new Theatre Club production is *Pygmalion* ✓
00 at the Maida Theatre. I **was** enjoyed it very much.
 1 It is a most amusing and I would certainly
 2 recommend it you for an amusing evening's
 3 entertainment. It was an evening filled with the
 4 laughter. It was a very superb production.
 5 Angela Brown was a marvellous in the role of
 6 Eliza, and yet Bruce Perkins was a superb
 7 Higgins. Percy Evans ought to be congratulated
 8 too for the scenery, which had looked magnificent.
 9 Afterwards, several of people said they had
10 been preferred the happier ending of the film
11 version *My Fair Lady* but me personally I prefer
12 the bitter-sweet original. I am agree that
13 this ending is more faithful to Shaw's intentions.
14 It filled me with enthusiasm feelings for his work.
15 Tickets are available from the box office.

WRITING

You have been asked to write a report of a film
or play you have seen for a students' magazine. Using
the summary of *Pygmalion* and the edited text above
as a guide, write a report in **120 - 180** words. Think
about these areas:

• The name of the play/film and the author/director.
• The kind of play/film it is and where it is set.
• The plot.
• How good the actors/direction/scenery are.
• What other people thought about it.
• Whether you would recommend it to other people.

5 A Sense of Adventure

THE BEST OF TIMES?

Look at the selection of photographs. What kind of holiday is shown in each?

LISTENING

1 Listen to Martin and Amanda's conversation. Which photograph are they talking about?

2 Managing conversations

Listen again and write down Amanda's side of the conversation. How does she get Martin to do most of the talking? How does she show that she is a good listener?

AMANDA: So (**1**)............ Martin?
MARTIN: The one of the seaside holiday and the Punch and Judy show.
AMANDA: (**2**)............?
MARTIN: Well I suppose it reminds me of when I was a child.
AMANDA: (**3**)............ you use to have holidays like this?
MARTIN: That's right, and my sisters and I used to play on the beach
AMANDA: (**4**)............?
MARTIN: You know, make sandcastles, that sort of thing, and hunt for crabs.
AMANDA: (**5**)............?
MARTIN: Yes, there were lots of rock pools where they used to live.
AMANDA: (**6**)............!
MARTIN: Yes, it was.

SPEAKING

1 Work in pairs and take it in turns to ask and answer these questions.

1 Which of the photographs would you most/least like to be in and why?
2 Do any of the photographs remind you of any experiences you have had of travel or holidays?
3 What are the ingredients of an ideal holiday for you?

Remember:
• give each other your full attention.
• react to what the other person says.
• be enthusiastic and interested.

2 Broadening out the conversation

Look at the list and decide which three things are the most important for you in a holiday. Then discuss your answers with your partner.

• excitement
• good food and drink
• romance
• good weather

• shopping
• adventure
• relaxation
• sightseeing

• sporting activities
• different culture and way of life
• comfort/luxury

VOCABULARY

Complete these sentences with words associated with **holidays** and **travel**. The first letter of each word is given.

1 We sent off to the tour operators for a *b*............ giving details of their holidays in Thailand.
2 Last year we went on a *p*............ *t*............ . Everything was organised for us: the flight, the hotels and all the entertainments. It was all included in the price.
3 They're going on *s*............ in Kenya. They'll be able to see lots of wildlife.
4 We brought back some local handicrafts as *s*............ . Each time we look at them we remember what a great time we had.
5 I wouldn't get a scheduled flight if I were you. A *c*............ flight would be much cheaper.
6 A holiday *r*............ is a town which welcomes and entertains tourists.
7 Bed and breakfast is £15 a night. If you want *h*............ *b*............, it costs an extra £6 which covers either lunch or dinner.
8 We really enjoy *s*............-*c*............ holidays where we rent a house and look after ourselves.

USE OF ENGLISH

1 Look at the short report of a family holiday. From what is written, do you think the family would choose the holiday again?

2 Read the report again and tick (✔) those lines which are correct. Where a line has an extra word which should not be there, write the word down.

  0 Last year we had a different kind of holiday. We ✓
00 **were** used to rent a house in the countryside.
  1 Even though it was lovely, but it was boring too.
  2 Instead, of last year we hired a caravan by the
  3 sea. We left from London early and took the
  4 ferry. We were shocked when we entered to the
  5 campsite – it was too much big. The best thing
  6 was the beach. It was such wide and sandy and
  7 safe for my brother. The caravan was enough
  8 large but it was hard to adapt ourselves to a small
  9 space. I was made friends at the teenagers' club.
10 We played games and had fires at night. A
11 French boy he taught me windsurfing. He was
12 really a funny. The worst thing was a noisy
13 funfair opposite of the site. One other thing
14 else was the traffic jams. Nobody could tell
15 us about how to avoid them. Otherwise I had a
16 wonderful time. I don't know about my parents!

WRITING

Write a short article for a travel magazine about a holiday or trip you have been on recently. Use the report you edited as a guide. Say

• why you chose the holiday, and where it was.
• what your travel arrangements were.
• what your first impressions were.
• how the holiday was organised.
• what the general atmosphere was like.
• which the good things and the less positive things were.
• what your final thoughts and recommendations are.

WHAT A NIGHTMARE!

FIRST THOUGHTS

What do you think the advantages are of travelling in a group on an organised tour compared with travelling independently?

LISTENING

You are going to hear five different women talk about travelling. Which of the sentences **A-F** best summarises what each one has to say? There is one sentence which you do not need to use.

A It's OK to break the law.   ☐ Speaker 1
B It was marvellous, but take warm clothes.   ☐ Speaker 2
C I need another holiday to get over this one. ☐ Speaker 3
D All you need is a good guide book.   ☐ Speaker 4
E My group was a nightmare.   ☐ Speaker 5
F Don't drink the water!

VOCABULARY

1 Look at the tapescript on p. 224 and see how the words in the box are used.

> priceless   hopeless   helpless   valuable   hopeful   waste of time   unhelpful
> worthless   invaluable   helpful   worthwhile

LANGUAGE STUDY

Obligation and necessity

1 Study these ways of talking about obligation and necessity. Match the sentences and the definitions.

1 You mustn't drink anything straight from the tap.
2 I needn't have taken half my clothes.
3 We didn't need to book.
4 You have to declare all your foreign currency.
5 It's one of those things you're supposed to do.
6 You must be here in the lobby by seven o'clock.
7 I must get the pictures developed.
8 You should take some warm clothing.

A makes a strong recommendation/ emphasises the authority of the speaker.
B gives advice.
C says something was done that wasn't necessary.
D is a prohibition.
E says something wasn't necessary.
F expresses a strong internal obligation.
G describes a general duty or requirement.
H describes a rule that may be disobeyed.

2 In pairs, discuss suitable responses for the following situations.

1 You saw a wonderful exhibition of African art a couple of weeks ago. Tomorrow is its last day. Strongly recommend that your friend sees it.
2 A hotel receptionist is explaining to a visitor what his/her job involves. What would he/she say about his/her duties and responsibilities? What about the things for which he/she was not responsible?
3 You are telling someone the rules of a student hostel. What would you say about washing-up, smoking, noise and guests? Which rules are important? Which ones can be disobeyed?
4 You receive a telephone bill warning you that if you do not pay it immediately you will be cut off. What do you say to yourself?
5 You were going to call for a taxi but your friend gave you a lift home instead. What would you tell your parents about the taxi?

WRITING

A letter of complaint

Peter Carr went on a *Club 20-30* holiday but did not enjoy himself very much.

1 Read his letter and note how many complaints he has to make. Which are serious?
2 Which words and expressions are useful for a letter of complaint.
3 What features of the layout and language of this letter make it formal?

CLUB 20-30

Make friends and enjoy yourself at one of our villa parties from a choice of over 15 continental resorts. Try Club 20-30 for action-packed holidays, sun-soaked days on the beach and fun evenings at parties and discos. Not for old folk over 30.

```
The Managing Director                          42 Railway Cuttings
Club 20-30 Holidays                            Birmingham
26 Spratt Street
London W1                                      1st July 1996

Dear Sir

I am writing to complain about a Club 20-30 holiday I went on at the resort of
Karamelli between 14th and 28th June.

According to your brochure, accommodation was supposed to be in a small villa.
However, when I got to Karamelli, I was taken to a modern hotel a mile from the sea.
Even though it had just been built, there were cracks everywhere and it looked as
though it was going to fall down. The walls were paper thin and you could hear
everything from the neighbouring room.

To make matters worse, there were only two other young people in the hotel and they
were both men. The hotel had been taken over by a package tour of old age pensioners
who insisted on playing bingo in the discotheque every evening. Where was the 'night
life' I had been promised?

On top of everything, when I mentioned my complaints to your company representative,
she was extremely rude to me and only reappeared at the end of my stay and became
abusive when I refused to give her a tip.

You can imagine how upset I am at having spent a considerable amount of money on this
holiday. In fact, I expect a full refund plus compensation for the inconvenience and
discomfort I suffered. I trust you will give this matter your immediate attention.

I look forward to receiving a satisfactory reply by return of post. If I do not
receive full satisfaction, I intend to write to the TV programme 'Value for Money'
and expose your operation.

Yours faithfully,

Peter Carr

PETER CARR
```

You went on the Rigby Activity Holiday advertised below. Read the advertisement carefully, and the notes which give details about why you were dissatisfied with the holiday. Write a letter complaining about the quality of the holiday. Write between **120 - 180** words in an appropriate style.

Notes
- *Instructors ex-soldiers – expected too much.*
- *Like a prison camp.*
- *Not enough surfboards / life jackets.*
- *Cabins cold – had to clean them.*
- *Not enough food.*
- *Cold and frightened! Left after one week.*

RIGBY ACTIVITY HOLIDAYS

Test yourself and learn new skills in the glorious Lake District. Holidays for people who don't want to laze around on a beach. Learn to sail and windsurf at our exclusive fully-equipped lakeside facilities. Rock climbing and survival skills taught by professionals. Beginners welcome. Get fit - learn confidence. Ten action-packed days for just £600. Holidays begin the first and third Saturdays of each month.

ONCE IN A LIFETIME

FIRST THOUGHTS

Imagine you have won a free two-week holiday anywhere in the world. Where would you go and what would you do?

READING

A holiday with a difference

Read the text and mark on the map the route the tour takes. Choose the most suitable answers to the following questions and then study closely the explanations on page 65.

1 The buildings in Dakar are
  A fairly new.
  B good to photograph.
  C boring.
  D a contrast.
2 The isle of Goree
  A imported slaves.
  B used to be important.
  C is a centre for slaves.
  D is cut off from the land.
3 The journey from Dakar to Bamako
  A moves from rainy to dry country.
  B takes three nights.
  C is not by bus.
  D passes through hills.
4 The town of Mopti is
  A just like Venice.
  B a market.
  C cosmopolitan.
  D west of Bamako.
5 Visitors are .... on the river Niger.
  A required to go
  B discouraged from going
  C recommended to go
  D obliged to go

WRITING

Imagine that you have to organise a tour of a region in your country. Write a brief description of the route the tour will take and the places of interest which will be visited. Think about

- how long the tour will be.
- the tour's main attractions.
- how the landscape will vary during the tour.
- how you will travel (try to vary it).
- good places for souvenirs.

THE IVORY COAST TRAIN

Two weeks by rail and local taxis in West Africa visiting Senegal, Mali, Burkina Faso and the Ivory Coast.

This escorted tour lets you experience two of West Africa's most important railways, the lifelines from the coastal countries of Senegal and the Ivory Coast to landlocked Mali and Burkina Faso. We use hotels and sleeper trains throughout the tour.

We spend time in the busy modern coastal capitals of Dakar and Abidjan. We also explore the remote region of the Niger river around Mopti, where ancient kingdoms once held power in this fascinating area of West Africa.

Our journey starts in Dakar, the capital of Senegal, which is situated on the Cape Verde peninsula. The modern buildings contrast with the lively African markets, which are a photographer's delight and a source of fine souvenirs such as tie-dyed cloth and exquisite jewellery.

We shall take a boat ride to the Isle of Goree which was once an important slave trading centre. Slaves were brought here from the interior and shipped to the New World until the abolition of this shameful trade. Goree's museum and the terrible House of Slaves shows visitors what life must have been like. We board the train in Dakar for a two-day journey through an ever-changing landscape. The train takes us across the dry region of Sahel to the lushness of Bamako, the capital of Mali. Bamako is a modern city dependent on the river Niger, which supports this arid area of West Africa. There are busy, colourful markets and many interesting areas for us to see and explore.

The next stage of our journey will be by local taxi from Bamako to Mopti with a night stop at Segou on the way. Mopti, an important market town, is often called the Venice of Africa because it lies in the middle of islands and waterways where the Bani and Niger rivers join. Mopti is an exotic and fascinating city. It is extremely cosmopolitan. Here you will see members of many different African tribes who come to Mopti to trade. A boat trip on the Niger is a must. There is a wide variety of river transport, ranging from marvellous old river steamers to narrow canoes called pirogues, the type we are going to use. There is a constant flow of river traffic carrying all forms of goods to and from the major ports with magical names like Gao and Timbuctoo.

Leaving Mopti, we travel by local taxi to Bobo-Dioulasso in Burkina Faso. The next day we will take the train to Abidjan, capital of the Ivory Coast. The train journey will take approximately 15 hours and goes from arid, landlocked Burkina Faso to the rich green lands of the Gulf of Guinea.

Abidjan is built in an area of lakes, forests and beaches. The city has clean, modern buildings but its market offers all the excitement of West Africa, with exciting spicy foods, colourful traders and African music. We will have a guided tour of the city and visit the excellent museum. Local craftsmen, who are famous for their wood-carvings, will give us the opportunity to buy souvenirs.

Our tour ends in Abidjan and in just two weeks you will have experienced many of the different faces of West Africa, travelling with the local people as they go about their everyday lives on West African railways.

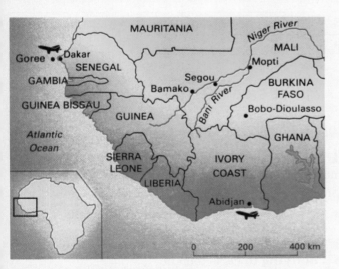

Top left *Mopti*
Left *Goree*

THE IVORY COAST TRAIN

Answers to the multiple choice questions

1. **A** CORRECT
   B WRONG (*The market is good to photograph*)
   C WRONG (*It does not say this anywhere*)
   D WRONG (*This sentence is incomplete because it does not say what the buildings are a contrast with.*)

2. **A** WRONG (*It exported them.*)
   B WRONG (*It still is important.*)
   C WRONG (*It used to be.*)
   D CORRECT (*It is an island.*)

3. **A** WRONG (*Although we know the Sahel is dry, we are not told if Dakar is rainy.*)
   B WRONG (*The journey takes two days. We are not told if this means two days or three nights.*)
   C CORRECT (*The journey is by train.*)
   D WRONG (*We do not know this from the text. We are told that the landscape changes, but not about hills.*)

4. **A** WRONG (*It is called the Venice of Africa, but that does not mean that it is **just** like Venice.*)
   B WRONG (*It is a market **town**.*)
   C CORRECT (*We are told that people of different nationalities and tribes mix together.*)
   D WRONG (*It is east of Bamako.*)

5. The correct answer is **C**, i.e. *Visitors are **recommended** to go on the River Niger.* Choices A, B and D suggest that there is some sort of obligation.

Student B[*]:
You are free this weekend. Your friend is going to invite you to his/her parents' house in the country. You love the countryside. You finish your course at five o'clock at a college near Charing Cross Station in London. Make arrangements to meet and ask what clothes you need to bring.

---

[*] This refers to the role play exercise on page 67.

FUTURE PLANS

FIRST THOUGHTS

1 How important is it to plan a holiday? Do you like to know exactly what you will be doing and where you will staying or do you enjoy the unexpected?

2 When friends go on holiday they sometimes come back as enemies. Why do you think this happens? Has it ever happened to you? What things can go wrong?

LISTENING

1 Listen to Julie talking to a friend about her planned holiday in the Lake

District. Put a tick by all the objects in the photo she says she is going to take with her this year.

PRONUNCIATION

1 ▭ Listen to the difference between the pronunciation of **l** in these two words: **hotel, hostel**. In both cases, the tongue rests behind the top teeth. However, in **hostel**, the back of the tongue is also raised.

2 ▭ Listen to these words from the listening and decide if they are like **hotel** or **hostel**.

	HOTEL	HOSTEL
1 holiday		
2 tell		
3 able		
4 lake		
5 kettle		
6 This'll		
7 Well		
8 We'll		
9 lot		

LANGUAGE STUDY

Ways of talking about the future

1 Working in pairs, match sentences **1-7** with the most appropriate description from **A-G**.

1 **She will be** 30 next June.
2 *Travel agent:* There aren't any flights left.
   Customer: In that case, **I'll go** by train.
3 **The bus leaves** at eight o'clock on Mondays.
4 **I'm flying** to Paris tonight.
5 **We're going to visit** Tunisia this summer. We've already booked the tickets.
6 Look at those clouds. **It's going to rain**.
7 **You will live** until you are 100.

A A future personal arrangement.
B A future prediction.
C A future prediction based on present evidence.
D A decision taken at the moment of speaking.
E An event which happens regularly.
F Something in the future which will definitely happen.
G Something that the speaker has intended to do in the future for some time.

2 Decide what you would say in the following situations. Use an appropriate way of expressing the future.

1 You feel tired and have decided to stay at home this evening. A friend rings you up to invite you to a party. How do you refuse?
2 A child you are looking after has just dropped its ice-cream and starts to cry. What do you say to comfort the child?
3 Tonight you're responsible for preparing the family's meal. How do you tell a friend that you can't go out with him/her?
4 A cousin is coming to stay for a few days. You promise to meet him/her at the station at seven o'clock. What do you say?
5 Your friend Samira is pregnant. Tell the news to your mother.
6 A friend is going to visit your home town. Predict what they'll like/dislike about it.
7 Your friend smokes too much. Warn him/her about future health problems.

SPEAKING

Role play

Work in pairs. Student A invites Student B home for the weekend.

Student B: Turn to page 65 for your information.

Student A:
Your parents live in the country. You are planning to visit them this weekend, and they have said that you can bring a friend. Invite your friend, Student B, to go with you. There are two trains on Friday evening: one at five o'clock and one at six. You think that the five o'clock train would be better because there will be more seats. They both leave from Charing Cross station in London. Your brother will meet whichever train you take. It is possible to go for long walks near your parents' house. Horse-riding and tennis are also possible.

WRITING

Compulsory letter

1 Your friend is going to Brighton in England to do an English course. He/she has written a letter to the school and shows you the letter before posting it. The style of the letter is OK but there are a lot of mistakes. How would you help your friend to correct it?

Dear Sir or Madam!

I am happy that I will come to your school next month to make an English course.

I write for to know details about the travel from London Gatwick to the school. Also I would like an information about how to go to the house of my host family after I will arrive. I hope it is an accommodation near to the school and that the family likes the youngs.

The flight is taking me three hours. I will be arrive at the Gatwick airport at two o'clock p.m. in the afternoon. How much time do I need for to arrive in Brighton? Can I take one bus? How many kilometres is it because maybe I can take one taxi. Would you recommend this to me or will it be too much expensive? Maybe there is a bus I could take.

Can you tell to me what class I will make? I want to do many progress during I am studying with you. I will enter the university next year and for this I need a good level. So I am studying hard when I am in England. How long time is necessary for to pass the Proficiency examination?

I salute you attentively,

2 You have arranged to do a course in a language school in an English-speaking country. Write a semi-formal letter to the school finalising travel arrangements and asking any final questions you may have about your accommodation and the course.

TRAVELLERS

FIRST THOUGHTS

1 What famous explorers or travellers has your country produced? Is there a modern traveller who is often in the news?

2 Why are most travellers and explorers men?

READING

You are going to read about two women travellers: Freya Stark and Ffyona Campbell. Look at the photographs and try to guess what is different about them.

1 Read Freya Stark's biography and complete the notes.

1893	born in England
....	injured in an accident
1921	....
....	sailed to Beirut
....	*Valley of the Assassins* published.
1947	....
1950s	....
In her eighties	....
At age of	................................Euphrates
At age of 87	....

2 What phrases are used in the text to describe when she did something?

3 Phrasal verbs in context.
Which phrasal verbs in the text mean: to recover from, to postpone, to continue?

WRITING

Use the notes below to write a biography of the explorer Christopher Columbus.

Columbus
1451 Born Genoa, Italy.
1476 Shipwrecked off coast of Portugal. Wanted to find short route to India for spice trade. Believed world was round and you could go east by sailing west.
1486 Approached Spanish monarchs for support.
3rd August 1492 Set sail in Santa Maria.
12th October 1492 Landed San Salvador. Returned to Spain and greatly honoured.
1493-1496 2nd voyage. Discovered Guadeloupe. Continued to Jamaica.
1498-1500 3rd voyage. Discovered Trinidad and S. American mainland.
1499 Sudden revolt against Columbus. Sent back to Spain a prisoner but pardoned and compensated.
1502-04 Final voyage. Returned ill.
1506 Died Valladolid, Spain.

Freya Stark

Freya Stark spent two-thirds of her life in Arabia and published 25 books. Born in England in 1893, she spent much of her happy childhood in Italy. When she was 12 she had an accident which left her badly scarred, and in her teens her parents separated. She was a nurse in the First World War and became engaged, but her fiancé married someone else while Freya was getting over typhoid. In 1921 she decided to learn Arabic because she believed, "The most interesting things in the world are likely to happen in the neighbourhood of oil." She put off a voyage to Lebanon because of illness but in November 1927 finally sailed to Beirut.

In 1934 she published her first success, *The Valley of the Assassins*. In 1947 Freya married an old friend but they separated four years later. In the 1950s she visited and wrote books about Turkey. During her eighties she carried on her travels and went to Afghanistan and Nepal. When she was 85 she took a trip down the Euphrates on a raft. Her last great journey was when, aged 87, she rode a mule through the Himalayas. She died in Italy at the great age of 100. She said her desire to travel was a result of her childhood: "We had nothing but our own intrinsic selves to rely on and came to look naturally at the intrinsic qualities of other people. Perhaps this is the most important of all assets a traveller can possess for it minimises barriers, whether of nationality, race or caste."

READING

You are going to read a magazine article about a woman long-distance walker. Seven sentences have been removed from the article. Choose from the sentences **A-H** the one which fits each gap (**1-6**). There is one extra sentence which you do not need to use. There is an example at the beginning (**0**).

> **A** The Western diet is so fatty compared with African food that even bread tastes rich to me.
> **B** She's also preparing for the final leg of her journey across Europe next year.
> **C** It also meant coping with loneliness.
> **D** So that's what I did.
> **E** I've put on three-quarters of a stone because my body is used to being so active and now it's not.
> **F** And her body will never be the same again.
> **G** She came close to giving up a number of times.
> **H** All to realise the dream she's had since the age of 16.

The Long and Wounding Road

Walking round the world is taking its toll on Ffyona Campbell's body. During her latest leg across Africa she took malaria, dysentery and typhoid in her stride. But she was horrified to hear the strain may have jeopardised her chances of being a mum. She has been spat at, stoned, mobbed, arrested and nearly raped. `0` `H` To walk around the world. She's now 26 and in the first trek, 10 years ago, she made it from John O'Groats to Land's End. She progressed to striding across America. Australia was next. That was a 95-day walk-over.

Africa has been the greatest challenge. It took two years to cross 10,000 miles. Leaving Cape Town in April 1991, she finally set foot in Tangier on September 1, 1993. `1` "A chiropractor I met after my Australian trek said the stress of walking would probably mean I'd be childless," says Ffyona. "I was really worried and upset, but I checked and found he was talking nonsense." But she has suffered a catalogue of illnesses and injuries on her journeys. Ffyona always carries a medical kit, including syringes and plasma to avoid contamination or the risk of AIDS.

After completing 30 miles a day in 90 degrees of heat through towns, rainforests and war zones, Ffyona is out of Africa and back in Stoke Newington, North London, adjusting to Western life. `2` "On the first day back in Britain, they put me in the Hyatt Hotel," she says. "And instinctively I thought, 'They'll have water.' When I got to my five-star room, I turned the sheets back to check for scorpions, purely out of habit."

"Everyone assumes I'll eat enormous meals after two years on a simple diet, but I can't. `3` In Africa, I lived on vegetables, fruit, pasta and occasionally meat such as gazelle, impala, tortoise and flying ants. "If I'd tried to tuck into a huge steak on my return, I'd have been sick in the same way British people often are when they eat abroad. Even though I was very careful, I still had an upset stomach for the first few days. `4` I haven't had time to exercise and I hate walking to the shops here." When Ffyona returned in a blaze of glory, her parents, Colin 54, a former pilot, and Angela 53, weren't there to meet her. "For the past two years, I'd dreamed of meeting them at the garden gate of their home in Devon. `5` "

Her quest has forced her to draw on vast reserves of self discipline. In Africa, she walked 30 miles a day, six days a week and rested on the seventh. `6` On her trip, which was largely paid for by sponsorship although she also raised money for charity, two drivers would meet her at certain points with camping equipment. Between campsites, she was on her own, and her first rule of survival was never fall for your driver. Something she did twice.

USE OF ENGLISH

1 **Part 2** of **Paper 3 (Use of English)** is a gap-filling exercise with an emphasis on testing grammar. Study this example and look at the categories of words (in **bold** type) which are often omitted.

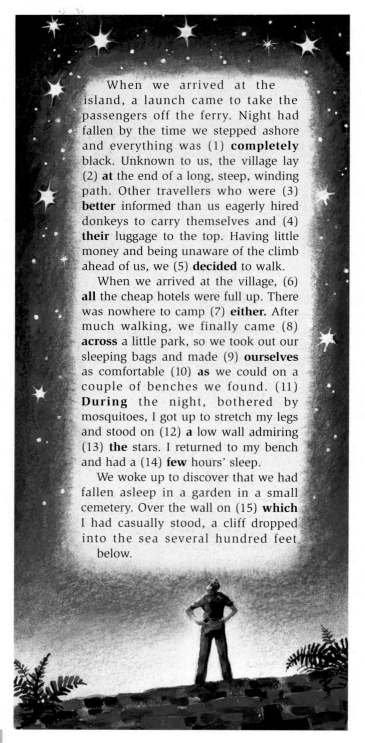

When we arrived at the island, a launch came to take the passengers off the ferry. Night had fallen by the time we stepped ashore and everything was (1) **completely** black. Unknown to us, the village lay (2) **at** the end of a long, steep, winding path. Other travellers who were (3) **better** informed than us eagerly hired donkeys to carry themselves and (4) **their** luggage to the top. Having little money and being unaware of the climb ahead of us, we (5) **decided** to walk.

When we arrived at the village, (6) **all** the cheap hotels were full up. There was nowhere to camp (7) **either.** After much walking, we finally came (8) **across** a little park, so we took out our sleeping bags and made (9) **ourselves** as comfortable (10) **as** we could on a couple of benches we found. (11) **During** the night, bothered by mosquitoes, I got up to stretch my legs and stood on (12) **a** low wall admiring (13) **the** stars. I returned to my bench and had a (14) **few** hours' sleep.

We woke up to discover that we had fallen asleep in a garden in a small cemetery. Over the wall on (15) **which** I had casually stood, a cliff dropped into the sea several hundred feet below.

1 adverb (modifying an adjective)
2 preposition
3 comparative adverb
4 possessive adjective
5 verb in the simple past
6 determiner/pronoun
7 adverb used with negative expressions
8 preposition (particle of phrasal verb)
9 reflexive pronoun
10 conjunction used in comparatives
11 preposition
12 indefinite article
13 definite article
14 determiner used with countable nouns
15 relative pronoun

2 The following three exercises concentrate on words which are often omitted in the gap-filling exercise. Complete the sentences using the words in the boxes once only.

1
A .... it was cold they went for a swim.
B .... he locked the car he remembered the keys were inside.
C They left early .... they wanted to get to the airport on time.
D We'll play tennis .... it doesn't rain.
E It was foggy .... the ferry didn't sail.
F .... Helen nor Peter can drive.
G She married him in .... of his age.
H .... you keep quiet or I'll ask you to leave.

spite	so	as	because	neither	if	either
although						

2
A There isn't .... food for four.
B That restaurant was .... expensive.
C We were upset as .... anyone came to the party.
D Jane is usually sad but .... she enjoyed herself.
E There were .... a few people at the match.
F We .... missed the train but managed to jump on it while it was leaving.
G She was .... annoyed at their rudeness.
H He asked if there was anything .... we needed.
I He knows he smokes far .... much, but he won't stop.
J I do apologise. It was .... my fault.

hardly	else	entirely	only	quite	almost	too
really	even	enough				

3 A Do you want .... one or that one?
B She was hiding in the room .... the time.
C There are just a .... tickets left.
D We had very .... money left by the time we came back from holiday.
E .... he and his father are extremely bad-tempered.
F Can you tell me .... the matter is?
G .... one would you like? The green one or the orange one?
H It was one of .... moments I shall never forget.

both	those	few	what	little	all	which	this

3 Complete this passage by choosing between the words in bold.

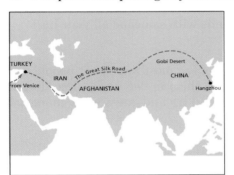

Marco Polo was born in Venice in about 1254. **(1) Both/All** his father and uncle were leading merchants who had **(2) already/still** met the Mogul emperor, Kublai Khan. When he was 17, Marco set off with them on an adventure **(3) who/ that** would last over 20 years. They passed through Turkey into northern Iran. In Afghanistan they stopped for a year, recovering from malaria. They continued overland **(4) through/along** the Great Silk Road and across the Gobi desert.

(5) So/Eventually, in 1275, they reached the summer capital **(6) when/where** they met the emperor, **(7) that/who** was impressed by Marco. The young man was sent on missions to report back on his master's vast empire. **(8) Although/However** the travellers wanted to return home, their opportunity only came 17 years later. They could go **(9) provided/whether** they accompanied a Mogul princess to Persia.

They took what, in those days, **(10) should/must** have been a dangerous sea voyage **(11) by/down** the east coast of China and Vietnam. They passed up **(12) a/the** west coast of India and finally reached Persia. When they arrived in Venice **(13) hardly/ almost** anybody believed **(14) they/them** to be still alive. Amazingly this story would have gone unrecorded if Marco had not been captured in a sea battle. **(15) In/During** his captivity he dictated his story to a fellow prisoner.

4 Complete the passage using only one word for each gap.

For a fortnight each summer we used to rent the same house by the sea. The house, **(1)**............ owner worked with my uncle, was on a cliff top overlooking the Channel. **(2)**............ it was only a couple of hours' drive away from our house, our preparations would **(3)**............ done justice to a polar expedition. Suitcases **(4)**............ taken down from the attic and filled **(5)**............ clothes for all **(6)**............ of weather. Somehow, all these things would find themselves pushed **(7)**............ the boot. Anything extra **(8)**............ placed under the seats. **(9)**............ everyone had climbed aboard, **(10)**............ was just enough space for me between my grandparents. On the way there three **(11)**............ always happened: we **(12)**............ stop at a pub to please grandfather, eat an enormous picnic, and I would **(13)**............ be car sick. These experiences probably help to explain **(14)**............ I always insist **(15)**............ travelling light, preferably by train.

6 Changes

BLOOD IS THICKER THAN WATER . . .

FIRST THOUGHTS

1 Look at these four photographs of typical family occasions. What are they and how are they different from what happens in your country?

2 How possible is it to stay friends with someone all your life?

LISTENING

1 Rosie York was asked to think of the most important people in her life now and five years ago. Then she had to arrange them in two circles according to how close she was to them. Study Rosie's *social circles* and try and guess what changes have taken place in her life.

Five years ago

Auntie Cathy
• Mum and Dad
(Me) • Simon (boyfriend)
• Grandma
• Lucy (friend)
• Clive (friend)

Today

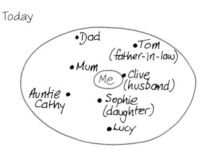

• Dad
• Tom (father-in-law)
• Mum
(Me) • Clive (husband)
Auntie • • Sophie (daughter)
Cathy
• Lucy

2 Listen to Rosie and see if your guesses were correct.

3 Listen again and answer these questions.

1 We can understand from Rosie that
  A she had been secretly in love with Clive.
  B Simon and Clive were strangers.
  C Clive had once gone out with Lucy.

2 Nowadays
  A Rosie has a reasonably good relationship with Lucy.
  B Rosie is proud of the way she behaved.
  C Simon is still in love with her.

3 Clive and Simon
  A hate each other.
  B have overcome their differences.
  C do not communicate.

4 Rosie's father
  A forgave her before the wedding.
  B thought Simon had a good future.
  C was more understanding than her mother.

5 Auntie Cathy
  A brought Rosie up.
  B can sympathise with Rosie.
  C had an easy childhood.

4 Look at the tapescript on p.225 and note down the words or expressions she uses which are to do with relationships, e.g. *go out with*.

VOCABULARY

1 Read the two letters between Miranda and Katrina, two sisters, and answer the questions.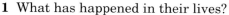

1 What has happened in their lives?
2 Who do you think is happier?
3 How do you think they feel when they read the letters?
4 Will there be any problems between them?

2 Complete the two letters by deciding which word **A, B, C** or **D** best fits each space. Work in pairs and use a dictionary if you like.

Dear Miranda,

I thought I'd write as we hadn't heard anything from you since the twins were (1)............ . We are so glad that you and Robert are (2)............ . It's nice to know that you would (3)............ them if anything happened to us. They are learning to (4)............ and are very (5)............ . Justin cries a lot at night but I think it is just a stage and he'll (6)............ it eventually. Everyone says that they both look (7)............ Simon. But mother says they take (8)............ me in character, although surely it's too soon to tell. The kids next door have gone (9)............ with measles. I hope ours don't catch it.

Anyway, less of this housewife talk. One of the reasons I have written is to ask you about the money we have (10)............ into since Aunt Vera (11)............ away. Our place is just too small and we've seen the house of our dreams. I wanted to mention it at her (12)............ but it didn't seem right...

Dear Katrina,

This is a hard letter to write but Robert and I are going to get (13)............ . It's time I (14)............ someone and you are my sister. I should have followed my instincts and called (15)............ the wedding. I don't want to reach (16)............ and be stuck with the wrong person. Robert has always been moody; he blames it on his (17)............ because he says his parents were (18)............ with him but (19)............ his elder brother James by giving him everything. James has always been a success and Robert has always been in his (20)............ . Perhaps I chose the wrong brother. They are always falling (21)............ about something. Robert was furious when James turned up in a new BMW. I accused Robert of being (22)............ and there was an awful row. It was the last straw!

Anyway, now I've told you everything. I'm looking forward to being (23)............ again, although I suppose I am lucky to have the money Aunt Vera left us in her (24)............ . I know you won't mind if I use it to set myself up somewhere new...

1 **A** named **B** christening **C** baptised **D** baptism
2 **A** step-parents **B** godparents **C** parents-in-law **D** foster parents
3 **A** bring up **B** rise **C** take care **D** look after
4 **A** creep **B** crawl **C** stride **D** stroll
5 **A** alive **B** vivid **C** lively **D** living
6 **A** grow out of **B** grow up **C** get up to **D** get on with
7 **A** likely **B** likeness **C** alike **D** like
8 **A** after **B** up **C** in **D** on
9 **A** along **B** out **C** through **D** down
10 **A** turned **B** come **C** looked **D** run
11 **A** passed **B** gave **C** looked **D** put
12 **A** cemetery **B** interment **C** coffin **D** funeral
13 **A** divorced **B** breakdown **C** split **D** parted
14 **A** confessed **B** told **C** found **D** discovered
15 **A** off **B** out **C** up **D** in
16 **A** middle ages **B** middle-aged **C** middle age **D** pension
17 **A** upbringing **B** overtaking **C** overlooking **D** undertaking
18 **A** unkind **B** cruel **C** severe **D** strict
19 **A** spoilt **B** rotten **C** stained **D** polluted
20 **A** shade **B** way **C** shadow **D** light
21 **A** over **B** down **C** out **D** off
22 **A** childlike **B** childhood **C** childish **D** children's
23 **A** lonely **B** solitary **C** single **D** bachelor
24 **A** testament **B** inheritance **C** heritage **D** will

SPEAKING

Imagine that the people in the letters are all characters from a TV soap opera. In pairs or groups think of a plot for the first few episodes. Try to include as much of the vocabulary from the other exercises as you can.

LOOKING BACK

FIRST THOUGHTS

How easy is it for older children when younger brothers or sisters are born?

READING

1 Read the description by Maeve Binchy, the Irish writer, of her childhood and answer these questions.

1 How does Maeve feel about her childhood?
2 What was her relationship with her parents like?

2 Read the text again and choose from sentences **A-I** the one which fits each gap (**1-7**). There is one extra sentence which you do not need to use. There is an example at the beginning (**0**).

> **A** We had a lot of books at home and I was very lucky to grow up in such a house of books.
> **B** I thought that I looked so gorgeous that I could hardly keep my eyes off myself.
> **C** Our house was always full of laughter.
> **D** That was a black time.
> **E** I think she tried to make up for this by ensuring that her own family would be a definite and very important entity.
> **F** I gave him a broad outline of her description.
> **G** She told me and I flatly refused to believe it.
> **H** The "me" was important because I loved receiving presents.
> **I** I got very used to walking as a child.

3 Does Maeve's story remind you of any funny or embarrassing experiences you have had?

My childhood

I have a very clear earliest memory. I, the first born, was three and a half and my mother was expecting another child. I was constantly asking God to send me a new brother or sister. | 0 | H | I was furious when the baby arrived, because all the attention moved from me to this small, red-faced thing in a cot. It was a great disappointment to me. I had been praying for this moment and now here was a "thing" which kept on crying with everybody saying how beautiful it was. "Honestly," I said, "I would have preferred a rabbit!"

| 1 | I was the eldest of four so there was always somebody in a pram to be wheeled out for a walk.

My mother had this view that if she made our home a centre for lots of our friends to come to then she would know where we all were and she would not have to worry about us. So our house became a meeting point for children of all ages. My mother didn't have much of a home life when she was young: her parents had died when she was a child and she had been brought up by relations. | 2 | I know that there is always the

LANGUAGE STUDY

Different forms of used to

1 Look at these three sentences and decide what difference there is in meaning.

1 When my father **used to tell** me to read the English classics, I resisted.
2 I **got used to walking** as a child.
3 She **is used to sleeping** late on Saturday mornings.

2 **Used to** and its different meanings can be confusing. Study these sentences.

1 *When Arthur was younger, he played tennis every weekend. Two years ago he hurt his back, so he stopped playing tennis. Now he swims instead.*
→ *He **used to play** tennis.*
used to + INFINITIVE (without to)
2 *Six months ago Janet left home to go to college. She missed her parents and felt very lonely.*
→ *She **was not used to living** away from home.*
be used to + VERB + ing
3 *Slowly Janet made friends and started to enjoy herself. After a few months, she no longer missed her family quite so much.*
→ *She **got used to living** away from home.*
get used to + VERB + ing
(Here **get used to** means *become accustomed.*)

3 Notice the pronunciation of **used to**.

Practise saying these sentences.
1 She used to smoke.
/juːstə/
2 I didn't use to live in London.
3 Did you use to play football?

4 Answer the questions using one of these forms.

- *used to* + infinitive (without **to**)
- *be used to* + gerund
- *get used to* + gerund

1 Is Bangladesh still part of Pakistan?
2 Do Chinese people find it difficult to eat with chopsticks?
3 Do politicians mind always being criticised in the newspapers?
4 Do your parents still wash you?
5 Why should British and Japanese people be careful when they first drive abroad?
6 Do contact lenses always stay uncomfortable?
7 Do Eskimos complain about the cold?
8 Do parents mind being woken up at night by their babies?

danger that you look back too sympathetically – rose-coloured spectacles and all that – but my childhood was a great joy.

My father always encouraged us to read. ☐3☐ Of course, as a teenager I always felt that when my father advised you to do something you should resist as much as possible, so, when my father used to tell me to read the English classics, I resisted. It was only when I reached my late teens that I started to read them and I began to think that they were good.

My mother was terrific at explaining the facts of life to us. I had known from a very early age how children were born because we had rabbits so there was no great mystery in birth, but I wanted to know how babies were conceived. ☐4☐ I thanked her very much and decided that this was absolutely impossible. Wasn't it terribly sad that my mother was going mad? I discussed the subject with my father.

"I'm very sorry to tell you, Daddy, that Mummy is going insane," I said.

"Why?" he enquired.

"I could not tell you the things that she has said," I replied tactfully, "but she has a very peculiar explanation of how children are conceived." ☐5☐ "Don't you think that we should get her a doctor?" I asked with great concern.

"Ah, no," he said, " I think a lot of that could be right."

I thought to myself, isn't he a wonderfully loyal man!

I went to my first dance when I was 17. ☐6☐ I wore a blue dress that my cousin had lent me, with a big blue velvet band set down the middle of the dress to let it out. I wore earrings which had made sores in my ears when I was rehearsing for the dance, so I had put sticking plaster on my ears and painted it blue to match the dress. I must have looked absolutely horrific.

Nobody – not one single person – danced with me that night. ☐7☐ There weren't many dark passages in my childhood but that most definitely was one.

75

USE OF ENGLISH

1 Read the story and think of a suitable title.

2 Look at the gaps in the text. What kind of word do you think needs to be created to fill each gap, e.g. verb, noun, adverb, adjective?

3 Now use the word written in capitals at the end of each line to form a word that fits in the space in the same line.

When I was about four years old I went to the post office with my mother <u>in order to</u> buy some stamps. I was hot and **(1)**............ in **COMFORT**
my pushchair so she let me wander about <u>on my own</u>. I noticed a small stocking hanging from a hook. It was there to collect money <u>on behalf of</u> a **(2)**............ organisation for the blind. My attention **CHARITY** was caught by the silver and copper coins which shone **(3)**............ **MYSTERY** in the light. I was <u>under the impression</u> I could just help myself! The stocking was slightly <u>out of reach</u> so, while my mother's back was turned, I lifted the stocking from its hook <u>by means of</u> a ruler I found on the counter.

   With some **(4)**............ I then emptied its contents into my coat **DIFFICULT** pocket. Of course, I was soon spotted. Everybody, with the **(5)**............ of my mother, thought this was funny. However, she **EXCEPT** could not join in the **(6)**............ – after all, her son was a thief! Nor **LAUGH** had she realised how **(7)**............ it was to let me <u>out of sight</u> for **DANGER** even a minute. She would have to keep a careful eye on me <u>at all times</u>. As I showed little **(8)**............ to hand over the the fruits of **WILLING** my criminal activity, she emptied everything from my pockets back into the stocking. This included, <u>by the way</u>, an additional **(9)**............ . I had had a few pennies of my own to buy sweets. The **CONTRIBUTE** manager who was <u>in charge of</u> the branch was something of an amateur **(10)**............ and did a drawing of me robbing an old lady **CARTOON** which was displayed in the post office for the next couple of years. Eventually, my mother saw the funny side of things.

VOCABULARY

Prepositional phrases

1 Look through the text above and find the prepositional phrases which have been underlined. Match each one with the correct meaning:

- incidentally
- believing something to be true
- using something to achieve an aim
- always
- responsible for

- independently
- to represent someone else
- for the purpose of
- not visible
- difficult to take

2 Complete the second sentences so that they have a similar meaning to the first sentences. You must use between two and five words including the word given. Do not change the word given.

1 You must never take your helmet off while you are horse-riding..
all
Helmets must be worn .... while horse-riding.

2 I am here as the council's representative.
behalf
I am here .... the council.

3 The car door was opened with a coat hanger.
means
The thief opened the door .... a coat hanger.

4 For once, I would like you to do without any help.
your
Can you do this .... for a change?

5 He wanted to say he was sorry; that's why he bought some flowers.
order
He bought some flowers .... he was sorry.

6 They waved until she disappeared over the hill.
sight
They waved until .... over the hill.

7 One other thing before I forget – Jane was on TV.
way
Oh, ..., I saw Jane on TV.

8 I'm sorry but I thought it was OK to park here.
under
I do apologise. I .... it was OK to park here.

9 Her responsibility was for the whole project.
charge
She .... the whole project.

10 The book was too high for me to get it from the top shelf.
out
The book was .... on the top shelf.

3 Look at the common prepositional phrases on page 76. Which ones are you familiar with?

LISTENING

1 Harriet Williams, an Englishwoman, was born in India and came to England in 1920 when she was ten. How do you think she felt about coming "home"? What do you think she found different?

2 Now listen to her talking about the major changes that took place during her childhood. Decide whether the following statements are **True** or **False**.

1 Her father had a terrible job.
2 Her father built airports and docks.
3 Their house in India had a large garden.
4 Her mother had to work hard to run the house in India.
5 She feels sorry that her brothers were sent away to school.
6 Her father became ill in 1925.
7 She had expected to see fewer white faces in England.
8 Her house in England seemed very small.
9 Her mother's cooking never improved.
10 In England, her father was no longer an important person.
11 Harriet believed ready-made clothes weren't good enough for her.
12 She thinks that coming back to England made her a better person.

3 Make sentences about Harriet using the various forms of **used to** we studied on p75.

LANGUAGE STUDY

Causative **have**

1 What is the difference between these two sentences?

1 *Harriet had her clothes made.*
2 *Harriet made her own clothes.*

We use the **have something done** form when we want to say that instead of doing something ourselves someone else does it for us. We usually use the form to talk about some kind of service we receive.
In sentence 1 someone made Harriet's clothes for her; in sentence 2 she made them herself.

2 Change these sentences using the **causative have**. Begin them with the words in **bold**.

1 A local firm re-decorated our kitchen. **We**
2 It's time for me to have a haircut. **It's time I**
3 A doctor took her tonsils out when she was six. **She**
4 A tailor had altered his suit for the wedding. **He**
5 A doctor is taking the woman's temperature. **The woman**
6 A plumber is going to fix our central heating. **We**

Can you think of other things we have done for us?

A SENSE OF PLACE

What is the most memorable building you have ever visited, e.g. a castle, a place of worship? Why was it special? What feelings and sensations did it cause? Was the time of day important?

1 You are going to read the first pages of the novel *Rebecca* by Daphne du Maurier. Look at the illustration of Manderley as it appears in the narrator's dream. What kind of place is it?

2 Now read the passage and answer the questions which follow by choosing the answer **A**, **B**, **C** or **D**.

Last night I dreamt that I went to Manderley again. It seemed to me that I was going in by the iron entrance gates. The private road was just a narrow ribbon now, its stony surface covered with grass and weeds. Sometimes, when I thought it lost, it would appear again, beneath a fallen tree or beyond a muddy ditch made by the winter rains. The trees had thrown out new low branches which stretched across my way. I came upon the house suddenly, and stood there with my heart beating faster and tears coming to my eyes.

There was Manderley, our Manderley, secret and silent as it has always been, the grey stone shining in the moonlight of my dream. Time could not spoil the beauty of those walls, nor of the place itself, lying like a jewel in the hollow of a hand. The grass sloped down towards the sea, which was a sheet of silver lying calm under the moon, like a lake undisturbed by wind or storm. I turned again to the house, and I saw that the garden had run wild, even as the woods had done. Weeds were everywhere. But moonlight can play strange tricks with the imagination, even with a dreamer's imagination. As I stood there, quiet and still, I could swear that the house was not an empty shell, but lived and breathed as it had lived before. Light came from the windows, the curtains blew softly in the night air, and there, in the library, the door would stand half open as we had left it, with my handkerchief on the table beside the bowl of autumn flowers.

Then a cloud came over the moon, like a dark hand before a face. The strange feeling went. I looked again upon an empty shell, with no whisper of the past about it. Our fear and suffering were dead. When I thought about Manderley in my waking hours I would not be bitter. I would think of it as it might have been if I could have lived there without fear. I would remember the flower gardens in the summer, and the birds that sang there. Tea under the trees, and the sound of the sea coming up to us from the shore below. I would think of the blown flowers from the bushes, in the Happy Valley. These things could never lose their freshness. They were memories that could not be hurt. All this I knew in my dream (for like most sleepers, I knew that I dreamed). In reality I lay far away, in a foreign land and would wake before long in the bare little hotel bedroom. I would lie a moment, stretch myself and turn puzzled by that burning sun, that hard clear sky, so different from the soft moonlight of my dream. The day would lie before us both, long but full of a certain peace, a precious calm we had not known before. We would not talk of Manderley; I would not tell my dream. For Manderley was ours no longer. Manderley was no more.

We can never go back again; that is certain. The past is still too close to us. But we have no secrets now from each other. All things are shared. Our little hotel may be dull, and the food not very good; day after day things may be very much the same. But dullness is better than fear. We live now very much by habit. And I – I have become very good at reading aloud! I have lost my old self-consciousness. I am very different from that person who drove to Manderley for the first time, hopeful and eager, filled with the desire to please. It was my lack of confidence, of course, that struck Mrs Danvers. What must I have seemed like, after Rebecca?

1 When the narrator arrived in her dream at the house called Manderley
   A she was unaffected by it.
   B the road was the same as before.
   C she got lost.
   D she was overcome by emotion.

2 Where was Manderley situated?
   A By the side of a lake.
   B In a kind of hole.
   C At the bottom of a cliff.
   D Below a grassy lawn.

3 What did the narrator feel once the moon was covered by cloud?
   A Someone was living in the house.
   B She would find objects she recognised.
   C The house was really empty.
   D The house still held lots of bad memories.

4 She knew that when she awoke
   A she would remember the house as it had been before.
   B she would be in Manderley.
   C she would feel sad and lonely.
   D she would have a more positive outlook.

5 The narrator was certain that
   A she would share her dream.
   B they would plan their return to Manderley.
   C the new day would not be spoilt.
   D the day would bring an untruth.

6 How is life with her companion different now from the way it was before?
   A They are no longer afraid.
   B They have few secrets from each other.
   C Life is far more exciting.
   D Their lifestyle is more luxurious.

7 How does the narrator feel she has changed?
   A She has discovered an acting ability.
   B She is more sure of herself.
   C She is more like Rebecca.
   D Mrs Danvers would find her less striking.

3 Discuss these questions.

1 What do you imagine had happened at Manderley?
2 What were the secrets that had existed between the narrator and her husband (her companion)?
3 How do you think the narrator has changed?

VOCABULARY

Forming nouns

1 In the text it says: "*But **dullness** is better than fear.*" This is the same as "A dull and ordinary life is better than being afraid." Look at these common adjectives; what are their related nouns?

angry poor bored tired happy kind
hungry wealthy free thirsty hot cruel
calm ambitious excited satisfied

2 Make sentences like the first example, using the noun forms.

WRITING

1 Look at the answer below to the following examination question: *Write a description of a book you have enjoyed, saying something about its plot and why you would recommend it.* Would it make you want to read the book?

2 Now complete the description by using just one word for each of the gaps.

One of my favourite books is *Rebecca* by Daphne du Maurier. It is a (**1**)............ of a love story and a murder mystery. It is set in England in the 1930s and most of the action (**2**)............ place in a beautiful house called Manderley, (**3**)............ is central to the story. The main characters are Max de Winter and (**4**)............ narrator who becomes his second wife. (**5**)............, it is Rebecca, de Winter's first wife, who dominates the tale. It revolves (**6**)............ the mystery of her death which is gradually revealed by the events of the book.
I would recommend *Rebecca* for (**7**)............ reasons. First of (**8**)............, it is like a cunning jigsaw puzzle. Secondly, it is populated by extraordinary characters, not (**9**)............ the evil Mrs Danvers (**10**)............ hatred of and cruelty (**11**)............ Max's new bride are quite chilling. The descriptions of the house and countryside are marvellously atmospheric Above all, I appreciate (**12**)............ she develops the character of the narrator, who from a timid girl (**13**)............ a confident young woman, able to (**14**)............ her freedom (**15**)............ the terrible events of the past.

3 Using the description of *Rebecca* as a guide, write your own answer to the question in **1**.

A CHANGE OF JOB

1 Look at the photographs. Which jobs are shown? Which ones do you like? Which could you never do?

Work

Sort the words and expressions below into these categories: Getting a job, Doing a job, Personal qualities, Leaving/Not having a job.

> retirement   reference   interview   to do overtime   to be sacked   to be unemployed
> training   skills   conscientious   to dismiss   to fill in a form   pension   reliable
> to be cut out for something   enthusiastic   having the right qualifications
> to do/work a shift   previous experience   to be made redundant   to go on strike

1 Look at this advertisement which appeared in *Sea World* magazine. What kind of people do you think would apply?

2 Opposite there are two letters replying to the advertisement. They have been jumbled up. One letter is informal because it is written to a relative; the second letter is a typically formal application. Reconstruct the letters by studying the opening and closing sentences for each and putting sentences **a-r** in order.

TIME FOR A CHANGE?

Chefs Afloat is looking for all levels of kitchen staff to work on luxury liners for this winter's winter cruises season. Recognised training and experience essential. Send a covering letter and C.V. to:
Mr Michael Edwards, *Chefs Afloat*...

3 Make a list of the formal words and expressions from Anton Steel's letter. Then find as many informal equivalents in Jo's letter as you can. Example:

formal	**informal**
h My employer will supply you with a reference should you require one.	**e** He says he'll write a reference for me if you like.

Dear Uncle Mike,

Thanks a lot for ringing Mum and telling her that you are looking for well-qualified staff for winter cruises.

Dear Mr Edwards,

I am writing to express an interest in the posts advertised in last Saturday's Sea World. I have enclosed a full C.V. for your consideration but here follow brief details.

a For the past two years I have been the head chef on a luxury yacht for a prominent businessman.

b I'd even be able to start almost straight away.

c I shall be returning to Melbourne and will be available for interview at your convenience.

d I am a 28-year-old fully-qualified chef with seven years' experience.

e He says he'll write a reference for me if you like.

f You'll probably remember that I finished at hotel school about three years ago when I was 18.

g If everything is satisfactory, I would be able to commence almost immediately.

h My employer will supply you with a reference, should you require one.

i One last thing, can you tell Mum what the pay and working conditions are like?

j At the moment I'm finishing off a one-year contract on a liner.

k I began my career on the Anastasia liner where I worked for four years.

l Consequently, I shall be seeking a similar position.

m As soon as it finishes I'll be free and looking for work.

n I am going back to Melbourne and could have a chat with you then, if that's OK.

o I learned how to be a pastry chef there but I've done all sorts of cooking since then.

p My current contract comes to an end next month.

q I trained at the Blue Ribbon Institute where I specialised in French nouvelle cuisine.

r Anyway, I've had a great time on this job and my boss has taught me a lot.

Hope to hear from you soon.
All the best,

Jo

PS I've included an up-to-date C.V. for your records.

You may contact me at my home address. I would appreciate it if you could forward my wife further details concerning salary and conditions.

I look forward to receiving your reply.

Yours sincerely,

Anton Steel

4 Compulsory letter Read the advertisements from *Student Job Finder* magazine. Choose one of the jobs and write a letter of application in **120 - 180** words in an appropriate style.

Remember to ask about
- interviews – when/where? • salary and conditions. • length of commitment (for temporary jobs)

APPLE PICKERS Pick apples on an English apple farm. Good head for heights necessary. Free farmhouse accommodation. Write to: Mrs A. Cox, ref. 690.

CHAMBERMAIDS AND PORTERS needed for five star central London hotel. Smart appearance essential. Must be prepared to work shifts. Full board and lodging and uniform provided. Write to The Manager, ref. 691.

Hi there! Know about music and all the latest sounds? Then we may need you as a shop assistant at Murph's Records, London. Write to Jackie, ref. 692.

AU PAIRS (both sexes) for English families. Free board and lodging and pocket money in exchange for baby-sitting and light housework. Write to Mrs Clancy, ref. 693.

7 The Natural World

COSTING THE EARTH

FIRST THOUGHTS

Discuss the pictures with a partner.

1 When and where were they taken?
2 What is your reaction to them?
3 Do they remind you of anything in your country or region?

VOCABULARY

Complete the sentences using one of the words from the box.

> ecology fallout pollution waste acid extinct
> contaminated dumped environment reactor

1 The world in which we live is our ....
2 Smoke, dirt and noise are all types of ....
3 If man continues to hunt whales, they will shortly become ....
4 Every day rubbish and chemicals are taken out to sea and .... It's disgusting and should be stopped.
5 In many parts of the world trees and lakes are being destroyed by .... rain.
6 At Chernobyl, there was an accident at a nuclear .... When it exploded, large areas of the surrounding countryside were .... and there was .... all over Europe.
7 .... is the science that studies the relationship between different life forms in nature.
8 When uranium is used up, it has to be kept in a safe place. It is extremely difficult to dispose of nuclear ....

READING

1 Read the text and decide what its aim is.

THANK GOD SOMEONE'S MAKING WAVES

The natural world is under violent assault from man.

The seas and rivers are being poisoned by radioactive wastes, by chemical discharges and by the dumping of dangerous toxins and raw sewage. The air we breathe is polluted by smoke and fumes from factories and motor vehicles; even the rain is poisoned.

It's little wonder forests and lakes are being destroyed and everywhere wildlife is disappearing. Yet the destruction continues.

Governments and industries throughout the world are intensifying their efforts to extract the earth's mineral riches and to plunder its living resources.

The great rain forests and the frozen continents alike are seriously threatened. And this despite the warnings of the scientific community and the deep concern of millions of ordinary people.

Despite the fact, too, that we can create environmentally-clean industries, harness the power of the sun, wind and waves for our energy needs and manage the finite resources of the earth in a way that will safeguard our future and protect all the rich variety of life-forms which share this planet with us.

But there is still hope. The forces of destruction are being challenged across the globe – and at the spearhead of this challenge is Greenpeace.

Wherever the environment is in danger, Greenpeace has made a stand. Its scientific presentations and peaceful direct actions at sea and on land have shocked governments and industries into an awareness that Greenpeace will not allow the natural world to be destroyed.

Those actions, too, have won the admiration and support of millions.

Now you can strengthen the thin green line; you can make your voice heard in defence of the living world by joining Greenpeace today.

Thank God someone's making waves.

GREENPEACE

2 Choose the best answers (**A, B, C** or **D**) to these questions.

1 Which of the following statements is *not* true?
  A Drinking water is polluted.
  B Radioactive waste pollutes the sea.
  C Sewage isn't processed.
  D Cars and factories pollute the air.

2 The writer..... forests and lakes are being destroyed.
  A is surprised that
  B is unsure why
  C wonders why
  D understands why

3 Rain forests are being destroyed because governments and industries
  A are unaware of what they're doing wrong.
  B are rich and powerful.
  C choose to ignore criticism.
  D basically care about the environment.

4 The earth's resources
  A should be left for people.
  B can be made to last longer.
  C will last forever.
  D belong to just humans and animals.

5 How does Greenpeace feel about the future?
  A Desperate.
  B Resigned.
  C Cautiously optimistic.
  D Deeply pessimistic.

6 Governments and industries
  A don't know what Greenpeace thinks.
  B are forced by Greenpeace to understand the problems.
  C can easily ignore Greenpeace.
  D misunderstand what Greenpeace thinks.

7 How does Greenpeace think that people can help?
  A By becoming members.
  B By speaking out.
  C By painting a green line.
  D By making waves.

LISTENING

1 Listen to part of a second advertisement for Greenpeace and complete the notes.

The earth is **(1)**............ million years old. It is easier to understand this if we imagine the earth as a **(2)**............ person. Of the first seven years we know **(3)**............ . Dinosaurs appeared just **(4)**............ when the planet was **(5)**............ . Last week, man-like apes evolved into **(6)**............ . Modern man has been around for just **(7)**............ . In the last hour **(8)** .... was discovered and the **(9)**............ began a minute ago. In the last minute Paradise has been turned into a **(10)**............ .

2 How effective do you think the advertisement is?

VOCABULARY

Word building

1 *Now you can* **strengthen** *the thin green line.*

Strengthen is a verb which is formed from the adjective **strong**. Work in pairs and complete this table.

ADJECTIVE	NOUN	VERB
wide		
strong		
deep		
weak		
short		
high		

2 Complete each sentence using one of the words from the table. Make any changes that are necessary.

1 They wanted to .... the bottom of the harbour to allow oil tankers in.
2 These country roads are dangerously narrow. They need ....
3 Greenpeace has .... our understanding of the environment.
4 Industry is laughing at the .... of the new regulations.
5 Only people over a certain .... can join the army.

LANGUAGE STUDY

The definite article

1 **The** *natural world is under assault from man.*

The can be used for many different reasons. Match each reason with an example sentence or phrase.

1 There was a man outside. **The** man was tall.
2 **The** moon and **the** earth both go around **the** sun.
3 I can't find **the** pen I bought yesterday.
4 Where's **the** cat? (*the cat that lives in this house*)
5 Paul is in **the** garden.
6 She plays **the** piano well.
7 It was **the** best film I have ever seen.
8 **the** rich, **the** poor, **the** unemployed
9 **the** United States of America, **the** Irish President

A with superlatives
B when only one exists
C when the object or person is mentioned for a second time
D when we make something definite by adding extra information
E with musical instruments
F with adjectives to describe a class or group
G when location means only one thing is being referred to
H with titles and place names that have the idea **of**
I when the object is known by everybody

2 When do we **not** use the article? Match the examples with their descriptions.

1 love, hate, beauty
2 Cats are beautiful.
3 petrol, sugar, milk, wood
4 home, work, hospital
5 New York, Brazil

A most names of towns, cities and countries
B uncountable nouns
C countable objects in general
D abstract nouns
E some places/locations

3 Complete the following sentences with either **a**, **the** or nothing.

1 .... life is getting easier for .... rich.
2 .... accidents are generally caused by people driving too fast. This is certainly true of .... accident I had last year.
3 Caroline plays .... violin really well.
4 .... park has many examples of .... wildlife especially .... birds .... deer.
5 .... pollution is destroying .... environment.
6 She is going to visit .... India and .... USA.
7 We have nothing to fear but .... fear itself.
8 .... price of .... petrol is going up. .... petrol I bought yesterday was .... cheapest in .... area.
9 .... wood is much dearer than it used to be. In fact, ... wood I used to make .... shelves in the living room was £6 .... metre.
10 She's .... fascinating woman. Did you know she's .... leader of .... opposition party?

4 Correct these sentences if necessary, by adding **a** or **the** or deleting.

1 The most people in United States have two cars.
2 Mary works in a university.
3 Did you have the nice time at a school today, Amanda?
4 The Rolling Stones are the most wonderful group I've ever heard.
5 What do you think of book I lent you?
6 She is going to be doctor.
7 They have two holiday homes, one in mountains and one at seaside.
8 All people who live in this town work at car factory.
9 Where's Mary? She is in sitting room talking on phone.
10 She's wearing jeans. In fact they're jeans she wore last week.

PRONUNCIATION

Saying the **th** sound and **the**

1 Ways of pronouncing *th*

1 **Th** has two pronunciations in English: /θ/ as in **thin** and /ð/ as in **the**. Many students have problems with these two sounds.
   Go back to the first Greenpeace advertisement and find out which **th** words have the /θ/ sound and which have the /ð/ sound.

2 Listen to someone reading part of the Greenpeace text aloud and mark where he makes mistakes with the pronunciation of **th**.

Despite the fact, too, that we can create environmentally-clean industries, harness the power of the sun, wind and waves for our energy needs and manage the finite resources of the earth in a way that will safeguard our future and protect all the rich variety of life forms which share this planet with us.

2 Ways of saying *the*

The words that follow **the** can change its pronunciation.

If **the** is followed by a consonant, it is pronounced /ðə/, e.g. *the sun*.
If **the** is followed by a vowel, then its pronunciation becomes /ði:/ and we often use the linking sound /j/, e.g. *the earth*.

Practise saying these examples from the text and group them according to how we say **the**. Where necessary, use the linking sound /j/.

A the seas   **C** the rain   **E** the environment
B the air   **D** the power   **F** the admiration

LISTENING

1 Some people say that the climate of the earth is changing because of man's activity and pollution. How true is this of where you live?

2 You are now going to hear an interview between Peter Whitehead, the presenter of a current affairs programme, and Frances Kelly, the leader of the Campaign for Clean Air. While you listen, decide if the following statements are **True** or **False**.

1 The government is acting too slowly for Frances.
2 Sulphur monoxide is produced by power stations.
3 Britain is one of the worst polluters.
4 Carbon monoxide causes heart problems in adults.
5 In the short term, carbon dioxide isn't dangerous.
6 There is little evidence to show these gases have a bad effect on the development of children.
7 The greenhouse effect will cause droughts.
8 Frances believes that the government has a limited responsibility.

3 Listen again and make full notes about the effects of the three gases sulphur dioxide, carbon monoxide and carbon dioxide.

BIG ISSUES

FIRST THOUGHTS

Look at this list of 'big issues' (important topics). If you had the power to do something about just one of them, which one would you choose?
- world hunger
- homelessness
- pollution
- nuclear energy and weapons
- the gap between rich and poor countries
- unemployment

SPEAKING

How do you think the people in the cars in the photographs feel?

VOCABULARY

Which words in the box are verbs, parts of a car, or words to do with the road.

> lane roundabout crash junction brake bonnet bend swerve overtake gear
> reverse indicate windscreen clutch skid services steering wheel

LISTENING

1 You are going to hear five different people describe experiences which are all to do with cars and travelling by road. Choose from the list **A-F** the best description of what each one says. There is one extra letter which you do not need to use.

A driving in bad road conditions
B an accident the speaker witnessed
C a holiday ruined by traffic
D an accident the speaker may have caused
E the advantages of a new car
F helping someone who has got lost

Speaker 1 ☐
Speaker 2 ☐
Speaker 3 ☐
Speaker 4 ☐
Speaker 5 ☐

2 Tell each other about any memorable experiences you have had travelling by car.

READING

1 You are going to read an article about the impact the motor car has had on everyday life. Choose from the sentences **A-I** the one which fits each gap (**1-7**). There is one extra sentence which you do not need to use. There is an example at the beginning (**0**).

> **A** It is a problem that can be solved given the right levels of commitment.
> **B** Immediate steps are needed to check the emissions from car engines.
> **C** The number of vehicles on our roads is set to double over the next thirty years
> **D** There are other victims too.
> **E** The average speed of traffic in central London is the same as in the era of the horse and cart of 80 years ago.
> **F** We do not need cars to show what we are worth.
> **G** This would make people think twice before getting into their cars.
> **H** Indeed, most teenagers now expect to have their own car once they hit the age of 18.
> **I** Lead in petrol has been shown to cause brain damage in young children.

The Curse of the Motor Car

We are all familiar with the story of Frankenstein, the professor who created a monster that eventually led to his own destruction. In my opinion, the mass-produced car, which was born in the early part of this century, is set to strangle us in the next.

Just consider the awful impact that the car has had on modern life. [0][E] Lives in many big cities have become miserable because of the congestion, noise and pollution from motor vehicles.

It is the young who have been put most at risk. It has become far too hazardous to let children cycle freely on the roads. There has been an enormous increase in the number of juvenile asthma cases and respiratory problems. [1]

Nevertheless, in my opinion, the impact of the car is nowhere more visible than in the small villages of what was once our countryside. As far as I'm concerned, it is these and their inhabitants that have suffered the most. Huge juggernauts thunder down narrow streets and the high street becomes a permanent traffic jam. Pedestrians risk their lives by stepping off narrow pavements. [2] The slaughter of wildlife has become so common as to cease to be horrific.

This story is all too familiar, yet there is worse to come. [3] Does it mean that we will be living in a wilderness of tarmac and concrete? Or is it perhaps time to tackle the monster ? Now, I am not suggesting that we can turn back the clock and un-invent the car in any way. What I *am* saying is that we have to find imaginative solutions to our transport needs if we are to avoid choking ourselves to death, or living in a wilderness made from concrete and tarmac. I do believe, however, that the problem can be dealt with on three levels: internationally, nationally and, last but not least, on a personal level.

On an international level, governments must co-operate to ensure that motor manufacturers are working to produce more efficient engines which demand less in fuel and which are much cleaner. They should set limits for engine sizes and production. [4] Manufacturers must be made to fit effective filters to all new vehicles. Damage to the ozone layer or acid rain do not respect national boundaries.

Let us now look at what can be done on a national level. Road tax should be up to ten times more for vehicles with engine sizes over, say, 2 litres. Cars without effective filters and catalytic converters should be taken off the roads immediately. The government should put up the price of petrol immediately. [5] Road pricing for journeys would also help with this. Next, it should develop a public transport policy that does not have the private motor car at its centre. It is a fact that building more roads actually increases traffic. Public transport such as reliable trains and buses should receive a far greater investment.

Lastly, what can we do as individuals? First and foremost, we need to rid ourselves of the mentality that we cannot do without our cars and that they are a reflection of our success and status in society. Fifty years ago it was unusual for a family to have a car. Now, along with washing machines and annual holidays abroad, it has become the norm. [6] Next, we should make immediate changes to our lifestyles and walk or use bicycles for shorter journeys. We should become politically active and make it clear that transport policy is a key issue in how we decide to spend our vote.

To sum up, I have tried to show that there are steps that can be taken to reduce the damage caused by the car. [7] However, only by acting as individuals first can we expect governments to act in their turn. By accepting responsibility and acting upon it, we can avoid our lemming-like journey down the one-way street to extinction.

2 Understanding the organisation of the text

1 What does the first line of each paragraph do?
2 What words or expressions does the writer use to
  a give his/her own opinions?
  b list his/her reasons and put them in order?
3 The writer uses questions in the text. Find them and decide why they are used.

LANGUAGE STUDY

The passive

*...the problem **can be dealt with** on three levels...*

1 Change these sentences from the active to the passive beginning with the words in **bold**.

1 Farmers spray **the trees** each week.
2 That factory is producing **more and more pollution**.
3 Someone saw **the company** dumping rubbish.
4 Demonstrators have broken into **the oil refinery**.
5 The owners had hidden **all the evidence** by the time the police arrived.
6 A scientist was re-designing **the reactor**.
7 We need to find **a solution**.
8 The prime minister is going to open **the enquiry**.
9 We shall notify **the police** about this matter.
10 Someone should have written to **the papers**.

2 The passive is formed by a form of the verb **to be** plus the past participle. How is the passive is formed with:

1 the present simple and past simple tenses
2 the present and past continuous tenses
3 the **going to** future and the infinitive
4 the present and past perfect
5 modals like **shall**
6 modals in the past like **might have**

USE OF ENGLISH

Complete the second sentences so that they have a similar meaning to the first sentences. You must use between two and five words including the word given. Do not change the word given.

1 We need to find an imaginative solution.
   need
   What we .... an imaginative solution.
2 They didn't let her watch TV.
   allowed
   She .... TV.
3 They have made the castle a tourist attraction.
   turned
   The castle .... a tourist attraction.
4 It hasn't rained for two years.
   time
   The .... two years ago.
5 She wouldn't let me pay the bill.
   paying
   She .... the bill.

6 Asthma cases have gone up.
   increase
   There has .... asthma cases.
7 Someone must find the answer.
   must
   The .... by someone.
8 Do you know the story of Frankenstein?
   familiar
   Are .... the story of Frankenstein?
9 She didn't find his behaviour at all surprising.
   hardly
   She .... his behaviour.
10 The air is clean since they fitted filters.
   used
   The air .... they fitted filters.

WRITING

The opinion question

1 The article *The Curse of the Motor Car*, gives the writer's opinion on the subject. In **Paper 2 (Writing)** there is often a question which asks you to do this. Success depends on four things:
1 having sufficient topic vocabulary
2 having sufficient ideas and opinions
3 having the structures and expressions to use in this type of essay
4 good essay planning and organisation

You are going to write this essay: *"In a world of plenty, people are still dying of hunger. What can be done to solve this problem?"* First of all we shall look at topic vocabulary.

2 **Vocabulary**

Join these split sentences.
1 They haven't got enough to eat because
2 The size of a population can be controlled
3 It didn't rain for two years and
4 All the animals
5 Wheat and rice are
6 Another word for help
7 There is a terrible **famine**
8 If you get a loan from the bank
9 The desert has become green

A is **aid**.
B two kinds of **crop**.
C died of **thirst**.
D through **contraception**.
E and people are dying of **starvation**.
F you are in debt and you have to pay **interest**.
G the **harvest** failed.
H since **irrigation** was introduced.
I there was an awful **drought**.

3 This text should give you some ideas for the essay you are going to write on hunger. When you have read it, match the pictures to the paragraphs.

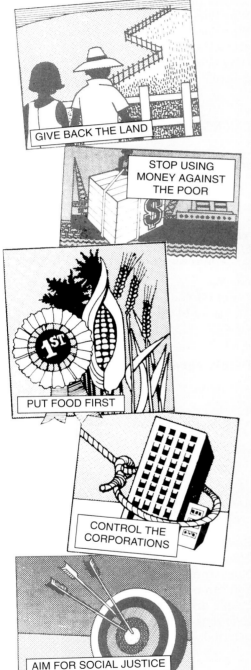

GIVE BACK THE LAND

STOP USING MONEY AGAINST THE POOR

PUT FOOD FIRST

CONTROL THE CORPORATIONS

AIM FOR SOCIAL JUSTICE

1 Debt has been crippling the Third World over the last five years. Countries can be forced to sacrifice as much as half their export earnings as repayments on debts to Western banks. And, before the West offers new loans, it insists on drastic cuts in welfare spending which hit the deprived hardest. Debt repayments should never amount to more than ten per cent of a country's export earnings.

2 Hunger only affects the poor – there are no hungry countries, just bigger or smaller numbers of hungry people within countries. The government's commitment to social justice isn't the icing on the cake – it is the cake itself. The only way to end hunger is to reduce poverty and inequality, and make feeding people a priority.

3 Much of the world's cultivable land is owned by people with large farms – particularly in the Americas. Left to itself, this situation will worsen, not get better, since it is the large farmers who can borrow and afford mechanisation and fertiliser. Land reform is not only essential for reasons of justice – it also increases food production, since smallholders farm much more efficiently than the big landowners. But sharing out the land will not work if inequality persists elsewhere in society.

4 The world is now a supermarket for the rich world's consumers – and the managers of that supermarket are the multinational agribusiness corporations. These companies control production prices, often holding small farmers under contract for their export crops. This way they can buy harvests at controlled prices while leaving the risks of bad weather and plant disease on the shoulders of the individual farmer.

5 Developing countries are still locked into a farming system created for the benefit of the rich world. Their best land and resources are used to grow cash crops for export rather than food. The trend away from crops for local consumption must be halted and farmers paid more for their harvests.

4 In pairs, plan your composition. When your teacher has checked your plan, write the composition. Use the expressions in the article about cars on page 87 to help you.

FREE TO CHOOSE

FIRST THOUGHTS

What would happen if cars and lorries were banned from city centres?

LISTENING

1 Read the situation and decide what you think should be done.

Marsham is a small town near London. In recent years its streets have become very congested. A traffic-free town centre could be achieved by building a bypass around the village. A number of people support the plan. Others are worried about the effect such changes would have.

2 Three councillors – Eric, Charles and Bernice – are discussing the proposals. Listen to their discussion and answer the questions by writing

E (for Eric)   **C** (for Charles) or   **B** (for Bernice).

1 Who is most worried about the effects of a bypass? ☐
2 Who is most concerned about improving conditions in the village? ☐
3 Who talks about what would happen to small shops? ☐
4 Who has a vision of how a new village centre could look? ☐
5 Who becomes very enthusiastic about change? ☐
6 Who is angry at the suggestions? ☐
7 Who says something needs to be done for the safety of pedestrians? ☐

3 Listen again and make notes in answer to these questions.

1 Why is Bernice worried about the proposed bypass?
2 Why does Charles think the bypass is essential?
3 Why does Charles think Marsham could be attractive to tourists?
4 Why doesn't Bernice want Marsham to be a tourist centre?

SPEAKING

Managing conversations

1 ▭ Listen to the discussion again and tick (✔) which expressions the speakers use for the following.

Giving an opinion
I think... ☐
I feel... ☐
I believe... ☐
In my opinion,... ☐
From my point of view,... ☐
As I see it,... ☐

Strongly agreeing
I quite agree. ☐

Absolutely! ☐

Partly agreeing
I see your point but... ☐
I agree up to a point... ☐

Disagreeing
I'm afraid I just can't agree ☐

Strongly disagreeing
What nonsense! ☐
What rubbish! ☐

2 Can you think of any other expressions that you could add?

3 Work with a partner and respond to these statements. Begin your response using one of the expressions we have just looked at.

1 Smoking should be banned in all public places.
2 Men are much better drivers than women.
3 Nuclear energy will kill us all in the end.
4 You can never trust a man with a beard.
5 People are old at 40.
6 Everyone should live together before they get married.

READING

Smokers' rights

1 Read the article and answer these questions.

1 Who is the school for and what is the row about?
2 What is the history of smoking at the school?
3 Who banned it and why?
4 How do the centre's users feel about this?
5 What do *you* think should be done?

ROW OVER CIGGIES BAN

A row has erupted after smoking was banned at a London language school. A room which used to be for smokers was turned into a non-smoking area. It was new school director Janine Murray who took the decision. What Janine insists is that the ban was introduced to protect staff and students from the effects of passive smoking. Murray maintained: "What smokers should realise is that if they want to commit suicide it's one thing; killing other people with their selfish habit is another. Most of our students are in their teens and early twenties – we shouldn't be enouraging them to wreck their lungs."

No smoke without fire

Colombian Mariana Gomes, a First Certificate student who is leading the fight to have the ban lifted, disagrees. She is planning a demonstration. Dark-haired Mariana vowed to fight the ban. "It's Mrs Murray who has caused all the trouble. The old director was much more easygoing. Studying for an exam is stressful work. Cigarettes can calm our nerves. All we want is one tiny room."

Smoke came out my ears

Teacher Bernie Green supports Mariana: "Even non-smokers on the staff are furious. What makes me angry is that people are kept here most of the day studying, so it's unreasonable to tell them they can't smoke. They are not kids."

2 Understanding the organisation of the text

What is the purpose of
a the headline?
b the opening sentence?
c the first sentence of each paragraph?
d each paragraph?
e the secondary headlines between the paragraphs?

SPEAKING

Work in groups of three and take one of these roles from the article you read: Janine Murray, Mariana Gomes or Bernie Green.

Look at the diagram which shows the floor where the smokers' room used to be. Try and find a solution which will satisfy everybody. Use as many ways of giving opinions and agreeing and disagreeing as you can.

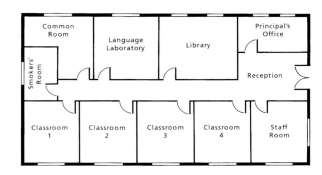

WRITING

A newspaper article

You were at the meeting where the future of Marsham was discussed. Using the article about the smoking ban as a rough guide, write a report of the meeting.
Before you begin:
• Invent ages and occupations for Bernice, Charles and Eric. Think carefully how you will describe them.
• Decide on the *angle* are you going to take on the story, i.e. are you going to favour Bernice or Charles?
• Think what headlines and sub-headings you could use to break the story up into interesting paragraphs.

WHERE ON EARTH?

FIRST THOUGHTS

1 If you could visit anywhere in the world, where would it be?

2 What is the most remote or isolated place you have ever been to?

USE OF ENGLISH

1 You are going to read an article about the Galapagos Islands. Before you read, find out if anyone knows who Charles Darwin was and why he was important.

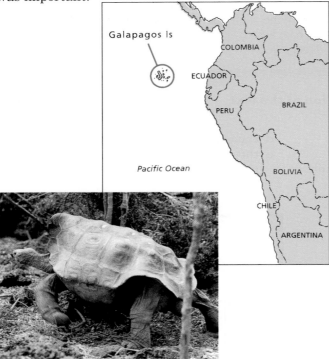

Galapagos Is
COLOMBIA
ECUADOR
PERU
BRAZIL
Pacific Ocean
BOLIVIA
CHILE
ARGENTINA

2 Now read Parts One and Two of the article, in exercises 3 and 4, and answer these questions.

1 Where are the islands and how were they formed?
2 Why were they left alone for such a long time?
3 What was the islands' first contact with man?
4 Why were the tortoises Darwin saw so special?
5 What problems did visitors to the islands indirectly cause? How were they solved?
6 What new dangers face the islands?

3 Read Part One again and decide which word **A, B, C** or **D** best fits each space. There is an example at the beginning (**0**).

Part One
One of the most (**0**) ..*remote*.. places on earth surely (**1**).......... to be the Galapagos Islands, which (**2**).......... in the Pacific Ocean 1100 kilometres (**3**).......... the west of Ecuador. These (**4**).......... islands made largely from volcanic rock were (**5**).......... to go their own way for millions of years without (**6**).......... interference. Most notably, the islands are (**7**).......... to the giant tortoise and iguanas. There are also turtles weighing up to 230 kilos and (**8**).......... a cormorant which cannot fly!

The islands were not (**9**).......... until a few hundred years ago when pirates came (**10**).......... them and buried their treasure there. Unpopular crew members were often (**11**)".........." there too! Later, in 1835, Charles Darwin visited the islands in (**12**).......... to study the wildlife and used his observations as the basis for his (**13**).......... of natural selection and evolution. He noticed, for (**14**).........., that many of the islands had their own (**15**).......... of tortoise which had evolved according to each environment in isolation over millions of years.

0 **A** far   **B** remote   **C** alone   **D** solitary
1 **A** should   **B** ought   **C** has   **D** is
2 **A** lay   **B** combine   **C** lie   **D** impose
3 **A** by   **B** in   **C** at   **D** to
4 **A** anti-social   **B** inhospitable   **C** unkind
   D awkward
5 **A** made   **B** allowed   **C** let   **D** engaged
6 **A** human   **B** humane   **C** humanity
   D mankind
7 **A** dwelling   **B** house   **C** residence   **D** home
8 **A** yet   **B** while   **C** just   **D** even
9 **A** disturbed   **B** molested   **C** annoyed
   D teased
10 **A** into   **B** across   **C** up   **D** by
11 **A** removed   **B** vanished   **C** disappeared
   D mislaid
12 **A** time   **B** case   **C** order   **D** purpose
13 **A** thoughts   **B** wonders   **C** theories
   D guesses
14 **A** once   **B** instants   **C** example   **D** chance
15 **A** style   **B** brand   **C** mark   **D** species

4 Complete the rest of the passage about the Galapagos Islands by using one word only for each space.

Part Two
In Darwin's time there were very **(1)**.......... natural predators and a balance **(2)**.......... the different species existed. Wild birds showed so **(3)**.......... fear that the first men could walk up to them and touch them **(4)**.......... them flying off. The biggest danger **(5)**.......... upon a time was the occasional fire which helped to **(6)**.......... the tortoise population down. However, the early visitors **(7)**.......... some unwelcome guests: they introduced rats, cats, pigs and dogs, **(8)**.......... grew in number and preyed upon the iguanas and ate the tortoises' eggs. **(9)**.......... creatures, part of an evolutionary process of millions of years, were in danger of **(10)**.......... lost in hundreds. Fortunately, radical steps were **(11)**.......... to hunt and destroy as many of these invaders as **(12)**.........., although the wild cats and rats have proved difficult to find. **(13)**.......... recent years, a new threat has appeared in the form of tourism. **(14)**.......... the government of Ecuador's best efforts, the tide of tourists, **(15)**.......... appears irresistible, may again upset the fine balance of nature of the unpopulated islands.

5 Can you think of any places of natural beauty or interest in your country which have been spoilt or destroyed by tourism? What steps could be taken to preserve them or to repair the damage?

6 Read this letter and tick the lines which are correct. Where a line has an extra word which should not be there, write it down.

Dear Angela,
  0 It was great to hear from you after such a long ✓
00 time. We had wondered what on **the** earth
  1 had happened to you; although I was astonished to
  2 get your letter. Your research it sounds very
  3 interesting – I can't imagine about being stuck
  4 on a small island with just birds for company.
  5 How long time did you spend there altogether? It
  6 sounds lonely. How did you arrive there in the
  7 first place? Whatever made you to go?
  8 The most people wouldn't be able to stand it but I
  9 think it is a very marvellous thing to do.
10 You don't say what was interested you the most.
11 If I were there I would do a research into the
12 giant tortoise! The man certainly has had a
13 devastating impact on it. I would ban tourists
14 for 50 years. Charles Darwin was the responsible
15 for making them too much famous!

WRITING

Compulsory letter

Angela Maybury has just returned home from the Galapagos Islands. You have written to her to ask if she would be willing to come to your school to talk at a meeting of the Natural History Club. Read Angela's reply carefully and the set of notes which you have made for yourself; then write a letter to her, organising the pre-talk appointment and answering her questions.

Write between **120 - 180** words in an appropriate style. Do not include addresses.

Thank you very much for your kind letter. I would be delighted to come along and talk to your club; I didn't realise there were so many young naturalists in my home town!

I will be returning to South America in about six weeks but I would be free to come along one evening. Early evening around five o'clock would be best for me. If you can give me a few dates to choose from, I'll see what I can do.

It would be very helpful, as I haven't done this kind of thing before, if you could tell me what you would like to know and the knowledge I can expect of the people who come to the talk. It might be an idea if we had a quick chat in person before I gave the talk. Any ideas?

I have lots of slides and video film which I could bring with me. Do you know if the school has a slide projector and/or video and screen which I could perhaps use?

Yours sincerely,

Angela Maybury

Notes

- *Children 12-17 little / no knowledge of islands.*
- *What made her go?*
- *What help did she receive?*
- *Were there other colleagues?*
- *Where were they from?*
- *Meet at my parents' house next Monday?*
- *Video – yes; school slide projector is broken.*

8 Judging by Appearances

JUMPING TO CONCLUSIONS

FIRST THOUGHTS

You have been invited to a party where you don't know anyone at all. Which people would you want to meet, and which ones would you wish to avoid talking to at all costs?

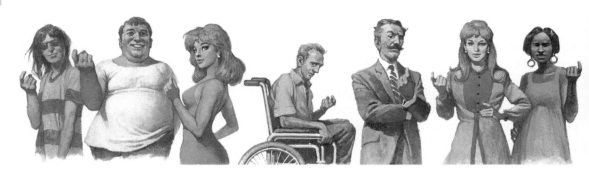

READING

1 Think of three things that you would like to find out about the art of face analysis. Then read the article to see if your questions are answered.

Secrets of the face

Is it really possible to judge someone's character from their face? The Chinese seem to think so. For over 2,000 years they have been practising Siang Mien, which is the art of judging character and predicting fortune from an analysis of the face. It developed in the ancient imperial court of China and consisted of jealously guarded secrets that were passed from masters to a few chosen apprentices. The secrets of face analysis were hidden away in special books which only a few could look at.

These secrets cannot have been that well guarded and must have got out because practically all Chinese practise some form of face analysis. Mothers tell their daughters that men with flat noses and small ear lobes will make shy and rather dull husbands.

So how does this analysis work? Well, to start with, people's faces can be classified according to one of ten basic shapes, each of which has its own special name. A triangular face, for example, is called a *fire-face*. One which is square is known as a *wall-face*, while one which is diamond shaped is a *jade-face*. There are even *bucket-faces*!

Once the basic shape has been decided, then parts of the face such as the eyes, nose, chin and mouth can be analysed in their turn. People who have not got conventional or beautiful faces should not worry, as ugly people tend to be lucky.

Anyway, let us see how *Siang Mien* works by using Princess Diana as a practical example. To begin with, we can say that she has got a *jade-face* which means that she must be strong-willed. This shape also belongs to people who are said to have had difficult childhoods. As you may know, the Princess's parents were divorced when she was a child and this time must have been a period of great unhappiness.

Turning to more specific features, we can see that one eye is a little larger than the other. It is a known fact that people with eyes of different sizes are often brought up by step-parents. They are also believed to be charming as well of being capable of great jealousy. We can see from this photograph that the top of her ears goes above the line of her eyebrows. People who have high ears such as hers are likely to become famous before the age of 30, while those who combine this with eyes of different sizes will be lucky.

2 Now read the article again and choose the best answers to these questions.

1 In China, who knew the secrets of *Siang Mien*?
  A Those who could read.
  B Experts and their students.
  C Ordinary people.
  D The emperor and selected courtiers.

2 Why has *Siang Mien* become common knowledge?
  A Because everyone practises it.
  B At some point, its secrets were given away.
  C The secrets remained well-guarded.
  D More people had access to the special books.

3 Chinese mothers think men with
  A big ears are exciting.
  B small ear lobes are kind.
  C flat noses are not interesting.
  D small ears and flat noses can't be trusted.

4 A jade-face is best described as
  A flat at the bottom and pointed at the top.
  B pointed at the top and bottom.
  C pointed at the bottom but flat at the top.
  D oval.

5 Why doesn't it matter if you're not good looking?
  A Because you'll worry less.
  B You may have some attractive features.
  C Fortune may smile on you.
  D People are attracted to interesting faces.

6 People with eyes of different sizes
  A often have step-parents.
  B are usually unhappy.
  C are often divorced.
  D are supposed to be generous.

7 Princess Diana
  A proves the truth of *Siang Mien*.
  B has low ears.
  C was over 30 when she became famous.
  D has an ordinary face.

3 tend to

According to the text, ugly people **tend to** be lucky. **Tend to** means generally but not always, e.g. *People from Scandinavian countries **tend to** have fair hair.* Now make some general statements about the people from your own country.

4 Discussion points

1 How far do you believe in this science?
2 Do you consider it to be convincing, ridiculous or amusing?
3 Could *Siang Mien* be dangerous in any way?

LANGUAGE STUDY

Making intelligent guesses

1 In the article it says *Princess Diana has got a jade-face which means she **must** be strong-willed.* **Must** is being used to make a deduction.

Match the example sentences of guesses with their definitions.

1 The killer can't be far away – the body is still warm.
2 She must be hiding somewhere in the area.
3 He must have been murdered at ten o'clock.
4 She can't have killed him. She was with her mother.

A A guess about a situation in the present (*positive*)
B A guess about a situation in the past (*negative*)
C A guess about a situation in the past (*positive*)
D A guess about a situation in the present (*negative*)

2 Make deductions about the situations in the pictures. If you are not sure use **might (not)** rather than **must** or **can't**.

A further passive construction

*They are also **believed to be** charming.*
*She is **said to have had** a difficult childhood.*

Change these sentences using this passive construction.

1 People **claim** the Mona Lisa is the world's most famous painting.
2 Experts **believe** it was a portrait of a noblewoman.
3 They **say** her smile hides a secret.
4 Many **believe** it is Leonardo's masterpiece.
5 Scientists **know** he was a wonderful engineer too.
6 Historians **think** he was unhappy in old age.

VOCABULARY

Adjectives of personality

1 Look at the adjectives of personality in the box. How many syllables does each word have? Mark the stress in the words of more than one syllable.

Example: *sélfish*

> selfish bad-tempered tough crafty sensitive sensible strict trustworthy dull shy mean reliable stubborn silly nice cheerful sympathetic clumsy loyal gentle

2 Fill the gaps with an adjective from the box. Use each word once only.

1 Janet is incredibly .... She always arrives on time and does her job well.
2 It's impossible to say anything to his grandmother. One word and she starts crying. She is so ....
3 I wonder why he is so ....? He's got lots of money but he hates spending it.
4 When she was a child, her parents were incredibly .... Whenever she did the smallest thing wrong they would send her to bed.
5 Ann is such a .... girl. She is always laughing and smiling.
6 You can't go on a country walk wearing high heels. Do be .... for once.
7 I'll give you a lift home if you're .... to me.
8 She was so .... When I told her my problems, I immediately felt better.
9 In westerns the hero is always .... He always beats his enemies and can put up with any hardship.
10 That's the second plate you've broken this week. Why do you have to be so ....?
11 I think he is an extremely .... boy. He laughs at stupid things and never concentrates in class.
12 Children are often really .... They hide behind their mothers when guests come.
13 Don't be ...., Cathy. You've got to learn to share things with other children.
14 She is 100% .... I'd leave my money, car, anything, for her to look after.
15 When I broke my leg, the nurse was so .... that she hardly hurt me at all.
16 Why do you get angry all the time? You are so ....
17 Bob is my best friend. He remained .... through all my problems.
18 He is such a .... person with his boring little job and his boring little wife.
19 He is terribly .... Once he has made up his mind, it is impossible to get him to change it even if it's obvious that he's wrong.
20 The general was really .... Just when the enemy thought they had won the battle, he played his best card.

3 In pairs, use the pictures and descriptions below to work out your partner's character. Then tell each other.

NOSE
long (1) = careful, worried
short (2) = cheerful, broad-minded
high-bridged (3) = active, curious
short and snub (4) = secretive
large = aggressive, tough
wide = careless, fun-loving

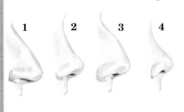

EARS
wide (5) = practical, sensible
large lobes (6) = independent, strong-minded
no lobes (7) = dull, dependent
sticking out (8) = imaginative
pointed = ambitious, crafty
small = instinctive, sensitive

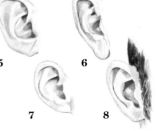
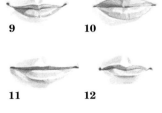

MOUTH
curving up (9) = gentle, naive
large (10) = generous, loyal
straight lips (11) = self-controlled
curved lips (12) = moody
small = trusting

EYES
slanting (13) = modest, tolerant
wide open (14) = friendly
close together (15) = energetic
deep set (16) = confident

LISTENING

1 Read the "lonely hearts" advert and check that you understand them.

MALE

1 PLUMP, fun-loving company director seeks warm, mature lady for companionship and cuddles.
2 FRIENDLY, leftish man into films, walks and history seeks bright woman to share fun times.
3 SHY foreign language student seeks sensitive blonde to bring him out of his shell.
4 TOTTENHAM HOTSPUR FAN seeks sporty girl to join him at home and away matches!

FEMALE

5 BRIGHT, professional woman, happy and successful, seeks honest and affectionate male to make her life complete.
6 GEMINI – attractive and articulate – seeks creative and compatible man.
7 CULTURE-LOVING lady seeks slim and attractive escort for opera and dinner parties.
8 SINCERE non-smoking vegetarian seeks meaningful relationship for now and for ever!

2 Clive and Jenny both work in the same office. Last Friday, just for fun, they decided to reply to an advertisement in the "lonely hearts" column of a magazine. It is Monday morning and they are comparing notes about their weekend dates. Listen to Clive and Jenny and answer these questions. For questions **1** to **4** choose your answer from choices **1-8 or A-G**. For the other questions choose from **A, B or C**

1 Jenny had a date with the man in picture
A ☐   B ☐   C ☐   D ☐

2 Clive met the woman in picture
E ☐   F ☐   G ☐   H ☐

3 Jenny's date described himself in advertisement
1 ☐   2 ☐   3 ☐   4 ☐

4 Clive's date described herself in advertisement
5 ☐   6 ☐   7 ☐   8 ☐

5 How did Jenny feel about meeting her date?
 A Embarrassed.
 B Relaxed.
 C Anxious.

6 How did Jenny feel about her date's conversation?
 A She was fascinated by what he had to say.
 B She wished he would change the topic.
 C She disagreed with what he had to say.

7 What did Clive discover about his date?
 A They recognised each other.
 B They had nothing in common.
 C They had a childhood connection.

8 What did Clive feel about his date's personality?
 A It was a surprise.
 B It matched her appearance.
 C It went with her job.

Physical description

1 When we describe someone we tend to follow this order in our description: height, build, age, hair, face, complexion, extra features, dress. Study this example.

My cousin, Paul, is a tallish man in his mid thirties. He is a bit plump and has got long straight hair which he wears in a pony tail. He has a round friendly-looking face with a little scar on his cheek from a childhood accident. He has got bright blue eyes and wears glasses. He has got a beard. He isn't very smart and tends to wear shabby clothes.

2 Height and build

Match these adjectives with the definitions.

Someone who is	frail stocky slim plump skinny	is	overweight. attractively thin. (old and) weak-looking. unattractively thin. shortish but well-built.

3 Age

1 What ages do these words and expressions describe?

   A elderly   **B** in your teens   **C** a youth   **D** a pensioner   **E** middle-aged
   F a toddler   **G** in your early/mid/late thirties

2 Tell you partner your age and the age of some family members without being exact about it.

4 Face

1 Find people in your class who have got round, oval and square faces.
2 What are scars, moles, wrinkles, lines and freckles?
3 What colour of skin do people have if they are pale, tanned or sallow?

5 Eyes

When we describe people's eyes we normally start with their size, followed by shape and colour, e.g. *She has got big round blue eyes.*

SIZE SHAPE COLOUR

Put these sentences into the correct order.

1 Susan has got brown/large/round/eyes.
2 Klaus has got blue/bright/eyes/small.
3 Mary has eyes/green/large.
4 Mariko has/almond-shaped/large/dark brown/eyes.

What are eyebrows and eyelashes?

6 Hair

When we describe people's hair, we normally give length first followed by colour and style, e.g. *He has got long dark hair in a pony tail.*

Match these adjectives with the pictures.

1 balding   **2** straight   **3** curly   **4** bald   **5** spiky   **6** wavy

A

B

C

D

E

F

What does hair look like if it is in a bun or in pigtails?

7 Clothes

Match these adjectives with the definitions.

1 casual	**A** old/worn a lot
2 scruffy	**B** carefully dressed
3 shabby	**C** well (expensively) dressed
4 smart	**D** informal
5 neat	**E** untidy/dirty

READING

Look at this short description of a character from a book. It is very effective, but how is it different from the description of Paul on page 98?

Eve was a small woman with a tiny waist and slender elegant legs. She had small hands with long tapering fingers. Her face was wide at the cheekbones and narrow at the chin, her forehead high, her upper lip short and her mouth full and lovely. Slightly tilted, her pretty nose was a little too small for her face. She had large hazel-green eyes and black eyebrows like Chinese brush-strokes, not unlike Sean's, and her thick, shiny, dark hair reached to the middle of her back. But she was very small, no more than five feet or five feet one at best. Liza didn't know her weight, they had no scales, but when she was sixteen Eve estimated seven and a half stone for herself and eight stone and a bit for Liza and that was probably right. Yet this tiny woman had somehow moved a man one and a half times her weight and nearly six feet tall.
And put him where? Somewhere in the wood, Liza decided, when she thought about it around that sixteenth birthday.

WRITING

You were a witness to a bank robbery in your town. You got a good look at the criminals when they took off their masks in the getaway car. Write about the robbery and include a full description of the criminals.

COLOUR CHOICES

FIRST THOUGHTS

When you select what to wear, are there colours you always choose? Are there any colours you always avoid because they don't suit you?

READING

What really suits you?

1 You are going to read an article about a method of selecting the colours that suit you best, based on the colour of your hair and eyes, and your skin tone. Before you begin, study the vocabulary in the glossary box opposite.

1 What are blusher, eyeshadow and lipstick?
2 What two common meanings does "wardrobe" have?

2 Read the first two paragraphs and find out what Margot Henderson does for a living and how her technique works.

3 Read the short profiles of the people Margot analysed and put them in order of how succesful Margot thinks their present colour choices are. Start with the best and go through to the worst. Match the people in the text with pictures 1-6.

4 Now choose the most appropriate heading from the list **A-H** for each part (**1-6**) of the article. There is an example at the beginning (**O**) and an extra heading you do not need to use.

A	Fashion victim
B	A hopeless case
C	Variations on a colour
D	Prettier in pink
E	Colour coded
F	A bit mixed up
G	Copy cat
H	Dare to be bold

0	E

In recent years there has been a growing interest in how we use colour in clothes and how to choose the colours which suit us best. Colour consultant Margot Henderson uses a system based around the kind of skin we have and the colour of our eyes and hair. The vast majority of people can then be placed into a number of broad categories or classifications called clear, light, soft, deep and warm.

Last week we picked half a dozen young people off the street for an instant analysis by Margot.

CLEAR

Hair: brown, black or dark grey.
Eyes: blue, green, hazel or brown.
Skin: porcelain, ivory, dark brown, clear yellow.

Kevin: | 1 |
Well this one obviously likes to play safe. He is dressed all in black and he is actually lucky that he can get away with it. He could afford to be a lot more adventurous. Clear people can basically mix dark and light items or go for something more dramatic. He should go for a bright red pullover or something like that to make himself stand out from the crowd. Five out of ten, but no marks for flair.

Susie: | 2 |
Susie has certainly made a good start. That purple top really does suit her and that gorgeous mauve jacket is just right. She should also try to experiment with bright reds or pinks as she could get away with it - she might even find that people take a lot more notice of her. She could be a bit more adventurous with the make up, though. Some daring bronze eyeshadow would really bring her eyes out. Seven out of ten.

LIGHT

Hair: blonde, light grey.
Eyes: blue, blue-grey, green.
Skin: peaches and cream, ivory or porcelain.

Jason: 3

Oh dear. What I can say? He is dressed in what is considered fashionable at the moment – all grey – but it just doesn't suit him at all, I'm afraid. There are so many sheep out there who just love to follow the crowd. He looks completely drained and washed out, doesn't he? He'd look much better in say brown or mushroomy colours. Pastels would also work for him too, I think. He should get rid of any pure white clothes he has in his wardrobe too. They have exactly the same effect as grey. Instead he should go for cream and off-white. Two out of ten.

Vanessa: 4

She has got some things right. The light blue polo-neck suits her beautifully, just the thing for her complexion and eyes. That dark navy blue blazer is just too much, though. It is too overwhelming. She really ought to steer clear of dark draining colours. A bluey green jacket would be much better. She's a bit of a mixture really.

As far as make-up goes, the red lipstick is far too dominant. She should opt for gentle pinks or rose. Pastel colours would suit her complexion better. All in all, I'd say she is about halfway there. I'd give her six or seven out of ten.

SOFT

Hair: light brown, medium brown, grey or ash blonde.
Eyes: brown, greyish blue, bluey green.
Skin: ivory, rose, beige, light olive.

Wayne: 5

I think this one is the best of the lot. He has either been to a consultant or else he has an extremely good sense of what suits him. He has done very well to stay with a central colour – in this case blue – and play with different tones. He could also go for earthy browns too. Very good indeed. Full marks.

Penny: 6

This is an example of just what you shouldn't do, I'm afraid. My guess is that she's got a friend and has just imitated her style without thinking what is best for her. That bright pink T-shirt is all wrong. It is just too dominating – she should wear something a lot more subtle. The bright green eyeshadow too is just too garish. It is screaming "look at me", but we lose her eyes beneath it. Something mauve or a light grey would suit her much better than this. No more than three. She needs help.

Glossary:

flair   imagination and style
gorgeous   very attractive
mauve   pale purple
get away with   succeed at something risky
bronze   dark yellowish brown
drained   with all the colour taken away
go for / opt for   choose
steer clear of   avoid
pastel   pastel colours are clear and pale
subtle   delicate, not obvious
garish   too brightly coloured
porcelain   cream
ivory   very white

5 List the colours that the three categories should and shouldn't use for clothes and make-up.

	Clothes		Make-up	
	✓	✗	✓	✗
Clear:				
Light:				
Soft:				

LISTENING

Margot, the colour consultant, and Ambrose, an interviewer, are discussing the right colours for them to wear. While you listen, complete the notes.

Before, Margot used to choose colours just because they **(1)**............ .
Margot thinks that **(2)**............ doesn't suit most people.
Margot has got **(3)**............ hair, **(4)**............ eyes and lots of **(5)**............ on her face.
Her colour classification is **(6)**............ .
When she realised how her old colours made her look, she got **(7)**............ .
Ambrose's colour classification is **(8)**............ .
He should go for blacks and greys and combine them with vivid colours like **(9)**............ red and yellow.
He should steer clear of **(10)**............ .

SPEAKING

Work in pairs or small groups. Based on what you have found out, advise each other about the right colours to wear.

PICTURES OF THE SOUL

FIRST THOUGHTS

Look at this selection of pictures drawn by different young children.

1 What is your immediate reaction to them?
2 What kind of character do you think the children have?
3 How possible is it to analyse character from people's drawings?

A   B   C

LISTENING

1 You are going to hear a conversation between three people who are discussing the pictures you have just looked at. Angela is a psychologist, Paul is a teacher and Joseph a social worker. Answer the questions by writing

A (for Angela),
P (for Paul) or
J (for Joseph).

1 Who thinks the technique could be useful for their job? ☐
2 Who said the child who drew picture A is happy? ☐
3 Who thinks picture B is nice? ☐
4 Who says picture B is by a child who wants to please adults? ☐
5 Who wants to know about the research behind the technique? ☐
6 Who thinks picture C is by an disobedient child? ☐
7 Who, by the end, seems to have changed their mind about the value of the technique? ☐

2 Managing conversations

Study these ways of keeping a conversation going.

Asking for clarification
What do you mean?
What makes you say that?

Checking you've understood correctly
So what you're saying is....

Saying you understand
I see; I think I understand.

Saying you don't understand
I'm sorry but I don't follow you

LANGUAGE STUDY

1 Study these constructions using **look**.

1 *This looks like the work of a child.*
look like + NOUN

2 *It looks neat and pretty to me.*
look + ADJECTIVE

3 *It looks as though / as if there is a lot of anger there.*
look as though/if + VERB PHRASE

2 Where necessary, correct the following sentences.

1 She looks like hungry.
2 He looks like his father
3 She looks like a teacher.
4 It looks as if it's going to rain.
5 The boys look like breaking into the car.

3 Practice

In pairs or groups, discuss these other pictures by young children. Which ones do you think have been produced by happy and unhappy children? Use the constructions based on **look**.

Keep the conversation going by using some of the expressions from **Managing conversations** on the opposite page.

USE OF ENGLISH

Word building

1 Look at the tapescript on page 228. What nouns are made from these adjectives?

- sympathetic
- miserable
- anxious
- angry

2 How are the following adjectives made negative?

- happy
- capable
- possible
- responsible
- legible
- honest

Turn the adjectives into nouns.

3 What negative prefixes are used with these adjectives?

legal loyal comfortable reliable kind obedient favourable literate patient

4 Complete this text about the painting *The Scream* by Edvard Munch by changing the word in capitals into a suitable form to fill each gap.

If ever a painting lent itself to the character **(1)**.......... of its artist it is surely *The Scream* by Edvard Munch. It expresses the **(2)**.......... of a solitary figure in emotional crisis. Beneath this, it is the deep **(3)**.......... of the artist that screams at us from the canvas. It is a **(4)**.........., neurotic, hysterical picture.
Yet, we should **(5)**.......... with Munch, a Norwegian, born in 1863, whose tragic **(6)**.......... was marked by the **(7)**.......... of close family members.
   This experience transformed a natural **(8)**.......... into an **(9)**.......... with love, sickness and death. *The Scream* expresses the profound pessimism and **(10)**.......... of its artist.

ANALYSE

MISERABLE
HAPPY
POWER
SYMPATHY
CHILD
LOSE
SENSITIVE
OBSESS
ANXIOUS

9 Teenage Cults

FASHION CLASH

FIRST THOUGHTS

1 Have you ever argued with your parents over the clothes you wear or the hairstyle you choose?

2 In groups, look at the pictures and tell the story. Then decide what the people might have said.

VOCABULARY

Clothes

Complete the sentences with an appropriate word connected with clothes.

1 These trousers are really *t*........... . I'll have to go on a diet.
2 Mind you don't wash it in hot water. You don't want it to *s*........... .
3 This jacket doesn't quite *m*........... these trousers.
4 She wanted to make room in her *w*........... so she threw away all her old clothes.
5 Go on! Buy that skirt. The colour really *s*........... you.
6 These trousers are really too big. They look *b*........... .
7 Passengers are advised to wear *l*........... , comfortable clothing when flying.
8 You can't possibly wear that striped shirt with a tartan tie. They *c*........... horribly.
9 Don't worry if these jeans are too big. We can always *t*........... them *i*........... at the waist and turn *u*........... the legs.
10 I'd like a blouse to *g*........... with this skirt. What would you suggest?

LISTENING

You will hear five different men talking about experiences they have had associated with clothes. Choose from the list **A-F** what happened to each one. Use each letter only once. There is one extra letter which you do not need to use.

A He had an accident while he was swimming.	Speaker 1	☐
B He decided not to buy something in a shop.	Speaker 2	☐
C He had an argument about school uniform.	Speaker 3	☐
D He was angry with a parent about an item of clothing.	Speaker 4	☐
E He wore the wrong thing to a party.	Speaker 5	☐
F He bought something which didn't fit that well.		

SPEAKING

In pairs find out from a partner if they have ever

• worn the wrong thing to a social occasion.
• had an argument with their parents about clothes or make-up.
• had problems in a clothes shop.

PRONUNCIATION

Rising intonation

1 ▭ In the Listening, speakers 3 and 4 repeat what someone else has said. They both use rising intonation to express disbelief. Listen again and try to copy their intonation.

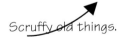

Scruffy old things.

Thirty pounds.

2 In pairs, practise showing surprise in these situations. Student A says something; Student B reacts, repeating what Student A says. Improvise!

A You have decided to accept your teacher's offer of marriage.
B You had a minor car accident on the way to school today.
C The car you were in knocked over a cyclist, but she's OK.
D You have decided to give up learning English and study Russian instead.
E You borrowed some money from Student B's wallet without asking.
F You can't pay your friend back until the end of the month.

NEW GENERATIONS

FIRST THOUGHTS

1 Can you match these names of teenage cults to the photographs. Which do you know?

A Skinheads   **D** Mods
B Goths   **E** Hippies
C Teddy boys   **F** Punks

2 What approximate order did they appear in?

READING

You are going to read a magazine article about Teenage Cults. Choose the most suitable heading from the list **A-H** for each part (**1-6**) of the article. There is one extra heading which you do not need to use.

There is an example at the beginning (**0**).

A The teenage idol theory
B The class theory
C The drug culture theory
D The capitalist domination theory
E The negativity theory
F The global village theory
G The reaction theory
H The technology theory

Understanding Teenage Cults

Ever since the early 1950s there have been attempts to explain why youth cults happen. None of them has been entirely convincing.

0	G

Teenagers want to show how different they are from their parents and, perhaps more importantly, their older brothers and sisters. If the last fashion had long hair and wide trousers, then the next one will have short hair and narrow trousers. There seems to be a lot of truth in this.

1	

Because of films, records, television and radio, teenagers are aware of what their contemporaries are doing all around the English-speaking world. Almost as soon as there were hippies in San Francisco, we had them too. A problem with this theory is that the time has to be right for a style to be adopted. The main influence on teenagers remains their friends.

2	

Teenagers imitate the people they look up to, chiefly film stars and pop performers. When David Bowie used eye shadow, so did many of his male fans. However, this only succeeds if the pop star is in tune with the way youth culture is already going.

3	

Many developments in teenage culture were possible only because of new technology. Electric guitars plus

LANGUAGE STUDY

Conjunctions

Conjunctions are used to join verbs, adjectives or parts of a sentence together. Choose the most appropriate conjunction, **A**, **B** or **C**, to complete the following sentences. The sentences must agree with the sense of the article you have just read.

1 Teenagers want to show they're different .... they react against their families.
   A because   **B** but   **C** so

2 .... do they react against their parents but against older brothers and sisters too.
   A Also   **B** Not only   **C** And

3 Young people know what's going on .... communications are so good.
   A yet   **B** since   **C** so

4 .... they are able to copy each other.
   A Even so   **B** As well   **C** That's why

5 .... teenagers copy pop idols, the stars have to understand what the young really want.
   A As well as   **B** Because   **C** For

6 Pop music is popular .... modern technology.
   A thanks   **B** because   **C** due to

7 There are other drugs .... alcohol and nicotine.
   A as well   **B** too   **C** besides

8 Businessmen invented youth cults .... to exploit the young
   A in order   **B** therefore   **C** also

9 ...., this does not explain cults such as the punks.
   A In addition   **B** Nevertheless   **C** Therefore

10 Skinheads feel victimised by society. ...., they form a culture of their own.
   A Consequently   **B** In order to   **C** And

amplification meant that you could have pop groups and pop festivals. The transistor radio made pop music inevitable.

 4

This theory suggests that the nature of a youth cult is determined by the drugs that it takes. Speed (amphetamine) equals aggression and energy – think of punks and skinheads. Pot (cannabis) equals relaxation and mysticism – think of hippies. Even ordinary society has its drugs such as alcohol and nicotine. But maybe the style came before the drug.

 5

Youth culture happened because commerce understood that teenagers had money to spend and worked out ways of making them buy more records, clothes and concert tickets. This does not account for cults that were anti-consumerist, like the punks and hippies.

6

This is a sophisticated left-wing theory. Youth cults assert the solidarity of young people who are victimised by society. Skinheads take aspects of working-class culture to an extreme. They almost enjoy people looking down on them.

There is no simple explanation. My own research points to these general observations. Firstly, cults don't arrive fully formed, flourish and then die; they are constantly changing and their message evolving. Secondly, teenagers only join a cult if it feels right, but most kids want to be something and cults give them something to be.

LISTENING

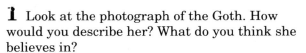

1 Look at the photograph of the Goth. How would you describe her? What do you think she believes in?

2 Listen to someone talking about Goths and make notes around these points.

- clothes/jewellery and make-up
- origins /influences
- philosophy/interests
- origin of their name

WRITING

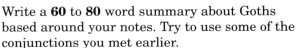

Write a **60** to **80** word summary about Goths based around your notes. Try to use some of the conjunctions you met earlier.

HANG YOUR HEAD IN SHAME!

VOCABULARY

Phrasal verbs

1 Match each phrasal verb with its definition on the right.

1	go along with	**A**	cause someone to be disappointed
2	talk over	**B**	put in order/put right
3	live up to	**C**	be brave enough to accept or deal with something
4	sort out	**D**	respect
5	put down	**E**	agree with/support
6	look down on	**F**	speak about something thoroughly
7	face up to	**G**	have a low opinion of someone
8	let down	**H**	reach someone's high standards
9	look up to	**I**	make someone feel unimportant

2 Fill the gaps with phrasal verbs from Exercise 1.

1 Stop running away from the situation. It's time you .... it.

2 He promised to pick me up from the station but he didn't. That's the second time he has .... me .... this week.

3 She was never able to .... her mother's high expectations of her.

4 I don't know why you .... him. You agree with everything he says and copy everything he does.

5 Why do you .... her .... every time she speaks? I'm not surprised she has no self-confidence.

6 Don't be such a snob, Marcia. Just because she doesn't have as much money as you, that's no reason to .... her.

7 After he had spent all evening .... the problem .... with his best friend he felt much better about things.

8 You can't expect me to .... the plan before I've had an opportunity to study it carefully.

9 Oh, no! It's going to take ages to .... these documents .... Why doesn't he ever file anything?

USE OF ENGLISH

1 When people have problems, they sometimes write to advice columns in magazines. Read this letter to Angela Strong and find out what the problems are. Now complete the passage by using only one word for each gap.

Dear Angela,

I was horrified **(1)**.......... I found out that my 12-year-old daughter had **(2)**.......... arrested for stealing some make-up from a high street chemist. **(3)**.......... happened because she had been dared **(4)**.......... some older children she looks up to. At **(5)**.......... she went along with what they wanted **(6)**.......... to do. However, once she was in the shop she was **(7)**.......... frightened that she started crying, which is **(8)**.......... attracted the attention of the shop assistant. The police **(9)**.......... called and she was given a telling-off at the police station.

(10).......... this terrifying experience she has been too afraid to go out on her **(11)**.......... and cries all the time. My husband doesn't seem to care **(12)**.......... much. He says she shouldn't have stolen in **(13)**.......... first place and was unlucky to be caught. Now it is **(14)**.......... she must learn to live with it. But I feel a failure as a parent and am afraid that my child will **(15)**.......... to crime later on in life.

Yours sincerely,
Ashamed

2 What advice would you give "Ashamed"?

3 Read the reply Angela Strong has written to "Ashamed". Do you think she offers wise advice?

4 Now edit the text. Tick those lines which are correct (✓). Where a line has an extra word which should not be there, identify the word and write it down.

Dear Ashamed,

1 I am tend to agree with your husband's reaction
2 You should try to put the incident behind of you.
3 Even though she is the one who has let you down
4 but she cannot forgive herself until you have
5 managed to forgive her. You seem to think that guilty
6 feelings are belong to you both. This is the real
7 shame. You should put an energy into making
8 your daughter feel better by talking over her problems.
9 This kind of situation is unfortunately quite a
10 common, you know. Most of kids, in my experience,
11 they do something like this at some stage. It is
12 a long time ago since this happened and if I can
13 give you some advice it is this: take her on holiday,
14 before she makes herself really ill, and enjoy
15 yourselves. I am confident that as soon as you will
16 leave your home environment the feelings of a
17 shame will begin to fade. Afterwards let her to
18 face up to people in her own time.
19 I am sure that you can sort every things out.

Yours sincerely,
Angela Strong

5 Look at this letter from Richard A. Complete it by changing the word in capitals into a suitable form to fill each gap.

Six years ago when I was a student I was short of money. Once a week I used to go home to see my parents. Although I had a good **(1)**............ with my mother I never got on well with my father. I could never live up to his high **(2)**............ of me. I had always been **(3)**............ at the things he valued and he was always putting me down with his continuous **(4)**............ .
One day I did a really **(5)**............ thing. I stole some money from him. I had started off by asking him if he could lend me some. He refused saying I was **(6)**............ with money. We then had a terrible row and he went out. I was so angry, I stole ten pounds from his wallet. When he noticed its **(7)**............, he asked me who had taken it.
After I told him he banned me from the house. I have been back there since but he still looks down on me for what I did. I want to make things up but I feel completely **(8)**............ . Half of me wants to say "Sorry Dad" while the other half still thinks he is behaving **(9)**............ by having kept up this attitude for so long. How can I bridge this endless **(10)**............ ?

Yours sincerely,
Richard A

RELATE
EXPECT
HOPE
CRITICISE
FORGIVE

RESPONSIBLE

APPEAR

HELP

REASON
UNDERSTAND

WRITING

Write a reply from Angela to Richard's letter. Remember that it should be in an informal, friendly style. Look through Angela's first letter to "Ashamed" and find the language she uses to give advice.

LANGUAGE STUDY

Reported speech

1 In his letter to Angela Strong Richard wrote *When he noticed its disappearance, he **asked me who had taken it***.

In pairs, look at these reported speech sentences and decide what is wrong with them.

1 He told the problem was difficult.
2 She said him to turn down the music.
3 He asked her how much money did he take.
4 He asked whether he can help.
5 She explained to him the problem.

Now work out the basic grammar rules for

A when we use **say** and **tell**, and how they are different grammatically.
B what happens to questions when we report them.
C what usually happens to tenses when they are reported.
D what happens to the word order of a sentence using **explain**.

2 Tense changes

Complete this chart of tense changes.

3 Changes with modals

1 What do **may**, **can** and **will** become in reported speech?
2 What happens to **would**, **could**, **should**, **ought to** and **must** in reported speech?
3 Change this first conditional sentence into reported speech.

Helen: *If you do that again, I'll hit you.*
She told him ....

Note Second and third conditional sentences stay the same in reported speech.

"*I thought you said you'd done this before.*"

DIRECT SPEECH	REPORTED SPEECH
1 Paul: She lives in London. *(present simple)*	Paul .... *said she lived in London.* .... (.... PAST SIMPLE ....)
2 Mary: .... (........................)	Mary told me she was working. *(past continuous)*
3 Karin: I've been to Spain. *(present perfect)*	She said .... (........................)
4 Peter: .... (........................)	He said he'd been living there for ages. *(past perfect continuous)*
5 Anna: I'd made a mistake. *(past perfect)*	She told me .... (........................)
6 Kate: We were watching TV. *(past continuous)*	She said .... (........................)

NOTE It is not always necessary to make these changes. For example, if something that is said is **still** true then we can use the present simple instead of the past simple.

Alan: *I live in Germany.* → He said he lives in Germany.

4 Other changes

1 Change these sentences from reported into direct speech. Think carefully how you are going to deal with the words in bold.

A She said she was going to leave **the following day**.

B He said that was the record he had bought **two days earlier**.

C They said the parcel would arrive in **two days' time**.

D He asked if anyone had come on **the previous day**.

E We told them their flat would be ready **the following month**.

F He said he had called **earlier** but nobody had answered the door.

G She asked him if **that day** was his birthday.

2 Now complete this table.

DIRECT SPEECH	REPORTED SPEECH
A this	....
B this/that	....
C today	....
D yesterday	....
E the day before yesterday	....
F before	....
G tomorrow	....
H the day after tomorrow	....
I next week/month/year	....

5 Reporting advice and suggestions

1 This is how you report advice:
She said, "If I were you I'd take an umbrella."
→ She **advised me to take** an umbrella.

2 This is how you report a suggestion:
She said, "Let's play tennis."
→ She **suggested playing** tennis.
    suggest +VERB + ing (GERUND)
or She **suggested that** they **(should) play** tennis.

Suggest is a complicated reporting verb to use because there are lots of possibilities. The best one to remember is **Suggest that someone should do something**.

3 Change these sentences with suggestions and advice into reported speech.

A "If you take my advice you'll go by train," Sue told Richard.

B "How about watching TV?" Arthur asked.

C Julian: Why don't you go to the cinema, Gina?

D Doctor: You should take more exercise, Miss Brown.

E Grandmother: If I were you, Fatima, I'd wear a scarf.

6 Complete the second sentence so that it has a similar meaning to the first. You must use between two and five words including the word given. Do not change the word given.

1 Carol: Could you be a little quieter, Peter?
such
Carol told Peter .... noise.

2 Sue: If I were you Richard, I'd take the train not the bus.
instead
Sue advised Richard .... of the bus.

3 The doctor advised me to take more exercise.
idea
The doctor told me it .... to take more exercise.

4 Robin advised me to buy shares in Sony.
I
Robin suggested .... shares in Sony.

5 He told me it was the first time he had ever flown.
never
"I .... ," he said.

6 Porter: Sorry, the train left five minutes ago.
missed
He told them they .... five minutes.

7 "I'll deliver the puppy the day after tomorrow," he promised.
in
He promised to deliver .... time.

8 "Do you know where my tennis racquet is, Mum?" Sharon asked.
seen
Sharon asked her mother .... tennis racquet.

9 In my opinion he should have a haircut.
am
As .... he should have a haircut.

10 Why do you think you are superior to other people?
look
What makes .... other people?

LISTENING

1 Rachel has telephoned a radio phone-in programme for some advice. The person in the studio is Dr Howard, who specialises in the emotional problems of young people.

Listen to Part **A** of the call and decide if these statements are **True** or **False**.

 1 Mark is unemployed.
 2 Mark left school a year ago.
 3 Mark is no longer the same boy.
 4 Rachel mentions three changes of character.
 5 Rachel doesn't like his friends.
 6 Rachel knows that Mark is taking drugs.
 7 A television has disappeared from the home.
 8 Mark likes listening to music.
 9 Money isn't safe in the home.
10 Mark's father is away from home a lot.

In pairs, discuss what you think is wrong with Mark. What advice would you give to his mother?

2 Now listen to Part **B** of the call. Note down the advice Dr Howard gives Rachel. In your opinion does she give good advice?

3 Write a short report on the phone-in programme for a students' newspaper. Explain what Rachel asked Dr Howard and the advice that was given in Part **B**. Finish the report with a few lines about your own opinion.

Begin the report like this:

"Last night's Dr Howard radio phone-in programme again focused on the problems young people face. There was one particularly disturbing call from a mother who was worried about her teenage son. She started by telling us........"

WRITING

1 In **Unit 7** we looked at the opinion question from **Paper 2 (Writing)**. In this unit we are going to look at two answers to the following: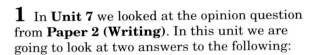

More and more young people are turning to drugs. Why is this so and what can be done about the problem?

Look at the first answer opposite and study the type of mistake that has been made.

There are some good ideas in this essay, but there are quite a few mistakes. Some, such as numbers 2, 3 and 8, can be forgiven because the language rules are quite complicated. Others, such as 5, 9, 13 and 14, are much more serious. They are basic mistakes and should have been avoided! When you write an essay it is essential that you check it for basic mistakes.

2 Working in pairs, look at the other answer to the same question and try to correct it. See if you can find any mistakes which you think are serious.

3 What can be learned from these examples? There are two main points.

1 When you have written a composition, you should read it through carefully to check for mistakes. In particular, you should check that the basic grammar is correct and that the different parts of sentences agree with each other.
2 You must get to know your mistakes. Lots of people make the same kind of mistake time after time. Look at your last four or five compositions and make a list of the kind of mistakes you regularly make.

4 Write your own answer to the question about drugs. Where you can, use expressions and ideas from the two compositions you have analysed.

ANSWER 1

1 'EVERYBODY KNOWS' WOULD BE BETTER.

5 DRUGS IS PLURAL: 'MAKE'.

6 WRONG WORD: 'LONELY' = ALONE AND UNHAPPY.

7 SHOULD BE PLURAL: 'PROBLEMS'.

9 WRONG EXPRESSION: 'IN MY OPINION' (ACCORDING TO SOMEONE ELSE).

11 SHOULD BE ADVERB: 'SEVERELY'.

13 SPELLING! ADDITION

14 WRONG VERB: 'SHOULD BUILD'.

Although almost all people know drugs are dangerous and can ruin them, there are many people who have addicted them. Some people have them because drugs makes them feel good. There are other people who have drugs because they feel alone or they want to escape from their problem and unsatisfied situation.

It is said that there is no solution to the drug problem. But even so, there are many things we can do to stop the use of drugs. According to me, the government should punished people who sell drugs severe. Moreover, they should warn people how dangerous drugs are and how do they harm people.

In adittion to this, the government would build a lot of hospitals for people who are addicts. On the whole, I think people should think about this problem much more and try to improve the situation.

2 HERE 'THEM' REFERS TO DRUGS. 'THEIR LIVES' IS AN ALTERNATIVE.

3 WRONG CONSTRUCTION. IT SHOULD BE 'WHO HAVE BECOME ADDICTED TO THEM.'

4 WRONG VERB. PEOPLE 'TAKE' DRUGS.

8 WRONG PART OF SPEECH: 'UNSATISFACTORY'.

10 'SHOULD PUNISH' – BAD MISTAKE!

12 NOT A QUESTION SO 'HOW THEY...'

ANSWER 2

The young people nowadays are in some ways lost. They don't expect much from life. Also they are living in difficult times. They keep trying to find out ways to enjoy themselves. In addition for them forbiden things is very attractive such as drugs alcohol etc.

So many of these young are getting addicted to drugs. Most of them start using drugs when they are adloescent. In that case they are trying to solve their familiar problems. The main victims are those who is too weak to stand certain situations such as the lost of one of their parents or their divorce. Drugs are very attractive at the first time. But after their "mask" falls and they become drug addicts.

I think both parents and governments should do something very strong to the solution of this problem. The parents have to give freedom to their children to talk about their problem and doubts. The goverment should open a national debate in all places to discuss the drugs.

The text you are going to read is from a story of a boy growing up in the middle of gang rivalries in the USA. It contains a lot of informal language and slang.

The boy, Pony, is part of a gang called the Greasers because they grease back their long hair. They come from a working-class part of town. Their enemies, the Socs, come from privileged families. They have short hair, drive Ford Mustangs and wear a perfume called English Leather.

FIVE SOCS were coming straight at us, and from the way they were staggering I figured they were reeling pickled. That scared me. A cool, deadly bluff could sometimes shake them off but not if they outnumbered you five to two and were drunk. Johnny's hand went to his back pocket and I remembered his switchblade. I wished for that broken bottle. I'd sure show them I could use it if I had to. Johnny was scared to death. I mean it. He was as white as a ghost and his eyes were wild-looking, like the eyes of an animal in a trap. We backed against the fountain and the Socs surrounded us. They smelled so heavily of whisky and English Leather that I almost choked. I wished desperately that Darry and Soda would come along hunting for me. The four of us could handle them easily. But no one was around and I knew Johnny and I were going to have to fight it out alone. Johnny had a blank, tough look on his face – you'd have to know him to see the panic in his eyes. I stared at the Socs coolly. Maybe they could scare us to death, but we'd never let them have the satisfaction of knowing it. It was Randy and Bob and the three other Socs, and they recognised us. I knew Johnny recognised them; he was watching the moonlight glint off Bob's rings with huge eyes.

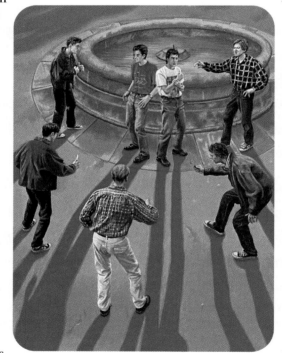

"Hey whatta ya know?" Bob said, a little unsteadily, "Here's the little greasers that picked up our girls. Hey, hey greasers."

"You're outa your territory," Johnny warned in a low voice. "You'd better watch it."

Randy swore at us and they stepped in closer. "Nup, pal, yer the ones who'd better watch it. Next time you want a broad, pick up yer own kind – dirt."

I was getting mad. I was hating them enough to lose my head.

"You know what a greaser is?" Bob asked. "White trash with long hair."

I felt the colour draining from my face. I've been cussed out and sworn at, but nothing ever hit me like that did. Johnnycake made a kind of gasp and his eyes were smouldering.

"You know what a Soc is?" I said, my voice shaking with rage. "White trash with Mustangs and madras." And then, because I couldn't think of anything bad to call them, I spat at them.

Bob shook his head, smiling slowly. "You could use a bath, greaser. And a good working over. And we've got all night to do it. Give the kid a bath, David."

I ducked and tried to run for it, but the Soc caught my arm and twisted it behind my back, and shoved my face into the fountain. I fought, but the hand at the back of my neck was strong and I had to hold my breath. I'm dying, I thought, and wondered what was happening to Johnny. I couldn't hold my breath any longer. I fought again desperately but only sucked in water. I'm drowning, I thought, they've gone too far. . . A red haze filled my mind and I slowly relaxed.

The next thing I knew I was lying on the pavement beside the fountain, coughing water and gasping. I lay there weakly, breathing in air and spitting out water. The wind blasted through my soaked shirt and dripping hair. My teeth chattered unceasingly and I couldn't stop them. I finally pushed myself up and leant back against the fountain, the water running down my face. Then I saw Johnny.

He was sitting next to me, one elbow on his knee and staring straight ahead. He was a strange greenish-white, and his eyes were huger than I'd ever seen them. "I killed him," he said slowly. "I killed that boy."

Bob, the handsome Soc, was lying there in the moonlight, doubled up and still. A dark pool was growing from him, spreading slowly over the blue-white cement. I looked at Johnny's hand. He was clutching the switchblade, and it was dark to the hilt.

1 Read the extract and then choose the answer **A**, **B**, **C** or **D** which you think fits best according to the text.

1 When Pony saw the Socs
 A he knew a fight was inevitable.
 B he thought he could talk his way out of trouble.
 C he realised it was too late to run away.
 D he put his hand in his pocket.

2 As the Socs approached, Pony
 A picked up a bottle.
 B knew friends would rescue them.
 C realised he was unarmed.
 D started to panic.

3 Pony knew that Johnny
 A was calm and unafraid.
 B could hide his feelings from the Socs.
 C could beat any Soc.
 D was ready for action.

4 What was the reason for the fight?
 A The Greasers were in Soc territory.
 B Both gangs had arranged it earlier.
 C The Socs were looking for revenge.
 D The Socs wanted to impress their girlfriends.

5 Just before the fight began
 A Pony had lots of clever things to say.
 B both sides got out their weapons.
 C both sides insulted each other.
 D Pony remained cool and calm.

6 When his face was in the fountain, Pony
 A managed to break free.
 B realised it was stupid to resist.
 C pretended to relax.
 D very nearly drowned.

7 After Pony found himself on the pavement
 A he was ready to continue the fight.
 B he was happy to be alive.
 C he got up almost immediately.
 D he couldn't control his body.

2 How do you think the story continues? What happens to Pony and Johnny?

VOCABULARY

1 The writer of the story adds atmosphere to the text through the choice of vocabulary. We know that the Socs "staggered", that Bob's rings "glinted" and that Johnny made a kind of "gasp". Which words describe a noise made when breathing, a way of walking and the way that light shines?

2 Using your dictionaries, find out which of the three categories above the verbs in the box belong to.

| limp pant sigh glow shuffle stroll snore stumble glitter gleam sparkle stride choke wheeze creep |

3 In pairs or groups, invent a short dramatic story incorporating as many of the verbs we have just met as you can.

10 | Us and Animals

PROBLEMS, PROBLEMS

FIRST THOUGHTS

What is the answer to this traditional riddle: *"Which creature has four legs when it is young, two legs when it has grown and three legs when it is old?"*
Do you know any more riddles like this?

SPEAKING

Here is another problem which has teased the brains of generations. Have you come across it before? Do you know the solution?

A farmer wants to cross a river with a dog, a goose and a cabbage. However, he has a problem! He can only take one item at a time in his old rowing boat.
* Unfortunately, the dog will eat the goose if it is left on its own.
* Also, the goose will eat the cabbage given half a chance.
How does he get all three to the other side of the river without any being eaten?

LISTENING

1 Listen to Magnus and Patrick discussing the above. How far do they get with the problem? What idea do they come up with to help them to solve it?

2 Now listen to their conversation again and complete the dialogue.

MAGNUS: Well, **(1)**............ he should do?
PATRICK: Well, it's tricky, isn't it? He **(2)**............ the cabbage across.
MAGNUS: No **(3)**............; the goose will get eaten by the dog.
PATRICK: Oh, yeah. **(4)**............ . Well how about this: first of all he takes the goose, because the dog won't eat the cabbage, will it?
MAGNUS: **(5)**............ . But then what should he do next? I know, **(6)**............ row back to the other side and then pick up the dog.
PATRICK: But **(7)**............ won't he still have the same problem? I mean, we can't leave the dog with the goose, can we?
MAGNUS: Oh no, of course not. I'm not sure what to do.
PATRICK: I know. I've got an idea **(8)**............ you know, work it out with a diagram. OK, this is the river (*Draws river*) and this button is the dog, the paper clip's the cabbage and erm, this coin can be the goose.
PATRICK: Great, now **(9)**............ .

3 Managing conversations

What language do Magnus and Patrick use to work together and discuss a solution?

SPEAKING

Look at the cost and enjoyment factors for different kinds of pets. Then discuss which kind of pet would be most suitable for the people in the photographs.

Edward Cohen, 68. Enjoys long walk; lives in country.

Kenneth Dukes, 52. High blood pressure.

Emma and Gemma Jones, 8. Mother allergic to cats.

Elsie Grey 75. Lives alone and can't go out.

	Companionship	Relaxation	Upkeep	Cost
bird	***	***	**	**
hamster		**	*	*
rabbit	****	**	***	***
dog	**	**	**	***
fish			**	**
cat	***	*	*	**

LISTENING

You are going to hear eight people in eight different situations. For questions **1-8** choose the correct answer **A**, **B** or **C**.

1 You are in a car with a mother and child. Where does the child want to go?
A Home.
B To bed.
C To her grandmother's.

2 You overhear a conversation in a butcher's shop. The speaker
A will wait for another phone call.
B will investigate.
C feels horrible.

3 You go into a lecture theatre in a local college. What is the lecture is about?
A Fish.
B Mammals.
C Birds.

4 You overhear a mother reading a bedtime story. What is the story about?
A A greedy tiger.
B An overweight elephant.
C A very hungry bear.

5 A patient is talking to a doctor. What is the patient allergic to?
A Cats and dogs.
B Feathers.
C All animal hair.

6 You turn on the radio news. What kind of crime is reported?
A A burglary.
B A drugs raid by police.
C A murder.

7 Two people are talking about an incident that happened in the first speaker's garden. How does the second speaker feel?
A Interested.
B Bored.
C Surprised.

8 A TV programme you listen to is for
A children.
B consumers.
C motorists.

IN THE WILD

FIRST THOUGHTS

Do you think we can learn anything about ourselves by studying animals and their behaviour?

READING

1 Read the article about Jane Goodall. Note down what human beings and chimpanzees have in common.

For 25 years now, Jane Goodall has been studying chimpanzees at Gombe in Tanzania. This has already become the longest project on animals living in the wild. However, she intends to carry on her research for the rest of her life, as chimps can live for anything up to 50 years. In this way, she hopes to observe the progress of an entire generation of chimps from birth to death.

The most surprising discovery of the early years of her research was that chimps used tools. For example, they poked small branches into holes in trees in order to extract insects to eat. Before this discovery, people had thought that chimps weren't intelligent enough to use tools. Another distinction between chimpanzees and human beings had been eliminated.

There are, of course, many easily observed similarities. Chimps kiss and cuddle like humans. Furthermore, they are self-aware and can recognise themselves in mirrors, which other animals are unable to do. Strong family relationships are seen to exist and even adolescent chimps run back to mother when they find themselves in trouble! What's more, chimps seem to have some kind of structured language in which they can express a number of abstract concepts.

However, not everything about chimps is so cosy and comfortable. Starting in the early seventies, Jane Goodall was horrified to observe a prolonged war waged by one group of chimps on another "tribe" which had broken away some years earlier. This observation altered her perception of chimps, making them seem, in her

JUNGLE WARFARE

eyes, even closer to humans. It had always been thought that humans were the cruellest of animals, and that what made us unique was our habit of making war on one another. The chimps' war showed that this was not the case.

It appears that there was no reason for the conflict other than a perhaps natural hostility to aliens. Even though the younger males were the most aggressive of the group, they were sometimes joined by a single, aggressive female. Chimps in the enemy group were hunted individually and cruelly killed. The excitement and enjoyment Jane Goodall witnessed were very similar to that shown by human beings taking part in war or criminal activity.

Despite the fact that a lion may kill a zebra for food or a bull may fight to assert its dominance over the herd, this "law of the jungle" must be distinguished from the behaviour of the chimps. It has been claimed that war was a key factor in developing human social organisation and the selection of the strongest and most intelligent. Jane Goodall believes that she may have witnessed this in its earliest stage of development.

During the war, some females left the losing side to join the aggressors. Although they were accepted, not one of their babies was allowed to live. This is a common pattern in other animals, and the adoption of infants from an alien group is unknown in other species apart from man. Nevertheless, older chimps may adopt younger brothers or sisters if the mother dies.

This may help us understand why stepfatherhood can be unsuccessful for humans and how difficult it may be to create artificial families. Child-beating is at its most common where stepparents are concerned. It may be just too difficult for most people to truly accept children that are not their own.

Goodall is currently studying how the early experiences of baby chimps affect them in later life – particularly how a badly mothered chimp will become a bad mother herself. Such research may give us clues about human behaviour and motivation. She writes, "Because chimps are less complex, it is easier to study these effects. The scars of childhood are less apparent where human beings learn how to hide their feelings."

2 Choose the best answers to these questions.

1 Why does Jane Goodall want to stay in the wild?
  A She wants to study a whole life cycle of chimps.
  B She feels she hasn't made much progress.
  C She wants to die with the animals she loves.
  D She wants to stay a record 50 years.

2 What do chimps and humans have in common?
  A Their sense of humour.
  B Family arguments.
  C A dislike of warfare.
  D "Grammatical" language.

3 What did Goodall find out about warfare?
  A It was an exclusively human activity.
  B Mature males were more interested in it.
  C Chimps showed no mercy to male enemies.
  D A number of females took part.

4 Why did the chimps fight?
  A Over territory.
  B To win extra females.
  C For fun.
  D Because there wasn't enough food for everyone.

5 What theory does Goodall's research appear to support?
  A Society has evolved partly because of war.
  B Chimps will soon catch up with humans.
  C Chimps have much in common with lions and bulls.
  D Mankind will destroy itself through war.

6 What conclusions did she draw about adoption?
  A It is unknown among chimps.
  B It never occurs in nature.
  C It occurs within chimp families.
  D It often leads to child beating.

7 Why is it useful to study chimp behaviour?
  A We can learn how to be better parents.
  B It is just like human behaviour.
  C It may help us understand ourselves better.
  D It is not as complex as our behaviour.

LANGUAGE STUDY

Contrasting ideas

1 In the article about Jane Goodall it says *Some females left the losing side to join the aggressors. **Although** they were accepted, not one of their babies was allowed to live.*

There are two ideas in the second sentence: *They were accepted.   Not one of their babies was allowed to live.*

Although is used to emphasise the contrast.

Let's look at other ways in which we can contrast ideas.

1 *She had a cold **but** she still played tennis.*
  But shows there is a contrast in the sentence. People don't normally play tennis if they have got a cold!

2 ***Even though** she had a cold, she still played tennis.*
  Even though + SUBJECT + VERB
  Even though emphasises the contrast more than **although**.

3 ***Despite** (her) having a cold, she still played tennis.*
  Despite + (POSSESSIVE ADJ) + VERB + ing
  ***Despite** her cold she still played tennis.*
  Despite + NOUN
  ***Despite** the fact she had a cold, she still played tennis.*
  Despite the fact (that) + SUBJECT + VERB

4 *She had a cold. **However**, she still played tennis.*
  However comes **between** the two ideas that are contrasted, and is followed by a comma.

5 *She had a cold. **Nevertheless**(,) she still played tennis.*
  Again, **nevertheless** comes **between** the two ideas that are contrasted.

2 In pairs, look at these sentences and correct them where necessary.

1 Although she is three years old she can't walk.
2 Despite the restaurant was empty, the stranger came and sat opposite me.
3 However, the wine was bad the food was good.
4 Although it was a beautiful day, we had a marvellous time at the beach.
5 Even though he was unhappy, he was rich.

3 Now join these sentences using as many of the methods we have looked at as possible.

1 It really enjoys going for walks. Their dog is very old.
2 They have a small flat. They have got a large dog.
3 They tried to housetrain the puppy. It didn't work.
4 Pigs are supposed to be dirty. They're quite clean actually.
5 The squirrels look tame. They may bite you.

Invent sentences/situations of your own to show that you understand these different ways of making contrasts.

FIRST THOUGHTS

Write down the names of the first three animals that come into your head and give the names to your partner. Then turn to p123 for the interpretation.

SPEAKING

1 Animals quiz

Name the creatures in the picture and answer the questions.

1 What is the largest mammal in the world?
2 What is the fastest mammal in the world?
3 What is the commonest mammal in the world?

4 What is the most poisonous snake in the world?
5 What is the largest bird in the world?
6 What is the rarest mammal in the world?
7 Which creature is the most dangerous to man?

2 Below are 15 animals that are often the object of our love and fear. Which do you think are the most beautiful?

| eagle | panda | elephant | cockroach | snake | crocodile | spider | mosquito |
| dolphin | lion | giraffe | seal | whale | rat | polar bear | |

When you have finished compare your answers with a partner.

LANGUAGE STUDY

The comparison of adjectives and adverbs

1 *It had always been thought that humans were **the cruellest** of animals.*

Decide if these sentences are wrong. Where necessary, correct them.

1 She speaks good French.
2 James is more big than Mark.
3 She is the most good at English in our class.
4 She runs fast.
5 He plays tennis good.
6 His car isn't so good as mine.
7 Jane is very lazy. She works hardly.
8 You look coldly. Shall I shut the window?
9 They play chess much more badly than us.

2 Now answer these questions about the grammatical rules for making comparisons.

1 How do we make the comparative and superlative of a short adjective like **tall**?
2 How do we make comparative sentences using **as**?
3 What happens to **good**, **bad** and **far** in the comparative and superlative?
4 How do we make adverbs from the following?
   A slow   **B** angry   **C** good
   D beautiful   **E** hard, fast
5 What are the comparative adverbs for **good** and **bad**?
6 When do we use adjectives and adverbs after verbs like **look**, **feel**, **seem**, **sound**, **smell** and **appear**?
7 What are the comparative adjective forms of **friendly** and **clever**?

3 Complete these sentences using a comparative or superlative form of the word in **bold**.

1 Angela is .... person in the class. **young**
2 Andrew speaks good French but Lucy speaks it .... **good**
3 The bill isn't .... as I thought it would be. **expensive**
4 He bought .... petrol he could find. **cheap**
5 Don't kick the ball so .... You'll break a window. **hard**
6 Her teacher speaks .... than ours. **slow**
7 They live .... from school than I do. **far**
8 Your son's behaviour is .... in the whole school. **bad**
9 It was .... film I had ever seen. **boring**
10 You don't look very .... Cheer up! **happy**
11 She sings .... than anyone else in the choir. **beautiful**
12 He sounded .... than he did yesterday. By tomorrow he'll have forgotten! **angry**
13 What's for supper? Something smells .... **good**
14 She works .... **quick** than Julian but not .... as Alison. **fast**

4 Write sentences comparing two countries or towns that you know. Say something about the character of the people who live there as well as the place.

5 Sentences with **too** and **enough**

Study this sentence taken from the article about Jane Goodall. How could we rephrase it using **too**?

*People had thought chimps weren't intelligent **enough** to use tools.*

NEGATIVE VERB + ADJ + enough + TO DO SOMETHING

Use **too** or **enough** to make sentences based on the following situations.

1 Annie was really tired last night. She didn't take the dog for a walk.
2 The birdcage was high up on the wall. The cat couldn't reach it.
3 The zebra was very slow. The lion caught it.
4 What a stupid dog! It will never learn that trick.
5 The children want to have rabbits as pets. They're only three and four.

USE OF ENGLISH

Complete the second sentence so that it has a similar meaning to the first sentence. You must use between two and five words including the word given. Do not change the word given

1 The dog barked all night but we still managed to sleep.
   fact
   Despite .... dog barked all night we still managed to sleep.

2 The cat can't catch the mice. They run too fast.
   for
   The mice run too .... the cat to catch them.

3 Cats aren't as expensive to keep as dogs.
   more
   Dogs are .... cats.

4 Man is the cruellest of all animals.
   cruel
   There isn't .... man.

5 His canary sings better than mine.
   well
   My canary doesn't .... his.

6 Is this the cheapest pet food you've got?
   anything
   Isn't .... this pet food?

7 Most of the animals survived the hard winter.
   though
   Even ...., most of the animals survived.

8 I have never seen a dirtier dog.
   ever
   This must be the .... seen.

9 She couldn't afford the Persian cat.
   expensive
   The Persian cat was .... buy.

10 The cheetah is the fastest animal in the world.
   as
   No animal runs .... the cheetah.

121

DO ANIMALS HAVE RIGHTS?

FIRST THOUGHTS

Look at the photograph and discuss the questions.

1 What are the people in the picture doing?
2 Where are they and how do you think they feel?
3 Can you make out what they are carrying?
4 What do you think they are hoping to achieve?

WRITING

The opinion question

1 You are going to read an answer to this question: *"The killing of animals for their fur should be banned. Do you agree?"*

Before you read the answer, try and predict the arguments that would be used by each side. What would those who support the use of fur say? What would their opponents say?

2 Understanding the organisation of the composition

1 Note down any topic vocabulary used in the answer, e.g. *trap*.
2 Find the language in the answer that does the following:
 A puts points in order.
 B says **and**.
 C balances points of view.
 D introduces a conclusion.

People in the fur industry believe that the practice of killing animals for their fur should continue. On the other hand, many people want to ban it altogether. Which side is right? First of all, let us look at the arguments used to support the fur trade and then look at those of its opponents.

To begin with, the fur industry claims that fur is a natural form of clothing that man has worn since prehistoric times. Next, it is beautiful to look at and wear. In addition, the need for fur allows hunters to continue their traditional way of life, besides providing thousands of jobs in the fashion trade. Animals bred on farms lead much more comfortable lives than those in the wild, which lead short and savage existences.

Opponents believe that there are now so many different kinds of clothing that it is no longer necessary, or indeed justifiable, to kill animals for their fur. In addition, while the industry provides jobs, they are based on unacceptable cruelty. For instance, wild animals may take days to die in cruel traps. Moreover, even though conditions on farms may be good, they prevent animals living as nature intended.

On balance, I believe that the killing of animals for their fur should be banned. Despite the fact that fur is beautiful to look at and wear, man should learn to share the earth with other animals, not just exploit them. After all, there is now artificial fur which can give the look of real fur without the cruelty.

LISTENING

1 You are going to hear two people giving their opinions on vivisection (experiments on live animals). Listen to what they have to say and complete the notes which summarise their points of view.

If you want to talk on the show call (1)........... . Professor Wright believes experiments are necessary because we can't observe (2)........... in scientific conditions. Three illnesses, diphtheria, smallpox and (3)..........., used to kill people. Nowadays, if someone is bitten by a dog with rabies they survive because there is (4)........... . It is important to test drugs on animals to check for possible (5)........... on humans.

Peter Savage believes we can't (6)........... the effect drugs will have on humans by experimenting on animals. Understanding the nervous system is possible by (7)........... . Diseases were declining because of better (8)........... . Penicillin and aspirin were discovered (9)........... . Animal experiments should be stopped because they are (10)........... .

2 Sounds in sentences

Listen to these sentences and phrases taken from the listening and note what happens to the parts that are underlined.

1 It's eleven o'clock.
2 ....it's time for another edition of Crosstalk.
3 I have two guests to open the debate.
4 I must state categorically...
5 ...in the old days.
6 ....rats and mice...

Now practise saying the sentences and phrases by closely following the model.

3
Read the story and mark where the links between the words would appear. Practise reading it, taking care to introduce any of the features of connected speech we discovered in Exercise 2.

Mr West used to be crazy about photography. One day he took his car and went to a safari park. He stopped to take some pictures. Two ugly monkeys jumped on the car roof and bent the aerial. He got out of the car and tried to make them go away. Three enormous lions came and ate Mr West for lunch.

VOCABULARY

Phrasal verbs

1
Replace each of the words in **bold** with one of the phrasal verbs in the box. Make any changes necessary.

1 They had the dog **killed** because it was old.
2 The farmer **found** some newborn kittens as he was working in a barn.
3 Jenny has **thought of** a wonderful name for her new goldfish!
4 We had to call in the vet because a new disease **suddenly started** among our herd of cattle.
5 When you have finished supper, can you **continue** feeding the pigs?
6 No, you can't have a cat! It's no use complaining. Your father will **agree with** me.
7 Can I **depend on** you to feed the rabbit?
8 Are you going to **suggest** a design for the stable?
9 The rat **attacked** the cat and bit it on the tail.
10 The puppy is covered in green paint! How did this **happen**, children?

come across	come up with	put forward
come about	back up	carry on	break out
turn on	put down	count on

2 Expressions with take + noun + preposition

Complete each sentence with an expression using **take**.

Example: *He took o ..ffence.at. what his uncle said.*

1 They took *p.......... .... a demonstration against cruelty to animals.
2 Could you take *c.......... .... my cat while I'm away on holiday?
3 She took *p.......... .... the poor motherless kitten and gave it a home.
4 He takes a great deal of *p.......... .... the way his horse looks, so he brushes its coat every day.
5 Julia is going to Kenya on business. I think she should take *a.......... .... being there and go on a safari.

3 Preposition + noun + preposition

Example: *Susie went to the pet shop in order to buy some food for her goldfish.*

1 They didn't go to the zoo .... account .... the bad weather.
2 He was given a puppy .... place .... the dog that had died.
3 The ambassador presented the zoo with the panda .... behalf .... the Chinese government.
4 The firemen rescued the kitten from the tree .... means .... a ladder.
5 .... addition ..... her nine cats, she has three parrots.
6 He wrote a long reply .... answer .... the complaint about his dog.

WRITING

Using your notes from the listening and from the composition on page 122 as a guide, write a **for and against** composition on this question: *"Research which involves live animals should be banned." How far do you agree with this view?*

Answer to First Thoughts on page 120.

The first name is the animal you would like to be; the second animal is what other people think you are. The third is what you really are!

ANIMAL FARM

FIRST THOUGHTS

Which adjectives belong to which creatures:

adjectives: crafty, brave, wise, stubborn, greedy, strong
creatures: pig, lion, donkey, fox, owl, horse

Do you think the animals deserve to be described in this way?

READING

Animal Farm

1 Read the summary of *Animal Farm*. How are the animals different from the adjectives we associated with them in **First Thoughts**?

Animal Farm by George Orwell is a kind of fairy tale for adults. It tells the story of a revolution by the animals at *Manor Farm*. **(A) We first meet its heroes: the naive but courageous Boxer, the horse, and the cynical donkey, Benjamin, at a political meeting.** Conditions at the farm are terrible. **(B) Major, an ancient pig, explains his political theory of Animalism.** Almost by accident, there is a revolution at *Manor Farm* and its cruel and drunken owner, Jones, is forced to flee. The pigs, the most intelligent of the animals, assume control and introduce the seven commandments (laws) of Animalism.

Nearby farmers, afraid the revolutionary ideas will spread, unsuccessfully try to win *Animal Farm* back. They are defeated thanks to the bravery of Boxer and Snowball, one of the leaders of the pigs. Things gradually change. **(C) The pigs justify taking extra food and privileges for themselves.** They start to adopt human ways and live in the farmer's house and take to drink. The pigs fall out and Snowball is forced to leave. Napoleon, aided by his propagandist Squealer, is supreme leader of Animal Farm. The animals struggle to build a windmill. **(D) Boxer is an example to the other animals.** He always promises to work harder. **(E) The exiled Snowball and his allies are blamed for all the disasters which occur.** Gradually, pigs and humans learn to accept each other. Old and worn out by work, **(F) Boxer is betrayed by the pigs and sent off to be killed.** Poor Boxer. **(G) Only one corrupted commandment remains.** The pigs announce that Animal Farm will become *Manor Farm* once again. **(H) In the end it is impossible to tell the pigs and humans apart.**

2 Read the nine extracts from *Animal Farm*. Match eight of the extracts **1-9** with the **bold** summary sentences **A-G** in exercise 1. There is one extract which has no summary sentence.

1 [ ] There was nothing there now except a single Commandment. It ran: ALL ANIMALS ARE EQUAL BUT SOME ANIMALS ARE MORE EQUAL THAN OTHERS.

2 [ ] Frequently it took a whole day of exhausting effort to drag a single boulder to the top of the quarry, and sometimes when it was pushed over the edge it failed to break. Nothing could have been achieved without Boxer, whose strength seemed equal to that of all of the other animals put together.

3 [ ] "Comrades!" he cried. "You do not imagine, I hope, that we pigs are doing this in a spirit of selfishness and privilege? Many of us actually dislike milk and apples. I dislike them myself. Our sole object in taking these things is to preserve our health. Milk and apples (this has been proved by Science, comrades) contain substances absolutely necessary for the well-being of a pig."

4 [ ] Twelve voices were shouting in anger, and they were all alike. No question now, what had happened to the faces of the pigs. The creatures outside looked from pig to man, and from man to pig, and from pig to man again: but already it was impossible to say which was which.

5 [ ] "I do not believe that Snowball was a traitor at the beginning," he said finally. "What he has done since is different. But I believe that at the Battle of the Cowshed he was a good comrade." "Our leader, Comrade Napoleon," announced Squealer, speaking very slowly and firmly, "has stated categorically – categorically, comrade – that Snowball was Jones's agent from the very beginning- yes and from long before the Rebellion was ever thought of."
"Ah, that is different!" said Boxer. "If Comrade Napoleon says it, it must be right."

"Even when you have conquered him, do not adopt his vices. No animal must ever live in a house, or sleep in a bed or wear clothes, or drink alcohol, or smoke tobacco, or touch money, or engage in trade. All the habits of man are evil. And above all, no animal must ever tyrannise over his own kind. Weak or strong, clever or simple, we are all brothers. No animal must ever kill any other animal. All animals are equal."

6 □

7 □ "Fools! Fools!" shouted Benjamin, prancing round them and stamping the earth with his small hoofs. "Fools! Do you not see what is written on the side of that van?" That gave the animals pause, and there was a hush. Muriel began to spell out the words. But Benjamin pushed her aside and in the midst of a deadly silence he read: " 'Alfred Simmonds, Horse Slaughterer, and Glue Boiler, Willingdon, Dealer in Hides and Bone-Meal. Kennels supplied!' Do you not understand what that means? They are taking Boxer to the knacker's!"

8 □ Jones saw him coming, raised his gun and fired. The pellets scored bloody streaks along Snowball's back, and a sheep dropped dead. Without halting for an instant Snowball flung his fifteen stone against Jones's legs. Jones was hurled into a pile of dung and his gun flew out of his hand. But the most terrifying spectacle of all was Boxer, rearing up on his hind legs and striking out with his great iron hoofs like a stallion.

9 □ Boxer was an enormous beast, nearly eighteen hands high, and as strong as two ordinary horses put together. A white stripe down his nose gave him a somewhat stupid appearance, and in fact he was not of first rate intelligence, but he was respected for his steadiness of character and tremendous powers of work. After the horses came Muriel, the white goat, and Benjamin the donkey. Benjamin was the oldest animal on the farm, and the worst tempered.

LISTENING

An expert talks about *Animal Farm*. Complete the chart of parallels Orwell wished to draw.

1 Manor Farm	....
2	Soviet Union
3 Mr Jones	....
4	Communist intellectuals
5 Major	....
6a	Lenin/Stalin + Trotsky
+b	
7 Boxer	....
8 Moses the Raven	....

WRITING

1 Read this examination question and the answer underneath. How effective is the answer ?

Who do you think is the most interesting person in the book you have read? Give a brief account of that person's character and explain why you found him or her especially interesting.

The character I would like to describe is the horse Boxer from Animal Farm. He is not all that intelligent but he has qualities which are far more important. He is loyal and hard-working and a good friend. After all, the pigs are intelligent but in the end they betray both the animals and the revolution.

Boxer, by contrast, is strong and virtuous and never lets anybody down. He shows tremendous courage in the battle of the cowshed, and alone of all the animals dares to question Squealer's judgement on Snowball. So he is not that stupid! Without him the windmills could never have been built. If he has a fault it is that he is too trusting. It made me sad to read how cruelly exploited he was by the pigs. The part of the story where he is taken away is very moving. In my opinion, although he is a little naive, he is the true hero of the book.

2 How does the writer

1 sum up Boxer's attributes?
2 deal with his negative points?
3 use examples from the story to illustrate and support his opinion of Boxer?

3 Using the composition you have just analysed as a guide, answer the question based around a book you have read recently.

11 Your Cultural Heritage

STONES FOR SALE!

FIRST THOUGHTS

When people think of London, they think of Big Ben. Which building or monument symbolises your capital city?

READING

1 Read the text about Cleopatra's Needle and find out

1 where it came from.
2 how it was transported to England and what happened on the journey.
3 what now lies underneath it.

By the River Thames stands the obelisk known as Cleopatra's Needle. It was originally cut from a quarry in Aswan, Egypt, in the 15th century BC, stood for over a thousand years in Heliopolis and was later transported to Alexandria. After a couple of centuries it fell over in the sand where it lay. In 1877, a British engineer performed the seemingly impossible task of transporting it to England. The Needle was put in a cylindrical container and towed by ship to England. After a hazardous voyage in which six sailors drowned, it arrived in London where it was erected. Beneath it are various articles left for future archaeologists to find. They include the day's newspaper, some coins, a razor, a box of pins, four bibles in different languages, a railway timetable and twelve photographs of the most beautiful English women of the time!

2 Discussion points

1 Cities and museums in Europe and the USA are full of objects taken from other countries. Should they ever be returned to their country of origin? Do you think they were "stolen"?
2 Is there a museum in your town or city which you sometimes visit? What do you like about it? How could it be improved?
3 What do you think the people who buried the objects under Cleopatra's Needle were trying to say about their society? What would you choose to bury in a small box so future archaeologists would have an idea of what today's society is like?

USE OF ENGLISH

1 Read the texts in Exercises 2 and 3 below and find out the connection between the famous landmarks. What are they?

2 Using the word given in capitals at the end of the line, form a word that fits in the space in the same line. There is an example at the beginning (**0**).

What do the Eiffel Tower, the White House and Nelson's Column all have in common. One thing is (**0**).obviously. that they are all famous landmarks. Another is that they have been at the centre of (**1**).......... by clever (**2**).......... with an understanding of human nature. The most (**3**).......... was surely Count Victor Lustig. In 1925 the (**4**).......... Lustig informed some businessmen that the Eiffel Tower was going to be demolished because it was (**5**).......... . Pretending to be an official, he asked them to bid for the scrap metal that would result. His (**6**).......... to one of them, a certain Monsieur Poisson, that his offer would receive (**7**).......... consideration if he, Lustig, received a "present" , was received with great (**8**).......... . Lustig had chosen Poisson on purpose as being the greediest and most (**9**).......... of them all. As soon as Lustig got the bribe he left France. Understandably Poisson was too (**10**).......... to do anything.

OBVIOUS
DECEIVE
CRIME
SUCCEED
PERSUADE
SAFE

SUGGEST
FAVOUR
ENTHUSIASTIC

HONEST
SHAME

3 Now complete the second text by deciding which word **A**, **B**, **C** or **D** best fits each space. There is an example at the beginning (**0**).

Scottish villain Arthur Ferguson had a different technique. He (**0**)would. stand around a London monument where quite (**1**).......... accident, or so it appeared, he would (**2**).......... the acquaintance of a wealthy tourist. When the (**3**).......... invariably turned to the monument, the tourist would ask Ferguson how he was so (**4**).......... . Ferguson would confess to being the official (**5**).......... for the sale of Britain's monuments. His greatest success was selling Nelson's Column for £6,000. It was only when the demolition company (**6**).......... address had been given to the tourist refused to knock (**7**).......... the piece of Britain's national (**8**).......... that the tourist understood he had been (**9**).......... in.

   Realising that (**10**).......... Americans were perfect (**11**).......... of his techniques, Ferguson emigrated to the States where he stood outside the White House. He told a Texan cattleman that the government was (**12**).......... ways of cutting its costs and that the building could be rented for a (**13**).......... $100,000 a year. In New York he sold the Statue of Liberty but (**14**).......... himself to be photographed. He was identified as someone who was already (**15**).......... suspicion and the police arrested him.

  0 A accustomed   **B** would   **C** should   **D** used
  1 A on   **B** from   **C** by   **D** with
  2 A make   **B** have   **C** do   **D** get
  3 A debate   **B** argument   **C** conversation   **D** row
  4 A well-known   **B** knowing   **C** knowledgeable   **D** knowledge
  5 A dealing   **B** responsible   **C** chose   **D** charged
  6 A that   **B** which   **C** who   **D** whose
  7 A off   **B** down   **C** over   **D** out
  8 A heir   **B** treasure   **C** inheritance   **D** heritage
  9 A put   **B** brought   **C** taken   **D** carried
10 A trusted   **B** trusty   **C** trusting   **D** trustworthy
11 A clients   **B** victims   **C** prey   **D** source
12 A seeking   **B** searching   **C** looking   **D** going
13 A just   **B** mere   **C** only   **D** little
14 A allowed   **B** made   **C** let   **D** forced
15 A with   **B** under   **C** on   **D** above

FESTIVALS

FIRST THOUGHTS

What festivals are famous in your country or region? What events do they celebrate?

LISTENING

You are going to listen to five different men talking about festivals and special events. Choose from the list **A-F** what each one has to say. There is one extra letter which you do not need to use.

Speaker 1 ☐
Speaker 2 ☐
Speaker 3 ☐
Speaker 4 ☐
Speaker 5 ☐

A He was moved by what he saw.
B He would never join in the race himself.
C He hadn't been to an organised fireworks display before.
D He thought it was an excuse for bad behaviour.
E He took advantage of it to play a trick on a colleague.
F He preferred the way it used to be.

READING

You are going to read a magazine article from the travel section of a magazine for young people. It is about the Carnival in Trinidad. Choose the most suitable heading from the list **A-H** for each part (**1-6**) of the article. There is one extra heading which you do not need to use. There is an example at the beginning (**0**).

A	A Blazing Start
B	A Costly Experience
C	African Influences
D	Simply the Best
E	Highly Recommended
F	A Stroke of Luck
G	The Meaning of Carnival
H	Music from Nothing

0 | **G**

- Ancient Roman festivals from pagan times were taken over by the Christians and became Carnival.
- The word *Carnival* comes from the Latin *carnem levare* which means "farewell to the flesh". Carnival was the last time people could enjoy themselves before Lent.
- French colonists with their tradition of masked balls were responsible for taking Carnival to the New World.

1 |

Milly and I were really lucky to have Julius as our guide. We met him over a drink in a bar on the day we arrived. He had actually worked in England for 13 years before escaping back to the sun. He was proud of his island's history and filled us in on it as well as introducing us to Carnival.

2 |

As I'm sure you know, the black population of Trinidad used to be slaves. When they won their freedom, they started to develop their own version of Carnival. This partly copied the behaviour of their old masters but also drew on traditions from their own strong West African roots. Julius explained all the features of the Trinidadian version which make it so different: the special processions, the masked rituals, the stick dancing and the drumming, all of which have transformed the event into what it is today. We certainly wouldn't have got so much out of our visit without him.

3

The first big event he took us to was an amazing procession with lighted torches which started at midnight on the Sunday, the day before Carnival. It is called the *can boulay* which comes from the French *cannes brulées* meaning "burnt canes". The slaves would have to fight fires in the cane fields on the big estates. It was an incredible and somehow frightening sight, a reminder of the bad old days.

4

Julius told us about a unique kind of Trinidadian band which doesn't use ordinary musical instruments. Instead, the musicians beat objects such as bamboo stems and bottles and spoons. This is because in the old days the white masters had been scared of the slaves communicating using drums, and so the beating of real drums was banned. The slaves had to make do with what they could lay their hands on! Another Carnival treat which Trinidad is famous for is its steel bands. It's incredible to think that such wonderful music can come from some old oil drums. Pans are made which are then beaten and tuned to notes on the musical scale. They let me have a go but all I managed to do was give Milly a headache!

5

Although all the Caribbean islands celebrate Carnival, Julius pointed out that none of them can match the scale of the Trinidadian festival. I believed him if the costumes were anything to go by. They were absolutely fantastic and take weeks to prepare. People dress up as vampire bats, devils with horns and tails and as African and South American warriors. Julius told us that the South American warriors are based on a Venezuelan tribe which used to trade regularly in the southern parts of Trinidad. It makes you realise just how close the island is to South America.

6

All in all, it was an absolutely unforgettable experience and Milly and I would recommend it to anyone. If you go to Trinidad, we hope that you'll bump into Julius too.

WRITING

Through foreign eyes

1 England's most famous festival is without doubt Bonfire Night which takes place on November 5th each year.

2 Adriano is studying in England. He has just been to Bonfire Night. Find out why he didn't enjoy himself. Then correct the letter.

Dear Melissa,

Sorry for not replying your letter but I have been in bed with one terrible cold after the Guy Fawkes night. I will never used to the weather here. I didn't know nothing about this festival before coming to England and I must say I think it is a very terrible thing.

The family where I stay are hospitable and made a big bonfire party and invited lots of their friends. A few weeks before, the children made a model called a Guy. He was the man who tried blowing up Parliament. The children were let to go out into the street for to ask money from the people who were walking by. I don't understand it! Both the mother and father have good jobs but they let their children to go beg! In my country it would be one big scandal.

Anyway, my English family did a very huge bonfire from wood and old furnitures at end of their garden. They invited lots of friends and their children too. It was freezing cold although everybody was outside. They cooked potatoes and the sausages in the fire and drank soup! It wasn't very sophisticated. In my country people would be embarrassed for to give guests such foods! I was never so cold in my life; I am not used to be. The fireworks was really nice even if a bit dangerous. At the end they threw the poor Guy on the fire, everyone clapped and laughed. I was really shocking! I thought English people was civilised but now I am not sure. I thought it was barbaric!!!

Lots of love,
Adriano

3 Write a description of a festival in your country from the point of view of a foreigner. Describe its origins, what actually happens and how you feel about it.

LANGUAGE STUDY

used to and would

The writer of the article says that *the black population of Trinidad **used to** be slaves* and that in the old days *the slaves **would** have to fight fires in the cane fields of the big estates.*

Both **used to** and **would** can describe regular habits and routines in the past:

He used to smoke.
He would always light his pipe after dinner.

Used to can also describe past states or situations:
They used to have slaves.
She used to have lovely brown hair.

Would cannot be used in this way, e.g. you cannot say *She would have lovely brown hair* or *When I was young, the town would be surrounded by fields.*

It is possible to use **used to** most of the time. However, we do not do this for reasons of style. Look at this example and say why we do not use **used to** all the time.

He used to get home at about six o'clock in the evening. Then he would sit down in his armchair, get out his pipe and sit puffing away at it. After that, Mother would tell him that tea was ready and he used to go into the kitchen to wash his hands.

Why can't we say *His father **would** work at the car factory?*

Prepositions following adjectives

In the article about Carnival it says that *French colonists **were responsible** for taking Carnival to the New World.*

The adjective **responsible** is often followed by the preposition **for**. If we follow a preposition with a verb, we have to put the verb into the gerund (**-ing** form).

Complete these sentences by following each adjective with an appropriate preposition. Sometimes there is more than one correct answer.

1 Are you interested .... antiques?
2 She was surprised .... how cheap the watercolour was.
3 Is he aware .... how long we have been waiting for the tour to start?
4 Pisa is famous .... its Leaning Tower.

5 When I was at school, I was really bad .... history.
6 We were impressed .... the guided tour.
7 Hurry up! I'm worried .... missing the boat.
8 This festival is similar .... the one in Rio.
9 I'm really tired .... looking at monuments.
10 The flood was responsible .... damaging the statue.
11 She was terribly disappointed .... the guide-book.
12 This portrait of her is completely different .... that one.
13 We're not keen .... visiting the ruins.
14 I'm sorry .... being so late. I had to go back for my camera.
15 Sorry .... the delay. We should still get to the museum before it closes.

READING

1 You are going to read an article called *Kids go through the Euroblender*. Look at the cartoon and discuss what the title means.

2 Choose from the sentences **A-H** the one which best fits each gap (**1-6**). There is one extra sentence and an example at the beginning (**0**).

A	In particular, the divide between the north, where the young leave home to live independent lives, and the south, where they remain part of an extended family, is narrowing.
B	A few are worried at the loss of national identity and traditions.
C	The concept of the extended family is on the way out in southern Europe. More and more young Italians and Spaniards, for example, don't see care of their parents as a personal duty in the way they used to.
D	English is their lingua franca and Inter Rail their passport.
E	They are puzzled by their parents' lack of enthusiasm.
F	It's a fake place. It doesn't have any history. There's more of a community in Europe.
G	They are interested in Japan, which they see as a hi-tech paradise and home of hip foods such as sushi.
H	Eurokids suggest that young Europeans are much more independently minded than was once thought.

Kids go through the Euroblender

EUROPEAN KIDS are turning their backs on American culture and displaying a much greater enthusiasm for European unity than their elders, according to a survey report. [0] [E] They watch US films but do not consider the US or its culture the source of all inspiration. MTV, which now reaches 41 million households in Europe (compared with 14 million two years ago), is an American import; however, one of its most popular shows is *120 Minutes,* which covers the European music scene.

The report also suggests that the young are more eager than previous generations to live a genuinely Euro-lifestyle. [1] This is why they are in such a hurry to learn English and they make 40 per cent more foreign visits than adults (in Spain, Portugal and Greece, the figure is nearer 60).

Materialism, money, greed and yuppies are out of favour. Crystals, tarot readings and anything Japanese are in. Home-grown youth culture is the unifying force of the new generation. "Eurokids" listen to European music, wear French and Italian jeans, watch European "video jockeys" on the satellite music channel and gather in tapas bars. When they do look beyond Europe it is to the east. [2]

Simon Silvester, the report's author, concluded that if young people had their way then full European unity would take place immediately. 78 per cent expressed approval of the EU. "Everywhere we went, we found the young talking enthusiastically about a united Europe," Mr Silvester said. As expected, there are a few exceptions. [3] " The researchers built up their portrait of the typical Eurokid by interviewing groups of people aged under 25 in Amsterdam, Barcelona, Brussels, Dusseldorf, London, Milan and Paris.

An informal poll of teenagers in south London thought the conclusions of the poll were accurate. Tessa Morris, 15, said "I'm definitely into the idea of Europe. It would be great not to have the hassle of passports. I like visiting Greece, Spain and Italy." Ali Mombasser expressed distrust of the US: "[4] " His views were echoed by Kate Chesshyre: "The Americans are so arrogant. Europe needs its own identity."

While older generations remain entrenched within their national identities, the report suggests, the under-30s in the EU countries are drawing closer together. [5] Rising living standards in southern Europe are opening up new frontiers for the young. Incomes are rising on average, and they can't wait to leave home and do their own thing.

Young Europeans delay getting married until later in life in both the north and the south," Mr Silvester said. This can best be seen in what is happening in the family. "[6] " He predicted that the life-styles of northern and southern kids would soon be indistinguishable.

3 From what you know, are young people in different countries becoming more similar? How do you feel about this?

WRITING

Write a short article or letter for an international students' magazine explaining how life has changed in your country since your grandparents' generation. Write between **120 - 180** words.

TAKING A TRIP

FIRST THOUGHTS

Imagine you are a tour guide in your town or city. You have to organise a tour for a group of young people from abroad.

In pairs or groups discuss how you would spend the day. Think about these questions.

- Where would you start the tour?
- How long would you need?
- Which places of interest would you visit? (Don't restrict yourself to monuments or museums – there might be interesting factories or agricultural sights too.)
- What recommendations would you make about how to spend any free time/where to buy souvenirs?
- What would everyone do at lunch time?

LISTENING

A day out in Cambridge

1 Listen to the tour guide's speech and work out the route of the tour on the map of Cambridge.

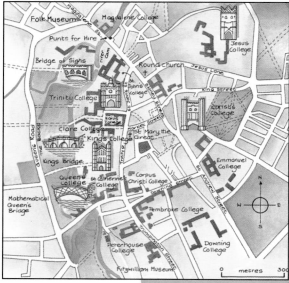

2 Listen again and complete the notes.

The tour leader's name is (**1**).......... Southgate.
She works for (**2**).......... .
The church is special because it is (**3**).......... .
The tour includes visits to four colleges: Trinity, Clare, (**4**).......... and (**5**).......... .
Visitors mustn't (**6**).......... or disturb (**7**).......... .
In the afternoon there will be a visit to the (**8**).......... .
A punt is a kind of (**9**).......... .
Everybody has to meet back at the starting point at (**10**).......... p.m.

VOCABULARY

remind, remember and **forget**

1 *Please may I **remind** you not to walk on the grass.*

Complete the following sentences with **remind**, **remember** or **forget**.

1 Do not .... to buy a textbook.
2 May I .... you that smoking is not allowed.
3 I shall .... that trip until the day I die.
4 Please .... me to your parents the next time you see them.
5 Can you .... her to send the postcards?
6 Passengers are .... to keep their valuables with them at all times.

2 Imagine you are going on holiday and a friend is going to look after your house or flat. Think of five things you would tell them to remember/not forget to do.

LANGUAGE STUDY

Study this verb pattern.
She reminded them to be back by 4.30.
SUBJECT + VERB + OBJECT + INFINITIVE

Now rewrite the sentences using the words in capitals.

1 "Would you like to come to the art gallery?" Sophie asked Ann.   INVITE
2 I finally agreed with Leila's suggestion that we should go to the son et lumière show.   PERSUADE
3 "Why don't you visit the ruins this afternoon?" his mother said.   ENCOURAGE
4 "Whatever you do, don't walk on the grass," the guide told us.   WARN
5 "Stop smoking at once!" the curator shouted at Lennie.   ORDER

LISTENING

You are going to hear the curator of a museum talking about some of the exhibits. Listen to her and answer the questions below.

1 Complete the table.

	NAME	USE
object one		
object two		
object three	flail	
object four		

2 We can understand from the curator that
   A the tourists are late.
   B the weather is poor.
   C it is fine.

3 The museum
   A sometimes can't find out what objects were used for.
   B has some exhibits that are still used.
   C eventually manages to find out what objects were used for.

4 Which of the pictures is object two?

5 Which of the pictures is object three?

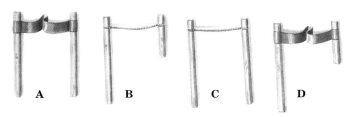

6 According to the curator, men who went poaching
   A were brave.
   B did it for sport.
   C risked deportation.

USE OF ENGLISH

Complete the passage about King's College Chapel by using one word only for each space.

King's College Chapel

The chapel, set in the grounds of King's College, by the River Cam, is **(1)**.......... question the most beautiful building in Cambridge. It is over five hundred years old and is a magnificent **(2)**.......... of late medieval architecture. It can best be appreciated in spring, from the back of the college, when the daffodils are out.

It was begun by King Henry VI in 1446, but was not completed **(3)**.......... the following century. This probably explains the use of different **(4)**.......... of stone in its construction. The exterior is **(5)**.......... elegant combination of stone and glass. We can best admire its beautiful stained-glass windows **(6)**.......... the inside. It **(7)**.......... craftsmen from Belgium over 30 years to put them in.

We can **(8)**.......... see *The Adoration of the Magi*, an imposing painting by the artist Peter Paul Rubens, **(9)**.......... was given to the chapel **(10)**.......... 1961. The painting **(11)**.......... the three wise men with the baby Jesus in the stable at Bethlehem. The chapel is also famous **(12)**.......... its choir of boy singers and the regular recitals it **(13)**.......... . At Christmas, people **(14)**.......... in the cold for hours to get a place for the carol concert which is broadcast **(15)**.......... over the world.

WRITING

Write a description in **120 - 180** words of an historic building in your town or region.

Say where it is and the best place to view it from.
Say something about its history and construction.
Say what special events were/are associated with it.

PRESERVING THE PAST

FIRST THOUGHTS

Look at these statements and decide whether they are **True** or **False** for you. Then compare your answers with a partner.

1 They used to make things much better in the old days.
2 I would rather drive an old Jaguar than a brand new BMW.
3 I would rather live in an old house than a new one.
4 People worry too much about preserving old things.
5 Artists these days just don't know how to paint.

VOCABULARY

1 Complete these sentences by using the adjectives in the box.

1 They have a beautiful .... writing desk; it must be three hundred years old.
2 Oh Dad! Why do you have to wear such .... clothes? How long have you had them?
3 You can't use this ticket, madam. It's ....
4 Greece has many .... monuments.
5 Buy a(n) .... car if you can't afford a new one.
6 She drives a(n) .... Rolls Royce from 1943.

old-fashioned	antique	vintage
second-hand	out of date	ancient

2 Complete the sentences using a word based around **heir/inherit**.

1 When his mother dies he will .... a fortune.
2 Prince Charles is the .... to the throne of England.
3 Monuments and parks are all part of our ....
4 He wasted his .... on gambling and fast cars.
5 This silver teapot is a family .... It has been in the family for five generations.

LISTENING

Listen to Matthew talking about a clock which is a family heirloom and decide if the following statements are **True** or **False**.

1 The clock reminds him of Big Ben.
2 He knows exactly when it came into his family.
3 He remembers the full name of its maker.
4 It was made in 1776.
5 He used to love hearing the clock when he was small.
6 The clock reminds him of his grandfather.
7 He thinks it is a little bit ugly.
8 He might inherit the clock one day.

LANGUAGE STUDY

Describing objects

1 Made **of, from** or **with**

Look at this entry from *Right Word, Wrong Word* by L.G. Alexander and decide if the sentences which follow are correct. Where necessary make alterations.

> **made of/out of** * **made from** * **made with**
> *Beer is made from hops and other ingredients.* (not **made of/out of*)
> (**made from** when the ingredients aren't immediately obvious.)
> -*Our new garden gate is made of/out of wrought iron.* (Not **made from**)
> (**made of/out of** when we can recognise the material)
> -*This cake is made with fresh cream.*
> (**made with** = using; compare **filled with** =containing.

1 This skirt is made from wool.
2 They had to drink coffee made from nuts.
3 The costume was made from an old pair of her father's pyjamas.
4 Water kept in bottles made with plastic tastes horrible.
5 Cider is a drink made from apples.
6 This table is made from an old wooden door.
7 This stew is delicious. Is it made of beef?

2 The order of adjectives

It is about eight feet tall, I should think. It's made of beautiful dark brown oak which is shiny from being polished. At the top there's a squarish box with a round face inside. It's covered in gold leaf, and is decorated with carving. It really is a lovely old object.

The rules for adjective order are complicated and few people agree about them. However, adjectives which describe the purpose of an object always go directly before the noun.

Example:

a superb	silk	wedding	dress
OPINION	MATERIAL	PURPOSE	NOUN

There is a also a *tendency* for adjectives to follow this order:
number → opinion → size / shape / age → texture → colour → decoration → origin → material → NOUN

3 In which of the categories above do these adjectives belong?

silver silk square old eighteenth-century rare long unique shiny decorated cotton wonderful French awful Japanese ivory oval fascinating smooth huge old-fashioned English ugly ancient small round jade rough carved priceless

4 It can seem awkward to have more than two or three adjectives before the noun. We can avoid this by moving some of the information to follow the noun.

- noun + **with** + e.g. *carving / decorations*
- noun + **made of/from** + material
- noun + **from** + country of origin
- noun + clause, e.g: *which was beautiful*

In pairs or groups, describe an object which is special to you or your family. Don't forget to explain why it is important.

WRITING

Lady Ffoulkes-Bracknell's house has been burgled! Lots of her most precious things have been stolen. She has made a list of the stolen property but is still too upset to write a letter to Scotland Yard. Using the notes below, write the letter on her behalf.

> To Inspector Jones, New Scotland Yard.
> Thank him for coming quickly.
> Have made a list of stolen property:
> Writing desk, antique, English. Made of oak. Carved lions on feet.
> Silver beer mug from Bavaria. 18th century – very valuable.
> French Louis XV clock. Delightful piece. Initials H.P. underneath. Gold and silver. Priceless.
> Antique duelling pistols. Italian?
> Tiger skin rug. Dirty-looking! Sentimental value. Grandfather shot it in India.
> Colombian statue. Tiny. Made of stone. Four hundred years old.
> 2 pairs silk pyjamas – blue and white stripes.
> Hope you can find property etc.

VOCABULARY

Re-arrange the jumbled letters to form words connected with painting and art.

1 There is an NOBIXEHITI of Picasso's work I would very much like to see.
2 The YELGALR is closed this month for repairs.
3 The artist mixed the paint on her ALEPETT and then placed the paint on the SAANCV with a thick SUHBR.
4 I don't like TABSRATC art very much. I prefer to know what I'm looking at.
5 The RAEFM is more interesting than the picture!
6 Old Masters such as Rembrandt and Breughel painted in ILOS. Some people say that ETRLOWACROUS are more delicate.
7 This is a fine ATORRIPT; the artist has caught her character perfectly.
8 There was an enormous LNACDPSAE of a hunting scene on the dining room wall.
9 Rodin is a OTCUSPLR who is much admired.
10 At the top of the steps, there used to be a big marble TUATSE of a man on a horse.

SPEAKING

Describing a painting

1 In **Part 2** of **Paper 5 (Speaking)** you are required to look at a pair of photographs. It can be useful to know how to describe and speculate about a picture for this part of the examination. Study this painting carefully and then read what a student said about it.

This is a painting of the countryside. In the front of the picture I can see two girls. They look very poor. They are wearing old clothes Maybe they are sisters – I am not sure. Behind them there is the countryside. Maybe it is England. It looks like England very much. Typically English, I think. I think that maybe it has rained because I can see a lovely, um , rainbow, it is called, in the sky. I can see some animals in the fields behind the girls. The smaller girl is saying the other one something about the rainbow. It is a nice picture. It has been painted maybe a hundred years ago. One of the girls has got a musical instrument with her. Wait a minute! I think she is blind and the small girl is taking care of her.

2 In pairs or small groups, discuss how you could improve the student's description. Think about

1 any obvious mistakes that have been made.
2 what you can say instead of *I can see....* and *maybe.*
3 what special words to describe paintings you could introduce.
4 what you could add to the description to make it more interesting.
5 how you could join up the observations better.

LISTENING

Listen to a native speaker talking about the picture by John Millais and answer the questions.

1 What words and expressions does she use
   A instead of *I can see* and *maybe*?
   B to describe the position of objects within the picture?
2 What extra subjects does she include in her description?
3 How does she move away from the picture?

WRITING

In **Part 2** of **Paper 2 (Writing)** you may be asked to write a description of something. Study this example.

One of my favourite paintings is "The Fall of Icarus" by Peter Breughel. If you remember, Icarus and his father made themselves wings and learned to fly. Icarus ignored his father's warnings and flew too near the sun. This melted the wax which held the wings to his body so he fell into the sea and drowned.

What is so interesting about this painting is that everyday life is going on while this disaster is happening. In the foreground there is a farmer totally unaware of what has just taken place. He concentrates on ploughing his field. Just behind him there is a shepherd boy looking up at the figure in the sky perhaps wondering what on earth it can be. Behind him, the cliffs curve away into the distance. In the background we can see the rest of the bay and a few boats.

In fact you have to look quite hard to see poor Icarus who is in the bottom right-hand part of the picture. You can see a splash and a pair of white legs sticking up as he disappears beneath the sea. Perhaps someone on the boat saw him, but I doubt it.

In a way it's strange that the artist didn't put Icarus in the middle of the painting. I suppose what he is saying is that "great" events often go unobserved and perhaps that life is more than a little absurd and ridiculous. What's more, it reminds us that we are the victims of our pride. Every powerful person or politician should have this picture in their office.

Now write about a picture you know well in the same way. Your composition must be between **120 -180** words.

SCRUPLES

FIRST THOUGHTS

Complete this questionnaire. If you wouldn't make any of the choices suggested, then add one of your own.

1 You can hear a terrible noise coming from your neighbour's house. It sounds as though he's murdering someone. Would you

- a do nothing?
- b call the police?
- c go round yourself and see what was happening?
- d ....

2 You discover a way of making free telephone calls anywhere in the world. Would you

- a tell all your friends?
- b keep the secret to yourself?
- c inform the telephone company?
- d ....

3 Imagine you're a shop assistant and you notice one of your colleagues stealing from the till. Would you

- a say nothing?
- b tell the person to stop or else?
- c inform the boss?
- d ....

4 While you are parking your car, you accidentally scratch the paintwork of a new car next to you. Would you

- a leave a note for the owner of the other car?
- b hurry off?
- c park as though nothing had happened?
- d ....

5 You are staying in an elderly woman's home when you notice a painting on the wall. She doesn't know that it is a Rembrandt. Would you

- a buy the painting for as little as possible?
- b tell her what the painting was worth?
- c offer her a fair price but not tell her everything?
- d ....

6 A tramp smelling of alcohol asks you for money. Would you

- a give him some knowing he will spend it on alcohol?
- b buy him a meal or a sandwich?
- c refuse to give him any?
- d ....

7 Your best friend's boyfriend/girlfriend invites you out for a date. Would you

- a refuse the invitation and tell your friend?
- b accept the invitation and keep it a secret?
- c refuse it and say nothing?
- d ....

8 Somebody pays you in cash for doing a job. Would you

- a declare it to the taxman?
- b keep the money without declaring it?
- c not declare it but give the customer a discount for cash?
- d ....

Compare the results of the questionnaire with a partner.

VOCABULARY

Phrasal verbs

Replace the words in brackets with a phrasal verb from the box. Make any other changes which are necessary.

The police are **1** *(investigating)* an incident which took place this afternoon. Two masked men **2** *(robbed)* a security van outside the national bank and **3** *(escaped)* with half a million pounds. Their getaway car **4** *(knocked down)* one of the guards as they **5** *(went towards)* the motorway.

She had **6** *(invented)* a wonderful alibi and managed to **7** *(make everyone believe her lies)*. The police only **8** *(discovered)* the truth because a jealous lover **9** *(betrayed her)* to the police.

The children are suspiciously quiet. I wonder what they are **10** *(doing)*? I think I'll go and have a look.

He **11** *(lost control of his emotions)* and cried. He confessed everything to his father. His father **12** *(didn't punish him)* because he believed the boy was genuinely sorry.

The alarm bell **13** *(started to ring)* when the gang tried to **14** *(enter)* the bank.

> find out   look into   run over   go off   get away
> break down   hold up   be up to   break into
> make for   let off   make up   take in   give away

Different types of crime

1 What are the crimes described in these situations? The words are given in the box.

1 He threatened to send the love letters to her husband unless she gave him £500.
2 The telephone box had been smashed and there was graffiti all over the walls.
3 An old man has been attacked and robbed in a city street. He is recovering in hospital.
4 Department stores lose millions of pounds each year through goods being stolen off the shelves.
5 Thieves broke into the house while the family was away on holiday.
6 The young woman was sexually attacked as she walked across the park at night.
7 He watched with satisfaction as the fire he lit burnt down the factory. "That'll make them wish they'd never given me the sack," he thought.

8 It was a perfect copy. It was so good, in fact, that it could even fool an expert.
9 The bank believed her to be trustworthy. They had no reason to suspect that she had transferred thousands of pounds to false accounts.
10 "If you want to see your child again, put £10,000 into an old suitcase and wait for further instructions."
11 George gave the man £50 in return for a small packet of heroin.
12 It was a beautiful day. The sun was shining and people were sitting outside the café enjoying the sunshine. Then the bomb went off.
13 "If only I hadn't brought those watches through customs," she thought as she sat crying in the police station.

> burglary   arson   vandalism   terrorism   forgery
> blackmail   smuggling   fraud   mugging   rape
> kidnapping   drug dealing   shoplifting

2 What do you call the criminals who commit the crimes above?

What verbs can be made from the list of crimes? Example: **burglary → burgle**.

What do we have to do if a verb cannot be made from the word for the crime?

SPEAKING

1 Decide individually which you think the three worst and three least serious crimes are from the list, then compare your answers with a partner.

2 Which of the crimes is the most common in your country?

A QUESTION OF JUDGEMENT

FIRST THOUGHTS

"Sometimes crimes are so terrible that the death penalty is the only suitable punishment." How far do you agree with this opinion?

SPEAKING

1 Work in pairs. Student A look at pictures 1 and 2; Student B look at pictures 3 and 4. Think about what your photographs show. How do they make you feel? Discuss your reactions with your partner.

1

2

3

4

2 In **Part 3** of **Paper 5 (Speaking)** you may be given some kind of problem to solve. Look at the following situation and, in groups of three, discuss the task.

You are on the parole board of a prison which is so overcrowded that you must release two prisoners. From the photographs and notes decide who you should set free.

 Alan Jones: Murder. Poisoned wife slowly. Neighbours say nice man; children love him. Wife had lots of affairs.

 **Mick Brown:** Vandalism and football hooliganism. Low intelligence. Violent when drunk.

 **Janet Green:** Shoplifting, 10th offence. A tramp. Likes to spend winter in prison.

 **Cynthia Carter:** Smuggling pet cats against quarantine regulations. Cutoms officers want an example made of her.

 **Miranda Morgan:** Drug addict and dealer. Two unsuccessful drug treatment programmes. Two-year-old child.

3 In **Part 4** of **Paper 5 (Speaking)** the interlocutor (the examiner who asks the questions) will ask you to develop the conversation you began and to report back on what you decided. Listen to Anna and Bruno talking to each other and the examiner.

1 Who do they each believe should be freed? What reasons do they each give?

2 How fluent are they? How well do they communicate their ideas?

3 What questions does the interlocutor ask to keep the conversation moving?

4 Look at the tapescript on p. 233 and correct any obvious mistakes Anna and Bruno have made.

How could you improve what they actually say?

4 Choose one person in your groups of three to be the interlocutor. Role play a discussion like the one you have just listened to, based on what you said in Exercise 2.

USE OF ENGLISH

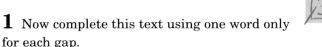

1 Now complete this text using one word only for each gap.

A blind bank robber who was desperate for money was **(1)**.......... a 12-month suspended sentence recently. David Worrell had just put his white stick on the counter before **(2)**.......... a note to the cashier saying he **(3)**.......... shoot her if she did not hand over the cash. The court heard that Worrell had lost his previous job **(4)**.......... of his condition and had been turned down for many **(5)**.......... .

Worrell, who pleaded guilty to attempted robbery, had queued up and passed a note demanding £2000. He **(6)**.......... to use the money to start his own disco business. The cashier sounded the alarm and refused to hand over **(7)**.......... money. Even if he had got **(8)**.........., a young blind person would **(9)**.......... been easy to identify. When he tried to escape, he walked straight into the bank's glass doors **(10)**.......... than through them. He was arrested. Between the incident and his trial, Worrell had succeeded **(11)**.......... starting his own successful discotheque. The judge said, "This sort of offence would **(12)**.......... result in a substantial term of imprisonment. You are a man of good character, with an **(13)**.......... severe physical disability but **(14)**.......... this you have been **(15)**.......... to generate a prosperous business."

2 Complete the text by deciding which word **A, B, C** or **D** best fits each space. There is an example at the beginning (**0**).

Even though the crime (**0**)...rate... keeps going up, society is soft on criminals. People who have (**1**).......... major crimes and even murderers sentenced to (**2**).......... are often released after serving just part of their sentence. Everyday (**3**).......... crime is destroying the (**4**).......... of life of many people, particularly in city areas. (**5**).......... you look there are examples of graffiti and mindless vandalism. Personally, I have had my car (**6**).......... into twice in the last three months. As far as I know the police are not looking into (**7**).......... of the crimes.

  Even when a friend recently caught a young thief, the police (**8**).......... him off with a warning because of his age. Doubtless, the child in (**9**).........., thinking he has got (**10**).......... with one crime, will be (**11**).......... to try another. Yet if you or I park our cars in the wrong place or exceed the speed limit slightly we have to pay a (**12**).......... . I know it's important to (**13**).......... into account the age of criminals. I also know that upbringing and drugs are (**14**).......... for many crimes. All the (**15**).........., the lives and rights of the victims of crime should be considered too.

0 **A** numbers **B** wave **C** rate **D** figures
1 **A** committed **B** done **C** completed
  D made
2 **A** live **B** living **C** life **D** lifetime
3 **A** little **B** petty **C** small **D** major
4 **A** standard **B** cost **C** level **D** quality
5 **A** Wherever **B** Forever **C** However
  D Whatever
6 **A** looked **B** turned **C** broken **D** made
7 **A** both **B** any **C** either **D** none
8 **A** set **B** allowed **C** let **D** got
9 **A** mind **B** trouble **C** discussion
  D question
10 **A** on **B** up **C** off **D** away
11 **A** attempted **B** dared **C** tempted
  D threatened
12 **A** fee **B** caution **C** ticket **D** fine
13 **A** take **B** put **C** make **D** carry
14 **A** guilty **B** reponsible **C** faulty **D** cause
15 **A** time **B** while **C** same **D** better

A LIFE OF CRIME

1 Comment on the situations **A-D** with an appropriate idiom **1-4**.

A Uncle Bill caused a great scandal a few years ago so we made him go to another town.

B They saw him climbing out of the bedroom window with the jewels.

C Every time he promises he'll "go straight" and every time he lets us down. He just can't help it.

D I wouldn't trust him if I were you. Even though he seems kind and innocent, he'll take advantage of you.

1 What do you expect? After all, *a leopard never changes its spots.*

2 I always thought he was *a wolf in sheep's clothing*!

3 There is always someone who is *the black sheep of the family.*

4 Really, so he was *caught red-handed*?

2 How true do you think it is that "a leopard never changes its spots"?

1 Before you read the article about Rose Jones, look at her photograph and describe her in as much detail as possible. Then read the article and answer these two questions.

1 What reason does she give for her life of crime?
2 Do you think her reasons are, in fact, reasonable?

2 Now read the article again. Seven sentences have been removed from the article. Choose from the sentences **A-H** the one which fits each gap (**1-6**). There is one extra sentence which you do not need to use. There is an example at the beginning (**0**).

A Rose thinks it is time she turned over a new leaf.

B Hunger drove young Rose to steal food and she quickly graduated to picking pockets.

C It was to be the first of many such visits.

D She lives in a damp, uncomfortable basement bedsit with no heating and no company except for her dogs and cats and the TV.

E Instead, she was given life imprisonment.

F She remembers taking a lipstick and a five pound note from some guests' luggage.

G She should have tried robbing banks.

H Her crime has been pickpocketing.

A life of crime

Looking at this little old lady it is hard to believe that she has spent 20 of her 76 years in jail. [0] [H] Just a short while ago she was caught practising her trade in Harrods – a favourite hunting ground for the pickpocket as it is frequented by the well-off. Her fingers aren't as quick as they used to be and she was spotted by a sharp-eyed store detective more used to catching shoplifters.

Luckily for her, the judge let her off. All the same, crime certainly hasn't paid for Rose Jones. [1] Nevertheless, she believes that it is better there than in prison. During her many spells in prison, she met Ruth Ellis, the last woman to be hanged in Britain and the notorious murderess, Myra Hindley, who would certainly have followed Ellis to the scaffold if hanging had not been abolished. [2]

Rose blames her life of crime on her childhood and harsh

LANGUAGE STUDY

Conditional sentences using if

1 *If Rose's mother hadn't died when she was small, her life would have turned out differently.*

Correct these sentences.
1 **First conditional:** *If it will rain, we will not play tennis.*
2 **Second conditional:** *If he would have a haircut, he would look nicer.*
3 **Third conditional:** *If she had have phoned you, I would have told you.*

2 Which sentences **1-5** express the ideas **A-E**?

A something quite likely to happen in the future
B an unreal situation in the past
C something in the past that affects the present
D an established fact
E something possible but unlikely

1 If you heat water to 100 degrees centigrade, it boils.
2 If he studies hard, he will pass the exam.
3 If you smoked less, you would save a lot of money.
4 If I had kept the receipt, I would change the tie.
5 If I had seen her, I would have remembered.

---

upbringing. She feels that if her mother hadn't died when she was small, her life would have turned out differently. As it was, her father remarried and her stepmother was cruel to her. ⬜**3**⬜ She was only six at the time. When she was 11, she started doing menial jobs in big houses. She perhaps wishes she had taken that opportunity to go "straight" but she didn't. ⬜**4**⬜ When her mistress accused her of stealing, she denied everything and, for once, got away with it.

Her life "inside" started when she was 17. Following a conviction, she was sent to a prison for young people. ⬜**5**⬜ Yet, in all her long criminal career, Rose has never made any real money. Either she gave it away or she spent it on trivial things. While she was in prison her husband stole the little money she had managed to save.

Nowadays, she has just about decided that her life of crime is over. After all, she finds it difficult to move around now without any support, which makes her line of work rather difficult. In addition, the popularity of credit cards means that people tend to carry less cash around with them than they were once accustomed to. ⬜**6**⬜ But is it possible to break the habits of a lifetime?

---

3 Change the verbs in brackets into the most appropriate form to make conditional sentences.

1 What you (**do**) if you (**be**) in my situation?
2 Behave yourself, Lucy. If you (**do**) that again you (**have**) to go to bed.
3 Their marriage only lasted three months. If he (**be**) less mean, she (**not leave**) him.
4 Good, everybody's ready. If we (**leave**) now, we (**miss**) the rush hour traffic.
5 If you (**smoke**) less, you (**have**) a lot more money. But I don't think you ever will.
6 If we (**close**) the car window, we (**not give**) them the opportunity to break in.
7 When Alice (**get**) here, you (**show**) her to her room?
8 I know it's a delicate situation, Inspector, but what you (**say**) if I (**give**) you a little present?
9 If you (**press**) that button, a receptionist (**come**) to help you.
10 The film was marvellous. If you (**come**) with us, you (**enjoy**) it too.
11 Imagine, darling. What we (**do**) if your husband (**have**) a little accident?
12 If I (**be**) the prime minister, I (**bring back**) capital punishment.

PRONUNCIATION

1 How do we say the following sentences in normal speech?

1 I will do it if you want me to.
2 If he had not come, we would have had a good time.
3 If I were you, I would see a doctor.
4 If only I had not said it!

What do we have to contract?
Which parts of the sentence should be stressed?

2 🔲 Listen and identify which conditional construction is being used in the eight sentences.

	FIRST	SECOND	THIRD	MIXED
1				
2				
3				
4				
5				
6				
7				
8				

LANGUAGE STUDY

Verbs followed by prepositions

1 *Rose's mistress* **accused her of** *stealing.*
Complete these sentences of verb-preposition combinations.

1 You accuse someone ..of...
2 You forgive someone ....
3 You arrest someone ....
4 You discourage someone ....
5 You blame someone ....   } doing something.
6 You punish someone ....
7 You prevent someone ....
8 You convict someone ....
9 You congratulate someone ....
10 You warn someone ....

2 Make all the changes necessary to produce past tense sentences from the following sets of words and phrases. Make sure that you choose the correct prepositions to go with each verb.

1 Her employer - accuse - her - steal - money.
2 Rose - blame - parents - not - bring her up - properly.
3 His mother - punish him - be rude - to their neighbour.
4 The lock - prevent - burglar - break into - house.
5 The jury - convict him - murder - his wife.
6 The shopkeeper - forgive - child - steal - sweets.
7 His son - be - arrest - sell drugs - to teenagers.
8 Her nephew - be - discouraged - talk - the police.
9 The judge - congratulate - police - catch - gang.
10 She - warn - children - play - park - after dark.

"Would you say your husband had any Swiss enemies?"

LISTENING

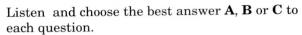
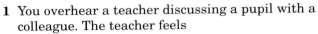

Listen and choose the best answer **A**, **B** or **C** to each question.

1 You overhear a teacher discussing a pupil with a colleague. The teacher feels
   A ashamed.
   B amused.
   C angry.

2 You are in a solicitor's (a lawyer's) office when he plays back a message left on his answering machine. The message is from
   A a friend.
   B a person with a complaint about a client.
   C a client.

3 A magistrate has just heard a case in which a youth has committed some driving offences. As a punishment she decides to give him
   A a prison sentence.
   B a fine and special supervision.
   C a heavy fine and a severe warning.

4 You are in a library when you overhear one side of a telephone conversation. The librarian is talking about
   A trees.
   B organising a demonstration.
   C protecting an old building which is under threat.

5 You are at Mrs Williams' house when one of her daughter's friends arrives on his bicycle. What does he do with it?
   A He brings it into the house.
   B He leaves it outside.
   C He goes back home for the lock.

6 A landlady is speaking to a student in a student hostel. The student has to
   A make a promise.
   B look for somewhere else.
   C smoke outside.

7 You are listening to a radio programme about a couple who live next door to noisy neighbours. The husband agrees to
   A call the police.
   B confront the neighbours.
   C put up with the noise.

8 A manager is briefing a new store detective in his department store. He tells him to
   A be firm.
   B chase anyone who tries to escape.
   C be ready to argue his case.

LANGUAGE STUDY

Ways of saying **if**

Look at the tapescripts on p.233-234. You will see that four ways of saying **if** have been underlined.
Complete the sentences using each of the ways once.

1 We'll have a picnic ...., of course, it rains.
2 I'll go .... he goes too.
3 I'll take you to the airport .... you pay for the petrol.
4 You'd better hurry .... you'll miss your train.

• Which form has the idea of "if not"?
• Which form is followed by a consequence?
• Which two forms are followed by strong conditions and mean "provided that"?

Forms of **wish**

1 Study the questions which follow each of these examples.

1 *I wish I had a million pounds.*
  a Is the speaker talking about the past, present or the future?
  b Does the speaker think he/she is likely to have a million pounds?

2 *I wish I had blue eyes.*
  a Is the speaker talking about the past, present or future?
  b Is the wish unlikely or impossible?

= We use **wish + past simple** when we want something in the present to change. Such a change is either unlikely or impossible.

3 *I wish I had worn gloves.*
  a Did the speaker wear gloves?
  b What do you think happened to him/her?

= We use **wish + past perfect** when we regret in the present what we did in the past.
Note: We can often use **if only** instead of I **wish**, e.g. *If only I'd worn gloves.*

4 *I wish he would stop smoking that awful pipe.*
  a Is the speaker talking about the present, the future or both?
  b Does the speaker really believe he will stop?
  c How does he/she feel about the situation?
  d Can we use this construction to talk about ourselves?

5 *I wish the train would come, I'm freezing to death.*
  a Is the speaker talking about the present, the near future or both?
  b Does the speaker want the train to hurry up?
  c Does the speaker really believe the train will arrive soon?

= We use **wish + would** either when something is annoying us and we would like it to stop, or when we want something to happen sooner rather than later.

6 *I wish I could swim.*
  a Can the speaker swim?
  b Would the speaker like to?

= We use **wish + could** when we want to talk about an ability.

2 Look at the tapescripts on p.233-234 and, in pairs, decide how **wish** is used on each occasion.

3 What might you say if you were the people in the following situations? Make sentences using one of the forms of **wish** we have looked at.

1 Liz is unhappy because she has got a small flat.
2 Alex is trying to lose weight but his diet hasn't made any difference.
3 Thieves have stolen Candy's fur coat. It wasn't insured.
4 You work with someone who whistles horribly all day long.
5 Anita drank too much again last night. She has got a terrible hangover.
6 She wants to take the top off a bottle of aspirin but she can't open it.
7 Katie is sitting by the telephone. She is waiting for Angus to ring.

4 Write some sentences about yourself using each of the forms we have looked at.

"Look, lady, all the wishing in the world isn't going to change anything."

145

ROUGH JUSTICE

1 Read the text and discover what the miscarriage of justice was.

2 Now complete the text by changing the word in capitals at the end of the line into a suitable form to fill the gap. Remember to ask yourself first what part of speech the word should be. There is an example at the beginning (**0**).

In 1974 five people died in an IRA (**0**) terrorist bomb attack. The police were under enormous pressure to catch the criminals.	**TERROR**
Desperate to solve the case, they (**1**).......... forced confessions from	**FAIR**
four ordinary and (**2**)......... Irish people.	**POWER**
Despite the (**3**)......... of the evidence against them and the	**WEAK**
(**4**)......... of their confessions, they got long sentences, capital	**RELY**
(**5**)......... having fortunately been abolished.	**PUNISH**
The (**6**).......... to the bombings by other IRA prisoners was not	**ADMIT**
enough to prove their (**7**).......... . It took a fifteen-year campaign to	**INNOCENT**
overcome the (**8**)......... of the judicial system to admit its	**WILLING**
(**9**)......... terrible mistake. Even though the five people received	**FRIGHTEN**
compensation, nothing can pay them back for fifteen wasted years.	
This story is one of the most (**10**)......... episodes in British justice.	**SHAME**

You are going to listen to three friends discussing the issue of crime and punishment. Answer the questions by writing **I** (for Ian), **C** (for Christine) or **V** (for Victor).

1 Who explains what rewarding crime means? ☐
2 Who makes excuses for young criminals? ☐
3 Who says punishment is as important as rehabilitation? ☐
4 Who says they don't agree with corporal punishment? ☐
5 Who believes prison is bad for criminals? ☐
6 Who is in favour of capital punishment? ☐
7 Which person has changed their mind about capital punishment? ☐

Complete the second sentence so that it has a similar meaning to the first. You must use between two and five words including the word given. Do not change the word given.

1 He managed to trick them with his lies.
taking
He succeeded .... with his lies.

2 They said the accident was her fault.
responsible
They held .... accident.

3 Someone stole the jewels. Perhaps it was Paul.
might
The jewels .... by Paul.

4 The jury decided he had murdered his wife.
guilty
The jury .... his wife.

5 "Are you saying I stole your wallet?"
accusing
"Are you .... your wallet?"

6 I used to believe he was innocent.
mind
I've .... his innocence.

7 Do you agree with long sentences?
favour
Are you .... long sentences?

8 The policeman didn't arrest him because he knew his parents.
off
The policeman .... because he knew his parents.

9 I regret driving so fast.
only
If .... so fast.

10 You ought to lock the door.
better
You .... the door.

WRITING

The opinion question

1 Two students wrote answers to this question.

It is often said that serious crime could be reduced if judges gave stricter sentences. How far do you agree with this view?

Working in pairs or small groups, read both compositions and decide which one gives the better answer to the question. Decide which one has

- the better ideas.
- the better range of expressions.
- the better vocabulary.

A

The number of serious crimes has increased in the past few years. Most of these crimes are committed for economic and social reasons. What can justice do to reduce them?

Each country has its own laws which is why the same crime can be sentenced in different ways. The first reason why judges should give stricter sentences is because more and more criminals are no longer afraid of being punished. They know that prisons are overcrowded and that most of them will be released early for good behaviour. Therefore justice should be more consistent and give sentences which will immediately frighten criminals.

The second reason is that in certain countries capital punishment has been abolished. This special sentence could be re-introduced for very difficult cases. For example, a terrorist responsible for the deaths of innocent people should not be kept alive.

On the other hand lots of crimes are committed because of poverty and unemployment. Delinquency cannot be cured by stricter sentences. Some people need to be directly helped in their lives at school, work, and in the family.

To sum up, for shocking crimes capital punishment should be used but carefully. Anyway, justice should be more competent and precise in order to take care against mistakes.

B

I do not think that stricter sentences would by themselves reduce serious crime. But I want harder and longer punishment because it shows that someone has done something wrong and will maybe keep people from doing the same thing.

What we have to do is ask ourselves what our morality is. We could do a lot so that our children do not grow up in a world without rules, order and morality. This is difficult but very important.

We can do a lot for criminals both during and after their time in prison. We have to educate them about what is right and wrong and make them understand. I know that this is sometimes done but we have to look after them even after they have left prison. Give them a job and somewhere to live. More things for them would cost more but they could be paid for by reducing the comfort in prison. It is not necessary for them to have videos or colour TV etc.

I can sum up by saying that I want stricter sentences together with more work to make them more functional in today's society.

2 Take the best elements from both compositions and write your own composition on the same topic. If you have any problems, refer to the composition work in Units 7 and 9.

13 Beyond Belief

YOU CAN'T TAKE IT WITH YOU

FIRST THOUGHTS

What sort of people would make the following comments? How would you reply to them?

1 "Ghosts and UFOs always have a logical explanation."
2 "I always take my lucky elephant into an examination."
3 "For every supernatural event there is a simple explanation."

LISTENING

The Chaffin Will affair

1 Listen to the story and find out what the connection is between a will, a coat, a Bible and a ghost!

2 Listen to the story again and complete the notes.

James Chaffin died in (**1**).......... . He left all his money to his (**2**).........., whose name was Marshall. The will had been written (**3**).......... .
Chaffin's ghost first appeared (**4**).......... .
It was wearing (**5**).......... . Chaffin's ghost gave an instruction to his son on the (**6**).......... visit.
The coat was with (**7**)..........; the note was hidden in a (**8**).......... . The Bible was looked at in front of (**9**).......... . The will appeared genuine so Marshall (**10**).......... .

Can you think of a logical explanation for this story?

LANGUAGE STUDY

Relative clauses

1 Relative clauses are used to join two ideas together in one sentence:
James Chaffin was a wealthy gentleman. He died in 1921. = James Chaffin was a wealthy gentleman who died in 1921.

The clause begins with one of these pronouns or other words: **who/that** for people; **which/that** for things; **whose** for possession; **where** for place; **when** for time and **why** for reason.
Look through the tapescript on p.234 and find the relative pronouns.
Now connect these pairs of sentences using a relative pronoun. Make any other necessary changes.

1 They looked in his overcoat. They found a letter in the lining.
2 The will had been written fifteen years earlier. It was not his last will.
3 They examined the Bible. They found another will in it.
4 That's Marshall Chaffin. His mother and brothers weren't left anything.
5 Chaffin left everything to Marshall. Nobody understood the reason.
6 Chaffin's ghost appeared to one of his sons. This son will never forget the experience.

2 Defining relative clauses

In **defining** relative clauses, the information which is given is essential to the meaning of the sentence and cannot be removed. It helps us to identify and **define** what we are talking about:
The woman who said she saw a ghost is very reliable.

Complete these sentences with a relative pronoun.

1 That's the hotel .... I went on my honeymoon.
2 So that was the reason .... they were late.
3 She's the woman .... husband won the lottery.
4 Is that the dog .... bit you?
5 I can remember the time .... all this was forest.
6 Are you the gentleman .... wanted more information about the trips?

In defining relative clauses the pronouns **who**, **which** and **that** can be left out if they are the object of the verb in the relative clause:
*Would you like to borrow the book (**which/that**) I told you about last week?*
*That's the woman (**who/whom**) I met at the party.*

Note: Whom is used in writing and in formal English rather than in everyday speech.

3 Look at these sentences and decide if the pronoun can be omitted.

1 The woman who you met at lunch is my next door neighbour.
2 The food which made me ill was badly cooked.
3 The man who owns that house is a doctor.
4 The university that she attended has a good reputation.
5 That mistake which we discovered was important.
6 Isn't that the girl who used to work in the café.
7 Those cigars which Andrew smokes smell awful.
8 The letter that arrived last night was for you.

4 Non-defining relative clauses

Look at this pair of sentences. Which one suggests there is only **one** son? In which sentence is the information essential, i.e. defining?

a *The son, who received everything, was extremely selfish.*
b *The son who received everything was extremely selfish.*

Non-defining relative clauses give additional information which is not essential to the main meaning of the sentence. They are used mainly in writing and are separated from the main clause by commas. Look at the tapescript on p.234 and search the text for non-defining relative clauses.

Remember:
- In non-defining relative clauses the pronoun cannot be omitted.
- We cannot use the pronoun **that** in non-defining clauses.

Join these sentences, adding commas where necessary. Omit the relative pronoun if you can.

1 That's the woman. Her son scatched my new car.
2 This is a photograph of the ghost. It was seen coming down the stairs.
3 Stonehenge was built thousands of years ago. It was a miracle of engineering.
4 It's a hard job. Not many people would choose it.
5 This is the boy. I met him on holday last year.

5 Pronunciation of non-defining clauses

The speaker pauses before the clause and then says it faster than normal but more quietly. This is because the information is unimportant or non-essential. Another reason is that the he/she may think the information is already known by the listener.

Listen to sentences **1**, **2** and **3**. Which one is being said, **A** or **B**?

1 **A** The woman whose husband had died was rich.
  B The woman, whose husband had died, was rich.
2 **A** Carole's daughter who lives in Scotland is a doctor.
  B Carole's daughter, who lives in Scotland, is a doctor.
3 **A** This bible which was found in the keeping of Chaffin's widow was examined in front of independent witnesses.
  B This bible, which was found in the keeping of Chaffin's widow, was examined in front of independent witnesses

In pairs, take it in turn to read the sentences. Your partner has to guess if you are saying **A** or **B**.

6 Relative clauses with prepositions

In speech we often put prepositions at the end of a sentence:
*He's the man I spoke **to**.*
*She's the lady I received the present **from**.*

In writing and formal English it is more appropriate to keep the preposition between the clauses, and to use **whom** (for people) and **which** (for things):
*He's the man **to whom** I spoke.*
*She's the lady **from whom** I received the present.*

7 Relative clauses with quantifiers

Quantifiers – words such as **some**, **all**, **none**, **both** and numbers – can be used with **of whom/of which** in non-defining relative clauses:
*She gave me the eggs, **a few** / **several** / **most of which** were broken.*
*The students, **both** / **some** / **all of whom** had missed the train, finally arrived.*
*He sent me some novels, **three** / **none of which** I had already read.*

8 Join these pairs of sentences using a relative clause and the written forms from 6 and 7.

1 That's the woman. I spoke to her yesterday.
2 Five students were asked. None of them knew the answer.
3 We got a lift to the cinema. Without it we would have missed the beginning of the film.
4 The guests arrived. They were all wearing their best clothes.
5 He is the friend. I borrowed the car from him.

ANYBODY THERE?

FIRST THOUGHTS

Young children often have imaginary friends. Why do you think this happens? What qualities would you want an imaginary friend to have?

READING

1 Doris Stokes was a famous medium. She claimed she was able to contact the spirits of the dead. Read her story quickly and find out

1 how she felt about her imaginary friends.
2 how her imaginary friends helped her.
3 when she had her first psychic experience.

Imaginary friends

by Doris Stokes

'My mother warned me that I'd end up in a mental hospital.'

We have all heard of children who have imaginary playmates. I get lots of letters from parents about them and I always say the same thing: don't say there is no one there. What you are putting down to imagination could be a spirit child.

One dad wrote to me to say he was getting very worried about his child. He told me his son had an imaginary friend called Robbie, and was forever saying things like, " Don't set off yet, Robbie's not in the car."

I told him, "Your child can actually see that boy, love. Don't say anything. He'll either grow out of it and go on to more worldly things or he'll develop into a very good medium."

I was about six or seven when I first saw the spirit children. I'd had rheumatic fever and had to be in a pushchair. I don't know how, but I knew that other people could not see Christopher and Pansy. I saw them a lot. And you know, I never could do maths – it was a mystery to me – but Christopher and Pansy helped me pass my exams!

So there's nothing frightening· about children having imaginary friends, especially if they've been very close. I remember one little lad telling his mum, "You don't have to turn off the light tonight. Grandma will do it."

His mum watched him go upstairs on his own that night and the lights went off! It scares the life out of some parents. But you just have to accept that his grandma loved him very much. She'd always tucked him in. It was a routine.

Most children are psychic up to the age of 11 or 12. My first psychic experience happened when I was four. I woke up to a commotion outside in the street.

There was a fire in the house nearby, and all the neighbours were crying. They kept saying "Poor Tom, what a terrible way to die." As I peered from between their legs, I saw a stretcher with little Tom on it, and Tom was also walking beside it. I told my dad I'd seen Tom and he said, "If you did, love, then you did." You see, I'd seen Tom's spirit walking beside him.

My mother warned me that I'd end up in a mental hospital. I did. Nearly 40 years later I was a nurse in one!

2 Choose the best answer (**A**, **B**, **C** or **D**) to these questions.

1 What does Doris say about imaginary playmates?
  A They are commonplace.
  B They are definitely imaginary.
  C They write letters.
  D There is no such thing.

2 What is her advice to the father who wrote?
  A Tell your son Robbie doesn't exist.
  B Your son is a good storyteller.
  C It could be a stage he is going through.
  D Make a special place for Robbie.

3 What was special about Doris's contact with Pansy and Christopher?
  A She only met them a few times.
  B She had been ill.
  C They ran and played together.
  D They helped her with their schoolwork.

4 Children who have psychic experiences
  A are generally frightened by them.
  B often see friends.
  C either see friends or grandparents.
  D always see someone who's been close.

5 What did the mother think when the light went out?
  A This is scary.
  B Grandmother always does it.
  C He's being naughty.
  D There's nothing to worry about.

6 What does Doris claim about the psychic powers of children?
  A Children over 12 aren't psychic.
  B Children tend to lose their powers after 12.
  C Children are only psychic until 12.
  D A few children are psychic at some point.

7 What happened after the fire?
  A Doris knew Tom wasn't dead.
  B She knew she had seen the fire before in a dream.
  C Her father had seen Tom's spirit too.
  D Her father said he believed what she told him.

8 Doris' mother
  A thought Doris was going mad.
  B became psychic herself.
  C thought Doris was psychic.
  D knew Doris was going to become a nurse.

VOCABULARY

Ways of looking

*she **peered** through someone's legs.*
Using these dictionary definitions, complete the sentences which follow with a way of looking.

gaze /geɪz/ to look steadily, often with admiration
peer /pɪə/ to look very carefully or hard, especially if it is hard to see
look /lʊk/ to turn the eyes so as to see, examine or find something
see /siː/ to use the eyes, have the power of sight
stare /steə/ to look at someone or something without moving your eyes
glance /glɑːns/ to give a rapid look
watch /wɒtʃ/ to look at some event or activity

1 They sat on the bench and .... the tennis match.
2 He quickly .... over his shoulder to see if anyone was following him.
3 She wound down her car window and .... at the sign in the fog.
4 Do you think you could .... at the engine for me? It doesn't seem to be working properly.
5 Have you ever .... a ghost?
6 The child .... at the woman's strange hat for a good five minutes.
7 They stood on the hill and .... at the river.

LANGUAGE STUDY

Abbreviating clauses

1 *I'd seen Tom's spirit **walking** beside him.*

Study these two examples. What are the differences between them?

1 We saw them. They were opening the door.
  → *We saw them opening the door.*
2 We saw a plane. It crashed into the mountain.
  → *We saw a plane crash into the mountain.*

2 Join these pairs of sentences in the same way.

1 We felt the ground. It started to shake.
2 Anna noticed a strange smell. It was coming from a cupboard.
3 Did you hear their dog? It was barking all night.
4 The police officer caught the thief. He was climbing through the window.

IT'S YOU AGAIN!

1 Some people and some religions believe in reincarnation. In other words, they believe that when people die their spirits are reborn in a different form. What do people in your class believe?

Proving the truth of reincarnation

Did you know?...

• Hypnotism has been used to help people recall their past lives. Two of the most interesting cases concern Jane Evans and a woman called Dolores.
• Jane claimed to remember seven lives including being a servant to one of the wives of King Henry VIII and a murder victim.
• Under hypnosis Dolores took on the character of a German woman called Gretchen and spoke German even though she'd never used the language before.

2 What is happening in the pictures? What is the connection with the notes in the box?

LISTENING

James, Malcolm and Yolanda are discussing reincarnation. Listen to their conversation and answer the questions by writing

J (for James),
M (for Malcolm) or
Y (for Yolanda).

1 Who is convinced that there is some truth in reincarnation?
2 Who finds the evidence for reincarnation quite strong ?
3 Who thinks that the use of hypnotism is ridiculous?
4 Who is the first to suggest a logical explanation for Jane Evans's past lives?
5 Who is interested in discussing other cases?
6 Who thinks Dolores's knowledge of German is significant?
7 Who thinks Dolores was trying to trick people?

PRONUNCIATION

Rising intonation

1 ▭ When James says he has been reading a book about reincarnation, Malcolm comments *Reincarnation! Ah, you surely don't believe in that.*

Notice the way he says **reincarnation**. His voice rises. This **tune** is often used to express disbelief.

Listen to the recording again and stop the cassette every time you hear this particular tune. Try to copy the intonation.

2 ▭ Listen to these six phrases. Is the speaker showing surprise, showing disbelief or making a simple statement? Write **S**, **D** or **ST**.

1 His own daughter. ☐
2 His own daughter. ☐
3 His own daughter. ☐
4 By car. ☐
5 By car. ☐
6 By car. ☐

LANGUAGE STUDY

Inversion

1 In the listening James says **No sooner had she** *told the story* **than** *some archaeologists found the cellar.* Notice that the sentence begins with **No sooner**. This is an adverb of negative force meaning 'as soon as' or 'just after'.

Look at these pairs of sentences. All the **B** sentences have an adverb of negative force at the beginning.

1 A As soon as she had told the story some archaeologists found the cellar.
　B No sooner had she told the story than some archaeologists found the cellar.
2 A She not only made a lot of mistakes but she also also avoided using verbs.
　B Not only did she make a lot of mistakes but she avoided using verbs.
3 A Shortly after she told them her tale they discovered the skeleton.
　B Hardly had she told them her tale than they discovered the skeleton.
4 A We had never seen such a thing before.
　B Never before had we seen such a thing.

2 Now answer these questions about the pairs of sentences in Exercise 1.

1 What difference in meaning, if any, is there between the sentences in each pair? Which is more dramatic/emphatic?
2 What happens to the subject and auxiliary verb in the **B** sentences? What other elements do we need to include with some of the forms?
3 When do you think we would tend to use the **B** forms more: in speech or in writing?
4 Which part of the **B** sentences would normally be stressed?

Note: In Unit 2 we saw that inversion is used when we make short replies.
Example: A: *I like chocolate.*　B: *So do I.*

3 Re-formulate the sentences, beginning with the adverbs in brackets. Make any other changes that are necessary.

1 The moment she arrived she started to complain. *(No sooner)*
2 He both sings and dances. *(Not only)*
3 I had never eaten such an awful meal. *(Never)*
4 When the match started, fighting broke out. *(No sooner)*
5 The moment I got into the bath the phone rang. *(Hardly)*
6 It was the most wonderful book I have ever read. *(Never)*

WRITING

Compulsory letter

You decided to go on a short break to The White Horse Hotel. Unfortunately nothing was as you had been led to expect. Using the notes, write a letter to the hotel manager about the night you spent there.

The White Horse Hotel
14th-century inn in the heart of the countryside.
Own friendly ghost!
All rooms with 21st-century facilities.

Notes　Bathroom: no soap / towels.
Food was terrible! Worst meal ever!
Went to bed – noisy, bed uncomfortable. Fell asleep at two o'clock. Moment fell asleep, woke up again.
Terrifying noises from ghost – not friendly at all.
Shook chains and made terrible groans.

CHILLING TALES

FIRST THOUGHTS

1 Which book, film or story has most frightened you?

2 What elements are important for an exciting supernatural story?

VOCABULARY

Extreme adjectives

1 In the discussion about reincarnation on p.152, James says *There are some **fascinating** stories in this book.*

Fascinating means **very interesting**. In this box there are other pairs of adjectives with similar meanings. Match them up. Can you think of any other pairs of adjectives that like these?

gorgeous   cold   boiling   huge   starving   tiny
big   terrified   tired   fascinating   sure
frightened   interesting   hungry   bad   positive
freezing   awful   wonderful   exhausted   small
hot   beautiful   good

2 Look at the sentences and decide which are right and which are wrong.

1 It's very cold.
2 It's very freezing.
3 It's absolutely freezing.
4 It's absolutely cold.
5 It's really cold.
6 It's really freezing.

How can we modify ordinary adjectives like **cold** and extreme adjectives like **freezing**?

3 Complete these sentences using an appropriate adjective from the box above.

1 After the walk, we were .... as we had not eaten all day.
2 The room was really .... He had to stand on the bed to close the door.
3 Can you close the door? It's .... in here !
4 Don't eat in that restaurant. The food is ....
5 "You look great after your holiday!" "Yes, I feel ...."

6 He was so .... when he saw the spider that he fainted.
7 What a(n) .... dress! It's the most beautiful one I've ever seen.
8 The book was so .... that she read it in one go.
9 They live in a(n) .... house. It's got ten bedrooms and six bathrooms.
10 I didn't sleep at all last night. I feel totally ....
11 I'm absolutely .... he used to be a policeman.
12 I'm not really very .... I had a big breakfast.

4 Anna is asking questions. Listen to how Martin, who always exaggerates, replies.

ANNA: Are you cold?
MARTIN: Cold? I'm absolutely freezing.
ANNA: Is that an interesting book?
MARTIN: Interesting? It's absolutely fascinating.
ANNA: Was the film bad?
MARTIN: Bad? It was absolutely awful.
ANNA: Are you tired?
MARTIN: Tired? I'm absolutely exhausted.

1 What happens to Martin's voice when he repeats the adjective in Anna's question? How does he pronounce the extreme adjective in the answer?
2 Listen again and copy Martin's intonation as closely as you can.
3 Working in pairs, take it in turns to practise the questions and replies. Then invent further exchanges using other extreme adjectives.

WRITING

The mysterious hitchhiker

In Unit 4 we looked at telling a story. Here is some more practice.

1 Read the two versions of the same story and note what the differences between them are. Think about vocabulary, grammar and style.

Version 1

ONE NIGHT a friend of mine was driving past one of the cemeteries outside Rome. By the side of the road he saw a girl of about 18 who was hitchhiking. He stopped to pick her up and, as she looked cold, lent her his jacket.

She told him where to go and he took her to a block of flats in a small street. As she got out, she held out the jacket but Carlo told her to keep it and that he would see her another time. She smiled and went into the building.

A few days later, Carlo went back to find her. When he told an old woman the girl's description, she told him that the girl used to live there but had died a couple of years before.

Three months later Carlo went to the cemetery to put some flowers on his mother's grave. As he was leaving the cemetery, he noticed his jacket on another gravestone. When he picked it up, he saw the photograph of the girl he had given a lift to.

Version 2

ONE COLD WINTER'S EVENING, Carlo, an old friend of mine, was driving past one of the huge cemeteries just outside Rome. It was freezing cold and he happened to notice a young girl hitchhiking by the side of the road. Even though it was winter, she was wearing just a thin dress.

Carlo pulled up and opened the passenger door to let her in. Her lips were blue with cold so he gave her the jacket he was wearing to put over her shoulders. After a few moments' silence, he asked her where she wanted to go and she whispered some instructions. He glanced at her and noticed for the first time that she was extremely beautiful. She had a delicate pale face with long blonde hair and large green eyes. He wondered what she had been doing standing by the side of the road and guessed that she looked so sad because she had had a row with her boyfriend who had left her there.

They drove on in silence, the girl making little gestures to show him which route to take. They finally turned into a narrow street in an old part of town. As soon as the girl got out, she took off the jacket and held it out to Carlo. He refused to take it because she still looked cold and he wanted an excuse to see her again. She smiled mysteriously and disappeared through a dark doorway, without saying a word... .

2 In pairs, write the end of the second version of the story, using words and expressions you have learnt in this unit.

3 Write a composition on this subject. *You were walking through the countryside one day with a friend when you came across a ruined mansion. Describe what happened.*

USE OF ENGLISH

1 Read the text below and decide which word **A**, **B**, **C** or **D** best fits each space. There is an example at the beginning **(0)**.

We were watching TV **(0)** ..when.. we heard a lot of barking coming from our kitchen. There, we came **(1)** .... Jasper, our dog, throwing a furry bundle around the room. This turned **(2)** .... to be Flopsie, the pet rabbit **(3)** .... to the children next door. We had already been in **(4)** .... with our neighbours as Jasper had dug up half of their garden. Jasper had obviously broken **(5)** .... the rabbit's hutch and killed it.

We knew that the neighbours were out and that we had to **(6)** .... quickly. I gave Flopsie a soapy bath and my wife dried and brushed its fur **(7)** .... it looked as good as new. Making sure the coast was **(8)** ...., I jumped over the fence and placed Flopsie lovingly in its home. Ten minutes **(9)** .... we heard the Greenaway's car come back and sat in our kitchen **(10)** .... with anticipation.

All of a sudden, there was a loud **(11)** .... of terror from outside. Naturally, we could not **(12)** .... it and went out with a look of concern on our faces. Mrs Greenaway stood white-faced **(13)** .... the fence with Flopsie in her arms. "What's the **(14)** ....?", I asked. "Is anything wrong with Flopsie?" "Flopsie's dead," she cried, "but what is extraordinary is that we **(15)** .... her last week!"

```
 0  A as       B while     C when      D that
 1  A across   B into      C out       D up
 2  A off      B out       C into      D down
 3  A possessed  B owing    C owned     D belonging
 4  A problems  B argument  C trouble   D difficult
 5  A up       B into      C off       D with
 6  A act      B make      C perfom    D behave
 7  A during   B once      C until     D that
 8  A empty    B free      C clear     D open
 9  A afterwards  B ago     C after     D later
10  A shivering  B trembling  C yawning  D gasping
11  A crash    B splash     C scream    D sigh
12  A forget   B defy       C ignore    D deny
13  A on   B in   C by      D off
14  A matter   B wrong      C happening  D up
15  A dug      B planted    C buried    D grave
```

2 Read the text below and think of the word which best fits each space.

Most ghost stories are set in mysterious old houses or castles. The ghosts themselves, **(0)** ..whose.. spirits wander the earth, **(1)** .... usually the victims of some horrible crime. This is not always the case as the **(2)** .... story shows.

When my friend Paul was a schoolboy, he often **(3)** .... to chat to Mr Scott, an elderly gentleman living on his **(4)** .... Mr Scott was a keen gardener. He would **(5)** .... be looking after his lawn or his flowers and Paul was in the habit of saying a **(6)** .... words to him over the fence.

One summer's evening, as Paul was making his **(7)** .... home from school, he saw, as usual, Mr Scott in his garden. **(8)** .... old man was busily weeding his flower beds. When he saw Paul, he invited him into the garden with a **(9)** .... of his hand. Slowly, they strolled round, admiring the flower beds. Then, to Paul's surprise, Mr Scott bent down and picked a bunch of his finest dahlias. "Here boy," he said. "Give **(10)** .... to your mother."

No **(11)** .... had he arrived home than he presented the flowers to his mother. He then told her that they were with Mr Scott's compliments. His mother's face went red **(12)** .... anger. "You wicked boy!" she shouted. "How dare you say **(13)** .... a thing! I bumped **(14)** .... his daughter in the supermarket this morning. She told me that the poor old chap passed **(15)** .... in his sleep last Friday."

USE OF ENGLISH

1 What do you know about the pyramids of Egypt and why they were built?

2 Quickly read the text and find out if there is any new or surprising information in it.

3 Now decide which lines are correct (✔) and which contain an extra word which should not be there.

  0 It seems that the mystery of why the Pyramids ✓
00 were built may have been solved. Until **a** quite
  1 recently people got used to think that they
  2 were just tombs for pharaohs. Instead, of
  3 the connection with astronomy seems too much
  4 more important. Egyptologists they have often
  5 asked themselves how long time it took
  6 to build them and why did build them in the first
  7 place. Experts came up with it a suggestion that the
  8 Egyptians may have believed in the River Nile
  9 was the earthly equivalent exact of the Milky
10 Way. Many are agree that the sizes of the three Giza
11 pyramids are in proportion to the three stars of
12 Orion. Nothing, then, was by the chance.
13 Rather, than the souls of dead pharaohs were
14 deliberately being projected through shafts to
15 reach at their goal of the Orion constellation.

READING

Creatures of the night

1 You are going to read some information about six creatures of the night. For questions **1-13** choose from the creatures (**A-F**). Some of the creatures may be chosen more than once. Where more than one answer is required, these may be given in any order. There is an example at the beginning (**0**).

The cries of which creatures warn of a death to come?

| 0 | A | | 1 | |

Which one is always hungry? | 2 | |

Which two can bear good will to humans?

| 3 | | | 4 | |

Which one makes the most awful noise? | 5 | |

If you see this one, you would be advised to move house. | 6 | |

Which one has no clear form? | 7 | |

Which creatures behaviour is compared with the behaviour of a similar creature? | 8 | |

For which creatures are we given special advice about how to protect ourselves? | 9 | | | 10 | |

Which creature might be used to punish an enemy?

| 11 | |

Which creatures harm, but do not kill, their victims?

| 12 | | | 13 | |

2 Which of the creatures do you think is the most/least terrifying?

Do any of them corrrespond with creatures from your own country or culture?

A The Banshee

Banshees are female spirits of the Gaelic and Celtic peoples. They are rarely seen but often heard. A banshee is said to be a woman with long black hair and eyes red from weeping and dressed in a green robe and grey cloak. She has an appalling cry, described by some who have heard it as a blend between the howling of a wolfhound, the cry of wild geese, the screams of an abandoned child, and the groans of a woman in labour.

The wail of a banshee has only one meaning – that a member of the family which hears it is doomed to die.

B The Duppy

A type of ghost raised by people of the West Indies to perform some service, usually of revenge. A duppy is raised by calling the name of a dead person continuously over their grave until the duppy arises through the earth and awaits instructions.

A duppy can only cause vomiting by breathing on the victim or convulsions by touching him or her. When it has performed the task, it should be rewarded by placing rum and tobacco on the grave.

Anyone who has reason to fear duppy-attack may keep them away by sprinkling tobacco seed around the house.

C Menahune

Night spirits of the Hawaiian Islands. They are unusual spirits because they are helpful rather than dangerous. Like the brownies of the British Isles, the menahune appear when the household is asleep and do all the housework. It seems, however, that the menahune are very particular about their employers. They do their work only for families which they feel to be especially pleasant and kind. Very few people have seen the menahune, which are believed to have pointed ears, shaggy black hair and tiny agile bodies.

D Abiku

An insatiable demon of the night which preys upon the Yoruba people of West Africa. Parents living in the little villages huddled deep in the forest are terrified of Abiku because his diet consists of children. He relishes nothing better than a plump, newborn child. As soon as the sun sets, parents rush their children into the huts, and sometimes hide them under mats or blankets so that Abiku will not find them.

Nobody seems able to give a definite description of Abiku, except he is as shapeless as smoke. Everyone agrees, however, on his principal peculiarity. He has no stomach, and is therefore obliged to eat continuously because he never knows the satisfaction of feeling full.

E The Azeman

A rare example of a vampire actually appearing in the form of a vampire bat. Fortunately the azeman is restricted to certain regions of north-eastern South America. The azeman is invariably a woman. During the day she appears to be perfectly normal, but after dark she changes into a bat and flies around the village in search of victims. In normal vampire bat style, she seeks a sleeper whose foot is exposed and sucks the blood. Luckily it is easy to prevent an azeman from entering one's hut simply by propping a broom across the doorway.

F Domovoi and Domovikha

These are Russian household spirits. On the whole they are benign spirits, who live beneath the stove or doorstep or in the cellar. When a family moves into a new home, it is wise to place a piece of bread beneath the stove to attract Domovoi. His wife accompanies him but lives in the cellar.

Domovikha never speaks, but one may hear Domovoi during the night. When he chatters and murmurs softly, the family may be sure that nothing unpleasant is likely to happen. But when he sobs or groans loudly it is a sign of misfortune, and Domovoi weeping is a sure sign of a death in the family.

Humans rarely see Domovoi and never see Domovikha. It may be that he resembles a small man covered with silky hair, who might be mistaken for a dog or cat. A Domovoi sighting is extremely unfortunate and, and if he does appear, it may be better for the family to move house.

LISTENING

Match the replies to the speakers

1 Listen to the replies given by five women to the question *If you came back in another life, what would you like to be and why?*

A A creator of religious harmony.   Speaker 1 ☐
B A pop star.   Speaker 2 ☐
C A top model.   Speaker 3 ☐
D A work of art.   Speaker 4 ☐
E An sportswoman.   Speaker 5 ☐
F Her country's leader.

2 What would *you* like to come back as?

14 Destination USA

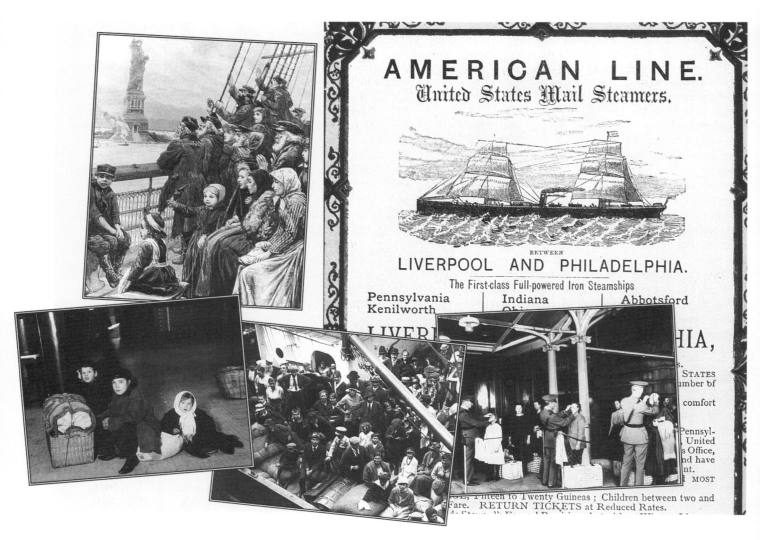

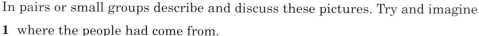

NEW HORIZONS

FIRST THOUGHTS

In pairs or small groups describe and discuss these pictures. Try and imagine

1 where the people had come from.
2 why they had left their old homes.
3 how they felt.

SPEAKING

Discussion points

1 Have you or anyone in your family ever considered emigrating?
2 What circumstances would make you leave your own country?
3 If you had to, which country would you emigrate to and why?
4 Do you have any relatives who have emigrated?
5 How easy or difficult would it be for a foreigner to settle down in your country?

VOCABULARY

1 What is the difference between to **immigrate** and to **emigrate**? What nouns can you form from them?

2 Complete the sentences using the words from the box. Make any changes to the word that are necessary.

1 The ex-president spent the rest of his life in .... in a distant country.
2 Thousands of .... filled the roads as they tried to escape from the war zone.
3 Unfortunately, some people escape only to find themselves the victims of .... in the host country.
4 I feel so .... I wish I could go home and see my family and friends.
5 They were extremely ....; they welcomed me into their home and made me feel like one of the family.
6 It was difficult for him to really .... with the others because the colour of his skin and his hair made him look strange.
7 At first she found it very difficult to .... The culture, food and weather were so different, but eventually she managed to .... most things.
8 They escaped from their country and asked for political .... in Canada.
9 You can't enter the country unless you have a valid ....

settle down   fit in   refugee   asylum   exile   get used to   prejudice   homesick
hospitable   visa

USE OF ENGLISH

1 Quickly read the text and find out who the couple in the picture are, what their problem is, and if their story has a happy ending.

2 Complete the text by changing the word in capital letters at the end of the line into a suitable form to fill the gap. There is an example at the beginning (**0**).

Green Card is a (**0**) romantic... comedy about a couple called George and   **ROMANCE**
Bronte. It is set in New York. George is a French (**1**) .... who can't   **COMPOSE**
get a Green Card (a working visa). Bronte is an American
horticulturist who wants to rent an apartment with a greenhouse.
(**2**)........... the apartment is only available to married couples, not single   **FORTUNE**
people. George and Bronte are introduced and in (**3**)........ they agree to   **DESPERATE**
a (**4**)........... of convenience. She gets the apartment and George is   **MARRY**
eligible for a Green Card. An (**5**).......... official is highly   **IMMIGRATE**
(**6**).......... of the arrangement and wants to interview them to check if   **SUSPECT**
the visa is (**7**)............ .   **JUSTIFY**
   The couple have to invent an instant history with (**8**)...........   **HUMOUR**
consequences. Before too long the (**9**)........... suspicions   **INVESTIGATE**
(**10**)............. and George makes a full   **DEEP**
(**11**).......... . He leaves the country but by now he and Bronte are   **CONFESS**
genuinely in love. The (**12**).......... is that even though George is   **SUGGEST**
forced to leave, they will continue their romance.

SPEAKING

Work in groups of four, **Pair A** and **Pair B**.

PAIR A: One of you is a US resident. The other wants a visa. You have to convince immigration officials that there is a family connection between you and that you know each other well, e.g. you are brother/sister/husband/wife. Swap information on these areas: favourite food, music, books, family members, pets, description of family home, education. Pair B, the immigration officers, will try to "break" your story.

PAIR B: See page 165.

A SENSE OF LIBERTY

FIRST THOUGHTS

When people think of the United States, they may think of the Statue of Liberty or Coca Cola! What do you think people associate with your country?

LISTENING

There is nothing that symbolises the United States more than the Statue of Liberty. Listen to the tour guide and complete the notes.

The Statue was a present from the people of France to the USA to mark the **(1)**.......... between the two nations. In her right hand Liberty carries a torch and in her left a tablet on which the date **(2)**.......... is written. The sculptor who made it was Frederic **(3)**.......... . It is made of **(4)**.......... sheets. It was finished in **(5)**.......... . It weighs **(6)**.......... . The statue is **(7)**.......... feet high without the pedestal. With the pedestal its height in metres is **(8)**.......... . There are **(9)**.......... steps to the observation point. The statue was dedicated by President **(10)**.......... .

READING

1 Read the text and answer the questions.

1 How many people emigrated from Europe between 1815 and 1914?
2 When was the Irish potato famine?
3 How many foreign-born Americans were there in 1890?
4 What was the number of black slaves in 1860?

2 Read the text again and choose the most suitable heading from the list **A-I** for each part **(1-7)** of the article. There is one extra heading which you do not need to use. There is an example at the beginning **(0)**.

A	Freedom to Pray
B	An Enduring Dream
C	One in Seven
D	The Balance Changes
E	The Journey to Despair
F	Jobs and Land
G	Flight from Hunger
H	Europe in Crisis
I	The Great Adventure

THE MELTING POT

0 I

The USA is a land of immigrants. Between 1815 and 1914, the world witnessed the greatest migration in its history: 35 million people, mostly Europeans, left their homelands to start new lives in America. Why did these people risk everything by leaving their homes and families to see what the New World had to offer? How had the Old World let them down? There are both push and pull factors which we should consider.

1

First, what forced emigrants to make the momentous decision to leave? One major cause of the exodus among European peasants was the rise in population which in turn led to land hunger. Another was politics. Nationalism saw increased taxation and the growth of armies, and many young men fled eastern Europe to avoid being conscripted. Also, the failure of the liberal revolutions in Europe caused the departure of thousands of refugees.

Al Pacino – his family came from Italy

2

Physical hunger provided another pressing reason. Between 1845 and 1848, the terrible potato famine in Ireland ended in the deaths of one million Irish people and the emigration of a further million who wished to escape starvation. Following the collapse of the economy of southern Italy in the 1860s, hundreds of thousands of Italians decided to start afresh in America.

Ronald Reagan in Ireland discovering his roots

3

Religion also encouraged millions to leave the Old World. We should remember that the Pilgrim Fathers had wished to escape the ungodliness of England, while the Russian Jews of the last century sought to escape persecution and death in their native land.

4

n short, people chose to leave their homes for social, economic and religious reasons. As a result, by 1890 among a total population of 63 million, there were more than 9 million foreign-born Americans.

5

But what were the attractions? First of all, there was the promise of land which was so scarce in Europe. Next, factories were calling out for labour, and pay and conditions were much better than back home. Men were needed to open up the West and build the long railroads, and settlers were needed to populate new towns and develop commerce. There was the space for religious communities to practise their faith in peace and comparative isolation.

6

This immigration meant that by around the 1850s Americans of non-English extraction had started to outnumber those of English extraction. As we know, there were losers. To start with, there were those unwilling immigrants, the slaves who had been used as a source of cheap labour for the tobacco plantations of the South. Nor should we forget the equally awful fate of the American Indians. By 1860 there were 27 million free whites, four million slaves and a mere 488,000 free blacks.

7

Nowadays, the USA is still seen by millions as the Promised Land. Gone are the days when you could buy US citizenship for one dollar. Yet, even though entry is strictly limited, refugees continue to find freedom there and people from poorer countries a better way of life. As always, the USA remains a magnet to the ambitious and the energetic who are ready to commit themselves to the land that gives them a second chance.

LANGUAGE STUDY

Numbers

By 1860 there were twenty-seven million free whites, four million slaves and a mere four hundred and eighty-eight thousand free blacks.

Where necessary, correct these sentences.

1 She lived for hundred years.
2 The population of the USA is over two hundred millions.
3 Five thousands of people visit the gallery every day.

4 My telephone number is twenty four, thirty three, eight hundred and ninety-five.
5 I would like one dozen of eggs, please.
6 The code for London is nought one seven one.
7 Dozens of people walked out of the film.
8 The book is one hundred eighty pages long.
9 Altogether that's three pounds and sixty-five.
10 The average family has two comma four children.
11 The drawer is an eighth of an inch too wide.
12 There were thousands of people at the party.
13 The Battle of Waterloo was in one thousand eight hundred and fifteen.
14 My car does thirty miles for one gallon of petrol.

LISTENING

Listen to the numbers and write them down.

1 **Phone numbers**
   A .... B....................

2 **Account numbers**
   A .... B....................

3 **Decimals**
   A .... B....................
   C ....

4 **Fractions**
   A .... B....................
   C .... D....................

5 **Dates**
   A .... B....................
   C ....

6 **Amounts**
   A .... B....................

7 **Scores**
   A Agassi won the match ....
   B Italy beat Holland ....

8 **Large numbers**
   A .... B....................
   C .... D....................

PRONUNCIATION

1 Listen to the phone and account numbers again and try to copy the rhythm and intonation. How are the numbers broken up?

2 In pairs, give each other these telephone numbers as if you were speaking over the phone.

A
1 635 4551
2 289 6412
3 00 88 4842 6780

B
4 0145 75551
5 00 36 5421 5331
6 4524

LANGUAGE STUDY

The gerund and the infinitive

1 Study these two sentences.
*They **chose to leave** their homes for social, economic and religious reasons.*
*Immigrants **risked losing** their lives in the West.*

If we want to follow **choose** with another verb, we must put the second verb into the **infinitive**.
We can't say ~~They chose emigrating~~.

If we want to follow **risk** with another verb, we must put the second verb into the **gerund**. We can't say ~~They risked to lose their lives~~.

2 Complete these sentences by putting the verb in brackets into either the **infinitive** or the **gerund**.

1 Have you ever considered .... (*emigrate*)?
2 The customs officer refused .... (*let*) him into the country.
3 They denied .... (*enter*) the country illegally.
4 The government agreed .... (*allow*) the refugees over the border.
5 They threatened .... (*deport*) her on the next flight.
6 He avoided .... (*cross*) the bridge by swimming the river.
7 The tourists offered .... (*hide*) her in the boot of their car.
8 Would you mind .... (*show*) me your passport, sir?
9 Have you finished .... (*fill in*) that form?
10 He pretended not .... (*understand*) the regulations.
11 Immigration officials tend .... (*be*) suspicious.

3 Now divide the verbs in the exercise into those that are followed by the infinitive and those that are followed by the gerund. Can you add to the list?

+ infinitive	+ gerund
choose	risk

4 Look at these pairs of sentences. Decide where there is
• little or no change in meaning
• an important change in meaning.

1 **a** It started to rain.
   b It started raining.
2 **a** He remembered to close the window.
   b He remembered closing the window.
3 **a** I like to play tennis.
   b I like playing tennis.
4 **a** I like to go to the dentist twice a year.
   b I like going to the dentist.
5 **a** They stopped to look at the map.
   b They stopped looking at the map.
6 **a** I meant to apologise.
   b It meant apologising.
7 **a** She tried to learn Japanese.
   b She tried learning ten new words a day.

5 Put the verbs in brackets into the **gerund** or the **infinitive**. Sometimes, both may be possible. Look carefully at the context you are given.

1 Don't forget .... (*go*) to the travel agent's, will you? The plane tickets need .... (*pick up*).
2 I shall never forget .... (*see*) the Statue of Liberty for the first time.
3 Oh, no! It's starting .... (*rain*).
4 I like .... (*play*) tennis but I wouldn't like .... (*play*) with her. She's such a bad loser.
5 Lucia started .... (*study*) English six years ago.
6 I meant .... (*tell*) you about the party but I completely forgot.
7 I didn't tell her about the party because it would have meant .... (*invite*) her and her boyfriend.
8 Do try .... (*make*) less noise. I'm trying .... (*concentrate*).
9 He remembers .... (*drive*) up to the crossroads but nothing else after the accident.
10 Have you ever stopped .... (*wonder*) why she behaves like that?
11 We really need .... (*do*) some shopping; we're running out of everything.
12 I've tried .... (*jog*) and aerobics, but I still can't lose weight.
13 I'm terribly sorry but I forgot .... (*post*) your letter.
14 Did you remember .... (*do*) your homework?
15 I'll stop .... (*lend*) you money if you waste it on cigarettes.
16 'I can't get this table through the door.'
   'Really? Have you tried .... (*take off*) the legs?'

LISTENING

One group who went West were the Mormans. They wanted to be free to follow thier beliefs. Listen to these two friends discussing the Mormons and decide if these statements are **True** or **False**.

1 Gina is no longer a Mormon.
2 Mormonism is a Christian religion.
3 It dates from 1727.
4 Smith was visited by Mormon.
5 There are similarities with the Old Testament.

6 The plates were written in Hebrew.
7 Mormonism quickly became popular.
8 The plates may have come from Israel.
9 The dead can be included in the church.
10 Mormons have more than one wife.

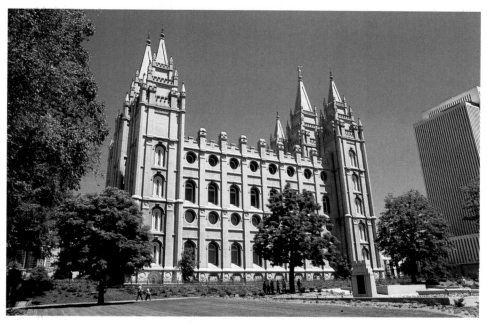

The Mormon Tabernacle, Salt Lake City

SPEAKING

(From page 161.)

PAIR B: You are immigration officers. Try to "break" Pair A's story and prove that they have no family connection and that they do not know each other very well. Interview each of **PAIR A** individually and make a note of the answers.

You can only ask questions on these areas: favourite food, music, books, family members, pets, description of family home, education.

When you have finished, swap roles and repeat the procedure.

FIRST THOUGHTS

Work in pairs. Discuss the differences and similarities between the two pairs of pictures.

1

2

USE OF ENGLISH

1 Read the first text and find its connection with the first two photographs you discussed.

2 Read the text again and decide which word **A**, **B**, **C** or **D** best fits each space. There is an example at the beginning (**0**).

The all time American hero has to be the cowboy seen in (**0**) countless Westerns and TV serials. Good guys wore white hats, (**1**).......... those the baddies wore were always black. In (**2**).......... you knew everybody would be white – (**3**).......... from the red Indians, who were there to be slaughtered. The (**4**).......... belief that the only cowboys were white is (**5**).......... by the facts. Even though you (**6**).......... ever see a black face in cowboy films, (**7**).......... a quarter and a third were Negroes.

The famous cowboy (**8**).......... as Deadwood Dick who has been played by white actors was in (**9**).......... an ex-slave and civil war veteran. Only such people (**10**).......... by a tough physical existence could (**11**).......... the challenges of life as a cowboy. Outlaws and sheriffs included their fair (**12**).......... of black men too. The wicked and (**13**).......... outlaw Belle Starr was half Negro and half Native American, (**14**).......... she was played by the white actress Barbara Stanwyck. Isn't it time we (**15**).......... a more accurate portrayal of the wild west on our screens?

0 **A** counted   **B** uncountable
   C countless   **D** numbered.
1 **A** yet   **B** while   **C** so   **D** then
2 **A** case   **B** addition   **C** time
   D fact
3 **A** apart   **B** except   **C** rather
   D instead
4 **A** varied   **B** large   **C** widespread
   D vast
5 **A** criticised   **B** contrasted
   C contradicted   **D** confirmed
6 **A** seldom   **B** nearly   **C** almost
   D hardly
7 **A** about   **B** roughly   **C** between
   D within

8 **A** known   **B** called   **C** referred
   D nicknamed
9 **A** really   **B** truthful   **C** reality
   D factual
10 **A** used   **B** hardened   **C** tough
   D accustomed
11 **A** make   **B** take   **C** do   **D** have
12 **A** portion   **B** amount   **C** share
   D ration
13 **A** famous   **B** well-known
   C reputable   **D** notorious
14 **A** despite   **B** yet   **C** although
   D then
15 **A** took   **B** had   **C** made
   D received

A

B

3 Quickly read the text and find the connection it has with the photographs above. Then think of one word to fill each gap.

Baseball, **(0)**....<u>rather</u>.... than American football, is the national game of the USA. So it is quite understandable that Americans are proud of it and **(1)**.......... it extremely seriously. It is hardly surprising **(2)**.......... that English claims that the game was based on rounders **(3)**.......... in upsetting a lot of people. Particularly as rounders is a gentle game for people not tough **(4)**.......... to play England's national sport – cricket!

The argument caused so **(5)**.......... controversy that a special commission was **(6)**.......... up in 1905 to establish the truth. **(7)**.......... surprisingly, it decided that baseball had been invented in New York in 1839.

Since then baseball has been taken up **(8)**.......... over the world. In recent years, South American countries **(9)**.......... come to dominate **(10)**.......... amateur game. Cuba has already won the championship no **(11)**.......... than 18 times.

The game has also **(12)**.......... on in Australia and Japan. So **(13)**..........so that these countries can now field quite impressive teams. These developments gave one of the **(14)**.......... blows to American sporting pride at the Los Angeles Olympics of 1984, where the Japanese **(15)**.......... to beat the Americans 6-3 in the championship final.

LISTENING

Gus is telling his friend Andy about the rules of American football. Listen carefully to their conversation and answer the following questions.

1 A field goal is worth
  A six points.
  B one point.
  C three points.
  D two points.

2 In American football, you can pass the ball forwards
  A as often as you like.
  B never.
  C twice in a *play*.
  D once in a *play*.

3 A *play* is
  A thirty seconds.
  B when the teams block and tackle.
  C the time between two scrimmages.
  D when the ball is passed between the players.

4 How many examples does Gus give of when the ball can change hands between teams?
  A 2.
  B 3.
  C 4.
  D 5.

5 Gus thinks that American football is
  A easy to understand.
  B twice as difficult to understand as cricket.
  C half as difficult to understand as cricket.
  D easier to understand than cricket.

FLORIDA FUN

FIRST THOUGHTS

A group of foreign school children, aged 15-17, are coming to spend a week in your country. Which places of interest would you recommend they should visit? Include if you can:

- a place of natural beauty, e.g. a famous waterfall or national park.
- a place where they can see wildlife.
- a place where they can have fun, e.g. an amusement park or theme park.
- somewhere to relax, e.g. a beach or resort.
- a place of historic interest, e.g. a castle/battlefield.
- a technical or engineering achievement, e.g. a bridge or dam.
- a place where you can see an old-fashioned/ traditional way of life.
- a museum or cultural event.

READING

You are going to read some information about the entertainment possibilities offered in Florida, USA. For questions **1-13**, choose from the attractions **A-J**. Some of the attractions may be chosen more than once. Where more than one answer is required, these may be given in any order. There is an example at the beginning.

Which attractions would you recommend for someone who:

- wants to know how films are made? [0] [A]
  [00] [J]
- wants the most frightening "on land" rides?
  [1] [ ]
- is fascinated by space and science and technology?
  [2] [ ] [3] [ ]
- loves all kinds of modern music? [4] [ ]
- wants to go surfing? [5] [ ]
- is concerned about the environment? [6] [ ]
- would like to see a spectacular parade?
- would like to see cartoons being produced? [8] [ ]
- would like to go on a world tour? [9] [ ]
- would like to watch human experts give a display of water sports? [10] [ ]
- wants to go shopping? [11] [ ] [12] [ ]
- would like to experience a ride on a water chute?
  [13] [ ]

Entertainment . . .

UNIVERSAL STUDIOS [A]

Visit Hollywood in Florida at Universal Studios – the largest working studio complex out of "Tinsel Town" itself. "Ride the movies" with King Kong, and the Ghostbusters team, take a bike ride with a difference in the ET Adventure or blast "Back to the Future" courtesy of Doc Brown... and don't miss "Jaws", Universal Studio's latest attraction.

SEA WORLD [B]

As oceans become more polluted and natural habitat continues to be lost, the conservation work carried out by Sea World becomes more important by the day. See threatened species such as the Florida manatee, giant sea turtles, sharks and dolphins - not forgetting "Shamu" the killer whale - and learn more about the fascinating undersea world and how we can protect it.

BUSCH GARDENS [C]

Turn upside down seven times on Busch Gardens' 60mph "kumba" – the largest and fastest steel roller coaster in the south-eastern United States! The "Scorpion" and "Python" offer even more thrills and excitement. At a gentler pace, explore some 300 acres of grounds where more than 3,400 animals live in the open – including chimps, gorillas, lions and giraffe.

WET 'N' WILD [D]

"Surf's up" at Wet 'n' Wild. You can "catch" 4ft waves at Surf Lagoon, "go for a spin" on the Ragin' Rapids or plunge the 76ft "freefall" of Der Stuke. The watery possibilities here are endless.

CYPRESS GARDENS [E]

More impressive each year, Florida's very first theme park offers 8,000 varieties of beautifully planted tropical gardens, the world famous Cypress Gardens waterski team, as well as the Gardens' newest attraction – Wings of Wonder Butterfly Conservatory.

...Florida style

CHURCH STREET STATION F

Downtown Orlando's complete entertainment, dining and shopping complex, Church Street Station offers you the choice of Dixieland Jazz at the legendary "Rosie O'Grady's", Country and Western, Rock & Roll – plus more besides.

KENNEDY SPACE CENTER G

Live the dream of manned space exploration. See the launch site for the Space Shuttle and many of the Apollo lunar missions, plus an array of rockets, lunar rovers and landers – even a space shuttle itself.

Walt Disney World Resort

MAGIC KINGDOM PARK H

Visit the Magic Kingdom Park and explore more than 50 attractions, entertainments and shops – making friends with your favourite Disney characters on the way. Take a ride on Big Thunder Mountain's Runaway Train, board the Jungle Cruise or laugh 'til you scream on Splash Mountain with its five-storey high-speed drop! Save time to watch the Main Street Parade, the world's most colourful procession.

EPCOT 95 I

EPCOT 95 invites you to voyage into the future and travel around the globe on a series of adventures exploring advanced science and the 21st century. Visit the Living Seas, the Universe of Energy, World Of Motion, Body Wars and Journey Into the Imagination. Then take a whirlwind trip around the 11 authentic "countries" of World Showcase before IllumiNations, a dazzling laser, fountain and fireworks display.

DISNEY-MGM STUDIOS J

Lights! Camera! Action! Disney-MGM Studios combines all the fun and excitement of thrilling attractions such as the Indiana Jones Epic Stunt Spectacular and the Great Movie Ride, with fascinating behind-the-scenes tours showing how motion pictures are made. See the Disney animators at work and watch live television in action.

LISTENING

An interviewer is talking to the Oldham family about their holiday in Florida. Answer the questions by writing **R** (Roger), **C** (Christine), or **K** (Katie).

1 Who talks about money the most? ☐
2 Who thought Sea World was the highlight of the tour? ☐
3 Who was unimpressed by the Disney experience? ☐
4 Who bought some boots? ☐
5 Who was afraid of being robbed? ☐
6 Who thinks American service is better than you would find in Europe? ☐
7 Who thinks there is no substitute for the American experience? ☐

SPEAKING

Pyramid discussion

Follow the instructions to get as much speaking practice as you can on the 'Entertainment Florida style' information.

1 On your own, decide which three places you would most like to visit.
2 Then decide on three with a partner.
3 Then make a decision as a group of five.
4 Then as a whole class!
5 Decide where you would go if you could only visit one place.

WRITING

The compulsory letter

You work at a travel agent's. A customer, Mrs Green, has asked you to suggest an itinerary for a six-day tour of Florida. Based on what you have read, and the notes below, write a letter in **120-180** words giving your suggestions.

Notes:
Mrs Green, 42. Science teacher at secondary school. Likes wildlife.
Mr Green, 44. Likes jazz. Interested in space and science. Wants to make Mandy happy.
Sandy Green, 15. He likes science and sea animals. Thinks he is too old for Magic Kingdom.
Candy Green, 13. She loves films. Keen on water sports and would like to try surfing.
Mandy Green, 13. She is crazy about Mickey Mouse and wild animals.

CULTURAL EXCHANGES

FIRST THOUGHTS

The influence of the USA has aided the spread of English. Some countries have laws to prevent the use of English words in their language. For example, advertisements and technical jargon which use English words may be banned.

What is the situation in your country?

Do you think that it is necessary to protect languages by legal means?

LISTENING

Tricia talks to Larry Monde about street gangs in Los Angeles.

1 Before you listen, discuss these two questions.

1 What do you think makes young people join gangs?
2 Are there any well-known street gangs in big cities in your country?
3 Describe the people in the two photos.

2 Now listen and complete these notes which summarise what Larry says.

The two main gangs are the Crips and the **(1)**........... .
The gangs are from the **(2)**........... area of Los Angeles and another area called Watts.
There are two main gangs but **(3)**........... of smaller gangs.
Gang members distinguish themselves by wearing a red or blue **(4)**........... .
It is very dangerous to go into the other gang's **(5)**........... .
A favourite method of murder is by shooting your enemies from **(6)**........... .
The only law in these areas is the law **(7)**........... .
Larry finds TV programmes about the gangs **(8)**........... .
Ordinary people are usually **(9)**........... .
Most gang members are black or **(10)**........... .

READING

Read the article about Euro Disney near Paris and find out why the writer thinks it was a bad idea to build it.

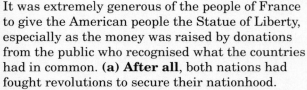

It was extremely generous of the people of France to give the American people the Statue of Liberty, especially as the money was raised by donations from the public who recognised what the countries had in common. **(a) After all**, both nations had fought revolutions to secure their nationhood.

Nowadays, it seems as though the gift has been returned with interest with the foundation of Euro Disney near Paris. **(b) Nevertheless**, many French people are unhappy with this "present", which they feel symbolises a kind of "cultural colonialism". To tell the truth, I would not welcome the presence of such a theme park in the middle of England, for the same reason. **(c) Mind you**, neither England nor France have ever been afraid to export their own culture and values.

(d) Anyway, it is not difficult to understand why they chose to build Euro Disney near Paris. It is a *geographically* logical site, in the centre of continental Europe, right by the sophisticated capital city with its own attractions and so on. **(e) All the same,** was it a *culturally* logical decision? There is the issue of "cultural colonialism" which I have already mentioned. What's more, do the French *need* Mickey Mouse when they have their own cartoon hero in the form of the brave little Gaul, Asterix? Euro Disney's rival the Parc Asterix has proved a popular destination for families wanting a day out. **(f) Incidentally**, Parc Asterix is an easy drive from Paris too. Millions of dollars have been poured into Euro Disney to provide a top class attraction but **(g) the thing is**, can visitors expect an authentic American welcome? The answer must surely be "no"! **(h) There again**, Euro Disney is a cheaper option for most Europeans than going all the way to the States.

(i) All in all I would rather create theme parks which celebrated my own heroes than accept those from elsewhere. **(j) In a nutshell**, this is because it is not always possible to transport culture – like some wines they do not travel well. **(k) By and large** I feel positive towards things American: I have many American friends, adore Rock and Roll music and American movies and even eat their fast food. When I am rich I will take my family to Florida to DisneyWorld and the Magic Kingdom. **(l) However**, until that day arrives we won't be going to Euro Disney. There is a time and place for everything.

LANGUAGE STUDY

Discourse markers

Now look at the twelve words and phrases in bold **(a-l)**. Which ones show that the writer is:

- saying 'don't forget'? **1**.......... **2**.......... **3**..........
- reconsidering an earlier argument? **4**..........
- saying 'but'? **5**.......... **6**.......... **7**..........
- changing the subject? **8**..........
- adding a minor point? **9**..........
- summarising / generalising? **10**.......... **11**..........
  12..........

VOCABULARY

British and American English

1 Match the American English words on the left with the British English equivalents on the right.

1	cable	A	holiday
2	diaper	B	note
3	apartment	C	chemist
4	truck	D	plaster
5	fall	E	biscuits
6	vacation	F	bill (*in a café*)
7	band-aid	G	lift
8	purse	H	telegram
9	check	I	petrol
10	cookies	J	nappy
11	drug store	K	tap
12	freeway	L	handbag
13	gas	M	underground
14	bill (*paper money*)	N	lorry
15	elevator	O	autumn
16	candy	P	motorway
17	subway	Q	sweets
18	faucet	R	flat

Can you think of any other American English words?

2 Change these sentences into British English.

1 Can you go to the drugstore, honey? We need some diapers for the baby and a band-aid for my finger.
2 Last fall, I was driving along a freeway when I ran out of gas. Luckily, a truck driver gave me a ride.
3 Our apartment is quite near the subway station.
4 It's my turn to pay the check. Pass me my purse; I've got a $20 bill in it.
5 Cookies and candy are bad for our teeth.
6 Nothing works round here! Not only is the elevator broken but so is the faucet in the bathroom.

AMERICAN DREAMS

FIRST THOUGHTS

1 Who are these three Amercian heroes? What unfortunate thing do they all have in common?

A

B

C

2 Martin Luther King was a black American leader at a time when there was segregation in the southern states of the United States. In other words, blacks and whites led separate lives, with black people being denied basic human rights and equal opportunities in education. This is part of a famous speech by Martin Luther King:

"I say to you today, my friends, that in spite of the difficulties and frustrations of the moment I still have a dream. It is a dream deeply rooted in the American dream. I have a dream that this nation will rise up and live out the true meaning of its *creed: 'We hold these truths to be self-evident: that all men are created equal.' I have a dream that one day even the state of Mississippi, a desert state *sweltering with the heat of injustice and oppression, will be transformed into an oasis of freedom and justice. I have a dream that my four little children will one day live in a nation where they will not be judged by the color of their skin but by the content of their character."

*creed: central belief
*sweltering: unpleasantly hot and humid
From what you know of the present-day situation in the USA, how far has King's dream become a reality?

READING

1 You are going to read a text by the film star Arnold Schwarzenegger. Before you read it, what do you know about him already? Where is he from for example? Which films has he starred in? How many careers has he had?

2 Now read the text and find out how different Arnold's dream is from Martin Luther King's.

I was born in a little Austrian town, outside Graz. It was a 300-year-old house.

When I was ten years old, I had the dream of being the best in the world in something. When I was fifteen, I had a dream that I wanted to be the best body-builder in the world and the most muscular man. It was not only a dream I dreamed at night. It was also a day-dream. It was so much in my mind that I felt it had to become a reality. It took me five years of hard work. Five years later, I turned this dream into reality and became Mr Universe, the best-built man in the world.

"Winning" is a very important word. There is one that achieves what he wanted to achieve and there are hundreds of thousands that failed. It singles you out: the winner.

I came out second three times but that is what I call losing. The bottom line for me was: Arnold has to be the winner. I have to win the Mr Universe title more often than anybody else. I won it five times consecutively. I hold the record as Mr Olympia, the top professional body-building championship. I won it six times. That's why I retired. There was nobody even close to me. Everybody gave up competing against me. That's what I call a winner.

When I was a small boy, my dream was not to be big physically, but big in a way that everybody listens to me when I talk, that I'm a very important person, that people recognise me and see me as something special. I had a big need for being singled out.

Also my dream was to end up in America. When I was ten years old, I dreamed of being an American. At the time I didn't know much about America, just that it was a wonderful country. I felt it was where I belonged. I didn't like being in a little country like Austria. I did everything possible to get out. I did so in 1968, when I was twenty-one years old.

If I believed in life after death, I would say in my before life I was living in America. That's why I feel so good here. It is the country where you can turn your dream into reality. Other countries don't have those things. When I came over here to America, I felt I was in heaven. In America we don't have an obstacle. Nobody's holding you back.

You have to choose at a very early date what you want: a normal life or to achieve things you want to achieve. I never wanted to win a popularity contest in doing things the way people wanted me to do it. I went the road I thought was best for me. A few people thought I was cold, selfish. Later they found out that's not the case. After I achieve my goal, I can be Mr Nice Guy. You know what I mean?

California is to me a dreamland. It has the absolute combination of everything in the world I was ever looking for. It has all the money in the world there, show business there, wonderful weather there, beautiful country, the ocean is there. Snow skiing in the winter; you can go in the desert the same day. You have beautiful-looking people there. They all have a tan.

I believe very strongly in the philosophy of staying hungry. If you have a dream and it becomes a reality, don't stay satisfied with it too long. Make up a new dream and hunt after that one, and turn it into reality. When you have that dream achieved, make up a new dream.

I am a strong believer in Western philosophy, the philosophy of success, of progress, of getting rich. The Eastern philosophy is passive, which I believe in maybe three per cent of the time, and the ninety-seven per cent is Western, conquering and going on. It's a beautiful philosophy and America should keep it up.

3 Read the text again carefully and choose the best answer (**A**, **B**, **C** or **D**) to each question.

1 How long did it take for Arnold to make his dream of being the best in the world a reality?
   A Five years.
   B Ten years.
   C Fifteen years.
   D Twenty years.

2 Why did Arnold retire from body-building?
   A He knew he had reached the bottom line.
   B He hated coming second.
   C There were younger people who wanted his titles.
   D There was no real competition.

3 What was Arnold's great need as a boy?
   A To be alone.
   B To be very big.
   C To be respected
   D To be a good speaker.

4 What did Arnold believe before he went to the USA?
   A He had been an American in a previous life.
   B He already knew a great deal about the States.
   C You can achieve your potential in the USA.
   D He was satisfied with life in Austria.

5 What does Arnold think about himself?
   A He has the potential to be kind.
   B He is totally ruthless.
   C He has a need to be popular.
   D He is emotionally cold.

6 How does Arnold feel about California?
   A It is just something from a dream.
   B You can be who you want to be there.
   C It has everything.
   D It is a superficial place.

7 What, in a sentence, is Arnold's philosophy?
   A Be satisfied with what you've got.
   B Don't eat too much.
   C Have a dream and make it come true.
   D However successful you are, always have a goal.

8 What does Arnold believe about Western philosophy?
   A It is passive.
   B It is aggressive.
   C It overvalues success.
   D The whole world should adopt it.

15 Our Common Future

WHAT DOES THE FUTURE HOLD?

FIRST THOUGHTS

Complete this questionnaire individually by circling your chosen answer. Then discuss your answers in pairs or small groups.

1 = impossible   2 = unlikely   3 = possible   4 = quite likely   5 = bound to happen

In or by the year 2025. . .

1	there will have been a catastrophic nuclear accident or war.	1 2 3 4 5
2	people will be living on cities in the moon.	1 2 3 4 5
3	English will still be the international language.	1 2 3 4 5
4	Canada and the USA will be one country.	1 2 3 4 5
5	a cure for AIDS will have been found.	1 2 3 4 5
6	Madrid will be the new fashion capital of the world.	1 2 3 4 5
7	most families will have a robot to help with the housework.	1 2 3 4 5
8	the USA will have had at least one woman president.	1 2 3 4 5
9	women will be completely equal to men.	1 2 3 4 5
10	Brazil will be a new superpower.	1 2 3 4 5
11	life expectancy in industrialised countries will be 100.	1 2 3 4 5
12	cash will have disappeared.Everything will be paid for by credit or cash card.	1 2 3 4 5

SPEAKING

Discussion points

1 Which predictions are the most/least likely to come true?
2 Who is the most optimistic/pessimistic in your group?
3 As a group, think of three other things you will be doing or will have done by the year 2025.

VOCABULARY

Technology and work

1 New technology

Join these split sentences.

1 A computer is
2 A computer's hardware consists of
3 The programmes used to run a computer
4 A robot is
5 A holograph is
6 A gene is the part of a cell of a living thing that
7 Genetic engineering
8 The term "virtual reality"

a a machine which can move and perform some of the physical work done by men.
b allows scientists to determine the development of a cell.
c a three dimensional image produced by light.
d the computer and its equipment.
e determines how it will develop and grow.
f describes computer images which appear almost like the real world.
g an electronic machine which is used to store and organise information.
h are its software.

2 Word building

Scientist (the noun for the profession) and **scientific** (adjective) are both formed from the noun **science**. How does the stress of these words change between the different parts of speech?

- Make profession nouns and adjectives in the same way from the following: *biology, physics, chemistry, ecology*.
- Form the adjective from *technology*.
- What profession noun and what adjective can you make from *technique*?

3 Work

Complete the sentences with a word or expression to do with work. The first letter of each word or expression is given to you.

1 Typing and knowing how to use a computer are two useful s........... .
2 The workers decided to go on s........... when the management refused their demand for higher wages.
3 When the car company introduced computers into the factory, five hundred workers were made r........... . They were no longer needed to perfom manual tasks.
4 The t........... u........... tried to negotiate with the management to save jobs but was powerless to do anything.
5 In England, people without jobs can go on the d...........; in other words the government pays them some kind of unemployment benefit each week.

LISTENING

1 You are going to hear five people talking about their visions of the future. Choose from the list **A–F** the description which best fits each speaker. There is one extra letter which you do not need to use.

A Talks about the future of home entertainment.
B Thinks science and technology will improve everyone's lives.
C Believes mankind will have to colonise other planets.
D Thinks that humans will have spare body parts made from computers.
E Suggests we won't be able to tell the difference betweeen what is real and what is "virtual".
F Fears there will be a terrible disaster.

Speaker 1 ☐
Speaker 2 ☐
Speaker 3 ☐
Speaker 4 ☐
Speaker 5 ☐

2 Whose vision of the future is closest to your own?

PRONUNCIATION

Word building

Look at the words that can be formed from the verbs **employ**, **compete**, and **qualify** and decide

- where the stress falls in each word.
- what part of speech each word is, i.e. is it a noun, verb or adjective? There may be more than one noun or adjective in each group.

1 employ
employ = VERB
employed =
employment =
employable =
employer =

employee =
employability =
unemployed =
unemployment =
unemployable =

2 compete
compete =
competitive =
competitor =

competition =
competitiveness =
uncompetitive =

3 qualify
qualify =
qualified =
qualifications =

unqualified =
disqualify =
disqualification =

LANGUAGE STUDY

More complex ways of describing the future

1 The future perfect

Study this sentence from the recording and answer the questions which follow:
By 2025 **we'll have conquered** *most diseases.*

- Will we conquer most diseases?
- Will this happen before, in or after 2025?
- Do we know exactly when this will happen?

With the **present perfect**, we look at the past from the viewpoint of the present.
Example: *I* **have been** *to Germany* which means *Some time in the past I went to Germany.*

With the **future perfect**, we project to a point in the future and look back from there.
Example: *By 2010, new technology* **will have revolutionised** *communications* which means *This revolution will take place some time between now and 2010. I am not exactly sure when it will happen; however, I predict that by 2010 it will have happened.*

Expand these sentences using the future perfect.

1 I - will - finish - this exercise - in five minutes' time.
2 By - end of century - doctors - find - cure for AIDS.
3 They - arrive - by - ten o'clock this evening...
4 ...but they - be - tired and hungry - they will not - sleep - eat.
5 By next April - he - be - out of work - six years.
6 A super-intelligent computer - invent - by 2020...
7 ..... and human labour - be replaced - by robots...
8 ...but they still - not find - a way to replace cleaners!

2 The future continuous

Our great-grandchildren **will be living** *on the moon.*

Match the descriptions of the uses of the future continuous with the example sentences.

1 an activity completely covering a period in the future
2 a future arrangement
3 a guess about something happening in the present

A It's six o'clock. Dad will be listening to the news.
B I'll be taking the 11.30 train.
C We'll be working in New York for the next two months.

3 The future after introductory time expressions

When this happens, *there won't even be the need for a screen or anything.*

1 Study what happens when two sentences expressing the future are joined by using an introductory time expression:
Doctors will find an answer to AIDS. They will be able to cure people.
→ *As soon as doctors* **find** *an answer to AIDS, they will be able to cure people.*
After the time expression, a form of a present tense has to be used.

2 Now join the sentences below using the words in capital letters. Make any other necessary changes.
Example: *Children will still be going to school. Scientists will be trying to invent machines to teach them at home.* WHILE
→ *Children will still be going to school while scientists* **are trying** *to invent machines to teach them at home.*

A Office workers will have jobs. New technology will make them redundant. UNTIL
B Robots will have been introduced. Factory workers will go on strike. AS SOON AS
C Computers will act as judges. They will be programmed with all the information. ONCE
D Oil will have run out. Scientists won't have discovered an alternative source of energy. BEFORE
E Super-intelligent computers will be invented. Technicians will need to maintain them. IMMEDIATELY
F All these changes will take place. Our world will be transformed. AFTER

4 Write a paragraph predicting what your life will be like by or in the year 2010. What will you have done? Will you be married and have children? Where will you be living? What will your job be?

MAKING A LIVING

FIRST THOUGHTS

1 How easy is it for young people to find jobs these days? Do they have realistic expectations?

2 Some people say that people are often over-educated for the jobs they do. How far do you agree with this? What effect could over-education have?

USE OF ENGLISH

Complete the passage by changing the word in capitals at the end of the line into a suitable form to fill the gap. There is an example at the beginning **(0)**.

There is no doubt that the world has become a more **(0)** *competitive* place. For the past twenty years or so the chase for paper **(1)**.......... has become even tougher. Young people without pieces of paper are immediately **(2)**.......... from applying for even the lowest jobs.

    All that seems to wait for them is long term **(3)**.......... . However, there are two ways out of this The first is to enrol on a training course in areas where there is a **(4)**.......... of people with the right skills and know-how. With determination and **(5)**.........., enough can be learned to dramatically improve the **(6)**.......... of young people whose prospects would otherwise be poor. The second is to contact big employers direct. Employers **(7)**.......... believe that the general education offered by most schools and colleges is out-dated and **(8)**.......... to today's new professions. This is why they are offering **(9)**.......... to applicants who demonstrate the necessary aptitude and **(10)**.......... . The future is much brighter than we thought.

COMPETE
QUALIFY

QUALIFY

SHORT
ENTHUSIATIC
EMPLOY

INCREASE

RELEVANT
APPRENTICE
COMMIT

READING

1 You are going to read an extract from the book *Brave New World* by Aldous Huxley. It is set in the distant future where people are no longer born but are "hatched" instead. Different classes of people with different levels of intelligence are biologically mass-produced according to society's needs. "Alphas" are the most intelligent and "Epsilons" the least intelligent. Most people take *soma* – a recreational drug. In this extract the Savage – someone from a "natural" world close to the one we know – discusses the situation of the Epsilons with Mustapha Mond – the World Controller. Read the passage and answer the questions which follow.

BRAVE NEW WORLD
Aldous Huxley

"I was wondering," said the Savage, "why you had them at all, seeing that you can get whatever you want out of those bottles. Why don't you make everybody an Alpha-Double-Plus while you're about it?"

Mustapha Mond laughed. "Because we have no wish to have our throats cut," he answered. "We believe in happiness and stability. A society of Alphas couldn't fail to be restless and miserable. An Alpha would go mad if he had to do Epsilon work – go mad or start breaking things. Only an Epsilon can be expected to make Epsilon sacrifices, for the good reason that for him they aren't sacrifices. His conditioning has determined the life he has got to live. He can't help himself."

The Savage sighed.

"The ideal population," said Mustapha Mond, "is like an iceberg eight-ninths below the water line, one-ninth above."

"And they're happy below the water line?"

"Happier than above it. Happier than your friends here, for example." He pointed.

"In spite of that awful work?"

"Awful? They don't find it so. On the contrary, they like it. It's light, it's childishly simple. No strain on the mind or the muscles. Seven-and-a-half hours of mild labour without excessive bodily effort, and then the soma distribution and games and other amusements provided for them. What more can they ask for?"

"True," he added, "they might ask for shorter hours, but would they be any the happier for that? No, they wouldn't. The experiment was tried, more than a century-and-a-half ago. The whole of Ireland was put on to the four-hour day. What was the result? Unrest and a large increase in the amount of soma taken. The Inventions Office is full of plans for labour-saving processes. Thousands of them." Mustapha Mond waved his arms as if to give an idea of the great pile of plans. "And why don't we use them? For the sake of the workers. It would be cruelty to give them too much leisure. It's the same with agriculture. We could produce every mouthful of food synthetically, if we wanted to. But we don't. We prefer to keep a third of the population on the land. For their own sakes – because it takes longer to get food out of the land than out of a factory. Besides, we have our stability to think of. We don't want to change. Every change is a threat to stability. That's another reason why we're so careful about using new inventions. Every discovery in pure science could lead to a revolution. Even science must sometimes be treated as a possible enemy. Yes, even science."

1 Why doesn't Mustapha Mond want to make everyone Alpha-Double-Plus?
   A Because it would be a joke.
   B Because Epsilons would have nothing to do.
   C Because it could be dangerous.
   D Because the change would difficult to introduce.

2 According to Mustapha Mond, Epsilons aren't unhappy because
   A they are used to making sacrifices.
   B they enjoy their work.
   C they realise unhappiness is a waste of time.
   D they can't think that way.

3 How does the Savage feel about Mustapha Mond's explanation?
   A Depressed.
   B Amused.
   C Fascinated.
   D Astonished.

4 What point does Mustapha Mond want to make when he talks about the iceberg?
   A All people are essentially equal.
   B You are happier out of the water.
   C Society needs people below the water line.
   D Most people are happy with an undemanding life.

5 What happened as a result of the Irish experiment?
   A Less soma was consumed.
   B There was trouble.
   C It was repeated elsewhere.
   D People wanted to work even less.

6 What does Mustapha Mond say about the inventions?
   A They are ignored.
   B They are continuously introduced.
   C Most are impractical.
   D They have reduced people's hours of work.

7 One third of the population works on the land because
   A synthetic foods are not sufficiently advanced.
   B it's good for the workers.
   C there is a world food shortage.
   D it is more efficient to produce food this way.

8 How does Mustapha Mond feel about science?
   A We must be cautious of its consequences.
   B It is man, not science, who is evil.
   C There is no threat from it at all.
   D He has little respect for it.

2 Discussion points

1 How far do you agree with Mond's philosphy?
2 How necessary is it for people to work?

LISTENING

Renate Gross is talking about the impact of technology on work. Listen to what she has to say and complete the notes.

According to Renate, the industrial revolution in Europe took place in (1)............. . A postal service has existed since (2)............ . However, nowadays postal workers (3)............ . According to Renate, the invention of (4)............ marked the end of the Middle Ages. It will only cost colleagues (5)............ to communicate internationally by computer. Computers will be more efficient, accurate and (6)............ than human beings. Old-fashioned jobs like (7)............ and thatchers and coopers have disappeared. She says that nowadays, clerical and (8)............ jobs are disappearing too. People who want to have a job in the future should become (9)............ . 50 years ago, if you had told someone about jobs involved in TV they would have said (10)............ .

READING

Nowadays, a lot of information is available on compact discs, which can be read with the aid of computer technology. This is called CD-ROM (compact disc read-only memory – you can read, copy or interact with what you see but cannot add to it or change it).

You are going to read some descriptions of CD-ROMs. For questions **1–15**, choose from descriptions (**A-K**). Some answers may be chosen more than once. Where more than one answer is required, these may be given in any order.

LEARN TO SPEAK SERIES   **A**
(Hyperglot Software)
Learn another language with these self-study language tutors. The emphasis is on learning words within a real-life context, rather than as strings of vocabulary. You can also record your own pronunciation and then compare it with a recording by a native speaker.

MICROSOFT ART GALLERY   **B**
(Microsoft Corporation)
Take a tour of London's National Gallery, with 2,000 paintings dating from 1300 to this century. Animation is used to explain the techniques of the great artists, and the history and social conditions of the artist's time put paintings into their proper context.

BATTLE CHESS   **C**
(Interplay)
A new experience in the game of chess, this title contains animated pieces that play out battles when a piece is taken. A detailed animated tutorial will teach beginners to play chess.

SPACE ADVENTURE   **D**
(Knowledge Adventure)
Take a highly interactive voyage into space, with plenty of video, sounds, and images. You can read about space missions, ponder how the universe was formed and what it is made of, and follow the search for extraterrestrial life.

TIME ALMANAC   **E**
(Compact Publishing)
This title is produced annually and consists of the previous year's articles and images from *Time* magazine as well as a collection of features from previous decades. Video clips are included, and you can test your knowledge of current affairs with the NewsQuest quiz.

THE WAY THINGS WORK   **F**
(Dorling Kindersley/Houghton Mifflin)
Based on David Macaulay's best-selling book, this
title uses hundreds of animation clips to explain the
workings of everything from aircraft to X-rays.

THE BIG GREEN DISK   **G**
(Media Design Interactive)
Designed to give users an overview of ecological
problems, this title explains the origins of the
difficulties facing the earth, details possible
solutions and includes interviews with leading
experts.

RETURN TO ZORK   **H**
(Activision)
This challenging adventure game features
excellent graphics, real actors, and full motion
video footage. The title is the fifth in the series.

WORLD VISTA   **I**
(Applied Optical Media)
More than a simple atlas, this title includes images
and sounds from over 200 countries. In addition to
history and politics, topics covered include
agriculture, health, education and crime. Users can
also learn common phrases in 25 languages.

**INTRODUCTION TO CLASSICAL
MUSIC**   **J**
(Attica Cybernetics)
Aimed at the novice listener, this title details the
various types of classical music and explains
musical terminology. Seven different search
methods are available to guide users through the
four hours of music clips.

**MACMILLAN DICTIONARY FOR
CHILDREN**   **K**
(Maxwell Electrotonic Publishing)
This product offers an entertaining way for children
to learn: every word has an audio pronunciation,
and some entries include animated sequences.

Which CD-ROM would you buy for someone who:
- likes games and quizzes? [1]   [2]
- is interested in the origins of the universe?
  [3]
- is interested in learning languages? [4]
- would like to have last year's magazine articles?
  [5]
- would like to know about the social context of
  works of art? [6]
- would like to know how machines function?
  [7]
- would like to check their pronunciation in another
  language against a native speaker? [8]
- is starting to learn new words? [9]
- had previous CD-ROMs in the same series?
  [10]
- would like to "participate" in a space flight?
  [11]
- would like an introduction to music? [12]
- might already have a book of the same title?
  [13]

14 Which CD-ROM might help you solve everyday
practical problems, B, D, E, or G?

15 Which one would be of best all-round educational
value, A, E, I, or K?

THE CURSE OF UNEMPLOYMENT

1 How effective is your government at creating new jobs?

2 If you were in charge, what action would you take to reduce unemployment among young people?

WRITING

The opinion question – a final look

1 *Many countries around the world have problems with unemployment. Young people in particular are often unable to find work. What can be done about this problem?*

Imagine that your answer to the question is the one below. You have five minutes to go before the end of the exam and now you must check your answer. In pairs, read the composition carefully and correct any mistakes you find.

(1)

Unemployment among young people is increasing constantly. The reason is that industry try to reduce the number of employees who are replaced by computers or person able to manipulate these computers.

I think the problem is that company look mainly after well-qualified people with a lot of experience because they expect to make serious business and don't give the chance to university students to introduce themselves.

On the other hand in the work area young people

(2)

tend to specialise too much in one limited area and haven't got any other knowledge. I think students should take an orientation that will allow them to get several kinds of job and mainly studies in connection with technologie, public relations, commerce and social activities.

Another fact is that student are quickly self-satisfied. Once they don't get a job in this specialisation don't go on looking for another job and choose the easier way "unemployment".

2 Look at this grading system. What grade would be fair for the composition you have just checked through?

GRADE	DESCRIPTION
Excellent	Natural English with just a few unimportant mistakes. Answers the question thoroughly and appropriately.
Very good	Good use of vocabulary and structure. Range of structure better than simple sentences. Mistakes are non-basic.
Good	A simple but accurate answer. Fairly natural English without too many mistakes.
Pass	Limited structure and vocabulary. Errors sometimes prevent understanding.
Weak	Vocabulary and grammar are not good enough to answer the question properly. No evidence of appropriate writing style.
Very Poor	Answer not long or clear enough to assess.

3 Know yourself

Look through the most recent compositions you have written and think about these questions.

1 What are your biggest problems? For example, do you do well when you write simply? Do you do badly if you try to express complicated ideas?
2 What are your "favourite" mistakes, for example:
  • spelling?
  • tenses?
  • agreement of subject and number, or person and tense?
  • punctuation and problems with handwriting?
3 In general, what marks would you give yourself for your compositions? Be honest!
4 What should you do in the examination? For example, should you try and write simple accurate English so that you are able to pass, or should you be a little more ambitious? Ask your teacher what he or she thinks.

4 Final advice

1 Remember – the First Certificate Examination is not a philosophy examination. Do not try to express ideas that are too complicated for your level of English.
2 Do not rush into writing. Spend at least five minutes planning your composition.
3 Leave at least five minutes at the end of each composition to check for mistakes.
4 Write slowly and clearly so that you do not have to copy out the composition again. This is a waste of time as you may just copy out your mistakes. Instead, spend this time checking your work. It can be a good idea to write on every other line so that if you have to make corrections you can do so clearly and cleanly.

5 Write a composition on this topic in 45 minutes:

Is new technology a blessing or a curse?

LISTENING

You are going to hear people talking in eight different situations. Choose the best answer, **A**, **B** or **C**, for each question.

1 You are in the reception area of an estate agent's. How does the man feel?
  A Relieved.
  B Annoyed.
  C Pleased.

2 You are in an electrical goods shop when you hear one side of a telephone conversation. The conversation is about
  A a customer complaint.
  B a technical problem.
  C late delivery of an order.

3 Listen to this woman talking about her son's interest in computers. She
  A believes his teacher.
  B thinks the programme is unsuitable.
  C believes games will help him learn quickly.

4 You are in a department store when you come across this man talking to a group of people. The man is
  A demonstrating a new product.
  B encouraging people to try something.
  C giving instructions to a new member of staff.

5 Listen to this advertisement for a radio programme. The programme is about
  A history.
  B sports.
  C science.

6 You are visiting an office when you hear two of the staff having a heated discussion. One of them is
  A trying to fix something.
  B angry with a colleague.
  C a technical expert.

7 In a school staff room you overhear two language teachers talking. How does one of the teachers feel?
  A Disappointed.
  B Confused.
  C Worried.

8 You are in a cafeteria when you hear two students at the next table. They are discussing
  A philosophy.
  B a joke.
  C food.

USE OF ENGLISH

1 Read the text and think of the word which best fits each space. Use only **one** word in each space.

Night had finally come. She knew that by now all the humans who worked in the factory **(1)**.......... have gone to their homes in satellite city. She realised that she **(2)**.......... to be careful. The robot guard passed by **(3)**.......... four minutes. As it disappeared around the corner, she jumped from **(4)**.......... the low wall where she had **(5)**.......... hiding and ran along the narrow corridor towards the main factory workshop. Her heart was beating **(6)**.......... fast she was certain that the robot guard would be able to hear it. Then, **(7)**.......... before she had time to realise, there in **(8)**.......... of her was the enemy. **(9)**.......... was the monster that had stolen the jobs of half the workforce.

The computer **(10)**.......... quite innocent as it stood silently in the middle of the office. She walked right up to it and **(11)**.......... herself that she was going to teach it a lesson it would never forget. **(12)**.......... her pocket she took a screwdriver and a hammer. **(13)**.......... she approached it, suddenly a strange mechanical cry **(14)**.......... from the front of the creature, the lights came on all **(15)**.......... her and the sirens began to wail.

2 Complete the second sentence so that it has a similar meaning to the first. Use the word given and between two and five words. Do not change the word given.

1 I haven't been to the cinema for ages.
since
It's .... to the cinema.

2 The garage is servicing my car on Monday.
serviced
I'm .... on Monday.

3 He couldn't reach the button because it was too high.
low
The button was .... him to reach.

4 They understand more than we do.
as
We don't understand .... them.

5 "Why don't you apply for the job, Ann?" said Sue.
should
Sue suggested .... for the job.

6 I haven't seen him for three years.
time
The .... was three years ago.

7 He is extremely rich but very mean.
fact
He is very mean .... extremely rich.

8 I didn't know the answer because I hadn't read the book.
would
If I had read the book .... the answer.

9 I don't agree with capital punishment.
favour
I'm .... capital punishment.

10 I'm sorry; I broke it by accident.
on
I didn't ....; it was an accident.

11 Patrick says Gemma is to blame.
according
It's Gemma's .... Patrick.

12 I'd prefer us to go to the cinema.
we
I'd .... to the cinema.

13 Somebody needs to tell him.
told
He .... someone.

14 She was so bored by the lesson she fell asleep.
boring
It was .... lesson she fell asleep.

15 Bob stills finds his new contact lenses uncomfortable.
used
Bob .... his new contact lenses yet.

16 His mother never let him go out.
allowed
He .... out.

17 It doesn't need to be finished this evening.
finish
It isn't .... this evening.

18 He has probably spent all the money he won.
likely
He .... spent all the money he won.

19 She didn't want to join in the dancing at the party
take
She didn't want .... the dancing at the party.

20 You had better not touch that switch.
would
If I .... touch that switch.

21 This fruit is a new experience for me.
time
It is the .... this fruit.

22 What a pity I broke the vase.
wish
I .... the vase.

23 Remind me to water the plants.
forget
Don't let .... the plants.

24 As I see it, someone should tell her the truth.
in
She should be .... opinion.

25 I'd rather you didn't smoke in here.
mind
Would .... in here, please?

26 The accident injured a lot of people.
number
A .... people were injured in the accident.

27 It was the most embarrassing experience of my life.
so
I had never .... before.

28 If you're not sure how to spell the word, consult the dictionary.
up
You should .... a dictionary if you're not sure how to spell it.

29 Very few people knew the full story.
known
The full story .... many people.

30 As the town council's representative I would like to welcome you.
behalf
I'd like to welcome you .... the town council.

31 You'd better take an umbrella. It might rain this evening.
case
Take an umbrella .... this evening.

32 We couldn't find a parking space anywhere.
find
We weren't .... to park.

33 We were given the directions by Paul.
who
It .... the directions.

34 They were still walking after two hours..
been
They .... two hours.

35 The bus comes in two hours; let's have lunch before it comes.
in
The bus comes in two hours; ...., let's have lunch.

36 The job was too badly paid so she didn't accept it.
down
She .... it was too badly paid.

37 I took my overcoat but it wasn't necessary.
taken
I .... my overcoat.

38 The film wasn't worth seeing.
time
The film was a complete ....

39 Who is looking after the children this afternoon?
of
Who is .... the children this afternoon?

40 They climbed out of the room using some bedsheets.
means
They climbed out of the room .... some bedsheets.

41 They believe the criminal has had plastic surgery.
believed
The criminal .... plastic surgery.

42 He plays the piano and sings beautifully too.
play
Not .... piano but he also sings beautifully.

Reviser Guide (for papers 1, 2, 3 and 5)

INTRODUCTION

This guide aims to help with your final examination preparation. You must become completely comfortable with the question and task types and the most effective techniques and examination skills for satisfying them. The guide contains reference material, examination advice and opportunities for examination practice. In the final phase leading up to your examination you will probably be working through practice tests. Make sure that you have a quiet place where you can concentrate and work to strict time limits.

Paper 1 READING

The reading paper is divided into four parts, each with its own text/s and accompanying tasks or questions. You have a lot to read and many tasks to complete in a limited time. Choosing an appropriate reading style for each part which will make it possible to complete the tasks in the time available.

1 Read the descriptions of appropriate styles and answer the questions underneath **(2)**.

- **skimming/reading for gist -** a rapid reading style used to extract the main idea or ideas of a passage.
- **scanning -** a rapid reading technique where you want to locate specific pieces of information.
- **intensive reading -** a slow, careful reading of the text or parts of the text with a high degree of understanding. We may often read this way when we want to find meaning and attitude which are not stated overtly.

2 What reading style would you be most likely to use if you were doing the following?

- looking up a number in a telephone book.
- reading a thriller at the beach or on a journey.
- trying to understand the handbook of a new and expensive camera.
- looking through a novel for a quotation.
- studying a usage note in a dictionary or grammar book.
- reading the first pages of a paperback in a bookshop to see if it interests you.

3 You answer questions by completing an answer sheet like this. Transfer your answers to the answer sheet after completing each part. NEVER wait to the end as you could run out of time.

Candidate Answer Sheet: FCE Paper 1 Reading

Use a pencil

Mark ONE letter for each question.

For example, if you think **B** is the right answer to the question, mark your answer sheet like this:

0 A B C D

Change your answer like this:

0 A B C D

	A B C D E F G H I
1	A B C D E F G H I
2	A B C D E F G H I
3	A B C D E F G H I
4	A B C D E F G H I

6	A B C D E F G H I
7	A B C D E F G H I
8	A B C D E F G H I
9	A B C D E F G H I
10	A B C D E F G H I
11	A B C D E F G H I
12	A B C D E F G H I
13	A B C D E F G H I
14	A B C D E F G H I
15	A B C D E F G H I
16	A B C D E F G H I
17	A B C D E F G H I
18	A B C D E F G H I
19	A B C D E F G H I
20	A B C D E F G H I

21	A B C D E F G H I
22	A B C D E F G H I
23	A B C D E F G H I
24	A B C D E F G H I
25	A B C D E F G H I
26	A B C D E F G H I
27	A B C D E F G H I
28	A B C D E F G H I
29	A B C D E F G H I
30	A B C D E F G H I
31	A B C D E F G H I
32	A B C D E F G H I
33	A B C D E F G H I
34	A B C D E F G H I
35	A B C D E F G H I

Part 1 MULTIPLE MATCHING
(Matching headings or topic sentences to texts)

Turn to the examples on pages 10-11 and 106-107
This tests how well you understand the gist (overall meaning) and the main points of the text you are given. It requires a more rapid, less intensive reading style. Usually, it is not important to have a detailed understanding of the text. Do not spend time trying to understand the meaning of every part of the text or every word within it.

Recommended procedure:

1 Quickly skim the text to get a general idea of what it is about. Don't try to answer the questions immediately.
2 Carefully read the headings and look for clues in the text e.g., synonyms, reference words, etc, to match.
3 Try to identify the extra sentence or heading you do not need.
4 Match the headings to the gaps. Start with the ones which are obvious and leave the more difficult ones to last. A poor choice or "guess" early on will cause problems later.

Part 2 MULTIPLE CHOICE

Turn to the examples on pages 50-51 and pages 64-65.
In this part you have to answer seven or eight multiple choice questions based around a text.
You will mostly have to read both text and questions carefully and intensively. Some of the differences between the choices can be very small. This question is as much to do with understanding the questions as the text! Make sure you do not spend too long on this part.

Recommended procedure:

1 Quickly skim the text to get a general idea of what it is about. Don't try to answer the questions immediately.
2 Read the questions which accompany the text carefully and closely.
3 Isolate the parts of the text that each of the questions belongs to. A highlighter pen is useful for this.
4 Methodically work your way through each choice for each question making sure that you do not jump to conclusions. Answers that can appear "obvious" may be wrong. Read both text and questions intensively.

If the answer is not apparent then you may have to make your choice through a process of elimination. i.e. "it can't be A because ......" See page 65 for a detailed analysis of how multiple choice questions work.
5 Transfer your answers to the answer sheet.

Part 3 GAPPED TEXT

Turn to the examples on pages 74-75 and pages 142-143.
This is where you have to match missing sentences or paragraphs to gaps in a text.
This is a challenging question and requires you to consider carefully the structure of the text and to follow closely the logic and arguments it presents. Read the text and explanations on page 16-17 once again to remind yourself of what the task involves. Pay particular attention to how "clues" are identified in the text.

Recommended procedure:

1 Quickly read the text through for a general understanding. Don't get stuck on the meaning of individual words and phrases.
2 Read the text again and make your initial selection of which sentence belongs with which gap. The best way of doing this is to start with the answers which you think are more apparent and obvious first. Always read the text on either side of the gap intensively and make sure that it fits logically and that reference words such as pronouns are natural.
3 Read the sentences/paragraphs which accompany the text again and try to identify the extra sentence which is there to distract you.
4 Now you will usually be left with a few sentences where you are less sure where they should belong. Read the remaining gapped text carefully looking for "clues" (see p 16-17) before making a final decision. Remember: a wrong choice usually means that you get two questions wrong!
5 Transfer your answers to the answer sheet.

Part 4 MULTIPLE MATCHING

Turn to the examples on pages 28-29 and pages 158-159.
This often consists of a number of related texts rather than a single text. The most appropriate reading style for this part is "scanning" i.e. reading rapidly searching for specific information or ideas. In this question you usually have a lot of text to read but the questions are fairly straightforward and un-complicated.

Recommended procedure:

1 Spend the first minute skimming the text/s to gain a general understanding of what it is or they are about.
2 Read the tasks which accompany the text/s.
3 Scan the texts rapidly, making your selection of answers on a separate piece of paper. Do not allow yourself to get stuck. If the answer is not apparent after say, 15 seconds, then go on and deal with the next question.
4 Transfer your answers to the answer sheet.
5 With any time remaining pick up any extra points you can. If in doubt, guess! Never leave an answer blank!

Paper 2 COMPOSITION

1 General considerations

- You must answer question 1, the compulsory letter question, and one other question from Part 2. For both questions you must:
- satisfy the task fully.
- write within the word limits.
- select the right "register" i.e. write in an appropriate style for the task and your "audience".
- be reasonably accurate.
- write within your limitations, i.e. do not be over-ambitious.
- write clearly and legibly.

2 Know yourself

Look through the most recent compositions you have written and think about these questions.

1 What are your biggest problems? For example, do you do well when you write simply? Do you do badly if you try to express complicated ideas?
2 What are your "favourite" mistakes? For example: spelling, tenses, agreement of subject and number or person and tense, punctuation and problems with handwriting.
3 In general, what mark would you give yourself for your composition? Be honest!
4 What should you do in the examination? For example, should you try and write simple accurate English so that you are able to pass, or should you be a little more ambitious? Ask your teacher what he or she thinks.

3 Final advice

1 Remember the First Certificate Examination is not a philosophy examination. Do not try to express ideas that are too complicated for your level of English.
2 Do not rush into writing. Spend at least five minutes planning your composition.
3 Leave at least five minutes at the end of each composition to check for mistakes..
4 Write slowly and clearly so that you do not have to copy out the composition again. This is a waste of time as you may just copy out your mistakes. Spend this time checking your work. It can be a good idea to write on every other line so that if you have to make corrections you can do so clearly and cleanly.

1 COMPULSORY LETTER

1 The compulsory letter requires you to complete an everyday writing task to achieve a particular aim, e.g. to obtain information. Look at pages 19 and pages 67 for examples.

Remember:
- you have to answer the question fully and take into account all the relevant information you have been given.
- English writing is usually direct and to the point. It is quite common to state our reasons for writing in the first sentence.
- to adopt an appropriate style. For example, a formal advertisement would require a formal reply.

2 Look at these examples of first sentences. What possible continuations do you think they could have?

More formal/Neutral
- I am writing to complain about/enquire about /ask about/tell you about/inform you of /confirm/cancel/ invite you...
- I am writing in reply to your advertisement which appeared...
- Please could you send me a copy of your brochure...
- Thank you for your letter asking/enquiring about/ agreeing to do...
- I would like to receive/hear/know/discover/find out...
- I was sorry/disappointed/interested to find out/hear/see that...
- Please find enclosed...
- Further to your enquiry about ...
- Concerning/Regarding/With regard to your letter/request/enquiry...
- I am pleased/delighted/sorry to tell/inform you that....

Informal

- It was lovely to get your letter...
- This is just a short note to tell you...
- It was great to hear from you...
- Sorry for not writing earlier but I've...

3 Here are some further set expressions which, if used correctly, can form a significant part of the letter. Match the beginnings of sentences 1-12 with the continuations below them.

1 Incidentally/By the way...
2 I am writing to complain about...
3 Guess what? They...
4 Anyway, that's all for now but...
5 You'll be sad to hear...
6 I look forward to...
7 I'm sorry for not having written earlier...
8 It was great news...
9 Unfortunately I won't be able to come...
10 Hope to see you soon...
11 Thank you for your lovely letter it...
12 Would you like to...

A because I have to study hard for my examinations.
B about your results. Well done!
C I'll write again next week.
D did you know that Marcel is coming to stay?
E come for dinner next Friday?
F then we can really catch up on each other's news.
G really cheered me up.
H offered me the job!
I that Felix the cat died last week.
J receiving a satisfactory explanation.
K the awful service in your restaurant.
L but I've been incredibly busy.

Which expressions
1 state the purpose of the letter?
2 give apologies?
3 help you "close" the letter?
4 give good and bad news?
5 are useful for formal letters?
6 help you to change the subject?

Can you add any other useful expressions to the ones listed above?

NOTE Remember these ways of beginning and ending letters:

*Dear **Sir/Madam,** .... Yours faithfully*
(You don't write the person's name)

*Dear **Mr and Mrs Green,** .... Yours sincerely*
(you write the person's title followed by their surname.)

*Dear **Simon,/ Miss Jones,** .... Best wishes.*
(For a fairly close friend or someone you know quite well.)

*Dear **Mum,/Julie,** .... Lots of love*
(For a member of the family, boyfriend or girlfriend. It is common for female friends to end a letter with **Lots of love**; it is usually more appropriate for male friends to end with **Best wishes** or **All the best**.)

3 Write the following letters

1 You have been invited to an old friend's birthday party. Write a letter explaining why family obligations prevent you from coming. Give some of your own news and suggest an arrangement for a future meeting.
2 Recently a friend gave you the name of an agency which specialises in organising working holidays abroad. This autumn, you would like to spend a month picking apples on an English farm. Write to the agency for further information and an application form. Give brief details about yourself and why you are interested in this type of work.

Style and vocabulary

1 We can make letters more or less formal through our choice of vocabulary and the expressions we use.
eg. *reply* (formal) and *answer* (neutral)
Match the formal words in the first box with their more neutral equivalents. Can you think of any other pairs like these?

Formal
a. receive/obtain/acquire   b. further   c. regret
d. telephone   e. search/seek   f. supply /provide
g. request   h. commence   i. enquire   j. attempt
k. available   l. require   m. convenient/possible
n. resolve   o. assistance   p. inform
q. dissatisfied   r. purchase

Neutral
1 tell   2 ring/call/phone   3 be sorry   4 another
5 free   6 help   7 ask about   8 look for   9 fed up
10 need   11 buy   12 OK   13 give   14 ask for
15 solve   16 get   17 begin   18 try

189

2 Study the differences between the formal expressions and their more neutral or informal equivalents.

1 I would appreciate it if you could -> Please could you
2 I look forward to your reply -> I am looking forward to your answer
3 I was most dissatisfied to receive your bill... I was really fed up when I got your bill.
4 Should you require further assistance do not hesitate to telephone me .-> If you need any more help just call me.
5 With reference to your letter/Regarding your letter-> In reply to your letter

3 "Translate" these formal sentences into more neutral English.

1 I would appreciate it if you could supply me with a further copy of your computer manual.
2 I am seeking summer employment in the tourist industry.
3 With reference to your letter of last month, I regret to inform you that we are unable to meet with your request for a refund of school fees.
4 Should you require any additional information do not hesitate to telephone our office.

NARRATIVE COMPOSITION

In Part 2 there is often an opportunity to write a narrative composition.
To write a good narrative composition you need to:
- answer the question showing that you have a clear understanding of your "audience", i.e. who you are supposed to be writing for.
- show the examiner that you can use a variety of narrative tenses.
- produce well organised, linked and logical work.
- be interesting.

1 Narrative tenses

Test yourself by trying to remember which form
1 is like the past in the past.
2 is used to describe simple facts and states.
3 sets the scene.
4 is used for events which follow a clear chronological sequence.
5 describes what was going on before an interruption.

Now check if you were right by turning to Unit 4 Storytelling pages 46-47, where this area is examined in depth.

2 Analysis

On page 56 there is this "model" composition:
Write a story ending with the words "We never saw him again".
Read the answer carefully and analyse when and why each narrative tense is used. Use the notes on the following page and those on pages 46-47.

3 Consolidation

Complete the passage by changing the verb in brackets into an appropriate past tense narrative form.

I shall never forget the time my wife and I (1).......... (take) the night ferry back from France. We (2).......... (decide) on a night crossing some months earlier so we (3).......... (have) an extra day. On the last day we (4).......... (get) up early and (5).......... (set off) on our long drive. Although it (6).......... (rain) slightly we (7).......... (not care) because we (8).......... (have) beautiful weather for the past three weeks. However, we (9).......... (drive) through Poitiers when we (10).......... (have) a puncture. We (11).......... (have to) take all our luggage out to get the spare tyre from the bottom of the boot.
After we (12).......... (drive) the rest of the day we finally (13).......... (arrive) at the port just before the ship's departure. We (14).......... (look forward to) a good night's sleep but they (15).......... (already give) our cabin to someone else because they (16).......... (think) we (17).......... (not going to come) . There (18).......... (be) nothing to do except try to sleep in the lounge. Unfortunately, earlier that day the English rugby team (19).......... (win) a rare victory over the French. While we (20).......... (try) to sleep, the English supporters (21).......... (celebrate) noisily for the entire voyage. When we (22).......... (land) in England five hours later we (23).......... (not sleep) a wink.

4 Extension

Turn to page 49 where there is the outline of the story of Prince Llewellyn and his faithful dog, Gelert. After it there are questions which helped you to expand the story and make it more interesting. Invent similar questions yourself which will help you to expand the story in exercise 3.

5 Verb tables

It is essential that you know the forms of irregular verbs in English. Mistakes with these can make a terrible impression and cost you marks.
Study the list of irregular verbs on page 216-217. They are grouped into "families". With a partner, test each other on their forms and spelling.

DISCURSIVE COMPOSITION

In this kind of composition you are usually asked to set out your ideas about an issue or to consider it from different points of view. This is often done within the context of writing a short article for a magazine or newspaper. We looked at this on page 25 and page 61. With this kind of composition, planning and organisation are essential. It is important to remember that successful compositions are the result of a process. Writers usually do something like this:

think about the title
write down a few ideas and words
prepare a simple plan
prepare a first draft
change some ideas/remove some old ones - add new ones/re-order
prepare a second draft

In the examination you may not have time to write completely different drafts. This means it is better to write on every other line (every second line) so that you can make corrections and changes without making your answer impossible to read.

ANSWERING THE QUESTION

1 Setting out ideas

Turn to page 87 and have another look at the reading passage "The Curse of the Motor Car". The writer organised it like this:

states situation/identifies problem.

▼

outlines solutions

▼

comes to a conclusion

There are other things you should notice.
- the way the first sentence of each paragraph tells us its topic.
- the way that the writer uses questions (we call them rhetorical questions) to help develop the arguments in the essay. Asking **rhetorical questions,** where you already know the answer, is an efficient way of dealing with different points.

2 Balancing ideas

Turn to page 122 and read the "model" essay which discusses the fur trade. The writer organises it like this:

states situation/problem

▼

states the arguments for one side

▼

states the arguments for the other side

▼

gives own opinions and comes to a conclusion

Notice the rhetorical question : "Which side is right?".

3 Discussing and balancing each point in turn

A third way of tackling this kind of question is to discuss the plusses and minuses of each point as you go through. This can lead to long and complicated sentences so only use it if you are very confident.

4 Key expressions for the opinion question

Ordering points and reasons:
First of all, Firstly, To begin with
Secondly, Next...
Lastly, Finally

Adding new, and perhaps surprising information:
As a matter of fact...
In your letter you claim the teacher had not been trained. As a matter of fact, Miss Greene is the most qualified member of staff.

Being Brief:
In brief, ... and so on. ... and so forth
We all know it is cruel to keep animals in zoos: they are taken from their natural habitat, live in cramped conditions and so on.

Concluding and summarising:
To sum up, On balance, In conclusion, All in all, In a nutshell, In short

Re-formulating:
In other words.
The police were completely ignorant of the facts of the case. In other words, they had no idea of what had really happened.

Saying *and*:
And, In addition, What's more, Furthermore

Generalising:
In general, By and large, On the whole

Referring:
Regarding..., As regards...

Giving examples:
For example, For instance, Let's take X as an example

Saying *but*:
But, while, however, although, even though, despite, despite the fact that, nevertheless
Make sure that you turn to page 119 and check that you really understand the important grammatical differences between these forms.

Other expressions:
After all... -> This means "don't forget" and we often use it to introduce an important point.
She is very young to go away on a school camp. After all, she is only twelve years old.

There again -> This is used to contradict something we have just said and often returns us to an earlier point.
She is very young to go away on a school camp. After all, she is only twelve years old. There again, the experience will help her to become a little more independent.

The thing is -> We often use this expression to introduce an fundamental, crucial point. (Often spoken.)
I know you would like to offer him the job but, the thing is, I just don't trust him.

Paper 3 USE OF ENGLISH

Parts 1 and 2 GAP FILLING

Part 1 GAP FILLING (MULTIPLE CHOICE)
Part 1 tests your knowledge of vocabulary and grammar through gap filling based around multiple choice vocabulary items.
Refer to pages 14-15 to remind yourself of what this question tests.

In Part 2, you have to complete a text with fifteen gaps using your own resources.
Both parts test similar things although there is more of an emphasis on vocabulary in Part 1.
With both parts it is essential that you read the entire text through for comprehension before attempting an answer. Challenging areas that both parts test are phrasal verbs and prepositional phrases. With a partner, study the list of phrasal verbs and information on prepositional phrases and dependent prepositions on pages 209-211 and 215-216.

Part 2 GAP FILLING (CLOZE TEST)

This is an extremely challenging question because it can test anything!

Syntax , i.e. sentence patterns and verbs.
Adjectives and verbs with dependent prepositions.
Prepositional phrases.
Particles and stems of phrasal verbs.
Conjunctions.
Quantifiers.
Articles.
Prepositions.
Auxiliaries.
Adverbs.
Personal and possessive pronouns and adjectives, relative pronouns and question words.

DO
- read the text for a general understanding.
- look at the words on either side of the gap.
- develop your awareness of the types of word which are often missing.
- practise this type of exercise often.

DON'T
- try to fill in anything until you have read through the text.
- get stuck on one gap. Move on to the next.
- expect a lot of nouns or main verbs to be missing.
- spend too long on this question!

Study page 25 and revise the exercises on pages 41 and 71.

Now fill in the numbered blanks in these two passages. Use one word only for each space.

A

Recently the company (0).<u>where</u>. I work started to use a computer to record (1)..........
the phone calls which were being made. The manager believed (2).......... employees
were making long-distance calls (3).......... the firm's expense. One of (4)..........
computer's first victims was a night cleaner. She (5).......... been having long
conversations (6).......... her relatives overseas. However, the greatest success was
(7).......... the building was broken (8).......... and valuable computing equipment was
stolen. The following morning someone had the (9).......... idea of printing out a list of
all the numbers (10).......... had been rung on that night. There was (11).......... one - to
a taxi company which had sent a cab to (12).......... up a smart-looking businessman
and a (13).......... of office equipment. The businessman had explained to the driver
that he had (14).......... working late and that he needed to take the computer home.
The driver was (15)........... to remember where the thief lived and eventually led the
police to him.

B

A pet shop owner had a parrot (0).<u>which</u>. once belonged to an old sailor. As you can
(1).......... imagine the parrot had an extremely rich vocabulary which is (2).......... it
was kept hidden away in the back of the shop.
Eventually, one day an old lady asked if she (3).......... buy it. Her husband had passed
(4).......... and she felt very lonely. The owner saw this was a marvellous opportunity to
(5).......... rid of it. However, (6).......... a decent and honest man he told her all (7)..........
it. She refused to be (8)........... off and the bird was sold. Hardly (9).......... it arrived in
her sitting room than it said the (10).......... awful words the woman had ever heard.
(11).......... wasting a second she took it to the kitchen and shut it in the freezer. When
it had got used to the darkness it saw a chicken plucked and (12).......... for the oven.
"Oh no," thought the parrot, "You (13).......... have said something really bad; I'd better
be more careful in future!" The old lady (14).......... rescued the half-frozen bird and
they spent many happy years together. The parrot, of course, (15).......... said a rude
word again!

Part 3 KEY WORD TRANSFORMATIONS

Study the exercises on pages 13 and 20 to review what this part of the test involves.
Prepositional phrases and verb/noun collocations are likely to be tested as well as
grammar.

Some dos and don'ts

> **DO**
> * make sure the meaning of the second sentence is the same as the first.
> * make sure that you include all the information of the first sentence in the second.
>
> **DON'T**
> * change the word in bold in any way.
> * exceed the number of words allowed.
> * add any extra information.
> * change the tense in active/passive transformations.

Part 4 TEXT CORRECTION

Look at the exercises on page 21 to remind yourself of this exercise type.

Study the categories below where extra and unnecessary words might be used.

Extra prepositions
near *to* London, opposite *of*,
reach *at*, catch *at*

Paul is going to home. Paul is at home. ✔
~~He arrived at home an hour ago.~~

We stayed in because of the rain. ✔
because it was raining. ✔
~~because of it was raining~~

Don't eat bread, have rice instead. ✔
~~Don't eat bread have rice instead of.~~
Have rice instead of bread. ✔

Unnecessary repetition of subject:
~~My sister she likes pizza.~~
~~Luigi, who lives opposite the bank, he is a student.~~

Unnecessary reflexive:
~~We dressed ourselves and left.~~
~~We adapted ourselves.~~
~~I didn't enjoy myself the film.~~
I hurt/cut myself. ✔ Enjoy yourself. ✔

Unnecessary auxiliaries
~~She got up, had dressed and ate her breakfast.~~
(The past perfect is not needed here.)
The film was enjoyed by everyone. ✔
~~Everyone was liked the film.~~

Embedded questions
I do not know where do they live.
Could you tell me where do you live?

Auxiliary trying to make an intransitive verb passive
~~The ship was disappeared in the storm.~~ (*Disappear* is intransitive so we cannot use it in the passive.)
The ship was lost in the storm. ✔ (The verb *lose* is transitive so we can make it passive.)
The bridge was raised. ✔
The bridge rose. ✔
~~The bridge was risen.~~

Unnecessary objects after intransitive phrasal verbs
~~We packed our bags and set off it.~~ Refer to page 54 where the grammar of phrasal verbs is examined.

Unnecessary words with expressions of quantity
Refer to page 34 to remind yourself of when the different forms are used.

too much too much money ~~too much expensive~~
a few/few of/a few of/several/several of.

Articles
Remember we generally don't use articles in front of abstract or concept nouns when they are being used in a general, non-specific way:
It was an evening filled with ~~the~~ laughter.
There is nothing more beautiful than the laughter of a child. ✔
The second sentence is correct because the 'laughter' is specific.

Adjectives wrongly used as nouns
He is young. ✔
~~He is a young.~~
He is a young man. ✔

Nouns which are normally uncountable
accommodation, advice, anger, behaviour, bread, business, cash, clothes, countryside, courage, damage, education, evidence, food, fruit, fun, furniture, gossip, hair, happiness, harm, help, homework, hospitality, housework, information, jealousy, jewellery, knowledge, laughter, leisure, luck, luggage, machinery, meat, money, music, news, nonsense, parking, patience, permission, progress, rubbish, safety, scenery, shopping, soap, spaghetti, strength, stuff, toast, traffic, transport, travel, violence, vocabulary, wealth, weather, work, writing.

Part 5 WORD FORMATION

In this part you read a text with gaps. Each gap must be filled by using the word at the end of the line in a suitable form. Look at pages 27 and 103 for examples of this task.

Do all you can to familiarise yourself with the items in these lists. It is by no means exhaustive! With a partner work through section after section and test each other on forms and spellings. Be aware when you are reading of other words which are clearly formed from a more common root and add them to these lists.

Often we can discover how to transform a root by looking it up in a dictionary. For example, in the *Longman Dictionary of Contemporary English* the entries for **happy** and **happiness** follow each other. However, **unhappy** appears under **u**. When a negative form is made by using a prefix, e.g. **mis-, un-, -in, dis-, -in, -im, -il, -ir,** then it will have an entry of its own far from the root. Similarly, the abstract noun **poverty** is quite distant from the simple adjective **poor**. In such cases the best option is to use a bilingual dictionary.

Paper 5 SPEAKING (INTERVIEW)

1 Examination Format

In most cases the speaking paper is conducted in pairs of candidates, i.e. two candidates at a time. There are two examiners (both of whom give marks): an interlocutor who conducts the test and asks questions; and an assessor who listens. The speaking paper is divided into four parts.

Part 1 PERSONAL INFORMATION

The interlocutor asks questions to obtain personal information about the candidates.

Part 2 DISCUSSING PHOTOGRAPHS

Each candidate is given two photographs to discuss. Candidates discuss the photos and the general topic. Candidate A has two photographs around one topic and candidate B two photographs around a different topic. Each candidate will also be asked to comment briefly on the other candidate's photographs.

Part 3 COMMUNICATIVE TASK

Candidates work together to complete a task based around picture prompts.
Tasks include planning, problem solving, prioritising and speculating.

Part 4 DEVELOPMENT

The interlocutor joins in and encourages candidates to extend and develop the discussion they began in Part 3.

2 Assessment

Candidates are assessed on the following:
• Linguistic resource (e.g. Grammar, Vocabulary)
• Pronunciation.
• Fluency
• Interactive communication

3 A sample examination

We are going to run though an entire imaginary interview. The candidates working together are Ana from Cordoba in Spain and Olivier from Orléans near Paris.

PART 1

INTERLOCUTOR: Good afternoon. Could I have your mark sheets please? Thank you. (Hands over mark sheets to the assessor.) My name is Rachel Brown and this is my colleague Peter Black. He is just going to be listening to us. So you are Ana and Olivier, aren't you?

ANA AND OLIVIER: Yes, that's right.

INTERLOCUTOR: Now, do make yourselves comfortable. First of all I'm going to ask you some questions about yourselves. Right, so let's start with Olivier. So, Olivier, where are you from?

OLIVIER: From near Paris, Orléans. I don't know if you know it?

INTERLOCUTOR: Oh yes. I went there once a long time ago. And what is it like?

OLIVIER: Orléans is a nice city. It is important for business and a lot of people travel each day to Paris to work. And of course it is important for tourism. It is famous for Jeanne D'Arc... Joan of Arc you say...

INTERLOCUTOR: Yes. Right, right... And Ana. You're from Spain, aren't you?

ANA: Yes that's right. From Cordoba in the south.

INTERLOCUTOR: Mm, lovely. Yes, I've been there many times, lovely. And what do you do there Ana?

ANA: Well, I am a student. I am studying psychology at university in Seville, which is a big city near Cordoba.

INTERLOCUTOR: Psychology ! That's interesting. And what do you plan to do when you graduate?

ANA: I am not sure yet. But perhaps I will try to work in a hospital.

INTERLOCUTOR: And Olivier, what are your plans for the future?

OLIVIER: Well. I have just finished high school and I would like to continue my studies and go to business school.

INTERLOCUTOR: I see, why is that?

OLIVIER: Well, eventually I would like to get a job as a lawyer or something like that.

INTERLOCUTOR: I see. And what do you both do in your free time?

ANA: Well, I don't have much free time because I have to study a lot and I have a part-time job as a waitress in a restaurant. But I like to play tennis and see my friends. I also go dancing a lot and practise traditional Spanish dancing..

INTERLOCUTOR: Sevillanas?

ANA: Yes, that's right.

INTERLOCUTOR: That must be very interesting. And Olivier, what about you ?

OLIVIER: I am keen on sport, I like to go windsurfing. I also like to take part in plays and act.

INTERLOCUTOR: Oh really! Right, I think we are ready to move on to the next part of the examination...

PART 2

INTERLOCUTOR: I'd like each of you to talk on your own for about a minute. I'm going to give each of you two different photographs. Here you are, Olivier, here are your two photographs. Please let Ana see them. They show different places where you can listen to music. (Hands over picture sheet.) Ana, I'll give you your photographs in a minute. Right, Olivier, I'd like you to compare and contrast these photographs. Which event would you rather go to? Remember, you only have about a minute for this, so don't worry if I interrupt you.

OLIVIER: Let me see, right. Well, they are both erm concerts. The first one is, I think, some kind of classical concert. The other one is a rock concert. It is in a park, on a hot summer's day. I think I prefer this one of the erm classical concert. I prefer classical music to pop music.

INTERLOCUTOR: And why don't you like the other one as much?

OLIVIER: I do not like the other one at all. It looks too crowded. In the background there is the stage but it is very far. It reminds me of the time I went to a concert like this. There were thousands of people and it was impossible to see anything.

INTERLOCUTOR: Right, right. Thank you Olivier. What about you, Ana, which event would you rather go to?

ANA: Well, I think I would prefer the pop concert. It looks a lot more fun. The other one is too formal and serious.

INTERLOCUTOR: Thank you. Now, Ana here are your photographs. Please let Olivier see them. They show people doing different jobs.
(Hands over picture sheet to Ana.)

INTERLOCUTOR: I'd like you to compare and contrast these photographs saying what you would find attractive or unattractive about each job, in other words what its positive and negative aspects . Remember, you have only about a minute for this, so don't worry if I interrupt you. All right?

ANA: Mm. Let me see. This first one looks like a kind of scientist. In the foreground there is a lot of apparatus...She is doing an experiment, I think. I think it must be worthwhile to be a scientist and to do research and find cures for illnesses. But I am not very good at physics or biology and I think it could be a lonely job. The other person looks like a businessman or erm stockbroker. He looks very busy and there are other people in the office . I imagine the job can be exciting, but perhaps very stressful too. All the same, I think I would rather be in the busy office.

INTERLOCUTOR: Thank you, Ana. And what about you, Olivier, which one would you prefer?

OLIVIER: I think I agree with Ana. I wouldn't like to be a scientist. I think it would be more interesting to be a businessman, I like to have contact with other people.

PART 3

INTERLOCUTOR: Now I'd like you to do something together. I'd like you to imagine that you have won first prize in a competition. It's a two week holiday in one of the places shown here. So just have a look at the pictures...
(Hands over picture sheet.)
I'd like you to talk to each other about three of these places. Say what they have to offer and how you would spend your time if you went there. Afterwards, say which you would choose. It is not necessary to agree with each other. All right? You only have about three minutes for this, so, once again, don't worry if I stop you and please speak so that we can hear you. So if you'd like to begin...

ANA: Right...let me see. There are lots of different holidays. There is one in the mountains, and another one, is it in India?

OLIVIER: Yes, I think so, and one on a tropical island, it could be Jamaica or somewhere like that. This one looks interesting. It's a pyramid, isn't it?

ANA: Yes. Isn't it one of the erm Mayan ones? From Mexico I think.

OLIVIER: Yes, I think you're right. And this last one. It looks like New York.

ANA: Manhattan.

OLIVIER: That's right. Anyway. What do they have to offer? Well, shall we look at New York first?

ANA: Yes. Well there are lots of museums and parks, and of course we could go shopping, there are some very famous stores. We could also practise our English.

OLIVIER: That's true. It is supposed to be quite dangerous isn't it? I don't think I would go there for a two week holiday.

ANA: No, neither would I. I like to relax more. Maybe for a long weekend. What about this one? The erm island holiday would be good for sunbathing and swimming.

OLIVIER: I agree, but don't you think it could be boring? In my opinion there are places which are just as nice in Spain and the south of France.

ANA: Yes, you're right. Where do you think we should go? How about this one?

OLIVIER: You mean the one of Mexico. Yes it could be very interesting. I have never been to that part of the world. I am interested in archaeology and ancient civilisations.

ANA: Me too. There is also a lot of culture and folk-lore I think. We would be able to buy some interesting souvenirs. And we could always go to the beach as well. What about India, though? I mean, I have never been there and they speak English too and the culture and people are very interesting.

OLIVIER: Mm... you're right but I think I would rather go to Mexico because...

INTERLOCUTOR: I'm sorry I am going to have to interrupt you...

PART 4

INTERLOCUTOR: ...So did you manage to agree on where to go?

OLIVIER: I'm not sure, I think we agreed to go to Mexico but then Ana changed her mind.

ANA: Yes. I would like to go to Mexico but I was about to say I would rather visit India. After all they speak English there so that would be different language for me too. There again, Mexico would be interesting.

INTERLOCUTOR: I see. Anyway, as I said you didn't have to agree. What I'd like to do now is to talk about holidays in general. How important do you think they are, Olivier?

OLIVIER: Very. I mean, in France everybody has a long holiday in the summer and I think it is very important to have a break from work.

ANA: I agree. It is also a good thing to go away too.

INTERLOCUTOR: Yes... And when you go away do you think it is it better to go on holiday with your friends or with your family?

OLIVIER: Ha ha! A difficult question. You can be freer if you go away with your friends but with your parents it is less expensive.

ANA: Yes, that's right. When I was about fifteen or sixteen I used to have lots of arguments with my parents about what to do.

INTERLOCUTOR: And is it different now. I mean have things improved?

ANA: Oh yes. Usually I stay with them for a while but I also have a holiday with friends.

OLIVIER: I think I am lucky because my parents give me a lot of freedom .

INTERLOCUTOR: And what are the bad things about going on holiday?

OLIVIER: The bad things? Well, being ill, I suppose or losing your money..

ANA: And also the arguments. It is terrible if you go on holiday and you don't get on with the other person or people.

OLIVIER: I couldn't agree more. I went away with a friend from school once and we argued all the time. After the holiday we weren't friends again.

INTERLOCUTOR: Oh dear! That's quite common, I think. And finally, if you could go anywhere in the world for a holiday where would it be?

ANA: Anywhere in the world? Well, that's difficult. I think I would go to Australia, maybe or New Zealand, I have always wanted to got there ever since I was a child.

INTERLOCUTOR: Oh really! Why's that?

ANA: I think I was fascinated by the idea of all the different animals you get there.

INTERLOCUTOR: And what about you, Olivier?

OLIVIER: Well, there are so many places I would like to visit. But Nepal and the Himalayas I think. There is still a traditional way of life there and I would like to experience it before it disappears.

INTERLOCUTOR: Well, thank you very much. That's the end of the test!

4 Conversational Strategies

Here is a list of expressions and strategies you may find useful for managing your interview. The examiner will probably use polite forms to ask you to perform tasks. It is important that you familiarise yourself with these.

E.g. Begin!

Would you like to begin. ✔

If you'd like to begin now. ✔

Signalling you are ready to start

OK. Well... Right...

Shall I/we begin? Are you ready?

"Right, Sylvia... Shall we begin?"

Talking about possibilities

We could...

"Well, we could put the TV in the corner and the have the sofa under the window."

Choosing a course of action

We should/we ought to... I think we should/ought to...

We had better... I think it is better if...

"Well, first of all I think we should make a list of guests. After that we ought to phone them to see what a convenient time for the meeting would be..."

Playing for time

Well, Er..., Let me see... Mmm...

Make sure you don't use hesitation words or sounds from your own language. They can sound strange in English!

Making choices

I prefer tea to coffee.

I'd rather have tea than coffee.

I'd rather we had tea than coffee.

We tend to use *prefer* for statements about our general preferences and *would rather* for situations where we are making a real choice:

"In general I prefer meat to fish but I'd rather have fish this time".

Expressing surprise

Wow! Really! Goodness!

What a surprise!

Expressing sympathy/disappointment

Oh dear. What a pity. Poor you.

Never mind.

Making suggestions

Why don't we do this?

How about doing this?

Let's do this.

We could always do this. (As a last resort)

Giving opinions

I think, Personally, In my opinion, As far as I'm concerned, As I see it,

Giving someone else's opinion

According to...

Asking for suggestions and feelings

What do you think? How do you feel about this?

What do you think we should do?

Agreeing

I (quite) agree, Absolutely! I couldn't agree more.

So do I/ I do too. (See page 23 in Unit 2 for a full examination of short replies.)

Requesting and getting people to do things

Could you/ Would you... Would you mind...

"Would you begin the task?"

"Would you mind beginning the task?"

NB Look at the answers to the questions.

"Can I ask you a personal question?"

Of course, go ahead. (It's OK)

" Would you mind if I asked you a personal question?"

Of course not, go ahead. (It's OK)

Offering/ordering

Would you like some more time/another minute?

Would you like to begin now? (A polite order the examiner may use.)

Do you think you could stop now? =Stop now!

Asking for permission

May I... Can I... Is it all right if... Do you think I could...

"Is it all right if/Do you think I could I have a few more seconds to think?"

Disagreeing

I don't agree, I (completely/entirely) disagree.

Yes but... I see your point but...

Confirming Yes, That's right...

Contradicting

Actually... In fact....

You're French, aren't you? Well, actually I'm Swiss.

Asking for clarification/repetition
What do you mean?
Could you explain/say that again?
Do you think you could explain say that again?
Would you mind saying/explaining that again?

Re-formulation
In other words...

Saying you understand/ don't understand
I understand, I see. Ah!
I'm sorry I don't understand. Sorry I don't follow you...

Re-capping what has been said
So, what you're saying /suggesting is...
Are you saying/suggesting that...

Apologising
I'm sorry, I'm afraid.
I'm sorry, I didn't catch what you said. Would you mind repeating it?"

Interrupting
Can I interrupt/say something?
Do you think I could interrupt/come in there?

Speculating
It might be, It could be, Perhaps, Maybe,
I'm not quite sure...
NB Candidates tend to overuse "maybe". If you can, use other forms of speculating:
I'm not quite sure what it is. It could be a scene of London, there's a title at the bottom... I can't quite make it out. Perhaps it is a picture of Paris.

Making guesses
It must be/It can't be
NB The opposite of "must be" is "can't be" .
He mustn't be English he has a funny accent.
He can't be English he has a funny accent. ✔

Describing
Although you are not required to describe the photographs you are given, you may wish to refer to them in the interview.
It looks... It looks like... It looks as if...
It looks old.
It looks like an old boat.
It look as if it's old / an old boat..

Describing position
In the bottom/top left/right hand corner
In the foreground/In the background...
There is a... I can see a...

Avoiding
Sometimes you may want to steer away from a topic you don't know very much about.

Well, I don't know much about X but I do know something about Y.
This reminds me of the time when I...

5 Final advice

When you are in an interview with another candidate, the important thing is not to appear passive. There are four other things that you should remember:

1 Don't let the other candidate dominate the discussion. Remember you have an equal right to participate and show what you can do. Don't be afraid to interrupt or take your turn. However, do remember that other candidate has the right to participate as well.

2 Don't automatically agree with everything that the other person may say as you will be restricted to saying "yes" all the time. Put different points of view so that you can occupy some of the speaking time. Make sure that you are confident with the conversational gambits on page 198.

3 Be animated! Show that you are following the discussion. Nod, smile and show you are actively listening to what is going on.

4 Don't go into the examination "cold". Speak to other candidates in English before you are interviewed. This will get you operating in English "mode" and help you to relax.

PRONUNCIATION

USING A DICTIONARY

A good dictionary not only gives you the meanings of words but it also helps you with their pronunciation. To use the dictionary effectively in this respect, you need to understand the symbols for the sounds (phonemes) of English and the system which is used for marking stress.

1 The sounds (phonemes) of English

Study the pronunciation table and think of one more keyword which will help you to remember the pronunciation of each of the sounds.

CONSONANTS		VOWELS	
Symbol	Keyword	Symbol	Keyword
These symbols are used for both the British and American pronunciations			
p	**p**ack	e	b**e**d
b	**b**ack	æ	b**a**d
t	**t**ie	iː	sh**ee**p
d	**d**ie	ɪ	sh**i**p
k	**c**lass	ɑː	c**a**lm
g	**g**lass	ɒ	p**o**t
		ɔː	c**au**ght, h**o**rse
tʃ	**ch**ur**ch**	ʊ	p**u**t
dʒ	**j**u**dg**e	uː	b**oo**t
		ʌ	c**u**t
f	**f**ew	ɜː	b**ir**d
v	**v**iew	ə	bett**er**
θ	**th**row		
ð	**th**ough	eɪ	m**a**ke
s	**s**oon	əʊ	b**oa**t
z	**z**oo	aɪ	b**i**te
ʃ	**sh**oe	aʊ	n**ow**
ʒ	mea**s**ure	ɔɪ	b**oy**
		ɪə	h**ere**
m	su**m**	eə	h**air**
n	su**n**	ʊə	p**oor**
ŋ	su**ng**		
		eɪə	pl**ayer**
h	**h**ot	əʊə	l**ower**
l	**l**ot	ɔɪə	empl**oyer**
r	**r**od	aɪə	t**ire**
j	**y**et	aʊə	fl**ower**
w	**w**et		
These symbols are used for the American pronunciations		ɑ	h**o**t, f**a**ther
		ɔ	h**o**rse, l**o**ng
		ɝ	b**ir**d
		o	h**oa**rse, c**o**urt

from the *Longman Active Study Dictionary of English*

• Now check your chosen words in a dictionary.

2 Word stress

Word stress is important for two main reasons. First of all, if you stress an English word in the wrong place, you may not be understood. Secondly, in *Paper 5: Interview* you are marked on stress! Study this dictionary entry for the word policeman.

This symbol (ˈ) shows where the main stress lies.

po•lice•man /pəˈliːsmən/ also **police officer** /pəˈliːs ˈɒfɪsəʳ/
-n -men /mən/ a male member of a police force
Look at the following words and decide where the main stress lies.

Example: advertise has three syllables
ad•ver•tise /ˈædvətaɪz/

1 ad • ver • tise • ment /ədˈvɜːtɪsmənt/
2 ad • ver • ti • sing /ˈædvətaɪzɪŋ/
3 in • dus • tri • al /ɪnˈdʌstrɪəl/
4 in • dus • try /ˈɪndəstrɪ/
5 ag • ri • cul • ture /ˈægrɪˌkʌltʃəʳ/
6 pho • to • graph /ˈfəʊtəgrɑːf-græf/
7 pho • tog • ra • phy /fəˈtɒgrəfi/
8 pho • to• graph • ic /ˌfəʊtəˈgræfɪk/
9 pho • tog • ra • pher /fəˈtɒgrəfəʳ/
10 co • mmu • ni •c ate /kəˈmjuːnɪkeɪt/
11 co • mmu • ni • ca • tion /kəˌmjuːnɪˈkeɪʃən/
12 pro • nounce /prəˈnaʊns/
13 pro • nun •ci • a • tion /prəˌnʌnsɪˈeɪʃən/

• Now check your answers in the dictionary.

3 Use the phoneme chart and the stress markings to help you work out what these common English words are.

1 /fɜːst/
2 /səˈtɪfɪkət/
3 /ɪgzæmɪˈneɪʃən/
4 /ˈkwestʃən/
5 /ˈɑːnsə/
6 /ˈlæŋgwɪdʒ/
7 /ˈdɪkʃənərɪ/
8 /əˈfɪʃəl/
9 /ˈɑːftəwədz/
10 /ˈtʃɒklɪt/
11 /ˈjuːʒʊəlɪ/
12 /ˈɪŋglɪʃ/
13 /ɪmˈpɔːtənt/
14 /θɪŋk/
15 /piːz/

4 Use your dictionary to check how to say the following words.

1 thorough
2 colleague
3 baggage
4 produce (verb)
5 whole
6 clothes
7 aisle
8 record (noun)
9 argue
10 vegetable
11 comfortable
12 cough

Key to page 189

Formal		Neutral	
a	receive/obtain/acquire	**16**	get
b	further	**4**	another
c	regret	**3**	be sorry
d	telephone	**2**	ring/call/phone
e	search	**8**	look for
f	supply /provide	**13**	give
g	request	**14**	ask for
h	commence	**17**	begin
i	enquire	**7**	ask about
j	attempt	**18**	try
k	available	**5**	free
l	require	**10**	need
m	convenient/possible	**12**	OK
n	resolve	**15**	solve
o	assistance	**6**	help
p	inform	**1**	tell
q	dissatisfied	**9**	fed up
r	purchase	**11**	buy

Key to page 190

I shall never forget the time my wife and I **(1)** took the night ferry back from France. We **(2)** had decided on a night crossing some months earlier so we **(3)** would have an extra day. On the last day we **(4)** got up early and **(5)** set off on our long drive. Although it **(6)** was raining slightly, we **(7)** didn't care because we **(8)** had had beautiful weather for the past three weeks. However, we **(9)** were driving through Poitiers when we **(10)** had a puncture. We **(11)** had to take all our luggage out to get the spare tyre from the bottom of the boot.

After we **(12)** had driven the rest of the day, we finally **(13)** arrived at the port just before the ship's departure. We **(14)** had been looking forward to a good night's sleep but they **(15)** had already given our cabin to someone else because they **(16)** thought that we **(17)** were not going to come. There **(18)** was nothing else to do but to try to sleep in the lounge. Unfortunately, easrlier that day, the English rugby team **(19)** had won a rare victory over the French. While we **(20)** were trying to sleep, the English supporters **(21)** celebrated noisily for the entire voyage. When we **(22)** landed in England five hours later we **(23)** had not slept a wink.

Recently the company **(0)** **where** I work started to use a computer to record **(1)** all the phone calls which were being made. The manager believed **(2)** that employees were making long-distance calls **(3)** at the firm's expense. One of **(4)** the computer's first victims was a night cleaner. She **(5)** had been having long conversations **(6)** with her relatives overseas. However, the greatest success was **(7)** when the building was broken **(8)** into and valuable computing equipment was stolen. The following morning someone had the **(9)** clever idea of printing out a list of all the numbers **(10)** which had been rung on that night. There was **(11)** just one - to a taxi company which had sent a cab to **(12)** pick up a smart-looking businessman and a **(13)** lot of office equipment. The businessman had explained to the driver that he had **(14)** been working late and that he needed to take the computer home. The driver was **(15)** able to remember where the thief lived and eventually led the police to him.

A pet shop owner had a parrot **(0)** **which** once belonged to an old sailor. As you can **(1)** probably imagine the parrot had an extremely rich vocabulary which is **(2)** why it was kept hidden away in the back of the shop.

Eventually, one day an old lady asked if she **(3)** could buy it. Her husband had passed **(4)** away and she felt very lonely. The owner saw this was a marvellous opportunity to **(5)** get rid of it. However, **(6)** being a decent and honest man he told her all **(7)** about it. She refused to be **(8)** put off and the bird was sold. Hardly **(9)** had it arrived in her sitting room than it said the **(10)** most awful words the woman had ever heard. **(11)** Without wasting a second she took it to the kitchen and shut it in the freezer. When it had got used to the darkness it saw a chicken plucked and **(12)** ready for the oven. "Oh no," thought the parrot, "You **(13)** must have said something really bad; I'd better be more careful in future!" The old lady **(14)** finally rescued the half-frozen bird and they spent many happy years together. The parrot, of course, **(15)** never said a rude word again!

Grammar reference

GRAMMAR

THE PRESENT SIMPLE

We use the present simple to talk about facts, states, habits and routines:

She is Greek. She comes from Athens.
He takes the bus at eight o'clock each morning.
Paul knows Emily.

We often use adverbs of frequency with the present simple. The position of the adverb can vary.

1 It is placed directly before the main verb:
   He often plays tennis
   He doesn't usually play football.
   Does he ever play tennis?
2 It is placed directly after the verb **to be**:
   He is often late.
3 It is placed after a modal auxiliary and before the main verb:
   She can usually play tennis on Mondays.

always	often	sometimes	occasionally	rarely	never
		usually			seldom
					hardly ever

While it is possible to use the adverb at the beginning, end or middle of a sentence, it is safest to put it as suggested above.

POSITIONS OF ADVERBS

Initial	Medial	Final
always	usually	usually
sometimes	sometimes	sometimes
occasionally	occasionally	occasionally
	hardly ever	
	rarely/seldom/never	

I usually get up at six o'clock.
Sometimes I get up at seven o'clock.
I get up at ten o'clock occasionally, but only if I'm on holiday.

If we want to begin a sentence with the words in bold above, then we have to invert the subject and auxiliary verb. (See **Inversion**.)

The present simple can be used with a future sense when we are talking about regular events and timetables:
When does the bus to Glasgow arrive? It arrives at six.

The present simple is used with verbs which express states.

1 verbs of cognition: **know, believe, understand, remember, mean.**
2 verbs of possession: **own, belong.**
3 verbs which express likes and dislikes: **adore, love, prefer, hate, detest, loathe.**
4 other verbs: **hear, seem, need, want, cost.**

With some verbs we can use either the present simple or continuous but there may be some change in meaning.
What do you think about capital punishment? (= what is your opinion?)
What are you thinking about? (= mental activity; what's going on in your head?)

He is a fool. (= he is a fool all the time - a state)
He is being a fool. (= he is a fool at the moment)
We can say
She is smelling the flowers, he is tasting the wine .
and *The flowers smell nice or the wine tastes good.*
We **can't** say
~~*The flowers are smelling nice, the wine is tasting good.*~~

THE PRESENT CONTINUOUS

The present continuous is used to describe:

1 activities which are happening right now:
   He is eating lunch.
2 planned future events:
   I'm watching TV this evening. (Present continuous + adverbial)
3 activities happening around now and temporary states (contrasting with permanent ones):
   Jenny works in New York but at the moment she is living in London. She arrived last month and is staying until August.

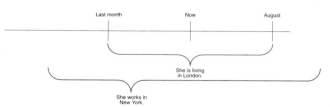

4 The present continuous is also used with **always** when we want to express annoyance:
   She's always smoking my cigarettes. (I don't like it; I wish she would buy her own.)

THE PRESENT PERFECT

The present perfect simple is used to talk about

1 the unfinished past; i.e. actions that began in the past and continue up to the present:
She has been a doctor for five years. (she is still a doctor)

2 the indefinite past i.e. actions in the past when the time is not stated or is left unclear:
I have been to Morocco. (but I haven't said when)

3 for recent events:
Oh no. I've lost my wallet. Has anyone seen it?
Here is the nine o'clock news. There has been an attempt on the president's life. A gunman tried to shoot her outside the presidential palace... (The information about the assassination attempt is news; the next sentence is in the simple past because it has a context.)

4 for recent events where the result is still present/visible:
Wow! You've lost weight.
You look different. Have you changed your hair?

5 for experiences up to now; this is often accompanied by **ever** or **never**:
Have you ever seen an alligator in the wild?

6 often with the following adverbs: **already, yet, just, lately**
Have you done your homework yet?
Yes, I've already finished it.

7 with superlatives:
This is the most interesting book I have ever read.

8 with "This is the first time..."
This is the first time I've visited Europe.
(Compare with : The first time I visited Europe I went on a one month bus tour.)

THE PRESENT PERFECT CONTINUOUS

We use the present perfect continuous

1 to talk about activities which start in the past and continue up to the present (and perhaps into the future):
She has been living in the same house for thirty years.
He's been learning English for seven years.

He's been learning English for seven years.

2 when we are interested in the activity rather than the result:
He has been writing for twenty years. (activity)
He has written seven books. (result)

3 when there is present evidence of an activity which started in the past:
Have you been sunbathing ? (You're like a tomato!)

4 for repeated actions up to the present:
I have been ringing that number all morning but it's always engaged.

MODALS

can   could   may   might   must   ought to shall   should   will   would

Modals are auxiliary verbs which are used, among other things, to talk about ability, possibility, obligation, necessity, to speculate, make requests, offers and suggestions.
Modals, particularly **could, would** and **might** are often used when we want to appear polite or tentative or when there is "social distance" between speakers. In this section we shall examine modals in terms of the individual modal or its "function".

CAN, COULD, MAY AND MIGHT

Look at the exercises on page 95 where this area is examined.

Can is used to
1 express abilities:
She can play the guitar.

2 express theoretical possibility:
Smoking can give you lung cancer.

3 ask for permission or make requests:
Can / Could / May / Might I use your phone?
Can / Could / May / Might you help me?
For past abilities **could** or a form of **be able to** and for future abilities **be able to** are used.

More specifically **could** is used to

1 describe general abilities in the past:
She could / was able to read when she was three.
NB We use **was able to** instead of **could** when a situation allows us to do something or when effort is required:
I drove around for ages looking for a parking space and finally I was able to / could find one.

2 speculate:
Where is my watch?
Have a look in the bathroom. It could / might be there.

203

3 to discuss options:
We could go to Mexico this summer, or there again we could go to the States.

May and **might** are generally considered to be more polite when asking for permission.

SHALL AND SHOULD

Shall is almost always used with *I* and *we*:

1 for offers:
Shall I make lunch for the children today?

2 to elicit suggestions:
What shall we do tonight? Any ideas?

Should is used to give advice or express opinions which we think are morally right:
You should wear a suit at the interview.
Rich people should help the poor.

Ought to can also be used and may be stronger:
You ought to write to your mother. (You haven't written for more than a month!)

Should is also used

1 to predict expected future events. (not **ought to**):
The train should be here in a minute.

2 to make a guess about something that you are sure has happened:
It's six o'clock. He should be at the airport by now.

In the past both **should** and **ought** take the perfect infinitive i.e. the **have done** form. We often use this to express criticism:
You should have closed the window.

MUST AND HAVE TO

Must and **have to** are both used to express obligation. You should make your choice with care.
Have to is used to describe duties and obligations:
I have to answer the phone, make appointments and welcome guests.
Must tends to emphasise the authority of the speaker. Note **must** can appear rude and **have to** is usually a safer choice:
You must wash your hands and face. (Parent to child. The parent has the authority to give the child an order.)
I must post that letter. (we say or think this when we are angry with ourselves)
You must see the Mantegna exhibition. (a strong recommendation)

Which one we choose depends on the situation and the authority of the speaker.
Check the exercise on page 62 to remind yourself of key differences.

SPECULATION

1 **Must**, **might** and **could** can be used for speculation; i.e. make conclusions we think are correct based on evidence or logic.
They almost look the same. They must be brother and sister.

2 The opposite of **must** with this meaning is **can't**:
She can't be English because she speaks with a French accent. She could/might be Canadian, I suppose.

3 If we are speculating about the past we follow the modal with the perfect infinitive, i.e: **have done**.
I can't find my house keys. I must have left them at George's place.
The opposite of **must** have is **can't have**.
You can't have left your keys at George's, you haven't been there today.

WILL AND WOULD

1 For **will** refer to ways of expressing the future and uses of **will** later in this section.
Would is commonly used as a reporting verb for **will**:
Peter rang. He said he would call again this evening.

2 In conditional sentences, refer to conditionals in this section.

3 For more polite offers and requests or when we wish to appear more tentative:
Would you like a drink?
Would it be OK if I borrowed your dictionary?

QUESTION TAGS

1 We use question tags when we wish to confirm or check something. A positive statement is usually followed by a negative tag; a negative statement by a positive tag. The tag uses either the verb **to be** or an auxiliary verb:
You're French, aren't you?
You come from France, don't you?
You've been to America, haven't you?

2 Intonation of the tag is important. Remember, it does not depend on what is true but what the speaker thinks is true. If the intonation falls, the speaker believes the statement is correct and is just checking. If it rises, it is a more genuine question:
Q: You're from France aren't you?
A: Actually, I'm from Switzerland.

Exceptions.
I'm late, aren't I? (not *amn't I*)
Be careful, won't you? (Because it is an imperative statement but talking about the future)
Let's play tennis, shall we?

USES OF THE ARTICLE

We use the indefinite article **a** when we are talking about a singular countable noun in a general, non-specific way or when we introduce it for the first time:
There was a car outside the bank.

We use the definite article **the**

1 when something becomes definite or specific because we refer to it once more:
There was a car outside the bank. The car had its engine running.

2 when what we are referring to is common knowledge:
Where's the dog? (the dog which lives in this house)

3 when something is unique:
The sun, the Eiffel Tower

4 for a species:
The koala bear is threatened with extinction.

5 with adjectives when we want to refer to a category or class of people:
The old, the disabled, the homeless.

6 with most geographical names rivers, seas and oceans, mountains, regions, and countries which have the idea of "of" in them:
The Nile, the Mediterranean, The Pacific, the Andes, the Arctic, the States.

7 for musical instruments:
The violin.
but:
She was given a violin on her birthday. (because it is one particular one)

8 for some places and amenities when we are thinking about them as buildings:
I'm going to the office.
She drove them to the swimming pool.

ZERO ARTICLE

We do not use the article

1 with uncountable nouns such as *milk, sugar, pasta* used in a general, non-specific way:
Milk is good for young children.
but:
The milk I bought yesterday had a strange taste.. (The particular milk I have just tasted.)

2 With abstract or concept nouns such as *fear, love, time, money, employment*:
A mother feels love for her child.
But:
Nothing can compare to the love a mother feels for her child. (Here we use the article because noun is made specific.)

CONDITIONALS

ZERO CONDITIONAL

The zero conditional is used when we state simple facts and truths:
If you touch that switch, a bell goes off.
If you put ice in the sun, it melts.

FIRST CONDITIONAL, **UNLESS, OTHERWISE** AND **PROVIDED**

We use the first conditional when we think something is likely to happen as the result of a future event:
If I we leave soon, we'll get there before it closes.

We often use time expressions **as soon as** and **when** in this construction:
As soon as / when she arrives we'll leave.

We also use it to express threats and promises:
If you do that again, I'll call the police.

We can also use **unless** to express the idea of **if not**. **Unless** comes before the condition:
Unless we leave now we won't find the shop open.

However, we can't use **unless** for **if not** all the time:
I will be pleased if I don't see her tonight.
I will be pleased unless I see her tonight.

Otherwise comes before the consequence.
We should / We had better leave now, otherwise the shop will close before we get there.

We use **provided** when we want to set a strong condition:
I'll take you to the airport provided you pay for the petrol.

See pages 143 and 145

SECOND CONDITIONAL

We use the second conditional when we want to talk about an event and outcome which are less likely to happen, or which is impossible:

If I won the lottery, I'd buy a yacht. (...but it's highly unlikely)

If I had blue eyes, I would be happy. (...but my eyes are brown and always will be)

We also use the second conditional when we are giving advice or making more polite/indirect suggestions or requests:

If I were you, I'd tell the police everything.

If I gave you a present, would you give me a work permit? (We can also use "suppose" here instead of "if".)

We use the second conditional with many stative verbs:

If you knew my father, you'd like him.

Not *"If you know my father you'll like him."*

THIRD CONDITIONAL

The third conditional is used to talk about the "unreal" past. All events are in the past and nothing can be done to change them; however, we imagine what the opposite might have been.

If I had told her the truth, she wouldn't have been angry. (But I didn't tell her and she was angry!)

Pronunciation
Even though it is rare for native speakers to speak in third conditional sentences, when they do they include a lot of contractions and weak forms.

If I'd told her the truth, she wouldn't've been angry.

MIXED CONDITIONAL

We use a mixed conditional when we describe the consequences of a past action on the present. It is like a combination of the third and second conditional:

If we hadn't missed the bus, we wouldn't be stuck here now. (They missed the bus and can't go anywhere!)

May, might and **could** can be used in both second and third conditional sentences when we are less sure about the outcome of an action:

If she told them the truth we might/could get into trouble.

FORMS OF **WISH**

Wish is used to express regrets, wishes and lost opportunities.

Revise the exercises on page 145 which deal with the various use of **wish.** In many respects, **wish** operates like the second and third conditionals:

I wish I had blue eyes. (But I don't and there is nothing I can do to change it.)

I wish I/you could play the piano. (But you can't.)

I wish the train would come soon. (But I don't think it will.)

I wish you would stop smoking those horrible cigarettes. (But I don't think you will.)

I wish I had met you twenty years ago. (But I didn't and there's nothing I can do to change this.)

NOTE If we want to express a wish about ourselves then we have to use **could**:

I wish I could stop smoking. (Not would.)

WAYS OF EXPRESSING THE FUTURE AND THE USES OF **WILL**

In English there are many ways of expressing the future. The form we choose depends largely on how we view the future event.

PRESENT CONTINUOUS + ADVERB OF TIME

I'm seeing Mary tomorrow. (for definite arrangements)

PRESENT SIMPLE

The train leaves at 7.15 . (for timetables and regular schedules)

GOING TO

Look at those clouds, it's going to rain. (for predictions based on present evidence; you can see the future coming!)

She is going to buy him a pullover for his birthday. (for intentions and plans which have usually already been decided)

THE FUTURE IN THE PAST WITH **GOING TO**

We can use **was/were going to do something** to talk about something we intended or planned to do but which we didn't do. = An unfulfilled plan or intention:

We were going to visit Corfu last summer but I had too much work.
I was going to post the letter but I forgot.

WILL

Don't ring for a taxi, I'll drive you to the station. (a spontaneous decision, often relating to the near future)
If you buy the food, I'll cook. (first conditional) (a promise)
We'll leave when / as soon as he gives us the order
I will be 20 next summer. (a simple fact over which we have no control)
You will regret it if you leave school at 16. (a prediction)
I'll be seeing him tomorrow. (Future continuous. Something certain that has already been planned.)
Please don't phone me tomorrow morning, I'll be working. (Future continuous is used to describe an action that will be happening over a period of time in the future.)
Hurry up! The film will have started by the time we arrive. (Future perfect. Something has already happened by a point in the future.)

NOTE: The negative of **will** is **won't** /wəʊnt/

Will has other uses which aren't strictly speaking to do with the future or predictions. In these cases **will** means **want**.
I will go to the discotheque if I want to, Daddy. (An expression of determination.)
Will you marry me.? (A request = Do you want to marry me?)
Oh no! The car won't start. (The car doesn't want to start.)

There are many expressions which are used to express the future, e.g. *It is bound to... It's likely to...*

We can also use the verb **to be** plus the infinitive:
The Queen is to go on a royal tour of South Africa.

Will can also be used to describe regular predictable behaviour.
What do you expect? The cat will scratch you if you tease it.

In the past **would** is used to describe regular predictable behaviour and actions and has a meaning similar to **used to**:
He would / used to come home from the factory and smoke his pipe.
These are repeated actions. For past states we cannot use **would** we only use **used to**:
She used to / would have lovely long hair when she was a girl.

REPORTED SPEECH

Refer to pages 110 - 111 for a thorough treatment of this area.
When statements or questions are reported we often go one step further into the past.
Direct speech: *Dina: I have eaten snails.*
Reported speech: *Dina said she had eaten snails.*

This convention of going one step further into the past is called "backshift". It is regularly tested in the examination.
Look at the table on page 110 to see what happens to major tenses when they are put into reported speech.
Look too at exercise 2 on page 111 which shows what happens to adverbials of time and place; e.g. *here* becomes *there*, *tomorrow* becomes *the following day.*

Remember, the tense of the verb does not change in these cases:

1 With the past perfect simple or continuous:
Direct speech: *Paul: I hadn't been to Paris before.*
Reported speech: *Paul said he hadn't been to Paris before.*

2 With the modals **would, should, might** and **could.** Otherwise you could seriously effect the meaning.
Mother: You should wear a suit, George.
Mother told George he should wear a suit. ✔
not
Mother told George he should have worn a suit.
(This suggests that George refused to wear a suit and his mother is criticising him for not having done so.)

THE INFINITIVE AND THE GERUND

THE INFINITIVE

The infinitive with **to** is used

1. after a number of common verbs: **want, need, hope, plan, intend, promise, tend, offer, afford, threaten, wish, would like, pretend, seem, manage.**

2. when we want to express purpose:
   He picked up the book to check the number.
   She closed the door quietly so as not to disturb her father.

3. in the pattern subject + verb + someone + to do something. Used with the following verbs: **encourage, expect, force, help, invite, order, permit, persuade, remind, teach:**
   They told her to call a doctor.

The infinitive without **to** (bare infinitive) is used after modal verbs like **can** and **must**; after **had better**, and after **make** and **let**.
NOTE: *You make someone do something* (active) but *Someone is made TO do something* (passive).

THE GERUND (-ING FORM)

The gerund is used

1. after verbs of liking and hating: **like, enjoy, love, don't mind/mind dislike, hate, can't stand** and **loathe:**
   I hate getting up early in the morning.

2. after common verbs such as: **admit, avoid, come, consider, deny, finish, go, involve, miss, postpone, risk, suggest:**
   She risked breaking her leg.

3. after prepositions and adjectives which are followed by prepositions: **bored with, keen on, interested in, tired of:**
   I'm interesting in hearing his complaints.

4. after phrasal verbs:
   I am looking forward to going on holiday.

5. with verb patterns which end with a preposition: e.g. **accuse someone of, congratulate someone on:**
   They congratulated him on passing his driving test.

Verbs with which the infinitive and gerund are both possible.

1. with little or no change of meaning:
   I like watching TV in the evening / I like to watch TV in the evening.
   NOTE: I like going to the dentist every six months. = I go every six months and I enjoy it.
   I like to go to the dentist every six months. = I think it is a good habit to go to the dentist every six months.

2. with an important change in meaning:
   I meant to tell her. (an unfulfilled intention)
   It meant telling her. (it involved telling her)

   I remembered to post the letter. (First I remembered, then I posted the letter.)
   I remembered posting the letter. (First I posted the letter and then I remembered.)

   I stopped to talk to him. (First I stopped, then I talked to him.)
   I stopped talking to him. (I finished our conversation (and went away.))

   I tried to lose weight. (objective or intention)
   I tried dieting, running and eating less. (methods)

THE PASSIVE

Refer to page 88.
We use the passive when the agent of the action is unknown, uninteresting, unimportant or obvious.

The passive is formed with the verb **to be** + the past participle of a transitive verb.

INVERSION

We usually invert the subject and noun in two main instances

1. in short statements of agreement. See page 23 for examples of this:
   I like chocolate. -> So do I. (Not *So like I.*)
   She doesn't like football. -> Neither does he. (Not *Neither likes he.*)
   Remember to use the correct auxiliary.

2. after adverbs and expressions of negative force when they come at the beginning of a sentence. e.g. **Hardly/ Not only/ Never/ No sooner.** See page 153. This is usually because we want to add emphasis or achieve a literary effect:
   *Hardly had we got home **when/than** the telephone rang.*

*Not only does she speak Russian fluently **but** she also speaks Arabic.*
Never had I seen such a boring film.
*No sooner had we heard the news **than** we phoned his mother.*

RELATIVE CLAUSES

Relative clauses are used to join two ideas in a single sentence. They tell us more about the subject or object. Relative clauses often begin with the following relative pronouns: **who/that** for people; **which/that** for things and animals; **whose** for possession; **where** for place; **when** for time; and **why** for reason:
*She is the person **who/that** spoke to you.*
*Here is the car **which that** I told you about.*
*He is a politician **whose** time has come.*
*This is the place **where** they got married.*
*Can you remember the time **when** we got lost?*
*She gave us an explanation **why** she couldn't come.*

DEFINING RELATIVE CLAUSES

Defining relative clauses give essential information without which the sentence would be incomplete:
The woman who borrowed my book had red hair.

In defining relative clauses we can leave out the pronouns **who, which** and **that** when they are the object of the verb in the relative clause.
Could you pass me the book (which / that) I bought this morning?

In formal and written English **whom** may be used as a direct object pronoun:
The man whom we had seen the previous evening was sitting at the same table.
Whom is also used after a preposition.
The woman with / about whom we spoke was very interesting.

NON-DEFINING RELATIVE CLAUSES

Non-defining relative clauses give extra, non-essential information. They can be taken out without affecting the principal meaning of a sentence. In writing they are separated from the main clause by commas. In speech, the speaker's voice will pause before and after the clause and often say the clause quickly and with a lower pitch than the rest of the sentence in which it is embedded:
Anna Maria, who had never visited London before, worked as an au pair in an English family.

The most important thing to remember is that the pronoun **that** cannot be used in non-defining relative clauses.

VOCABULARY

PHRASAL VERBS

Phrasal verbs or multi-word verbs consist of a verb plus one or two particles. (A particle may be a preposition or an adverb, or an adverb plus a preposition.) They operate as one item.
She told Paul off. = She criticised/scolded Paul.
The phrasal verbs we are interested in *Think First Certificate* are those which are idiomatic or non-literal; i.e. their meaning is not immediately obvious from the separate meanings of its parts.

There are four basic types of phrasal verb.

Type 1
Intransitive, i.e. they cannot be followed by a direct object:
Don't turn up late. (= don't arrive late)

Type 2
Transitive separable
With type 2 phrasal verbs an object pronoun can only come between the verb and the particle:
She took her on. ✔
She took on her.
A full object can come either between the verb and the particle or after the particle:
She took Anna on. ✔
She took on Anna. ✔

Type 3
Transitive inseparable
With this type of phrasal verb, the object or object pronoun both come after the particle:
She got over the operation.
She got over it.
She got the operation over. She got it over. (This means something different i.e. She finished it.)

Type 4
Phrasal prepositional - transitive inseparable
Type 4 phrasal verbs have two particles: an adverb followed by a preposition.
These are easy to use as they are transitive and inseparable like type 3 phrasal verbs:
She looks up to her grandmother.

SOME COMMON PHRASAL VERBS AND THEIR MOST COMMON MEANINGS

Here is a list of very common phrasal verbs. They are not the only phrasal verbs in English and you should use a good dictionary to learn others.

break down (type 1) stop working: *The bus had broken down.*
lose control of one's emotions: *He broke down and cried when he heard the news.*

break into (type 3) enter illegally: *They broke into the house while everyone was sleeping*

bring up (type 2) raise/educate: *His grandparents brought him up when his parents divorced.*
mention/raise a topic: *Someone brought up the subject of parking at the end of the meeting.*

call back (type 2) return a phone call: *Mrs Brown will call you back as soon as she is free.*

call off (type 2) cancel: *The match was called off because of the dreadful weather.*

carry on (type 3) continue: *When I leave just carry on with your work*

come across (type 3) find by chance: *They came across their father's medals in an old suitcase.*

come into (type 3) inherit : *When his grandmother died he came into a fortune.*

count on (type 3) rely upon: *You can always count on Pauline in a crisis.*

cut down (type 2) reduce: *She cut down the number of cigarettes she smoked.*
She cut the number of cigarettes she smoked down to ten a day.

cut off (type 2) to end/disconnect a service (often used in the passive): *The telephone was cut off because they hadn't paid the bill.*

face up to (type 4) accept/face a situation, usually unpleasant: *You have just got to face up to the fact that she doesn't love you any more.*

fall through (type 1) when something that has been organised fails to happen: *The peace negotiations fell through over a minor point.*

fill in (type 2) complete: *Do you think you could fill in your date of birth on the form, please?*

fill up (type 2) make full: *They filled up the car the night before the journey.*

find out (type 2) discover facts or information: *They phoned the station to find out the times of the trains to Cambridge.*

get across (type 2) communicate: *However hard he tried he couldn't get what he meant across.*

get away with (type 4) escape without punishment: *You let that child get away with everything; he is going to be a problem when he grows up.*

get by (type 1) survive: *Even though they don't have much money they manage to get by.*

get down (type 2) (no passive) depress: *This weather at this time of the year really gets me down.*

get on (type 1) have a (good) relationship: *Since their discussion they have got on a lot better.*

get over (type 3) recover: *Since I got over my cold I have got lots more energy.*

get through (type 3) make contact by phone: *I've tried ringing them all evening but I just haven't been able to get through.*

give away (type 2) distribute: *She gave away all her money to the dogs' home.*
reveal/ betray: *He was shot for giving away his country's military secrets.*

give in (type 1) surrender: *Her father finally gave in and allowed her to go to the disco.*

give out (type 2) distribute: *They gave out thousands of leaflets at the demonstration.*

give up (type 2) stop doing: *He gave up skiing after he broke his leg.*

go off (type 1) explode: *The bomb went off outside the restaurant.*

go on (type 1) happen: *There's a terrible noise outside, what is going on?*

go out (type 1/4) have a romantic relationship: *He asked her if she would like to go out. She refused to go out with him.*

go up (type 1) increase: *School fees are going up next term.*

grow up (type 1) to become an adult: *While I was growing up we used to live in that house over there.*

hold on (type 1) wait: *Is Julie there? Hold on, I'll go and look for her.*

keep on (type 1) continue/persist: *Why do you keep on bothering me? Can't you see I'm trying to work?*

keep up (type 1) maintain the same level: *Can you walk more slowly please? I just can't keep up.*

let down (type 2) disappoint: *He promised to take me to the airport but at the last minute he let me down.*

let off (type 2) not punish: *The judge let him off with a warning because of his age.*

live up to (type 4) meet expectations: *He spent his whole life failing to live up to his father's expectations.*

look after (type 3) take care of: *Do you think you could look after the children while I go shopping?*

look down on (type 4) to consider someone else as inferior: *People looked down on him because he had once been to prison.*

look for (type 3) search: *Have you seen my keys? I've been looking for them everywhere.*

look into (type 3) investigate: *The police are looking into the painting's disappearance.*

look up (type 2) consult a reference book: *I couldn't find her number so I looked it up in the telephone book.*

look up to (type 4) admire/respect: *She always looked up to her grandmother because of her kindness and wisdom.*

make out (type 2) see with difficulty: *What does this word say? I can't make it out.*

make up (type 2) invent: *When he was a little boy he used to listen to the wonderful stories made up by his uncle.*

pick up (type 2) learn (informally): *She picked the language up by working as an au pair in a family.* collect: *Don't bother to take a taxi, I'll come and pick you up.*

put down (type 2) to make someone feel inferior through criticism: *Why do you always put him down? He'll never have any self-confidence.* to kill an animal to end its suffering: *The racehorse broke its leg so the vet had no choice but to put the animal down.*

put off (type 2) postpone: *I am afraid my mother is coming this weekend so we'll have to put off our game of tennis.*

put through (type 2) connect on the phone: *If you'd like to wait a moment I'll put you through to her extension.*

put up (type 2) give (temporary) accommodation: *I'm flying to London on Friday morning, do you think you could put me for the night on Thursday? I don't mind sleeping on the sofa.*

put up with (type 4) endure/tolerate: *I can't put up with your complaints any more, I'm leaving.*

run out (type 1) finish/consume: *Oh no, we've run out of coffee, I'll go to the shop and get some.*

run over (type 2) hit with a car/vehicle: *Drive slowly along here, you don't want to run anyone over.*

set off (type 1) start on a journey: *We loaded the car, got in and set off.*

sort out (type 2) organise, find a solution: *When the computer broke down it took an engineer ages to sort out the problem.*

speak up (type 1) speak louder: *Do you think you could speak up, the line is very bad.*

split up (type 1) separate when a relationship ends: *Have you heard? Gemma and Lionel have split up.*

take after (type 3) inherit a characteristic: *He is so stubborn, he really takes after his father.*

take in (type 2) to deceive: *Don't be taken in by her lies, she just wants to cheat you.* to give shelter to: *The farmer took the travellers in during the snowy weather.*

take off (type 1) (of a plane, rocket, helicopter) leave the ground: *The plane took off on time.* (type 2) to imitate: *When he was at school he was good at taking off his teachers.*

take over (type 2) gain control: *They took the company over by buying over half the shares.*

take up (type 2) begin a new activity: *We're thinking of taking up German in the autumn.*

tell off (type 2) criticise/scold: *His mother told him off for being cruel to the cat.*

talk over (type 2) discuss: *He felt better for talking his problems over with his mother.*

turn down (type 2) refuse: *She eventually decided to turn the job offer down because the salary was too low.*

work out (type 2) calculate/arrive at a decision: *After a couple of hours they worked out that there was something wrong with the printer.*

WORD-FORMATION

Prefixes and suffixes

1 forming nouns
people and professions
-ant (assistant); -ee (employee), -ess (waitress), -er (builder), -ian (mathematician), -ist (novelist), -or (visitor)
2 other nouns
-al (dismissal), -ance (abundance), -cy (consistency), -ence (confidence), -ful (handful), -hood (childhood), ing (playing), -ion (addiction), -ism (symbolism), -ity (sensitivity), -ment (contentment, -ness (tiredness) -ship (directorship).
3 forming verbs
-en (strengthen), -ise (privatise), -ify (modify)
4 forming adjectives
-able (suitable), -al (logical), -ary (preliminary) -ful (shameful), -ed (painted), -ful (helpful), -ible (sensible), -ic (sarcastic), -ish (foolish) -ive (decisive), -ing (boring) -less (hopeless), -like (childlike), -ly (friendly), -ous (dangerous) -y (sunny)

Concept noun	Personal noun	Adjective	Verb
addiction	addict	addictive/addicted	to become addicted
advertisement (thing)	advertiser	advertised	advertise
advertising (business)			
advice /æd'vaɪs/	adviser	advisory	advise /æd'vaɪz/
analysis	analyst	analytical	analyse
application	applicant	....	apply
athletics	athlete	athletic	....
competition	competitor	(un)competitive	compete
crime	criminal	criminal	to commit a crime
death	the dead (person)	dead	die
criticism	critic	(un)critical	criticise
economy	economist	(un)economical	economise
employment	employer/-ee	(un)employed	employ
finance	financier	financial	finance
friendship	friend	(un)friendly	make friends/befriend
history	historian	historic/historical	....
industry	industrialist	industrial	industrialise
invention	inventor	inventive	invent
investigation	investigator	investigative	investigate
management	manager	managerial	management
mathematics	mathematician	mathematical	....
music	musician	musical	to compose music
negotiation	negotiator	negotiable/-iated	negotiate
optimism	optimist	optimistic	....
organisation	organiser	(dis)organised	organise
photograph (thing)	photographer	photographic	photograph
photography (activity)			
poetry (activity)	poet	poetic	write poetry
poem (thing)			
politics	politician	political	politicise
pollution	polluter	polluted	pollute
practice	practitioner	(im)practical	practise
product/production	producer	produced	produce
profit	profiteer	(un)profitable	profit
reality/realism	realist	(un) realistic	realise
science	scientist	(un)scientific	....
symbolism	symbol	symbolic	symbolise
terror/terrorism	terrorist	terrorist	terrorise
survival	survivor	surviving	survive
theft	thief	stolen	steal
training	trainer/ee	(un)trained	train
use	user	useful/less used	use

Verb	Adjective	Noun
to be able	(un)able	ability
accept	(un)acceptable	acceptance
adapt	adaptable	adaptation/adaptor
admit	(in)admissible	admission
annoy	annoyed/ing	annoyance
apologise	apologetic	apology
attract	(un)attractive	attraction
avoid	(un)avoidable	avoidance
believe	(un)believable	belief
bore	bored/ing	boredom
broaden	broad	breadth
care	careful/-less	care/carelessness
centralise	central	centre
(dis)comfort	(un)comfortable	comfort
compare	(in)comparable	comparison
comprehend	(in)comprehensible	comprehension
consider	(in)considerate	consideration
be convenient	(in)convenient	(in)convenience
corrupt	corrupt	corruption
decide	(in)decisive	decision
deepen	deep	depth
disturb	disturbed/ing	disturbance
en/discourage	en/discouraged/ing	dis/encouragement
enjoy	(un)enjoyable	enjoyment
excuse	(in)excusable	excuse
experience	(in)experienced	experience
explain	(in)explicable	explanation
forgive	(un)forgivable/forgiven	forgiveness
harm	harmful/-less, (un)harmed	harm
heighten	high	height
hope	hopeful/hopeless	hopeful/lessness
ignore	ignorant	ignorance
imagine	(un)imaginative/imaginary	imagination
interest	(un)interested/ing	disinterested interest
lengthen	long	length
memorise	memorable	memory
obey	(dis)obedient	(dis)obedience
persuade	persuasive	persuasion
possess	possessive	possession
predict	(un)predictable	prediction
prefer	preferable	preference
reason	(un)reasonable	reason
recognise	(un)recognisable	recognition
regret	regrettable	regret
rely	(un)reliable	(un)reliability
satisfy	(un)satisfactory (dis)satisfied	satisfaction
strengthen	strong	strength
succeed	(un)successful	success
terrify	terrified/terrifying	terror
think	thoughtful/less	thought
tolerate	(in)tolerant, (in)tolerable	toleration
vary	varied/various/variable	variety
weaken	weak	weakness

Adjective	Noun	Adjective	Noun
accidental	accident	(dis)honest	(dis)honesty
afraid/fearful	fear	hot	heat
(un)adventurous	adventure	hungry	hunger
ambitious	ambition	innocent	innocence
annoyed/ing	annoyance	(un)intelligent	(un)intelligence
angry	anger	jealous	jealousy
anxious	anxiety	(un)kind	(un)kindness
arrogant	arrogance	lazy	laziness
ashamed/shameful	shame	(il)legible	(il)legibility
bored/boring	boredom	(il)logical	logic
brave	bravery	lost	loss
bright	brightness	(dis)loyal	(dis)loyalty
chaotic	chaos	miserable	misery
childish/childlike	child/childhood	muscular	muscle
clumsy	clumsiness	moody	mood
(un) comfortable	(dis) comfort	(im)patient	(im)patience
(in) convenient	convenience	notorious	notoriety
cruel	cruelty	(dis)obedient	(dis)obedience
dangerous	danger	obsessive	obsession/obsessiveness
dark	darkness	painful/less	pain
disappointed/ing	disappointment	(im)patient	(im)patience
disastrous	disaster	(im)polite	(im)politeness
(in)effective	effectiveness	poor	poverty
(in)efficient	efficiency	(im)possible	(im)possibility
embarrassed/ing	embarrassment	powerful/less	power
(un)enthusiastic	enthusiasm	(ir)regular	regularity
excited/exciting	excitement	proud	pride
exhausted/exhausting	exhaustion	(un)reasonable	reason
(in)famous	fame	(ir)religious	religion
fascinated/-ing	fascination	(ir)responsible	irresponsibility
(un)fashionable	fashion	(un)safe	safety
(un)favourable, favourite	favour	(dis)satisfied	
(in)flexible	flexibility	(un)satisfactory	(dis)satisfaction
free	freedom	(un)selfish	(un)selfishness
frightened/frightening	fright	(dis)similar	similarity
furious	fury	sorry	sorrow
generous	generosity	spacious	space
(un)grammatical	grammar	stressful	stress
grateful	gratitude	stupid	stupidity
guilty	guilt	terrified	terror
hungry	hunger	thirsty	thirst
(un)fair	fairness	tired	tiredness
fluent	fluency	tragic	tragedy
(un)happy	(un)happiness	(un)willing	willingness
(un)healthy	health	wealthy	wealth
high	height	wise	wisdom

Noun	Verb
abolition	abolish
accusation	accuse
admission	admit
(dis)agreement	(dis)agree
(dis)appearance	(dis)appear
(dis)approval	(dis)approve
argument	argue
attendance	attend
blood	bleed
breath	breathe
cancellation	cancel
choice	choose
complaint	complain
delivery	deliver
denial	deny
discovery	discover
discussion	discuss
distinction	distinguish
entrance	enter
exaggeration	exaggerate
explosion	explode
failure	fail
food	feed
identification	identify
improvement	improve
inheritance	inherit
involvement	involve
judgement	judge
loss	lose
punishment	punish
recovery	recover
refusal	refuse
relief	relieve
relationship	relate
requirement	require
resignation	resign
revision	revise
solution	solve
signature	sign
starvation	starve
suffering	suffer
temptation	tempt
threat	threaten
(mis)treatment	(mis)treat
(mis)understanding	understand
warning	warn
weight	weigh
wreckage	wreck

DEPENDENT PREPOSITIONS

This is an important area as it is often tested in the gap filling questions. Prepositional phrases, are also likely to be tested in the key word transformation part of **Paper 3 Use of English**.

Below is a small selection of adjective + preposition and verb + preposition combinations. It is by no means complete. For a more complete selection refer to a grammar book.

adjectives + prepositions

afraid of, angry about something, angry with someone, annoyed about, anxious about, ashamed of, aware of, bad at, bored with, careful of, excited about, fond of, glad about, interested in, jealous of, keen on, right about, sorry about, worried about/by

verb + preposition combinations

agree about something/with someone, agree to, apologise to someone for/about something, apply to, approve of, arrive at/in, belong to, choose between, deal with, differ from, dream about, insist on, know about, laugh at/about, listen to, look after, look at, object to, pay for, refer to, rely on, resign from, succeed in, suffer from, wait for

verb + object + preposition

accuse someone of (doing) something, admire somebody for, blame somebody for, compare somebody/something with, congratulate somebody on, discuss something with, explain something to somebody, forgive someone for, remind somebody of something/to do something, stop somebody from doing something, tell somebody about

Prepositional phrases

as far as I am concerned, at all times, at first sight, at length, at the moment, at your convenience, by accident, by all means, by and large, by chance, by heart, by means of, by mistake, by oneself, by surprise, by the way, for a change, from time to time, in case of, in/under the circumstances, in conclusion, in confidence, in control, in danger of, in favour of, in general, in the long run/short term, in other words, in time, of course, on behalf of, on condition that, on no account, on my own, on purpose, on second thoughts, on the other hand, on the whole, on time, out of action, out of breath, out of date, out of fashion, out of order, out of practice, out of sight, out of the way, out of touch, out of work, to a great extent, to the point, under the impression, under the weather, up to date, up to you, with the exception of, with regard to, with reference to, without a doubt, without exception.

Common phrases and collocations

Break a promise/ the ice
Catch fire
Change your mind
Draw a conclusion
Have a look/a good time/a go/a try/an argument (with someone over/about something)/a word with someone, have something to do with
Make an appearance/an apology/a mess of something/an appointment/an assumption/a choice/a decision/a difference/a date/a discovery/a mistake/a profit/a start
Make a fool of someone/oneself/the most of something/a promise/sense of/sure of something/do with
Do someone good/a favour/yourself justice/something for a living
Find it difficult to do something
Find difficulty in doing something
Find fault with
Get a move on/the impression
Give a description/birth to/a choice/an example/a description/a hand/the impression/someone a call/someone the sack/your word
Hold a meeting/someone responsible for something (often passive)
Jump the queue/to conclusions
Keep a promise/the peace/your eye on something or someoneone/one's word/your head/in touch with
Like the look of
Lose your temper/touch with
Pay attention to/someone a compliment/the price/penalty of doing something
Mind your own business
Play a trick on someone
Set an example/fire to something
Take someone's advice/advantage of/the blame for something/care of/charge of/a chance/exception to/a fancy to/someone or something for granted/someone by surprise/someone's place/the opportunity to/notice of/offence at/notice of/part in/pleasure in/pride in/pity on/something to pieces
Tell the difference between/a lie/the truth

TABLE OF IRREGULAR VERBS

The following irregular verbs have been grouped into "families" according to the number of changes that occur, their endings or by pronunciation. This may make them easier for you to learn.

1 Simple past and past participle the same. Ending in /t/ or /d/

Infinitive	Simple past	Past Participle.
bend	bent	bent
build	built	built
burn	burnt	burnt
dream	dreamt	dreamt
find	found	found
feel	felt	felt
flee	fled	fled
get	got	got (gotten US)
grind	ground	ground
have	had	had
hear	heard	heard
hold	held	held
lay	laid	laid
lead	led	led
learn	learnt	learnt
leave	left	left
lend	lent	lent
light	lit	lit
lose	lost	lost
make	made	made
mean	meant	meant
meet	met	met
pay	paid	paid
say	said	said
send	sent	sent
sell	sold	sold
sit	sat	sat
spell	spelt	spelt
spend	spent	spent
stand	stood	stood
tell	told	told
understand	understood	understood

Can you usefully sub-divide this large group into smaller groups? e.g.pay/paid/paid, say/said/said

2 Past simple and past participle ending in /ɔːt/
   NB spelling change.

catch	caught	caught
teach	taught	taught
bring	brought	brought
buy	bought	bought
fight	fought	fought
seek	sought	sought
think	thought	thought

3 -eep, -ept, -ept

creep	crept	crept
keep	kept	kept
sleep	slept	slept
weep	wept	wept

4 no change

bet	bet	bet
broadcast	broadcast	broadcast
burst	burst	burst
cost	cost	cost
cut	cut	cut
hit	hit	hit
put	put	put
read /riːd/	read/red/	read/red/
shut	shut	shut
split	split	split

5 No obvious "family"!

be/am/is/are	was/were	been
become	became	become
come	came	come
do	did	done
dig	dug	dug
draw	drew	drawn
go	went	been/gone
run	ran	run
see	saw	seen
shine	shone	shone
stick	stuck	stuck
strike	struck	struck
win	won	won

6 past participle -own

blow	blew	blown
fly	flew	flown
grow	grew	grown
know	knew	known
show	showed	shown
throw	threw	thrown

7 past participle -en

beat	beat	beaten
bite	bit	bitten
break	broke	broken
choose	chose	chosen
drive	drove	driven
eat	ate	eaten
fall	fell	fallen
forbid	forbade	forbidden
forget	forgot	forgotten
freeze	froze	frozen
give	gave	given
hide	hid	hidden
mistake	mistook	mistaken
ride	rode	ridden
rise	rose	risen
shake	shook	shaken
speak	spoke	spoken
steal	stole	stolen
take	took	taken
weave	wove	woven
wake	woke	woken
write	wrote	written

Can you form any useful sub-groups?

8 ea /eə/ -ore /ɔː/ -orn /ɔːn/

bear	bore	born
swear	swore	sworn
tear	tore	torn
wear	wore	worn

9 -i - -a- -u- (vowel + nasal consonant)

begin	began	begun
drink	drank	drunk
ring	rang	rung
shrink	shrank	shrunk
sing	sang	sung
sink	sank	sunk
swim	swam	swum

Tapescripts

PAGE 8 Listen to these six situations and choose the best answer: A, B or C.

Question one

A: So remember. You never get a second chance to make a first impression. Look the person in the eye, smile and shake their hand. Say something like, 'It's a pleasure to meet you Mr Jones or Mrs Brown...' Use the other person's name it makes them feel good... Perhaps pay them a compliment. For example: That's a lovely brooch you're wearing. Where did you get that beautiful bag?' You'll win their confidence and in no time at all...

Question two

B: So what did you think..
C: Of her ? The last one?
B: Yeah...
C: Well... Erm, she was really lively, wasn't she?
B: Yes. her pronunciation wasn't that good though......
C: But a clear communicator.
B: Absolutely, and good vocabulary .
C: She made a couple of basic grammar mistakes.
B: All the same, I think she performed well .
C: Yes. Definitely a pass.
B: Oh yes. Would you say she was a strong pass?.
C: I'm not really sure. I know, shall we come back to her again in a minute?
B: Yes, why not?

Question three

D: So if I could have your details.
To change? From this course to the one in September...
Oh dear, I am sorry. No, no, that shouldn't be a problem. Let me check..
Um... Well, we should be able to squeeze you in.
No, no the fees will be the same. Don't worry, just concentrate on getting better.

Question four

E: It's Mrs Greenaway, isn't it?
F: That's right. Goodness me, it's Carmen..
E: That's right.
F: I hardly recognised you. You've changed.....Carmen Fernandez.
E: You've got a good memory.
F: How lovely to see you.
E: Ha, ha...
F: So what... How long have you been working here, then?
E: Since I left the college.
F: That's seven...
E: Eight years actually...
F: And what's kept you here...
E: Well I married an English man and had a child...
F: Well done ha ha.. And your English, it's perfect...
E: Well, it's thanks to you...
F: You're too kind...
E: And are you still working there?

Question five

G: Anyway, I really must be going...I've got an essay to write...
H: It's been lovely talking to you...
G: Yes.
H: And you sure you're settling in...
G: Yes mum.
H: And there's nothing you want...
G: No. No. Everything's fine.
H: I'll give you a ring next week.

G: After six...
H: After six and you know...
G: Right then... Speak to you next week... Bye... Phew...Sorry about that...Give me a minute... I'm coming....I'll just get my racquet. ...Oh no!

Question six

Now you can take incoming calls but you can't make calls from here I'm afraid. Now about the kitchen... It's fine if you want to have a snack or something like that, a sandwich or something, eggs you know, and of course you can make hot drinks. Help yourself to tea or coffee it's just here in this cupboard...but nothing too elaborate... Sorry but, you know, sometimes people think they can take over the whole kitchen. Three course meals and that. There was this boy last year from ...

PAGE 9 Adriana is a First Certificate candidate from Italy. Listen to part of her interview and complete the Examiner's questions.

Examiner: OK Jean-Luc. I'll come back to you in a minute. Now it's Adriana, isn't it?
Adriana: That's right.
Examiner: So, er, where are you from, Adriana?
Adriana: From Italy.
Examiner: I see. Whereabouts in Italy?
Adriana: From near Florence.
Examiner: Mm, lovely and, er, what do you do?
Adriana: I'm a student. I'm finishing high school.
Examiner: Huh, huh. And what do you want to do after high school?
Adriana: Well, I'd like to study archaeology.
Examiner: Really? Why archaeology?
Adriana: Well, we live quite near some, erm, ancient ruins and...I have always been fascinated by them.
Examiner: I see...And erm...tell me, what do you do in your spare time?
Adriana: Studying and meeting friends. Oh, and playing basketball.
Examiner: Do you play in competitions or just for fun?
Adriana: Just for fun. Nothing serious.
Examiner: Oh really. And, erm, how long have you been learning English?
Adriana: For four years now.
Examiner: Right...And, erm, why do like Italy?
Adriana: Well, it's a Mediterranean climate so it's hot and sunny most of the year.
Examiner: Lucky you, and erm why are you taking the First Certificate?
Adriana: It's an important qualification to have and also because in summer my city is full of foreigners. So, it's important to know English.
Examiner: Huh,huh. Right, right.

PAGE 18 Andrew Williams and his wife run 'Linguapal', an agency which organises exchange visits for young people. Listen to this interview with Andrew.

Interviewer: So how does it work?
Andrew: Well, basically a school or an individual responds to one of erm our advertisements and we send them a form and ask them to write a letter all about themselves and why they want to do an exchange.
Interviewer: I see. And what's the point of the letter?
Andrew: Well, one thing, it helps us to choose the right people. We reject quite a few people on the basis of the letter. You know, ones who have obviously got the wrong kind of attitude. Some just can't be bothered to write a letter at all.

Interviewer: I see. What kind of thing do you deal with on the form?

Andrew: We try to get as much detail as we can about the background and interests of the applicant. There are forty-three questions which cover everything from religious persuasion to family pets. As far as possible we want to match up people in terms of age and interests but also in terms of family background. We ask participants to give a description of their homes, what their parents do for a living and so on. A parent has to sign the form saying that they have checked it and that everything is accurate. Afterwards we make our decision on the basis of the form and the letter.

Interviewer: Why do you want so much background about family circumstances?

Andrew: Well we don't want people to go and stay in exactly the same kind of family, but on the other hand we don't want there to be enormous social differences or inequalities. As far as I am concerned it just causes problems.

Interviewer: Why? What can go wrong?

Andrew: Well, it can lead to all kinds of problems and embarrassment. For example, if someone from a less well-off family goes to stay with someone who is comparatively very rich then it can cause anxiety and jealousy for obvious reasons. Someone from a rich family might take it for granted that they would have their own bathroom or that there would be servants. Children who have perhaps stayed with a very well-off family get incredibly anxious about what the other person will think when they come into their house.

Interviewer: Doesn't this mean that you are just helping to reinforce social differences between people?

Andrew: I know what you mean. When I started the agency I thought I would be able to take advantage of the situation for a bit of social engineering but I quickly realised that it just didn't work. For a young person to go abroad - perhaps for the first time - to a strange family is already stressful enough. We don't want to add to anyone's problems.

Interviewer: And have you ever got it wrong?

Andrew: Well, we have difficulty in making an exact match but I've made a couple of mistakes too. On one occasion I sent someone who was a strict vegetarian to a home where the father was a butcher.

Interviewer: Oh no!

Andrew: And another time someone with a terrible allergy to horses was sent to a family where everyone was keen on riding. However, I should say that in the second case they erm hadn't said anything about allergies in the box provided.

Interviewer: Well, it sounds as though you really try to take everything into consideration.

Andrew: We try to do our best.

PAGE 20 Listen to these five young people who have all been on exchange visits.

Speaker 1

My biggest fear was that I wouldn't be able to make myself understood. And in fact when I turned up at the family I couldn't understand a word. This was because in the home they spoke a dialect, you know, from their region. Anyway, when I was around they always made sure they spoke erm ordinary Spanish, you know, Castilian. I was really homesick at first but after a week I didn't want to come back. And I had a really great time.

Speaker 2

Well, I got erm very upset because I was standing in a shop waiting my turn, when people kept on jumping the queue. I started to get a bit angry but then my friend told me that in her country queuing, you know, like we do over here, was less important. And I

must say that this is a bit of an English obsession.

Speaker 3

Well, let me see, I think the worst thing was on the first night. They had prepared this wonderful meal and we had erm artichoke as a starter. You know, the vegetable. Well, I tried to eat everything, instead of just the tips of the leaves. I was so embarrassed, you see I'd never eaten one before. I felt I'd made a real fool of myself.

Speaker 4

For me, the erm biggest shock was the toilets. I went to this village miles from anywhere and the toilet wasn't like ours, it didn't have a seat. In fact you had to squat down to use it. I just didn't know what to do at first, and the first time I erm tried I dropped a set of keys down it.

Speaker 5

That's easy. The thing that got me was the way, you know, everybody kissed. I just couldn't believe it. I come from a family where nobody ever touches anyone or hardly ever, and I found it difficult to feel comfortable with all the kissing and handshaking and stuff. I was quite used to it by the end though.

UNIT 2 **Time Out**

PAGE 22 1 John, Eleanor and Richard are discussing what to do this evening.

John: I'm really fed up, I mean, we've been stuck here all day. Why don't we go out?

Eleanor: You're right John, what shall we do then?

Richard: But there's something good on telly.

John: Come on, Richard! Something good on telly.

Eleanor: Telly telly, it's all you think about...

John: You'll end up with square eyes...

Richard: All right. ...What do you want to do then?

John: Well we, could go to that new café. What's it called

Eleanor: Video Café.

John: Yeah, that's right, Video Café..

Richard: It's boring. We might as well watch telly.

Eleanor: It'll be packed too... Full of smoke. I'd rather we did something else.

Richard: So would I.

John: There's that Burger em Tex-Mex place... what's it called Ranchero..

Eleanor: Yuk, you know I can't stand burgers...

John: How about ...there's ... I know it's a film... there's a really good film with Sylvester Stallone on. I've heard it's really good... Cliffhanger. Why don't we er...

Richard: I've already seen it...

Eleanor: I have too.

Richard: I don't like these action films much.

Eleanor: I don't either.

John: All right then. Richard. How about...? Look I'm getting fed up with this. I suggest something to you and you... you just knock it down...

Richard+Eleanor: Ah! You poor old thing...

Richard: Hold it... . I know, we could always go to the rink. There's an ice-hockey match on...

Eleanor: Ice-hockey...I've never been to an ice-hockey match.

John: Neither have I... A bit brutal isn't it?

Eleanor: Yeah. Um, let's go...

Richard: Well, there you are you see. A new experience...What do you think?

Eleanor: OK... but I'll hold you responsible if I don't like it.

John: Me too.

Richard: Brilliant. And I didn't even want to go out.. Anyway.. What's the time? It starts at eight.

Eleanor: It's half seven now.

John: It's time we left, we're going to have to get our skates on if we're going to get there on time.

Richard: Get our skates on...Ha ha... That's almost funny, John.

Eleanor: Anyone seen my car keys?

John+Richard: Oh no. Not again!

PAGE 24 1 Listen to these three descriptions. Which sports are being described?

1

I guess you could say that this is our national sport - we certainly have got the right weather for it. It has the reputation of being a pretty rough and tough game. Anyhow, as its name suggests we play it on ice, on skates, and the object of the game is to score by hitting the puck into the net. You have to be really well dressed up and padded and protected for this 'cos it's easy otherwise to get badly hurt.

2

This sport has a long and traditional history in my country. It's a mixture of meditation and concentration, and accuracy. It's important to breathe properly. Obviously you need a bow and arrow and to aim at the target.

3

I don't know whether you can really call this a sport but it is something that people from my country have been very good at. We have had lots of grand masters and international grand masters. It is an ancient game, I think it originally came from Persia, now Iran. It is about strategy and it requires a very good memory of other games and intense concentration. You play it on a board with sixty-four squares and the object of the game is to capture the enemy's king. Each player has sixteen pieces which move around the board in a certain way.

PAGE 29 3 Listen to these five women talking about books they have read recently.

Speaker 1

It was awful ... I mean it was all ... such an improbable story... I loathed the hero... you know killing people all over the place ... running round the desert... he wouldn't have lasted two minutes in real life... I don't know what possessed me to read it ... or for that matter to get to the end ... suppose I thought it might get better but it didn't. Dreadful rubbish. I got rid of it, threw it away in disgust you know. You'd have to be a bit sick in the head I imagine to enjoy it ... A book for men - definitely.

Speaker 2

It was pretty good, I suppose...Very clever plot ... And a bit too realistic in a way. The detail, you know some of the erm the detail about cutting up bodies, 'cos she was a pathologist was rather disgusting really, but the book took me over. I can't say I lost any sleep over it but it was a bit ... um gruesome.

Speaker 3

It was absolutely riveting, I mean I couldn't put it down. Poor old Malcolm, he kept shouting down the stairs, 'When are you coming up?' and I just said 'Five more minutes dear.' He was really fed up. Finally I got to bed at about two. Still it was worth it. He was asleep of course snoring his head off...

Speaker 4

It was good. I won't deny it, but all the while I was reading it there was a little voice sort of saying: 'You know it's not the real thing.' It was good, terribly clever and everything and she took off the style

of the original quite well, all the same, but it didn't have the same feel erm you know the flavour of the of the first one by the er original writer what's her name, du Maurier, that's right. I suppose I was silly to have erm expected it.

Speaker 5

Well, I wouldn't exactly say it was the best book I've ever read. All the same I think she really does manage to express, um, what every, well you know, normal people's lives are like... all of her characters... even though they were in a family set up, they all seemed somehow so erm alone if you know what I mean... very astute... well observed but a bit depressing. I'd only recommend it to someone who was feeling, erm you know not feeling down. You'd need to feel quite strong inside, not for the vulnerable; most people's family lives are bad enough as it is without reading about more...

PAGE 31 Pronunciation sentence stress

1 Listen to the sentences and decide which of the words are strong and weak. Put a line under the strong syllables and a circle around the weak ones.

Example: Len Deighton's been a photographer.

A He's been living in France.
B He's been writing books for ages.
C What have you done to my car?
D How long have you been a dancer?
E How long have you been learning English?
F It's late. Where have you been?
G I've been trying to phone.

2 Listen to the sentences again and try to copy the speakers' pronunciation as closely as you can.

UNIT 3 Survival

PAGE 35 2 Listen to the radio programme on surviving in cold weather and decide if you would have survived.

Presenter: Now, I'd like to move on to the next item. The weather certainly seems to have taken a turn for the worse and it looks like we're in for some heavy snowfalls in the next few days. Now, of course, every year there are cases of motorists who break down and get caught out in really bad weather. Tragically, some die and this is even more tragic when we consider that most of these deaths could be avoided. Now we have in the studio this evening Julie Mitchell from the Canadian Automobile club and she's going to tell us how to stay alive if we get caught out in the snow and our car breaks down. Hi, Julie.

Julie: Hi.

Presenter: So, what should we do?

Julie: Well, the first thing that you should remember is that your car is your most important piece of survival equipment you have if you get caught in a drift. So don't leave it unless you can actually see the place you want to get to. People have died when they needn't have because they have gotten impatient, left their cars and got lost in the snow.

Presenter: So, rule number one is stay in your car unless you can see where you are going.

Julie: Your destination.

Presenter: Right. Anything else we should remember?

Julie: Oh, certainly! First of all, use your common sense. If you have to drive and know you're going to hit bad weather, make sure you have blankets, a sleeping bag and a shovel in case you have to dig yourself out, and ideally food and hot drinks.

Presenter: Is there anything we can do to help ourselves if we're stuck, apart from keep warm, that is?

Julie: Oh, sure. You've got to keep warm but you've also got to keep the car well ventilated - there have been cases of drivers suffocating in their cars. So have the window on the side away from the wind open a little, say, half an inch or so.

Presenter: OK. What about using the car heater to keep warm?

Julie: Oh, I'm glad you asked me about this because this can be fatal unless you take extreme care. The risk of death from exhaust fumes is high. The cold takes hours to kill you but exhaust fumes can kill you in a matter of minutes. Before you run your engine, make sure the exhaust is completely free from snow. Otherwise, the fumes will escape into the car. Anyway, only run the engine for ten minutes every hour and every time make sure the exhaust is free.

Presenter: Any final tip?

Julie: Yes, if you know you're setting off in bad weather, ring up your destination just in case something happens on the way. That way, if you're late, your friends will know something is wrong and will be able to tell the police to go out and look for you.

Presenter: Thanks Julie for coming in and I hope our listeners out there...

3 Now listen to the interview again and complete the notes.

PAGE 40 Devil's alternatives

Listen to two friends discussing the questionnaire and find out what choices each of them makes.

Damien: Honestly... Have you seen this?

Lucinda: Yeah.

Damien: What'll they come up with next?

Lucinda: There are some pretty sick people around.

Damien: Right...Fun though. All the same what would you do?

Lucinda: What! Come off it...I wouldn't even...

Damien: Come on..You know. Suppose you had to?

Lucinda: Well...Clean the toilets... definitely.

Damien: Now that's interesting. I'd never have guessed it.

Lucinda: What do you mean?

Damien: Well, I've always thought you were, you know, confident...

Lucinda: With some things maybe, but I'd rather die than stand up in front of that many people..

Damien: Me, I'd do it.

Lucinda: Oh yeah.

Damien: Sure... I mean... It's over in ten minutes..

Lucinda: Anyway...What about this other one.

Damien: What's a bungee jump?

Lucinda: You don't know?

Damien: That's why I'm asking.

Lucinda: Well, it's a sort of ... you know... it's when you tie a cord, kind of cord around your legs and then you jump off a bridge or something like that. It's kind of, you know, elastic...

Damien: Gosh! What like in Samoa was it when they used to do it. Um... as a ... you know a... a sort of coming of age ... initiation ceremony...

Lucinda: This is the modern version... you keep bouncing up and down... it's much safer.

Damien: Should hope so too.

Lucinda: Modern technology.

Damien: Well. You know, they seem just as bad as each other...

Lucinda: I'm not sure... Snakes brr... that's my absolute nightmare, I couldn't do that if you paid me a million pounds.

Damien: Just imagine them sliding and slithering all over..

Lucinda: Oh do shut up... No the bungee jump, even though I'm

terrified of heights.

Damien: That's funny, I'm the complete opposite, I mean, I'd go for the snakes ...

PAGE 40 Managing Conversations

Listen to their conversation again and count how many times 'I mean' and 'You know' are used.

PAGE 42 Listen to these eight extracts.

Question 1

When the plane crashed all the lights went out. Everybody panicked, except Jemima Blond. Her years of training meant she could control her fear. She remembered her sergeant major's words, 'Crawl along the floor where the air is cleanest.' The terrorists stood up and fought for the exit, their screams turning to coughing and silence, while Blond was able to get out of the smoke-filled cabin. She got to the door, her lungs bursting, and with a mighty kick, managed to force it open. As she fell to the runway, the plane exploded above her.

Question 2

The search is continuing for members of the capsized fishing boat. The Royal Navy has taken charge of the rescue operation and Sea King helicopters are combing the area. Lifeboat services from Sidmouth have already succeeded in rescuing nine of the crew but hope is fading fast for the remaining two.
We will now go over to the village of Sidmouth for a live report from the centre of rescue operations.

Question 3

Come on! Damn you Billy. Don't give up now, boy. The sheriff and his posse ain't that far behind. When Momma was dying I gave her my word that I'd take care of you and I ain't gonna break that promise. There ain't no water here, but you'll be able to have all you can drink when we get somewhere safe. Come on, when you was a kid you could walk for miles. You can do it. We'll be at the hideout soon. On your feet, don't make me lose my temper.

Question 4

Woman A: Yes...yes.. anyway, this car, it just came from the middle of nowhere. It just smashed straight into my door, on the passenger's side.

Woman B: You poor things...

Woman A: Jeremy, didn't have time to react or avoid him...

Woman B: And is he OK?

Woman A: He was shaken, that's all.

Woman B: And what about the other driver?

Woman A: He was angry but the police said it was definitely his fault. They gave him a formal warning that they are going to prosecute.

Question 5

What do you mean, you weren't able to do it. Didn't we go through it last time? Look, we can find out the value of X in the first equation, like this, can't we? Stop looking out of the window and pay attention. That means we can put that value into the second equation to discover the value of Y. Simple! If you carry on like this then I just don't know if you're going to make it...

Question 6

Father: Before you go off, I want a word with you. Whales, whales, whales... that's all you think about.

Son: Dad...

Father: You don't have to go to the other side of the world to find a good cause you know.

Son: Come on Dad...What about the animals?

Father: I think you should spare a thought for some of the old people in this town and how they survive. If you really want to make a difference why don't you go and give old Mr Johnson a hand with the housework? I know that helping an old person isn't as romantic as saving the whales but ...

Son: All right, all right, I don't want to have an argument about this.

Question 7

That's it. Now, roll the dummy onto its side. OK. Now what you have to do is check that the airway is clear. One of the problems is that people can sometimes choke 'cos they've swallowed their tongues or false teeth and things... so always make sure that you check that there aren't any obstructions. That's it... don't worry, you can't hurt it...

Question 8

So now it gives me enormous pleasure to introduce my next guest whose recent book 'Without a Paddle' tells us about how an ordinary teacher survived when she just drifted for 43 days in an open boat, when most of us would have just given up. She had to come to terms with the fact that she might die there, thousands of miles from anywhere. So let's put our hands together and have a round of applause for the courageous and resourceful Kay Bradshaw.

UNIT 4 **Storytelling**

PAGE 48 An Alternative Cinderella

Narrator: Once upon a time there were three sisters who lived with their widowed father. The two eldest ran a beauty parlour and a clothes shop. They were both interested in finding a rich husband. The youngest daughter, whose name was Cinderella, looked after the house. Her father had refused to set her up in business as he wanted someone to look after him. Cinderella did not mind too much as she was doing a correspondence course in accountancy and marketing.

One day Cinderella decided to enter a competition in a woman's magazine because it offered some good cash prizes. If she won one of them, it would help her finance the setting up of her own hamburger restaurant.

Around that time the newspapers were full of stories about a big party that was going to be held at the palace. It was said that the Prince, a real playboy, wanted to find a wife and settle down. From the moment they heard about the ball, the two eldest sisters spent days and days trying to make themselves look beautiful. As for Cinderella, she wondered what all the fuss was about and didn't have the slightest interest in going to the ball.

One morning, while she was doing some work for her accountancy course, there was a knock at the door. She opened it and saw an extraordinary woman standing there with a ridiculous-looking tiara on her head. The woman who called herself Fairy Godmother, or FG for short, told Cinderella that she'd won first prize in the magazine competition she'd entered.

The prize was a 'charm course' worth hundreds of pounds, as well as books and records. Cinderella wasn't really that keen on doing the course but she realised she could probably make a small profit if she sold the prizes. However, in return for the prizes she would have to dress up in lots of fine clothes and be driven to the palace where she'd spend the night at the ball and be photographed for the woman's magazine.

The big day arrived and a shiny Rolls Royce came to pick her up. The man from the car hire firm said he was only on duty until midnight. Moments later a woman arrived bringing a fur coat and a diamond necklace which would be Cinderella's just for

the evening. When she turned up at the palace, she noticed that one of the servants was stealing food from the buffet tables. The palace itself was cold and draughty and the king himself was a man with a sad smile. Cinderella felt sorry for the man and told him why the food was disappearing so fast. The king then told her about his financial problems. He was almost bankrupt and he had organised the party in the hope that he might find a millionaire's daughter for his son. Cinderella suggested lots of ways of making money: re-organising the kitchens, opening the palace to the public and so on.

By this time it had turned midnight. The car hire man drove away and the woman came to collect her fur coat and necklace. The king showed Cinderella around the palace and they eventually came back to the ballroom where the party was still going on. The prince, who by this time was hopelessly drunk, took one look at Cinderella and asked her to dance. She kicked off her glass slippers, which were killing her, and joined him on the dance floor. Soon afterwards, she left the palace and hitch-hiked home.

The following day the newspapers were full of the big story about the prince who had fallen for a beautiful and mysterious woman who had disappeared. Her glass slippers, which she had left behind, were the only clues that would lead him to her. When Cinderella read the news, she was absolutely furious. Nevertheless, she saw quite a bit of the prince because she started work at the palace as financial adviser. In no time at all the palace was making a profit again. Naturally, Cinderella refused to marry the prince but she did help him cut down on his drinking and involved him in useful social work in the community.

PAGE 48 Pronunciation

Past tenses

1 Regular verbs in the past

Listen to these nine regular verbs and put them in the correct columns.

stayed	stayed
asked	asked
waited	waited
invited	invited
promised	promised
carried	carried
contained	contained
decided	decided
frightened	frightened

2 *Was* and *Were*

Listen to this short dialogue which contains *was* and *were*. When are *was* and *were* strong and when are they weak?

Man: Where were you last night?
Woman: I was at the office.
Man: Were you?
Woman: Yes, I was. I was working late.
Man: You were with Paul.
Woman: No, I wasn't.
Man: Yes, you were.

PAGE 54 Listen to the story of Alexandre Aufredi.

In the 1190s in the port of La Rochelle on the west coast of France, there lived a merchant called Alexandre Aufredi and his wife Pernelle. Although Aufredi was a successful man, he was dissatisfied. There were two main reasons for this: firstly he was proud and stubborn and next he wanted to become the most important merchant in his town. He dreamed of the fortune that could be made by trading over the ocean. Against the advice of his more cautious friends he decided on a risky venture. First of all he had four strong ships built and loaded them with goods that could be exchanged or bartered. Then he chose his most trusted steward to accompany the fleet which sailed away with much ceremony. He kept some money so he and his wife could live comfortably until the ships returned. At first, Aufredi continued to be well-regarded, but as time went on he was forced to borrow money

Two, three, four years went by and still the ships had not returned. In the meantime, Aufredi's money had run out. Finally, a rumour started that the ships had been lost and all his creditors rushed to get their money back. The good man was forced to sell his house and Pernelle sold her rings and jewels one by one until, finally, they were forced to beg.

After seven years a small fleet of boats carrying gold and precious wood sailed into the port. At last Aufredi's fleet had returned! Many people had even forgotten about Aufredi's existence but he was eventually discovered begging in a church doorway. The steward - for this was the mystery stranger - could hardly believe that the silver-haired beggar dressed in rags had once been his proud master. Yet Alexandre and Pernelle's suffering had not been for nothing for in the end Aufredi was suddenly, by far, the wealthiest man in La Rochelle .

The news that Aufredi and his wife were now incredibly rich spread like wildfire. However, the couple resisted the well-wishes of their old friends. Instead, they gave most of their fortune to the poor of the city. At the end of his life, Aufredi set up a foundation whose charitable work continued into the twentieth century.

PAGE 56 A Tall Story

Carol: I heard this wonderful story the other day which I must tell you.

Arthur: Oh my god, not another one of your stories.

Carol: You're going to hear it anyway so...

Arthur: Go on then, I'm all ears.

Carol: Well, you see there's this woman and she's driving off to meet a friend in town one day. She's in a bit of a hurry and she doesn't notice the cat asleep in the driveway. Anyway, you can guess what happens next.

Arthur: I think can, yes.

Carol: She's backing out of the driveway when she hears this little cry as she goes over something.

Arthur: The cat.

Carol: Right first time.

Arthur: Go on.

Carol: Anyway, so she gets out of the car and sees the cat lying there stone dead. And she doesn't know what to do. She's already late for her meeting with her friend and she's thinking 'Where am I going to put Java?'

Arthur: What's Java?

Carol: Oh, Java's the name of the cat. Well, she can't leave it there and she can't put it in the dustbin 'cos the kids might see. Anyway, to cut a long story short, she looks in the car and sees this plastic bag from a rather smart department store.

Arthur: I don't believe a word of this.

Carol: No it's all true. Cross my heart. So she puts the cat in the bag and drives off to meet her friend. Well, when she's parked the car she decides to take the bag with her into the department store where she's meeting her friend. You see, she thinks her friend will have some clever idea about what to do with the cat.

Arthur: You've got to be kidding!

Carol: No, no. She goes into the shop, oh, and spots rather a nice-looking handbag on the counter and puts down the plastic bag for a sec to have a quick look at it. Can you guess what happens next?

Arthur: No. I hate to think.

Carol: She puts the handbag down and looks for the plastic bag. It's gone, of course. And just then she hears this scream and commotion out in the street. She goes to the door and sees this middle-aged woman lying in the street - she'd fainted - with the plastic bag with poor old Java in it beside her on the pavement. You see, she was a shoplifter and when she'd got outside, she hadn't been able to resist having a peep at was inside the bag.

Arthur: Ridiculous. Still, it makes a good story.

PAGE 59 Listen to this extract from *Pygmalion*.

Mrs Pearce: A young woman asks to see you, sir.

Higgins: A young woman! What does she want?

Mrs Pearce: Well, sir she says you'll be glad to see her when you know what she's come about. She's quite a common girl, sir. Very common indeed. I should have sent her away, only I thought perhaps you wanted her to talk into your machines. I hope I've not done wrong; but really you see such queer people sometimes - you'll excuse me I'm sure, sir -

Higgins: Oh, that's all right, Mrs Pearce. Has she an interesting accent?

Mrs Pearce: Oh, something dreadful, sir, really. I don't know how you can take an interest in it.

Higgins: Let's have her up. Show her up Mrs Pearce.

Mrs Pearce: Very well, sir. It's for you to say.

Higgins: This is rather a bit of luck. I'll show you how I make records. We'll set her talking; and I'll take it down in broad Romic; and then we'll get her on the phonograph so that you can turn her on as often as you like with the written transcript before you.

Mrs Pearce: This is the young woman, sir.

Higgins: Why, this is the girl I jotted down last night! She's no use. I've got all I want of the Lisson Grove lingo, and I'm not going to waste another cylinder on it. Be off with you, I don't want you.

The flower girl: Don't you be so saucy. You ain't heard what I come for yet. Did you tell him I come in a taxi?

Mrs Pearce: Nonsense, girl! What do you think a gentleman like Mr Higgins cares what you came in?

The flower girl: Oh, we are proud! He ain't above giving lessons, not him, I heard him say so. Well, I ain't come here to ask for any compliment; and if my money's not good enough, I can go elsewhere.

Higgins: Good enough for what?

The flower girl: Good enough for you. Now you know, don't you? I'm coming to have lessons I am. And to pay for 'em too; make no mistake.

Higgins: Well!!! What do you expect me to say to you?

The flower girl: Well, if you was a gentleman, you might ask me to sit down, I think. Don't I tell you I'm bringing you business?

Higgins: Pickering, shall we ask this baggage to sit down, or shall we throw her out of the window?

The flower girl: Ah-ah-oh-ow-ow-ow-oo! I won't be called a baggage when I've offered to pay like any lady.

Pickering: But what is it you want?

The flower girl: I want to be a lady in a flower shop 'stead of sellin' at the corner of Tottenham Court Road. But they won't take me unless I can talk more genteel. He said he could teach me. Well, here I am ready to pay him - not asking any favour - and he treats me as if I was dirt.

Mrs Pearce: How can you be such a foolish, ignorant girl as to think you could afford to pay Mr Higgins?

The flower girl: Why shouldn't I? I know what lessons cost as well as you do, and I'm ready to pay.

UNIT 5 *A Sense of Adventure*

PAGE 60 1 Listen to Martin and Amanda's conversation. Which photograph are they talking about?

Amanda: So which one is your favourite, Martin?

Martin: The one of the seaside holiday and the Punch and Judy show.

Amanda: Oh really, why's that?...

Martin: Well, I suppose it reminds me of when I was a child.

Amanda: So what you're saying is … you used to have holidays like this.

Martin: That's right, and me and my sisters used to play on the beach.

Amanda: And what kind of thing did you do?

Martin: You know, make sandcastles, that sort of thing, and hunt for crabs.

Amanda: Hunt for crabs?

Martin: Yeah, there were lots of rock pools where they used to live.

Amanda: Oh, sounds brilliant.

Martin: Yes, it was...

2 Managing conversations

Listen again and write down Amanda's side of the conversation. How does she get Martin to do most of the talking? How does she show that she is a good listener?

PAGE 62 Listen to these five women talking about travelling.

Speaker 1

All in all it was fantastic. The only thing is that I was terribly ill in Bombay for a while. You know, stomach trouble. If you go, you mustn't drink anything straight from the tap. I'd been incredibly careful but I think it was the ice cubes in one of the drinks I had that must have done it. I was totally helpless for two days. It's a good job I was on an organised tour. Jackie, the guide, was amazing, she was just so helpful. She'd seen it all before she said.

Speaker 2

Oh, we had an absolutely wonderful time; the weather was fantastic, really mild. I needn't have taken half my clothes. It was nice going out of season 'cos there were hardly any other tourists there. We didn't need to book, we just turned up. We bought a couple of guide books before we went. This one was completely hopeless, you know out of date and inaccurate. This one, Roper's guide, was invaluable. I don't know what we'd have done without it.

Speaker 3

Well, I took plenty of cash, US dollars, with me. At the airport there's this sign which says you have to declare all your foreign currency and change a lot at the official rate. It's one of those things you're supposed to do but nobody in their right mind takes any notice. I got twice as much as the official rate on the black market. Don't bother to take one of the official guides either, they're a complete waste of time and unhelpful, all they're interested in is getting hold of your hard currency. Don't change too much into local money either, it's completely worthless outside the country.

Speaker 4

What a difficult lot. I told them, I said you must be here in the lobby by seven o'clock. I was hopeful we could make a quick getaway. We were going to the Tower of London. That was the first stop. You know what it's like when you get there. They all want to see the priceless crown jewels. Sometimes people have to wait an hour to get in. Anyway, I also warned them about not leaving anything valuable lying around. You know what it's like with thieves and pickpockets about. Well, to cut a long story short, it was a disaster from start to finish.

Speaker 5

You need to go there to really appreciate it. The people are lovely, really friendly and hospitable. The couriers took really good care of us. You don't have to worry about anything. But for me the highlight of the trip was the visit to Petra. I must get the pictures developed. It was a long way to go but one of the most worthwhile things I've ever done. The temples and buildings are just cut into the rock you know. Incredible. One thing, is if you go, you should take some warm clothing. You wouldn't think it, being in the desert and everything, but it gets bitterly cold at night. I was frozen but I managed to buy a jumper at a street market...

PAGE 66 Julie talks about her holiday plans.

Friend: What are you doing this summer for your holiday, Julie?

Julie: I'm going off with some friends. We're going to the Lake District for about ten days or so.

Friend: Oh, you camping?

Julie: No, we'll be staying in youth hostels most of the time. We're going to do a lot of walking but we'll be able to get to a youth hostel by the end of each day.

Friend: Oh, tell me, what will you be taking with you, then?

Julie: Well, a pair of really good walking boots for a start and quite a lot of clothing. You can never be sure what the weather's going to be like. Well, it can be lovely one moment and grotty the next. When you're up high too, it can even snow on a summer's day!

Friend: Sounds a bit dangerous. Do you have to take any special equipment or anything with you?

Julie: No not really. Oh, we have to take those survival blankets which you can wrap yourself up in, you know, just in case, but apart from that nothing special.

Friend: Oh yeah, I know. One of those silver things you see them wearing at the end of marathons.

Julie: That's it. Oh, a map and compass, of course, sleeping bags for the youth hostel, waterproof jacket and trousers, oh and a camping gas stove and kettle so that we can brew up. But no tent. I took one last year but I needn't have bothered. I didn't use it once.

Friend: So you've done this sort of thing before.

Julie: Oh yeah. This'll be my fourth visit to the Lakes. How about you? Have you got any plans?

Friend: Well, I'm not sure. I might be going to Greece or Turkey.

PAGE 66 Pronunciation

Listen to the difference between the pronunciation of /l/ in these two words:

hotel	hostel
hotel	hostel

In 'hotel' the sound is made towards the front of the mouth. In 'hostel' , the back of the tongue is raised. Now listen to these words from the listening and decide if they are like 'hotel' or 'hostel'"

1	holiday	holiday
2	tell	tell
3	able	able
4	lake	lake
5	kettle	kettle
6	This'll	This'll
7	Well	Well
8	We'll	We'll
9	lot	lot

UNIT 6 **Changes**

PAGE 72 Rosie talks about her life.

Interviewer: Rosie, you agreed to draw two social circles. Now would it bother you at all to go into them?

Rosie: Well, I suppose it could be a bit embarrassing but, well, I'll try and be as straightforward as I can.

Interviewer: I guess the first question that anyone would ask, is what happened to Simon?

Rosie: I was afraid you'd ask that. Well, to cut a long story short, I'd been going out with him since I was 16. When he was 18, he went away to university and, when he was away, I fell in love with Clive.

Interviewer: Where had you met Clive?

Rosie: Clive was Simon's best friend from school. I'd known him a long time.

Interviewer: And he'd been going out with Lucy?

Rosie: Yes, that's right. Well, they split up over something silly and the following weekend there was a party on, and Clive and I went together 'cos Simon was away. Well, it seemed the natural thing to do. Then quite simply, we realised we loved each other.

Interviewer: How did Lucy and Simon take this?

Rosie: Well, Simon was really upset for a while but he soon found a new girlfriend at university. I think he got over it pretty quickly really. As for Lucy, well, she was furious because she said it had only been a lover's quarrel and that I'd pinched Clive off her.

Interviewer: Well, in a way, hadn't you?

Rosie: Yeah, I know it sounds awful and I felt rotten at the time but I couldn't help myself. Later on I made it up with Lucy and we still see each other from time to time.

Interviewer: And what about Simon and Clive?

Rosie: Well, they fell out completely and haven't spoken to each other since.

Interviewer: And what about your parents? There seems to have been something of a change there.

Rosie: Well, my dad really liked Simon - he was going off to study to be a doctor and he's quite smart and was always polite - whereas Clive was unemployed at the time and wore an earring and things. Well, there were some terrible rows. Dad even refused to come to the wedding. We're just about talking to each other now but relationships are very tense still. Since Sophie was born, I've been getting on much better with my mum. I get on really well with Tom, my father-in-law, and I've grown much closer to my auntie Cathy.

Interviewer: Why's that?

Rosie: Well, I was brought up to think of her as the black sheep of the family. She'd been a bit wild when she was young and got kicked out of her home and I think she could understand what I'd been through.

Interviewer: And your grandmother?

Rosie: Oh, she passed away two years ago.

PAGE 77 Harriet Williams talks about her childhood.

Harriet: As you know, I was born in India. My father had a terribly important job - he was in charge of building projects for an entire region and supervised the construction of dams, roads, bridges and suchlike. I didn't see much of him as a child as he was often away. And when he was home, the house would be full of engineers with plans and papers.

The house I remember very clearly. You wouldn't call it a mansion but it was extremely large and painted white with a veranda and lovely grounds for me to play in. We had servants and all the years we were there my mother never had to lift a finger to do anything. I had a number of nannies and, being the only daughter, I was spoilt by everyone. My two elder brothers, poor lambs, were packed off to boarding school in England at the age of seven and I was brought up with a tremendous sense of my, and my family's, self-importance.

In the summer, the women and children would go to the hills but the men worked on through the heat on the plains. And it was during the summer that my father fell ill and could not continue with his job. We had to return to England. That was in 1920 and I remember being very seasick on the journey home.

In India everyone talked about going home but the reality for me was a terrible shock. When we landed, it was cold and grey and I was surprised at seeing so many white faces around me. I realised I wasn't special any more. We travelled first class up to London but it was nothing compared to travelling first class in India. And I was so disappointed in our house. It seemed so cramped and dingy. I felt that I had really come down in the world. We only had one servant and she didn't live in. My mother tried to do the cooking - oh, she did her best but at first she made a terrible mess of everything.

But the worst thing about coming back was what happened to my father. From being responsible for major projects and hundreds of people, he suddenly became just one of many working in the ministry. He never got used to it and somehow seemed to physically shrink in the last few years before he retired.

As for myself, oh, we had always had the best in India but in England we had to make do with ordinary things. In India I had my clothes made and I remember, I am ashamed to say, being terribly upset at having to buy clothes from a shop, off the peg as it were. I thought this was awfully common. And at first I expected to be waited on hand and foot but gradually I came round to the idea of doing some of the housework.

Looking back on it, it seems incredible how dramatically my life changed. Actually, I think the change did me good because my upbringing in India had made me into such a little snob and coming home to England taught me what ordinary life was really like.

PAGE 77 Pronunciation

Long and short vowels

1 Listen to six words and decide which one you hear.
1 reach   2 feel   3 pull   4 fool   5 shot   6 cot

2 Decide what the speaker is saying.

1   When did she leave?
2   Was she shot?
3   Can you fill it?
4   He's a little full.
5   What a pretty port!

UNIT 7 **The Natural World**

PAGE 83 Listen to part of a second advertisement for Greenpeace.

Planet Earth is 4,600 Million Years Old.

If we condense this inconceivable time-span into an understandable concept, we can liken Earth to a person of 46 years of age.

Nothing is known about the first 7 years of this person's life, and whilst only scattered information exists about the middle span, we know that only at the age of 42 did the earth begin to flower.

Dinosaurs and the great reptiles did not appear until one year ago, when the planet was 45. Mammals arrived only eight months ago. In the middle of last week, man-like apes evolved into ape-like men, and at the weekend the last ice-age enveloped the earth.

Modern man has been around for 4 hours. During the last hour Man discovered agriculture. The industrial revolution began a minute ago.

During those sixty seconds of biological time, Modern Man has made a rubbish tip of Paradise.

He has multiplied his numbers to plague proportions, caused the extinction of 500 species of animals, ransacked the planet for fuels and now stands like a brutish infant, gloating over this meteoric rise to ascendancy, on the brink of a war to end all wars and of effectively destroying this oasis of life in the solar system.

PAGE 85   Pronunciation

3 Listen to someone reading part of the Greenpeace text aloud and mark where he makes mistakes with the pronunciation of *th*.

Despite the fact, too, that we can create environmentally-clean industries, harness the power of the sun, wind and waves for our energy needs and manage the finite resources of the earth in a way that will safeguard our future and protect all the rich variety of life forms which share this planet with us.

PAGE 85   Peter Whitehead interviews Frances Kelly.

Peter Whitehead: The Campaign for Clean Air has just issued a report on air pollution and we have in the studio Frances Kelly of the CCA who's going to tell us something about the dangers we face from air pollutants.

Frances Kelly: Hello.

Peter Whitehead: Let's start with sulphur dioxide which causes acid rain. I thought the government was doing something about that.

Frances Kelly: Well, they are but slowly. Sulphur dioxide emissions from power stations are still going on and the resulting acid rain is still killing off fishes and plant life in lakes and destroying the forests. And we in Britain are among the worst culprits when it comes to this kind of pollution.

Peter Whitehead: What are the other pollutants?

Frances Kelly: Carbon monoxide and carbon dioxide. Carbon monoxide, which is mostly produced by motor vehicles can, even in small doses, cause sickness and a slowing of the reflexes and there is strong evidence to show that it has an effect on the growth of children.

Peter Whitehead: And carbon dioxide?

Frances Kelly: Well, in a way this is the least dangerous of the pollutants we've mentioned but in the longer term it may be the most damaging.

Peter Whitehead: Why?

Frances Kelly: There is clear evidence that the build-up of carbon dioxide in the atmosphere is the main cause of the Greenhouse Effect. This will have dreadful results like the melting of the polar ice caps and the subsequent flooding of low-lying areas.

Peter Whitehead: So what you're saying is that the increased amounts of carbon dioxide in the atmosphere is making it warmer.

Frances Kelly: Yes, that's right and the results will be catastrophic.

Peter Whitehead: And what should we be doing about this?

Frances Kelly: Frankly, the government has got to impose far stricter controls on these emissions and bring in tough legislation to deal with the problem.

Peter Whitehead: Frances Kelly, thank you very much.

Frances Kelly: Thank you.

Peter Whitehead: After the news we hope to be talking to the Minister for the Environment, Patrick Hilliard....

PAGE 86   Listen to these five people describing experiences which are all to do with cars and travelling by road.

Speaker 1

With a flick of the switch the canopy folds back and there you are with the wind in your hair and the sun in your face. This is what driving should be all about. This re-styled 900 restores some of the fun and traditional pleasures to modern day motoring. Its sleek design and state of the art sixteen valve engine under the bonnet mean that you can effortlessly glide along the motorway although you'll have to keep an eye on the speedometer as it can go deceptively fast .

Speaker 2

Well, it was dreadful really, we were right near the main road and each time a lorry came by the whole building shook. I mean, it looked nothing like the brochure. We'd expected a quiet little cottage in the middle of nowhere and instead we got a massive, you know, erm dual carriageway, outside the back door. And the smell, I mean, you needed to wear a gas mask.

Speaker 3

Never seen anything like it, it was just like a skating rink... cars were skidding all over the place. I'm really lucky to have that ABS thing, you know the, erm, the device that stops your car from going out of control if you brake - it's like a - a computer controls the braking on the wheels. I used it once or twice and believe me, I don't think I'd ever go for a car that didn't have it. Anyway a lot of people just gave up and erm left their cars by the side of the road. Gave three of them a lift as a matter of fact.

Speaker 4

Right, thought it would be you? Have you run into a bit of trouble then? Yeah that's right, junction eighteen, just after the service station, you'd better check it on the map though. So once you leave the motorway - a couple of miles past the services - erm, make sure that you, er, get into the right hand lane so that you can turn right. At the first roundabout, do a right and carry on a bit. There's a junction at the end and a petrol station, you can't miss it.

Speaker 5

He didn't indicate or anything. He just shot out, must have been dreaming. Anyway, the car behind was just as much to blame. He overtook on the bend and bang that was it. The second one swerved but, well, it was unavoidable by then. One of them smashed his windscreen and there was glass all over the road from the lights. I expect I'll be called as a witness, but as far as I'm concerned they're equally to blame. There was also this stupid girl, with a dog which wasn't on a lead, that can't have helped either.

PAGE 90   2 Three councillors, Eric, Charles and Bernice, are discussing the proposals to build a by-pass around Marsham.

Eric: OK, OK, now everyone has finally turned up let's get this meeting underway, shall we? Bernice, perhaps you'd like to begin.

Bernice: Right. Thank you, Eric. Well, as I see it, if we stop traffic coming through the centre of the village, then it'll be the beginning of the end for it. I mean there are an awful lot of people who stop off in the town and use the facilities we provide. Before long we'd be a ghost town. Lots of other villages have died out because they are no longer on the road to anywhere.

Eric: Charles. What do you think?

Charles: I'm afraid I just can't agree... With the by-pass we'll be able to improve the quality of life of people in the village immeasurably. We can't carry on like this, you know loads of huge lorries coming through the village. After all, it's these people, the, erm, villagers, we should be worrying about rather than the needs of passing motorists.

Eric: This is all very well in theory, and I don't think anyone would argue with you that the traffic makes the erm High Street unpleasant, but the thing is I'd like to bring up the effects that the by-pass could have on the village. I mean, Bernice is right... without the passing trade then lots of small shops will go out of business. Local people use them too but without the extra business they just wouldn't be able to survive.

Charles: I see your point, Eric, but other businesses will grow up in their place. Just think what the centre of the village would look like without the traffic. As I see it, we'll be able to have restaurants and cafés and a lot more people would come to the village for its tourist attractions.

Bernice: What nonsense, you're living in a dream world, Charles. What tourist attractions?

Charles: Well, there's the church, that's seven hundred years old... and there's the old medieval covered market and there are lots of lovely old buildings which are really picturesque.

Eric: And I suppose we could look into the plans we had before to open up the craft centre and the museum. Oh, and there are the ruins of the castle too. Just think of all the jobs and businesses it would create. We could have a souvenir shop and lots of things could be...

Bernice: Goodness me, Eric, I really don't believe it. You're as bad as he is... The place would lose its character as a real working village. I want to do my shopping not buy souvenirs. I can't eat a souvenir. A working village, with lots of people passing through, that's what I want...

Eric: Well, that's all very well, but what's the point if the people who live here can't actually enjoy it any more. I mean, you risk your life each time you step off the pavement at the moment. It's only a matter of time before someone gets killed.

Bernice: Well, I quite agree with Eric for once. We need to do something to make it safer but I'm sure that if it comes down to people still having shops and a job or turning into a sleepy picture postcard village, I think I know what they'll go for. Just think of the erm the garden centre and the garage as you come into the town. They employ loads of people...

3 Listen again and make notes.

UNIT 8 *Judging by Appearances*

PAGE 97 Clive and Jenny discuss their weekend dates

Clive: Hi Jenny.

Jenny: Hi.

Clive: How did it go then?

Jenny: Pretty mixed really.

Clive: Oh yeah?

Jenny: Yeah. He wasn't exactly the man of my dreams.

Clive: What happened then?

Jenny: It was pretty nerve-wracking, actually, waiting outside the station for him to turn up. Like being 14 all over again.

Clive Yes. I know what you mean. Still, he didn't stand you up, did he?

Jenny: No, no. He turned up all right.

Clive: So what did he look like?

Jenny: Well, he had reddish hair, glasses - quite good-looking, I suppose, - not very tall, about your height, in fact.

Clive: Charming!

Jenny: I didn't mean it like that but I guess I was expecting someone much sportier, someone who likes the outdoor life.

Clive: Well dressed?

Jenny: Not particularly. Bit scruffy really. Wore a leather jacket and a pullover.

Clive: Really?

Jenny: Yeah.

Clive: And what was he like?

Jenny: Not that exciting I'm afraid.

Clive: Why not?

Jenny: Well, at first I thought he was OK, but then we went off to a pub and all he could talk about was politics.

Clive: But you're into that, aren't you?

Jenny: Yeah, but not all the time. He went on and on. He said he had a great time but I couldn't get away fast enough.

Clive: Oh dear.

Jenny: He wants to see me again. Asked me if I wanted to go to a demo on Saturday.

Clive: You're kidding.

Jenny: No. I'm not going. Anyway, how about you?

Clive: Well, I have to admit that I almost chickened out.

Jenny: Typical.

Clive: Well, I didn't and I had a great time.

Jenny: Did you? Tell us all about it then.

Clive: We just went out to an Italian I know and had a nice meal and chatted away merrily. You know, we found out that we'd lived in the same street as kids.

Jenny: How amazing!

Clive: But we couldn't remember each other.

Jenny: Was she pretty?

Clive: Very. She was very chic - all in black, short black hair and not much make-up.

Jenny: She sounds a bit serious to me. Not really your type.

Clive: No, no, not at all. She had a great sense of humour. Funny, you don't expect that from someone who's an accountant.

Jenny: Going to see her again?

Clive: Yeah, she said to give her a call.

PAGE 101 Margot, the colour consultant, and Ambrose, the interviewer, are discussing the right colours for them to wear.

Margot: Well, in the old days, I think I used to go for stuff, for colours just because they were fashionable, you know the in colours of the time.

Ambrose: Like black these days.

Margot: Um, that's right. And I mean lots of people, I'd say most, look dreadful in black, it just doesn't suit them. I mean, people who are pale and blonde just look so washed out if they wear it .

Ambrose: But they do, 'cos of fashion.

Margot: Yeah that's right.

Ambrose: So could you tell listeners what sort of impact this has had on your life.

Margot: Sure, well, let me start with my details. I've got reddish, chestnut hair and hazel eyes and like lots of red-haired people I've got quite a few freckles.

Ambrose: Huh huh...

Margot: So all of this makes me, erm my classification, is 'warm'.

Ambrose: 'Warm' that's interesting, so what does this mean?

Margot: Well, before I used to wear a lot of blues and greys but I was advised they didn't suit me and so I just, I got rid of them.

Ambrose: Brave of you...

Margot: And instead I switched to greens, golden browns and so on.

Ambrose: That's why you're wearing these colours yourself.

Margot: Right,

Ambrose: So what advice would you have for me then? Does it work for men too?

Margot: Yes of course! Well, you've got brown eyes and hair and black skin which makes you a 'deep' person..

Ambrose: Deep! I like that...

Margot: Hah hah, this means that you can wear black and greys, but my advice to you would be to offset them, erm contrast them with really bright, vivid colours like turquoise, red or yellow. Steer clear of pastels as they just won't suit you at all.

Ambrose: You're right you know 'cos I remember once I bought this ...

PAGE 102 Pictures of the soul

Joseph: Yes. You're right. I can see this could be quite a useful tool for people like us, social workers and teachers. It's often difficult for us to assess the personality of some of the kids we have to deal with...

Paul: I'm sorry, Joseph, but I'm afraid I have less sympathy for the idea. It seems rather like erm black magic to me...

Joseph: Well, I'm sure it isn't, Paul. Erm, do you think, you could actually talk us through some examples.

Angela: Well, as a matter of fact I've brought some along to show you. Let's look at the first one, shall we?

Paul: OK

Angela: Well, this, looks like the work of a happy child and well-balanced individual.

Joseph: What makes you say that, Angela?

Angela: Well, there's a lot of life in it. There are people and animals

Joseph: Mm, it's very energetic, there's an awful lot of activity in it, isn't there?

Paul: I think you're reading too much into this one picture, Joseph.

Angela: Well, I take your point but let's compare it with the second one. Well, my guess is the child must be deeply unhappy.

Paul: What do you mean? How can you be so sure?

Angela: It would be dishonest of me to say I was 100 per cent sure. All the same, the picture is just too neat and cautious, there are no white spaces either, there are just erm buildings with nothing else. There's a lot of anxiety there.

Paul: Really? It just looks neat and pretty to me..

Joseph: But that's just it. This is a picture from a kid who desperately wants to please adults, you know parents and teachers.

Paul: So what you're saying, Joseph, is that it's too controlled, that there is no spontaneity in it .

Angela: Exactly... In fact, I'd say it expresses a fundamental misery.

Paul: This is all very well, but how can you really tell? How can you be that sure? You know it could be a bit irresponsible to make a very important assessment or judgement about a child on the basis of their drawings.

Angela: I agree. There's no point in the exercise if it's unreliable you know erm hit or miss.

Paul: Right... So how did you actually go about working it out? Surely it's impossible to come to any conclusion without seeing a lot of drawings from the same person.

Angela: Oh. I see. I think I understand what you're getting at. There has been a lot of research done. Psychologists have studied thousands of pictures by kids and matched them up .

Joseph: I'm sorry, but I don't quite follow you...

Angela: What I mean is, is that the same kind of child tends to produce the same kind of drawing and patterns.

Joseph: Mmm... I see.

Paul: Mm, this is interesting. Let's have a look at one more, shall we?

Joseph: It's difficult to make out what's going on.

Angela: Yes, you're right... There is a lot of scribbling and quite a bit of confusion in it...

Paul: It look as though there is a lot of anger there...

Angela: There is some writing too but it's completely illegible...

Paul: So what does it all mean, then?

Angela: Well, you're right about anger, Paul. We generally associate this kind of drawing with children who are disobedient, you know who don't do as they're told. They're often incapable of concentration .

Paul: Well, I must say, the more I hear you talking about this, the more I think there could be something in it. How could I found out a little more about the whole thing? Are there any books you could recommend?

UNIT 9 Teenage Cults

PAGE 105 Listen to these five men talking about experiences they have had connected with clothes.

Speaker 1

Well, it was really awful, you know. It was a wedding reception erm in the middle of town in a posh hotel. So, I was feeling really rather pleased with myself. I had on this beige Italian suit - very expensive and a beautiful tie and silk shirt. Everything went beautifully. But when I walked into the ballroom where the reception was being held I almost died. Everybody else, and I mean everyone was dressed up in evening dress. I swear everybody stopped talking when I went into the room. Well, what would you have worn at two o'clock in the afternoon? And the bride's mother - if looks could have killed. I don't think I appeared in any of the photographs.

Speaker 2

So anyway, I found this lovely pair of trousers, they were made of a kind of soft cotton, and I went to a changing room and tried them on. I thought they looked OK but that they were a bit loose round the waist - I wouldn't have that problem these days. Anyway when I got out of the changing room the assistant came up to me and asked me how they felt. I said fine but asked whether they would stretch or shrink when they were washed. Quick as a flash he said to me 'Well, what do you want them to do?' We both laughed and I bought them anyway.

Speaker 3

I was really upset... I'd had those jeans for ages and they were really faded and looked, you know, really cool and fashionable. Anyway, I got home after school and went to change out of my uniform and I couldn't find them anywhere so I asked mum if she's seen them. 'Those scruffy old things,' she said, 'I threw them out,' she said. They were an absolute disgrace.' Scruffy old things! They were my favourite! I was really upset. If I ever have kids, I'll never do that, I thought it was really mean.

Speaker 4

Well, I really liked it, the colour really suited me, the only thing is that the sleeves were a bit too long. So I asked if they could take the sleeves up for me a couple of inches. The girl in the shop said it would cost me thirty pounds. I just couldn't believe it. 'Thirty pounds!' I said. After all, I was ready to spend almost a hundred on a jacket. The girl said that it was because they had to send the jacket out to an erm outside, you know alterations place, tailor. In the end I left it - just as well really, it would have clashed horribly with the trousers.

Speaker 5

It was a really beautiful day and the others suggested going for a dip. Now I hadn't brought my things with me but in the end, well, I borrowed a pair of trunks from Keith. They were a bit on the large side but I didn't think anything of it. I ran into the sea and started swimming around and we all played with a ball, you know, throwing it to each other.. Then out of nowhere a huge wave came along and everybody was swept off their feet. Well, you can guess what happened. The trunks flew off and I was left stranded in the sea. The others thought it was hilarious. I had to beg them to bring the trunks back to me. Everybody on the beach was laughing too. They knew what was going on.

PAGE 105 Pronunciation

Rising intonation

1 In the listening speakers three and four repeat what someone else has said. They both use rising intonation to express disbelief. Listen again and try and copy their intonation.

Thirty Pounds!
Scruffy old things!

PAGE 107 Listen to someone talking about Goths and make notes.

Shall we move onto something else. Well, of course these are Goths. You can tell from the, erm the costume and make up. They're really interesting. When they started up in the early eighties nobody thought that they would, um, you know, last.

They were a mixture of quite a lot of other fashions... you know the emphasis on black, well this was something that was very much punk. There was also another fashion at the time - I don't know whether you remember it or not - well it was called the New Romantics - people dressed up in erm, you know, velvets and lace and stuff like that. Soft and rich fabrics. It looked a little bit like fancy dress I guess. It took its erm inspiration from, what, aristocratic fashion from two hundred years ago.

Anyway, as I was saying the Goths were really a mixture of all these things. But what makes them different I suppose is their philosophy. They are into mystical things and wear silver jewellery, often with a religious significance. They can look really striking with their white skin and swept back hair, you know they brush it right back.

Another thing is that they have a rather negative view of life. You know, you expect young people to be optimistic and full of life and enthusiasm, but Goths aren't like that.

They are quite pessimistic and interested in death. They have this attitude that everything is erm doomed and somehow tragic. They also have this fascination with TV programmes like the Munsters and the Addams family. It seems to appeal to kids, and I think there are always lots in every generation, who like to look on the dark rather than the bright side of life. You can erm go almost anywhere in England now, even to the smallest village and find a few Goths together as a small group, very much isolated from other kids of the same age.

The name Goths, of course, comes from the neo Gothic period, you know Dracula, Frankenstein, Mary Shelley and all that.

PAGE 111 The radio phone-in

Part A

Presenter: Our next caller is Rachel who is from South London. Go ahead Rachel.
Rachel: Hello, Doctor Howard.
Dr Howard: Hello, Rachel. How can I help you?

Rachel: Well, you see it's about my son, Mark. He's almost 18 and he hasn't been able to find a job since he left school.
Dr Howard: When did he leave?
Rachel: It'll be a year in July.
Dr Howard: And what seems to be the problem?
Rachel: It's like this. Mark used to be such a nice, outgoing sort of boy but over the last few months he's changed quite a bit.
Dr Howard: So, can you describe what has happened?
Rachel: Well, after he was turned down for several jobs he got depressed and withdrawn which was bad enough, but now it's got much worse - he's become really moody and aggressive.
Dr Howard: Moody and aggressive?
Rachel: Yes, and he's started mixing with some boys I don't like very much. But to tell you the truth, I think he's started taking drugs.
Dr Howard: What makes you think that?
Rachel: Well, as I said, there are his change of moods. One minute he's very depressed and the next minute he becomes very excited - you know, he can't sit still. Another thing is stuff has disappeared from the house. Some of my jewellery has gone and some money and so has Mark's cassette player.
Dr Howard: Does he know you know about the cassette player?
Rachel: Yes, he does. He told me he'd let a friend borrow it. I was really surprised because he's always been so keen on music. When I asked him about it a couple of days later, he just told me to mind my own business. Another thing is that he just doesn't look after himself any more or care what he looks like. And I've noticed strange smells in the house too.
Dr Howard: May I ask you, Rachel, are you still married?
Rachel: Yes I am but my husband spends a lot of time away. He's in the merchant navy, you see.
Dr Howard: From what you've said the change in your son has been quite dramatic. What I suggest...

Part B

Rachel: Yes I am, but my husband spends a lot of time away. He's in the merchant navy, you see.
Dr Howard: From what you've said the change in Mark has been quite dramatic. What I'd suggest is that you try and sit down with him and have a quiet chat about things. Approach him as a friend rather than as a mother. Try to get to the bottom of things and see how he feels. Something else which I would suggest is that you get in contact with one of his old teachers or your family doctor and ask them to have a chat with Mark. Someone he respects and could have a chat with.
Rachel: And what if that doesn't work?
Dr Howard: Well, if you do feel he is taking drugs, then I should contact the police.
Rachel: Turn my own son in to the police!
Dr Howard: It may seem harsh but it's probably the best course of action in the long run.
Presenter: OK, thank you Rachel. I hope things sort themselves out for you and Mark. Our next caller is...

UNIT 10 **Us and Animals**

PAGE 116 Listen to Magnus and Patrick discussing the problem.

Magnus: Well, what do you think he should do?
Patrick: Well, it's tricky isn't it. He could start by taking the cabbage across.
Magnus: No that won't work, the goose will get eaten by the dog.
Patrick: Oh, yeah. You've got a point. Well how about... first of all he takes the goose, 'cos the dog won't eat the cabbage, will it?

Magnus: That's a good idea...But then what should he do next? I know, why doesn't he row back to the other side, then pick up the dog..

Patrick: But wait a minute, won't he still have the same problem? I mean we can't leave the dog with the goose, can we?

Magnus: Oh no, of course not. I'm not sure what to do.

Patrick: I know. I've got an idea We could always you know, work it out with a diagram. OK, this is the river and this button is the dog, the paper clip's the cabbage and erm, this coin can be the goose...

Patrick: Great, now let's try again shall we ...

PAGE 117 Listen to these situations and choose the correct answer.

Question 1
Child: Oh no!
Mother: What's wrong, sweetheart?
Child: It's Teddy, he's not here. Teddy's not here?
Mother: What?
Child: I left it at grandma's.
Mother: What do you mean... you left it?
Child: In the bedroom. I want it...
Mother: But we're almost home. Are you seriously saying that you want me to drive all the way back to grandma's house...
Child: Please.

Question 2
Butcher: Hello, Higgins the butcher... Yes, hello Mrs Adams... A problem with the order? Right... you didn't get the chops or the sausages... what?... and the chickens? I really don't know what could have gone wrong...
Look, if it's OK with you ...I'll check the order... Mm... I've got a horrible feeling it could have... yes, that's it, gone to the wrong place. Yeah. Right you are. I'll look into it straight away and give you a ring in a couple of minutes... bye for now...

Question 3
Presenter: So strangely, it is the male who plays an important part in the incubation and hatching process. There isn't a nest as such for very obvious reasons: the environment is unable to support vegetation. As you can imagine the eggs cannot be left for a second because of the inhospitable Arctic conditions. So what happens in this instance is the female goes off in search of food while...

Question 4
Adult: And so, can you guess what happened next? Yes, Mrs Large went down to the kitchen and crept in ever so quietly, and then she stood on a stool to get the cake. See she was so hungry even though she wanted to get nice and thin... and there inside there was only one slice left. Yes... all her naughty children elephants had gobbled it all up. So you can imagine how she felt.

Question 5
Doctor: So what happens?
Patient: Well, erm, I get all, you know, wheezy and things, can't breathe properly, and my eyes start to itch.
Doctor: I see. And it's just horses you say.
Patient: Yeah.
Doctor: Does it run in the family?
Patient: Sort of. My mum, she was allergic to anything, you know dogs, cats and things. That's why we never had pets, but with me it just seems to be horses..
Doctor: What about feathers and dust?
Patient: Ah well, now you came to mention it, I do sneeze a lot.

Question 6
News presenter: Last night, laboratories on the Madingley road were broken into and many of the animals were released. Computers and experimental equipment were also destroyed in the raid. The Animal Liberation Front has accepted responsibility for this action. A security guard was badly injured in the attack. Members of the scientific profession and doctors investigating new drugs in possible cures for cancer have condemned the raid as totally irresponsible and say that it has put work in these vital areas back at least two years..

Question 7
First man: It was amazing really, there I was, just standing by the sink, you know, doing the washing up,
Second man: Oh yeah...
First man: When along comes this fox, I couldn't believe my eyes. It just trotted up the path as bold as brass. It finished off Toffee's food which we'd put outside, can't stand the smell.
Second man: Goodness..
First man: And then it turned and looked at me, straight in the eye, yawned and trotted off the way it had come..
Second man: Well I never.

Question 8
Right, now as we approach the time of year when we are often looking for small presents, we would like to start a safety drive about these cute little things. They're called Foalings, they're little miniature horses, they're made of plastic and have manes and tails in bright fluffy material. Now these are fine, they are made to the highest standards in the States, the problem is these copies which are flooding street markets. Now they're made in the east and even though they may look the same, let's see what happens, see, the head just pops off - very dangerous for small children. Now look at how the manes catch light if they're near a flame. So they're potentially lethal toys...

PAGE 123 The debate on vivisection

Presenter: Good morning everybody. I'm Joe Templer. It's eleven o'clock which means it's time for another edition of *Crosstalk*, the phone-in programme which looks at today's hot issues. The subject of today's discussion is whether vivisection - that's experimenting on live animals - is ever justified. Now if you want to take part in today's debate the number to ring is 0171 - if you're outside London -833 3974. But before that, in the studio I have two guests to open the debate. They are Professor Anna Wright from Queen Margaret Hospital and Peter Savage of the Free the Animals Movement. Good morning to the both of you.

Anna Wright: Good morning.

Peter Savage: Good morning.

Presenter: OK then, if you'd like to put your point of view first, Professor Wright.

Anna Wright: Thank you. Now I must state categorically that for advances in medicine we count on being able to carry out experiments on animals. Without them, there would be no progress. We are unable to observe human beings in scientifically controlled conditions so, unfortunately, we have to rely on animals. Medicine's made enormous advances based on the results of vivisection. For example, our knowledge of the nervous system is largely due to vivisection. It has allowed us to find cures for many illnesses. Diphtheria, smallpox and TB used to be killers in the old days but not any more. If you were bitten by a dog with rabies, you had very little chance of surviving. Now there is an antidote. Cancer recovery rates have greatly improved thanks to the work done on animals. And I'm afraid drugs have to be tested on animals prior to their release on the market to check for side effects. Nobody takes any pride in causing suffering and I can assure the listeners it is kept to an absolute minimum.

Presenter: Thank you very much, Professor Wright. Over to you , Peter.

Peter Savage: Thanks. I'd like to start by saying that I'm speaking on behalf of animals. On the issue of testing drugs on animals for side effects in human beings, as we know from the thalidomide case, it's very difficult to predict what the effect a drug will be on human beings from tests done on animals. They just don't tell us the whole story. As for understanding the nervous system, I think most experts would agree that this could have been done equally well by careful observation and nothing more. Professor Wright points to the reduction in the number of deaths from diseases like diphtheria, TB and smallpox. This is utter nonsense because these diseases were in decline already and they've been on the decline primarily because of improvements in hygiene, not animal experiments. No, the whole thing is rubbish. If we look at penicillin and aspirin, two of the most famous modern drugs, these drugs were found by accident. So much for medical research! And Professor Wright's argument completely ignores the moral dimension. The point is experiments on animals should be stopped because they are cruel and inhumane. Dogs are made to smoke cigarettes and mice have shampoo and cosmetics squirted in their eyes to see what will happen. Dogs don't smoke and rats and mice don't wash their hair. Very often these animals have suffered so much they have to be put down. Basically, we should take care of animals not take advantage of them.

Presenter: Thanks, Peter. OK then. So it's over to you, the listeners. Our first call...

PAGE 123 Pronunciation

Sounds in sentences

1 Listen to these sentences and phrases taken from the listening and note what happens to the parts that are underlined.

1. It's eleven o'clock.
2. It's time for another edition of Crosstalk.
3. I have two guests to open the debate.
4. I must state categorically.
5. in the old days
6. rats and mice

PAGE 125 Listen to this expert talking about Animal Farm.

Of course, one of the reasons that *Animal Farm* is so interesting is that you can read it on two levels. On one level you can read it purely and simply as a fairy tale for adults - I wouldn't recommend it to children as some pretty awful things happen to the animals, most of all Boxer.

At, perhaps, a deeper level we can read it as a criticism of what happens to revolutions in general and what happened in the Russian revolution of 1917 in particular. There are some obvious parallels and comparisons which can be drawn: Major, who talks about Animalism, is obviously Karl Marx, the creator of communism, while the pigs represent the communist intellectuals. Manor Farm is Imperial Russia and Animal Farm the new Soviet Union. The quarrel between Snowball and Napoleon reminds us of the conflict between Stalin and Trotsky. The pig Napoleon, is, of course a kind of composite character and equals both Lenin and Stalin. Jones the farmer is the old Russian Tsar. Moses the raven - the big black bird who talks about the animal heaven of 'Sugarcandy Mountain' obviously represents the church. The other farmers who try to win the farm back are the heads of other European countries at that time, who were completely against communism. Frederick quite obviously represents Germany's Adolf Hitler. Boxer stands for the Russian working class which is worked and exploited both by the Tsar and later by his new communist masters.

I think Orwell chose to tell his story as a kind of fairy tale so that he could make his point more readily. Full histories of the period, of which there are many, run to many hundreds of pages. Instead, Orwell makes his point beautifully, creates some believable and memorable characters and presents us with a poignant parable of what seems to happen with nearly all revolutions.

UNIT 11 Your Cultural Heritage

PAGE 128 Festivals

Listen to five different men talking about festivals and special events.

Speaker one
I wish they'd just ban it. I mean it's just an excuse for hooligan behaviour. There's no fun it... I don't think it's funny throwing flour and water all over people. There was also this thing of cutting off men's ties with erm big pairs of scissors. You know it's a terrible thing... if you complain, then they just accuse you of being a bad sport but it was really excessive. It's just out of control...They have these big plastic club things too, which they hit you over the head with, you're supposed to laugh but well it's just not really very funny.

Speaker two
You should have seen his face when he found out. I mean, we'd arranged for all the girls from the offices in Spain and Brazil to send him cards, with lots of hearts and kisses all in erm lipstick. 'We love you Milton' they said. You know, 'Can't wait to make you mine'. Anyway he was as proud as a peacock, inviting everyone into his office. There they were on his desk, he thought he had these admirers from all over the world. It was hilarious. We could hardly keep a straight face. When he found out he took it very well though. He was a good sport I like someone who can laugh at himself.

Speaker three
The climax of the thing was this procession through the erm town. It was absolutely beautiful emotional occasion. There were these tiny children - some of them can't have been much older than six, anyway there they were on skis carrying lamps with the grown-ups not that far behind with real erm blazing torches - all of them were singing traditional hymns and carols. The spectators joined in too, I would have if I'd known the words and the language! We were right near the front and so we could see everything...

Speaker four
It used to be much better in the old days. It was more you know intimate when it started off. In the tent there would the performers, the musicians and a maximum of about fifty people in the tents listening to them. There was much more of a relationship between people if you know what I mean. Nowadays it's all crowds and queues and lots of the performers use microphones and there are security guards, it's the opposite of what you'd expect a folk festival to be.

Speaker five
They must have been mad to do it. I mean some of the people were no more than boys and could run pretty fast but as for the others. Well, there was a really fat English bloke and he just couldn't keep ahead. The bulls they just ran over him. He was in a terrible state and they took him off in an ambulance. Still, by and large it was fun to watch and I guess it gave the bulls the chance for revenge.

One of the worst things for the runners was the fear of tripping up and falling over. You had to be able to jump as well. Still, it must have been really exciting for them but I wouldn't have done it for love nor money. There isn't really anywhere to escape to.

PAGE 132 A Day Out in Cambridge

Good morning, ladies and gentlemen. Please let me introduce myself. My name is Amanda Southgate and I would like to welcome you to the wonderful town of Cambridge on behalf of Culture Tours. I'm your guide today and it gives me great pleasure to introduce you to the most important sights of this town. We start our tour here at the Round Church, one of the few round Churches in England. After that, we visit Trinity and Clare colleges and then walk along the backs to admire the daffodils which are now in bloom. Then we shall visit King's College and its beautiful chapel. After a brief look at Queen's college we stop for a picnic lunch. Please may I remind you not to walk on the grass and to keep to the footpath. Visitors are not allowed to enter lectures or living accommodation.

This afternoon there will be a visit to the Folk Museum which shows how people used to live in the old days. Finally there will be an opportunity for you to experience a trip on a punt, which is a kind of boat you push along with a pole. I would not recommend you to try it yourself - it is easy to fall in the river.

One last thing I would like to say before we begin the tour is if anyone should get lost don't forget to be back here at the Round Church at 4.30 in order to catch the coach back. Many thanks for being so patient. Now let us begin the tour.

PAGE 133 At the Museum

Curator: Hello everybody. I'm glad you've been able to make it. It's a shame about the weather though, isn't it? Anyway, if you'd like to follow me into the first room, I'll tell you a litle bit about some of the exhibits there.

Well, as you can see, there are a number of farming and domestic implements here which we have collected over the years. Of course, none of them are used any longer. In actual fact, we can sometimes have quite a job finding out just exactly what they were for! Now this first one I suppose you'd describe as a giant comb. And that's just what it is - not for human beings though, but for wool. Once the wool had been sheared from the sheep then it would have to be combed to make it ready for spinning. Now if you look over here, you can see something which looks just like a huge frying pan with a very long handle. We had an Italian visitor in here last year who thought it was for baking pizza in a deep oven but it's actually a warming pan. In the old days you'd pop it into your bed to make it nice and warm. You'd take some coals from the fire or a hot brick, then you'd put it into the copper pan and make sure the lid was tight. Then, as I say, pop it in the bed. This one is an original but I should warn you about some of the ones you may come across in antique shops. They're quite often reproductions. So don't be taken in.

Now, this next object is rather strange looking. It is called a flail and as you can see, it is a couple of poles of about equal length which are held together by a strap. Now this was used before the days of modern agricultural machinery to beat the corn to separate the wheat from the chafe, the bits you didn't want. The men used to put the cut corn on the ground and then they'd swing the flail and beat it until they had separated all the wheat out.

The last thing in this room I want to draw your attention to before we move on to our Roman collection is this evil-looking contraption in the corner. Now this is in fact a man trap. It just shows how much crueller the world was in the nineteenth century. Farm workers and their families often had very little to eat, so to supplement their meagre diets they would go onto the farm owner's land to hunt for rabbits and other game, poaching in other words. And the farm owners would set these traps to stop them from doing this. Not very pleasant. And if someone did get caught in a trap, then their leg would certainly have been broken. After that, it would be a short step from the courthouse onto one of those terrible prison ships bound for Australia.

PAGE 134 A Family Heirloom

Listen to Matthew talking about a clock which is a family heirloom.

Right, a family heirloom. Well, I suppose the most important heirloom in my family is erm a grandfather clock. You know, it's one of those really tall clocks with a big pendulum and chimes. It's a little like having Big Ben in your house. Anyway, it has been in my family for quite a long time from what I can gather. My father says he can remember it in his grandfather's house and I can certainly remember it in, my grandfather's from when I was a boy. It's got the manufacturer's name Jonathan someone, I can't remember the second name and is dated 1776. It used to sit at the bottom of the stairs in the hallway and I can remember when I was a kid I used to be scared of the loud ticking, you know tick-tock that it made. And when it struck the hour well I almost used to jump out of my skin, it used to make an incredible noise. I can remember being with my grandfather and him winding the thing up. It was a ceremony that he performed once a week and it's probably my strongest, er clearest memory of him. It is about eight feet tall I should think, it's made of dark brown oak which is shiny from being polished. At the top there 's a squarish box with a round face inside. It's covered in gold leaf. and is decorated with carving. It really is a lovely old object. There's a sun and a moon in it but they have never really worked from what I can gather. It really is a lovely old object with its polished wood which has been polished for years and years. Anyway, the idea is that the clock goes from generation to generation, from the eldest son to son, so one day, I might inherit it.

PAGE 137 The picture by John Millais

Woman: This is a painting of a country scene. I think it was probably painted about a hundred years or so ago. Anyway, in the foreground there are two girls. They both look very poor. Their clothes are old and shabby, and there's tears and patches in them. They're sitting by the side of a field and, well, I suppose they look as though they are having a rest. The elder of the two girls has got some sort of - oh, I think it's an old fashioned accordion. She's young, quite pretty, with red hair. She's sitting with her eyes half closed, most likely because of the sun. In the background there are fields with a few animals in them and some farm buildings on the top of a hill and the most beautiful rainbow in the sky. It must have been raining but the sky is quite dark and it looks as though it might rain again. The little girl is quite enchanted by the rainbow. She seems to be telling her friend, or perhaps it's her sister, to have a look too. The other girl doesn't appear to be that interested. Oh, wait a minute. She's got something round her neck. It says 'Pity the blind'. I see. I get it. The elder of the two girls is blind and the younger one is trying to tell her all about the rainbow. Quite sad really. The colours of the painting are marvellous. Just like you get after it's been raining. There's so much beauty all around but all the blind girl can feel is the warmth of the sun on her face. She can't even appreciate the butterfly which has settled on her. I suppose she must play the accordion and hope that people give her money. Yes, it's a lovely painting, it's lovely, although in general I'm not a fan of this kind of art. I prefer Impressionist pictures, people like Monet, Cézanne. I recently went to see a big exhibition...

UNIT 12 Crime and Society

PAGE 141 The examination

Listen to Anna and Bruno talking to each other and the examiner

Interlocutor: So what have you two decided then?
Anna: Well, we are agree for the first. We think that the first should be Mick Brown.
Interlocutor: Why's that?
Bruno: Well, he is not very intelligent and maybe he needs help from a psychologist?
Interlocutor: Psychiatrist.
Bruno: Psychiatrist. The prison will be a bad place for him. He will become worst...
Interlocutor: And what did you think?
Anna: Well I am agree with him but we had a problem for to choose the other. I mean I think Janet Green must go free. OK, she is a poor lady but the prison is not like a hotel...
Bruno: But I thought this was not kind, it was a cruel thing. Another thing she has done this crime ten times. I chose Alan Jones...
Anna: Alan Jones! But he has killed his wife. It doesn't matter if the neighbours they say he is a nice man. His wife is died because of him...He must stay inside.
Interlocutor: So who did you choose?
Anna: Cynthia..
Interlocutor: Bruno, can you tell me why she chose Cynthia?
Bruno: Well, she said Cynthia hasn't done a strong crime... I can see her point but I still think Alan must go free.
Interlocutor: Right; that's interesting. Now, what do you think would happen in your country?
Anna: I'm not sure. Maybe, Janet, the weather is warm here so it doesn't matter if she has to sleep erm outside...
Interlocutor: Hah hah...And what about you, Bruno?
Bruno: Well, we are from the same country but I think Cynthia and Mick maybe can go free. You know murder is murder and Alan... he would stay in the prison a long time.

PAGE 143 Pronunciation

Listen and identify which conditional construction is being used in the eight sentences.

1. I'd have come if I'd known.
2. Would you mind if he borrowed Dave's car?
3. What'll we do if the police come?
4. If we hadn't done that, we'd be all right.
5. I'll tell him if you threaten me.
6. We'd have plenty of money if we'd been insured.
7. I wouldn't do that if I were you.
8. If only you'd told me, I wouldn't have said it.

PAGE 144 Listen to these situations.

Question 1

I really couldn't believe it you know. When I asked her why she hadn't done her homework again she came up with this fantastic excuse which was so wild that I thought it might have been true. She said her dog had eaten it. I wish I hadn't believed her though because I noticed that there were a number of kids sniggering, you know laughing behind my back... it was 'cos she didn't even have a dog.

Question 2

This is Connolly solicitors. I am afraid there is no one here to take your call at the moment but if you would like to leave a message or send a fax please do so after the tone... BEEP
Right, this is Felix, Felix Mortimer leaving a message for Jeremy Connolly. Jeremy, I got your message and I wish I could help you out, but the car's out of action at the moment - in the garage having the window fixed... someone erm, smashed it to get to the radio. The times in which we live, eh. One of your clients maybe! See you soon. Once again, sorry I couldn't say 'yes'.

Question 3

You have been found guilty of driving while under the influence of alcohol. This is a serious offence for which the court fines you £200 and bans you from driving for one year. For failing to report a serious accident the court had contemplated a period of imprisonment. However, on taking your age into consideration, we have decided on a suspended sentence and probation. This means that every week for two years you will have to visit the probation officer and tell them what you have been up to for the past week. It's their job to supervise you and do what they can to guide you. So, you'd better watch your step young man, <u>otherwise</u> you will go to jail. Nothing is more certain.

Question 4

What a terrible thing to do. I mean those oaks had been there for five hundred years, that's since the time of Shakespeare. Yes, that's what I thought too, part of our heritage...Whatever possessed the council to allow it.. .. If only we'd known about it earlier... Yes that's right, a demonstration, we could have chained ourselves to the trees or something...
Vandalism. Absolutely. I'm really angry. They're just destroying the countryside..

Question 5

Mrs Williams: Forgotten your lock...
Damien: Can I just leave it outside?
Mrs Williams: No, no, definitely not, of course you can't risk it. Your parents would be furious if you left it outside. Look, you'd better bring it into the hall.
Damien: Are you sure?
Mrs Williams: Yes, <u>provided</u> you check that there isn't any mud or anything on the tyres first.
Damien: Look, I could pop back home for the lock.
Mrs Williams: No, no, it'll be fine, just wheel it in. That's it. Mind those handlebars. I don't want them to damage the wallpaper.
Damien: Thanks, Mrs Williams.
Mrs Williams: You're welcome. I'll call Marcia... Marcia, Damien's here, dear.

Question 6

Landlady: Yes, I'd like to have a word with you, please. Now, the reason we let you have the room was <u>on condition that</u> you wouldn't cook or smoke in the room.
Peter: Yes...
Landlady: Now I've just been up and it smells smoky.
Peter: It was Mike, the boy from down the hall..
Landlady: I see, but it's up to you to make sure no-one smokes in your room. Another thing, I found lots of empty food cartons there.
Peter: Honestly, I wasn't cooking, it was erm take-away food.
Landlady: Whatever, Peter, the smell's just the same..
Peter: But...
Landlady: No buts, <u>unless</u> you can guarantee that this isn't going to happen again, you'll have to look for somewhere else.

Question 7

Wife: Can you hear it.?

Husband: Look just try to relax, will you...

Wife: Honestly it's not fair. This is the third one this month...and I've got to go to work tomorrow...

Wife: I wish you'd do something.

Husband: Do something! What do you think I can do, you know what they're like. Look, just relax and you'll soon fall asleep.

Wife: No wonder the other people were so keen to move. They're a menace these people...

Husband: I know, I know. Look I'll give the police a ring, just so long as you accept I'm not going round there myself. I felt really humiliated last time. I wish I knew how to deal with them but I don't.

Wife: I wish I was a man. I'd soon show them who was boss.

Question 8

Now the important thing is to look confident. If you look as though you'll take no for an answer, then they'll probably try to make a fuss. Just look at them and say 'I have reason to believe that you have attempted to remove articles from this store without paying, I'd like you to accompany me to the manager's office.' Now most of the time they come as meek as anything. You know they're scared or shocked. Now if they pull a weapon or look threatening, then just let them go and leave the rest up to the police. We're here as a deterrent as much as anything.

PAGE 146 Listen to three friends discussing the issue of crime and punishment.

Ian: I really do think that everyone is far too soft on crime nowadays.

Victor: Soft on crime, I suppose so, but what should we do then?

Ian: Well for a start I think we've got to stop rewarding the criminal.

Victor: What do you mean, Ian, rewarding the criminal?

Christine: Well, Victor, I suppose he means this business of sending kids off on holidays and stuff like that.

Ian: Thank you, Christine, exactly... It's a terrible business in this country. I don't know where else they would do such a thing.

Victor: Yeah, but come on, Ian. Lots of these kids who commit crimes they've come from really terrible upbringings and probably come from broken homes and criminal backgrounds themselves...

Christine: And so on, we all know the excuses. But they've got to be shown the difference between right and wrong.

Victor: But don't you think that one way of doing this is by taking them away under supervision and letting them sort their problems out more?

Christine: Maybe yes. I can see the logic behind that but they've still got to pay. There should be retribution, you know, punishment as well as rehabilitation.

Ian: Right... And so what would you do, Christine?

Christine: Use corporal punishment.

Victor: What you mean beat them?

Christine: Yeah. Like in the old days. A short sharp shock. Give them something to remember.

Ian: But that's erm pretty barbaric, isn't it? I'd draw the line at that . It's better to put them in jail. After all they get some erm guidance and help.

Victor: Jail makes people worse in my opinion. Universities of crime.

Christine: They need a bit of discipline... very often these kids have just been allowed to get away with anything, their parents have no control over them whatsoever.

Ian: So I suppose you're in favour of capital punishment too then...

Christine: Well, as it happens I'm not.

Ian: Oh really? Well, I am... in certain circumstances..

Victor: Now that's barbaric, Ian.

Christine: Mm .. don't get me wrong ..I'm against it not because it's cruel. Frankly, capital punishment is too good for some people.

Victor: So why...?

Christine: Well, I think that.. you know I've changed my mind about this, but it was the Guildford Four case..

Victor: Oh the erm IRA people.

Ian: But they weren't.

Christine: Right. Anyway. There was tremendous feeling against them at the time. I remember my dad saying - I was just a little kid - they should all be hanged. But that would have been terrible wouldn't it.
I know they spent along time in jail but the thing is they were innocent...

Ian: At least they're free now and have got their ordinary lives back

Victor: Yeah, if they'd been hanged, that would have been the end of it wouldn't it?

Ian: Yeah, I've lost faith in the system a bit, but all the same someone did blow up those pubs...

UNIT 13 **Beyond Belief**

PAGE 148 The Chaffin Will Affair

Storyteller:

One of the most famous and extraordinary cases of contact with the dead was the so-called Chaffin Will affair. In 1921, a certain James Chaffin died, leaving his entire fortune to his third son, Marshal, in a will which had been written a full fifteen years earlier, in 1905, and signed in front of witnesses. His wife and two other sons were virtually cut off without a penny. Marshal was not inclined to split up the inheritance he had come into any more fairly. Four years went by and then, strangely, James Chaffin's ghost started to appear before one of his other two sons. The apparition had on an old overcoat which Chaffin had often worn in life. On the ghost of Chaffin's second visit to his son, he told him that he would find a will in the overcoat pocket . The coat was actually in the possession of the third brother. Once it was found, they came across a note sewn in the lining of one of the pockets saying they should look in an old family Bible. This Bible was found in the keeping of Chaffin's widow and examined in front of independent witnesses. Sure enough, there in the Bible they discovered a later version of the will, one which divided the property and money evenly between the widow and the three sons. The will appeared to be genuine and Marshall was not prepared to challenge it in court.

PAGE 149 Pronunciation of non-defining relative clauses

1 The woman, whose husband had died, was rich.
2 Carol's daughter, who lives in Scotland, is a doctor.
3 This Bible, which was found in the keeping of Chaffin's widow, was examined in front of independent witnesses.

PAGE 152 A discussion of reincarnation

Yolanda: What's that book you're reading, James? You seem very engrossed in it.

James: Oh sorry, yes, it's about reincarnation. Quite riveting.

Malcolm: Reincarnation! Ah, you surely don't believe in that.

James: That's why I'm reading this book - I'm trying to make my mind up about it.

Yolanda: I'm absolutely positive there's something in it.

Malcolm: But how can we know one way or the other? I mean, there's no proof, is there?

James: That's what I used to think but now I'm not so sure. There are some fascinating stories in this book, you know.

Malcolm: Oh yeah. Like what?

James: Well, first of all, if we are reincarnated, this means that we must've been someone else in a previous life, right?

Yolanda: Right. Go on.

James: You see, people investigating re-incarnation came up with the idea that if you hypnotised someone, they might be able to go back in time and tell you about their previous lives. And one of...

Malcolm: What a load of old rubbish! Do you believe this?

Yolanda: Come on, Malcolm. Let James finish what he has to say.

James: Thank you, Yolanda. Now as I was saying, one of the people they hypnotised was someone called Jane Evans and she managed to recall something like six or seven lives. She'd been a Jewish girl who was murdered during the middle ages, a servant to one of Henry VIII's wives and a nun in a convent in the USA.

Malcolm: Blimey! She's been busy. I mean, come off it! She'd probably read some stories about these characters somewhere or other. I'm sure there's a logical explanation for all of this.

James: Well, maybe you're right. She could have read something which entered her subconscious. That's certainly true in the case of one of her lives. She claimed to be the servant to a French merchant. And all of the details she could remember of this past life were readily available in books. Strangely enough though, she forgot to mention the fact that the merchant was married and had five kids.

Malcolm: There you are. What did I tell you?

James: Hold on a minute! Going back to the Jewish girl, what's incredible about this past life is that she could say exactly where the girl had been killed, under a church in a, in some kind of cellar. No sooner had she told this story, than some archaeologists found it. Quite by chance - they were doing some other work on the church - when they came across it and they found some skeletons down there!

Malcolm: Skeletons! You'd surely expect to find skeletons under a church, or at least I would.

Yolanda: I'm afraid I agree with Malcolm, James. Were there any other cases?

James: Well, there's another one that's very interesting. A housewife called Dolores was hypnotised and she took on the character of someone called Gretchen Gottlieb. Now, she was murdered in Germany in a forest during the last century and what's interesting about this case is that, when she was hypnotised, Dolores spoke in German and yet she'd never learnt the language at school or anything. What's more, when she came out of hypnosis, she couldn't speak any German at all.

Yolanda: What was her German like?

James: Well, not very good, I'm afraid. It was pretty incorrect and she avoided using verbs. Some of her answers didn't make sense and some of the time she hadn't understood questions she'd been asked.

Malcolm: So did this Gretchen actually exist?

James: Well, they tried to verify the story but they couldn't confirm it either way. There weren't any records or anything like that.

Yolanda: Do you think Dolores was trying to take the researchers in?

James: Well, according to the book they were sure she was acting in good faith, but well, you never know.

Malcolm: In good faith! If you believe that, you'll believe anything.

PAGE 153 Pronunciation

2 Listen to these six phrases. Is the speaker showing surprise, showing disbelief or making a simple statement?

1 His own daughter.
2 His own daughter.
3 His own daughter.
4 By car.
5 By car.
6 By car.

PAGE 154 Vocabulary

4 Anna is asking Martin questions. Listen to how Martin, who always exaggerates, replies.

Anna: Are you cold?
Martin: Cold? I'm absolutely freezing.

Anna: Is that an interesting book?
Martin: Interesting ? It's absolutely fascinating.

Anna: Was the film bad?
Martin: Bad? It was absolutely awful.

Anna: Are you tired?
Martin: Tired? I'm absolutely exhausted.

PAGE 159 It's you again!

Listen to the replies given by five women to the question 'If you came back in another life, what would you like to be and why?'

Speaker 1

Goodness me what a question. Well definitely not a housewife that's for sure. I think I must have been very bad in a previous life to have to do what I have to do every day. I don't know really, maybe something valuable, perhaps a painting or something like that... Yeah... that way I'd really feel as though I was appreciated and people would like to look at me, you know... I wouldn't have to worry about the shopping or cooking meals either.

Speaker 2

Mm, I think one of the problems affecting the world today is world peace, and I think that you know the normal solutions like wars and generals just, well, aren't the answer. I think if I came back what I'd like to be is someone like a spiritual leader who would be able to unite people and help world peace that way. I'd get people to tolerate and recognise the good in all the major religions.

Speaker 3

I suppose a runner or someone like that. I've competed at amateur level and won a couple of races with my club, but I guess what would give me the most satisfaction of all would be to win a gold at the Olympics. You know, the buzz must be incredible - just to know that you're the best in the world and nobody else can touch you. I can almost imagine what it must be like standing up on the podium listening to the national anthem as they put the sash around my neck.

Speaker 4

'Cos it's the lifestyle that would suit me most I think. It must be incredible, going from Paris to Milan, Milan to New York and to be in demand all the time. There'd be the clothes as well. What an opportunity to wear the very latest fashions. Another thing I think is really good these days is that you can change your career, you know, once you retire at the age of thirty something you have another career in the movies or maybe even become a pop star.

Speaker 5
A statesperson definitely. You know someone who was around when there were enormous changes taking place in government and things. I have strong convictions and beliefs about how the country should be run and it would be marvellous to be president or prime minister and to have a go at shaping the erm destiny of the country.

UNIT 14 **Destination USA**

PAGE 162 **The Statue of Liberty**

OK, OK everybody, in a minute we'll be getting off the boat, but before we do, I want to tell you a little bit about the Statue. Now, although it's almost certainly the most famous symbol of America and its people, it was in fact given to us by the people of France to commemorate the friendship between the two countries. In her right hand, as you can see, is the torch of Liberty and in her left hand is a tablet which has the date July 4th 1776 on it. That's the date of American independence, of course. OK, let's give you a few facts and figures about the Statue. The idea of the Statue came from a French historian and the money for it was raised by the French people. It was designed by Frederic Bartholdi. That's B-A-R-T-H-O-L-D-I.

The Statue was made of copper sheets which were hammered together by hand. They had to be put together over a huge framework of four supports which were made by Eiffel, the guy responsible for the Eiffel Tower in Paris, France. It was finished in 1885 and then taken to pieces to be shipped from France to the USA, and it weighs 25 tons. Now the Statue itself is 151 feet high, but if you add the pedestal, that's what the Statue stands on, then it makes 305 feet, which is 93 metres. If you want to go right, if you want to go right to the top, then I'm afraid you've got to walk. There's an elevator up through the pedestal, but from then on you have to use a spiral staircase to reach the observation point in the lady's crown, and it's 171 steps. Just to finish off, before we dock, when the Statue had been reconstructed, it was dedicated by President Grover Cleveland on 28th of October 1886. OK, we're nearly there...

PAGE 163 **Saying numbers**

Listen to the numbers and write them down.

1 Phone numbers
A: 01223 68991
B: 00 88 1 4476 1085

2 Account numbers
A: 87640328
B: 925487234

3 Decimals
A: 3.2
B: 2.54
C: 0.38

4 Fractions
A: 1/4
B: 2/3
C: 3/8
D: 5/16

5 Dates
A: 11/11/1918
B: 14/7/1789
C: 1/3/1963

6 Amounts
A: $6.92cents
B: £10.03p

7 Scores
A: Agassi won the tennis match 6-0, 3-6, 6-1
B: Italy beat Holland 2-0

8 Large numbers
A: 23,927,421
B: 9,867,364
C: 989,774

PAGE 165 **Two friends discuss the Mormons.**

Chrissy: You're a Mormon, aren't you Gina?
Gina: Well, yes, I was brought up as a Mormon, if that's what you mean, but I don't go to church as often as I should.
Chrissy: Is it part of the Christian Church?
Gina: Oh, yes.
Chrissy: I'm sorry to be so ignorant but when did it all start?
Gina: You can date if from 1827.
Chrissy: What happened then?
Gina: That's when the prophet Joseph Smith was visited by an angel called Moroni.
Chrissy: Moroni?
Gina: Yes, and he took Smith to a place where there were some gold plates buried and these plates had a holy book inscribed on them, the Book of Mormon. Mormon was Moroni's father, by the way.
Chrissy: This sounds a bit like Moses receiving the Ten Commandments.
Gina: Exactly. The thing is, with God's help, Smith was able to read what was written on the plates 'cos it had been written in a kind of Ancient Egyptian. And after that, the cult really caught on and lots of people joined it.
Chrissy: And what happened to the plates?
Gina: They were destroyed.
Chrissy: I see. And how come this happened in America?
Gina: Good question. The Bible talks of lost tribes of Israel and the idea is that one of these tribes made it to America and that's how the plates came to be buried there.
Chrissy: What's special about being a Mormon? I mean, in what ways is it different from other forms of Christianity?
Gina: First, baptism is very important, not just for the individual but also for the ancestors of the individual.
Chrissy: The ancestors?
Gina: Yes, you can bring your ancestors into the Church when you join. And there are very strict rules on drinking. You can't, you can't drink any stimulants, coffee, tea, alcohol. And no cigarettes.
Chrissy: Sounds a bit tough.
Gina: Maybe, but it's been shown that Mormons live longer than the average American because of their healthy lifestyle.
Chrissy: And what about marriage? Is it true that the men can have more than one wife?
Gina: They used to but it's not allowed any longer.

Now listen to the recording again.

PAGE 167 **The rules of American football**

Andy: Before we go to this game, can you tell me a little bit about the rules?
Gus: Sure. What do you want to know?
Andy: Well, I know there are eleven men on the field for each team at one time, but what I really wanted to know is how you score points.

Gus: OK. First of all, you can score points in five different ways. The first is with a touchdown. When you cross your opponent's goal line then you get six points.

Andy: Although they don't actually touch the ball down, do they?

Gus: No they don't.

Andy: You have to in rugby.

Gus: Is that right? And a second way is after the touchdown you can get an extra point by kicking the ball between the posts.

Andy: That's just like rugby union except you get two points.

Gus: And the third way is a field goal - and that's worth three points - which is when you kick the ball between the posts while the ball is in play, not after a touchdown.

Andy: I've got it. And that's it?

Gus: Well, there are two other ways but they're a little complicated and unusual so I won't go into them right now.

Andy: OK. And what about the playing of the game? You can pass the ball forward in American football, correct? You can't do that in rugby.

Gus: Yes, but only once in each play. After that it has to be passed backwards like in rugby.

Andy: But I've never seen it happen in the games I've watched on TV.

Gus: No, it is a little unusual.

Andy: Now the *plays*, what exactly are they?

Gus: A *play* is basically the bit of action between the two scrimmages. So, imagine a player gets tackled with the ball. The game stops and then restarts with a scrimmage - that's when the two teams face each other and everybody blocks and tackles. Then there's maybe a bit of action lasting anything from two to twenty seconds until the next touchdown or tackle or the ball goes out of play.

Andy: I see. Oh, one more thing. How does the ball change hands between the teams?

Gus: It can be intercepted when it's thrown of course, or taken off the other team but the basic idea of the game is to gain yardage and you have to gain ten yards in four plays. If you don't achieve that, then the other team is given the ball.

Andy: It's all pretty complicated.

Gus: No, no, basically it's a very simple game, easy to understand. Now when I went to England, someone took me to a cricket match. Now that's a complicated game.

Andy: No, it's not. If you know baseball, then really it's quite easy...

Now listen to the recording again.

PAGE 169 A Holiday in Florida

An interviewer is talking to the Oldham family about their holiday in Florida.

Interviewer: So how come you chose to go to Florida?

Christine: Well, Roger's company had had a very good year and he got a substantial bonus. And the kids were the right age.

Roger: Kate was 13 and Nick 11... So we thought now or never... and of course for once the erm exchange rate was quite favourable, and we had the money at that point in time, so...

Interviewer: Umm... And er, what did you do?

Christine: Well all the usual really... you know, Disney - which includes the Magic Kingdom, Epcot centre, Sea World and erm... the studios.

Interviewer: MGM or Universal?

Christine: MGM, although Universal are pretty near too.

Roger: Yeah, if you ever do it, you should remember to get erm, not a day ticket, but a er passport I think they call it, you know, yes, a passport which entitles you to visit the three centres... It'll save you a fortune.

Interviewer: Right, that's worth remembering... And what did you think of it, Kate?

Kate: Just brilliant. I mean we had a great time.

Interviewer: And what was the best bit for you?

Kate: The ice creams I think.

Interviewer: No, I meant of the places you visited...

Kate: Well... they were all brilliant. Nick liked the Disney thing best, but I think for me, Sea World was the best...

Interviewer: But don't we have things like that in Europe?

Kate: Yeah... but no so big.

Interviewer: Anyway. And what about the grown-ups?

Christine: Well, of course we went primarily for the kids... The Disney experience, the erm Magic Kingdom left me a bit cold I must admit... the rides terrified me... it did nothing for me... but there were lots of other things I loved like the Epcot centre... you know the erm, science and technology part.

Roger: And of course there was the shopping... all the goods you know like Levi's and, what's the name of those boots you got?

Christine: Timberland.

Roger: ...you know all the branded names, they're still expensive but nowhere near what you'd have to pay over here.

Interviewer: And what about all these stories you hear about foreign visitors being targeted and robbed.

Christine: Yes, I must admit I was very scared about that and there were some really horrible people hanging around the airport but once we er got away from the area and were sure that no-one was following us then it was great.

Roger: Umm, the average American is so much warmer and more polite than over here. The way they look after you in hotels and restaurants is just so much better all round.

Interviewer: Just one more thing... Didn't you ever consider going to Disney near Paris? I mean, after all it's more or less on the doorstep now, isn't it? And you've got Paris and the Louvre and everything you can also go to.

Kate: Yes... but... the thing is, for the authentic American experience you've just got to go to the States.

Christine: And we'd been to Paris loads of times.

Interviewer: So you're glad you did it?

Roger: Oh yes, it was great, it cost a fortune but, after all, well, you only live once don't you?

Now listen to the recording again.

PAGE 170 Street gangs

Tricia talks to Larry Monde about street gangs in Los Angeles.

Larry: Larry here.

Tricia: Hi, Larry it's Tricia.

Larry: Hi, Tricia. What can I do for you?

Tricia: Look, I was wondering if I could pick your brains for a couple of minutes.

Larry: Sure. What about?

Tricia: Well, I'm doing a school project at the moment about erm gangs, you know, street gangs and I thought, now Larry, he's from Los Angeles and he'd be able to tell me something about the erm Crips and the Bloods.

Larry: Right, right. Well I'll do my best but I'm not an expert. To tell you the truth, I wasn't actually born in LA.

Tricia: OK then. Well, I've got a few topics written down.

Larry: OK fire away!

Tricia: Well the first thing I want to know is how big the gangs are and where they operate.

Larry: Well, mm, let's start with the second one. The erm most important area for the gangs is a bit of town called er South Central, which is where you'd expect, it's south of um downtown.

Mind you there's another area called Watts - you know there were some pretty awful riots there...

Tricia: And what about the size?

Larry: Well, let me put it this way... there aren't two enormous gangs as such where everybody knows everybody else, it's like there are hundreds of gangs but they are affiliated, they have loyalty to one of the two big ones.

Tricia: I see... So, how do you know who belongs to which?

Larry: Well, you either wear a red baseball cap or a blue one. I can't remember which is which... The thing is, if you're a gang member you make sure that you don't stray into another gang's territory.

Tricia: Why, what'll happen?

Larry: Well, you could get beaten up or even worse...

Tricia: What do you mean?

Larry: Well, you could actually get murdered.

Tricia: That's terrible!!

Larry: Huh, huh... And there's all sorts of tit for tat, you know revenge killing. A favourite pastime is for these drive by murders.

Tricia: What are they?

Larry: Well, you and your buddies, you get into your car and drive into the other gang's territory and you erm, spot a rival gang member in his blue or red baseball cap and you shoot him.

Tricia: As simple as that... for no reason.

Larry: By and large yes... Law of the jungle... That's how you erm, get accepted as a full member of the gang.

Tricia: Terrible...

Larry: Sure is, you know you sometimes get these programmes on TV where they look at the problem. Most of the kids who get involved are from deprived areas where the gangs dominate...

Tricia: The gangs dominate. What do the police do about this?

Larry: As a matter of fact there's not much they can do. What's more a lot of places are um no-go areas. The police have just about give up there. Anyway, to go back to what I was saying before, TV programmes are pretty depressing. Whole classes from high school end up dead or in jail. It's just hopeless.

Tricia: Mm... how awful. Anyway, what's it like for, you know, ordinary folk?

Larry: In a nutshell, not as bad as you'd think. Well, for the most part the gang members stick to their own part of town and prey on each other, you know a lot of it is drug related anyway, so unless you get caught out where you shouldn't be, you'll be OK...

Tricia: And just one last question, Larry... Does it break down on ethnic lines at all?

Larry: Not really, although most of the gangs are black, you get some erm Hispanic ones too. Mind you they could be either Crips or Bloods. You can't jump to any conclusion just 'cos of the colour of their skin.

Tricia: Right, Larry, that's really great. For someone who's not an expert you sure know an awful lot about the topic.

UNIT 15 Our Common Future

PAGE 176 Listen to these five people talking about their visions of the future.

Speaker 1

Well, I think it is going to be brilliant. I mean by 2025 we'll have conquered most diseases and people will be able to live longer and more fulfilled lives. Genetic engineering will mean there will be plenty of food for everyone and that illnesses will be cured by erm, you know, changing someone's DNA. Also robots and computers will be doing everything. All this knowledge we've got - it's going to do us so much good, you know.

Speaker 2

Mmm. I'm not sure, I have this fantasy, though, that it'll be very tough to tell reality from the virtual reality. I mean... technology will have become incredibly sophisticated. You won't be able to tell the difference between what is real and what is, you know, virtual. People will have virtual families and virtual relationships but without all the nasty bits like rows, illness, death. You'll be able to get a new partner and start again whenever you want. Other than that, well, I think things'll be pretty much the same as they are now.

Speaker 3

My guess is we'll or rather our great-grandchildren will be living on the moon or somewhere else like that. There'll be techniques for putting people into suspended animation and sending them off into space for maybe even hundreds of years so that when they wake up they'll be on some planet many light years away from the earth. One of the reasons for this will be pollution on earth. If we don't get away and start to colonise, then it's highly likely that human beings will just die out. It'll be like Adam and Eve all over again. I was reading this fascinating book which was going on about how they were, in fact, astronauts from another planet...

Speaker 4

I suppose I'm a bit of a pessimist. I mean I think it'll be an absolute miracle if we get through the next twenty years without blowing ourselves up. There's bound to be some sort of catastrophe... I think it's a great shame really that we have all this advanced technology but people haven't really evolved at all, have they? Just look at history from thousands of years ago. The motives and emotions people had then are exactly the same as nowadays. Technology may have improved but, well, human beings certainly haven't got any wiser, have they?

Speaker 5

I really can't think that far ahead I'm afraid. Things just seem to change beyond the imagination of most ordinary people. My dad told me that the first telly his family had was a big ugly box and in black and white - black and white, can you imagine? He had no idea we were going to have colour TV. You know, it won't be long before we have a screen we can hang on the wall just like picture... and now they're talking about 3D TV, you know holograms that'll just be projected into your room, and erm, I've even heard that there won't even be a TV screen or anything like that any more, they'll just project the image onto the retina of the eye. Amazing.

PAGE 180 Renate Gross is talking about the impact of technology on work.

Renate: One thing is for sure, the erm, rate of change isn't going to slow down, if anything it's going to increase. What we are going through is a change which is more dramatic than the first industrial revolution which took place in western Europe in the eighteenth century. Now while the industrial revolution changed things in the space of a hundred years we are going to experience far greater changes in the space of twenty or thirty.

Ian: Can you give me an example?

Renate: Sure. I think the most obvious one is that of the postal service. You know there has been a postal service - guys delivering letters - in its various forms since the time of the ancient Egyptians. All this is changing. Right now lots of postal workers who thought they were in safe jobs have been made redundant because of all the faxes which are being sent. Not only that, you can send information down fibre optic cables and it reaches its destination immediately.

Ian: Yes, it is amazing, isn't it.

Renate: Absolutely, the erm, the invention of print more or less saw an end to the middle ages, and the computer revolution will probably see the drawing to a close of the age we are now in ...

Ian: Will books vanish?

Renate: No, not straight away, they're convenient and portable and relatively inexpensive. What's more this Internet, the thing they call the Information Superhighway, this means that say a professor in Japan will be able to communicate with a colleague in Bangladesh, by computer at the cost of around a local phone call. Fantastic...

Ian: But what about the erm, you know, more traditional professions?

Renate: Ha ha. Well, there's no such thing as a safe job any more. It won't be long before we have computers programmed with say legal or medical information which will be able to try a criminal case more efficiently, accurately and fairly than any human practitioner. The old style professions which used to look as though they were a job for life, well they're fast becoming a thing of the past. You know, you read a book about the middle ages and you come across blacksmiths who made horseshoes, thatchers who put straw on your roof and coopers, the erm, barrel makers. Not to mention people like the letter writers who read and wrote letters for a largely illiterate population. Anyway the point I'm making is that these jobs disappeared. We'll lose lots of modern professions and lots of more basic clerical and secretarial jobs, although to a large extent this has already happened.

Ian: So what do you think the results of this are going to be?

Renate: Um... a mixture of good and bad I think. People who are prepared to be flexible and learn new skills, and who are intelligent enough, will continue to be in demand but for many others the challenge could be too much. My advice to people in the old style professions would be to get computer literate, after all, a few people are going to be needed to produce the programme, er, you know the software and suchlike. I think I should also say that new jobs are always going to be created by developments in technology. If you'd said to someone sixty years ago that their job was going to be either making, selling or repairing boxes which would show pictures in your living room, well they'd have said you were mad.

Ian: They'd have locked you up.

Renate: ...and thrown away the key...

PAGE 183 Listen to these eight different situations.

Question one.

Man: Hi... I've been trying to send a fax but I haven't had much luck... In the end I gave up and I've er delivered it by hand.

Woman: A fax? Right, oh dear that's because the number's changed. Have you got a pen. I'll give you the new one...

Man: Oh that's marvellous. Someone might have told me. Yeah, go ahead.

Question two

Shop assistant: So what happens next? When you press the return?
Well, my guess is there could well be something wrong with the disk you're using. Have you got another one handy? Yeah? Right, try putting that one in and see if it's any better...
That's right... Sometimes they get corrupted... But you've got a back up, you know a second copy...
Good. Listen, I've got a customer, give me, or I tell you what, I'll give you a ring when I've finished with them. OK... yes, I promise I'll do it without fail.
Sorry to keep you waiting, now how can I help you?

Question three

Woman: So anyway, we got this thing for Murray. 'Deviant Destroyer' it's called, and quite frankly I'm worried. It has these really graphic images of violence and, well, you know things on it... I think it's all pretty sick myself. I kind of wish we hadn't got it for him. His teacher said that these games would erm, make him comfortable with the technology, the nursery slopes of computing she called them but me I'm not so sure after all he's only nine and he's well far too young for this kind of stuff.

Question four.

Demonstrator: And the amazing thing about the Newman is that it actually recognises your handwriting. This means that things you erm write on the screen in your writing will actually be recognised and translated into ordinary letters. Let's have a look. There we are. Fantastic eh! It can even read my writing. Now the Newman is even compatible with your PC so all you need to do is plug it in when you get home and you'll be able to transfer stuff as easily as anything. Let's just see how it works shall we? Now, just for this week there is a special promotion and we're offering a ten percent discount off the list price and ...

Question five

Male link man: Now here is Isabella Greenhaigh with news of next's week's edition of Pandora's Box.

Isabella Greenhaigh: And in the next Pandora's Box, the programme that brings you the future now, we'll be going to Tokyo where exciting new developments are taking place with so called smart buildings. There is a special feature too on genetic engineering and the strides which have been made to detect Worrell syndrome in the early stages of pregnancy. All this plus the usual round up of science news. So tune in next Thursday at 8.15 for another fascinating edition.

Question six

Man 1: Broken down. What do you mean it's broken down? Look it's the fourth time this week I've been asked to come and sort it out.

Man 2: But he doesn't know what to do with it.

Man 1: Look, he knows just as much as I do. Honestly. he can't keep calling me every time there is a paper jam, you know.

Man 2: But he says he doesn't know how it works.

Man 1: Well, I don't believe it. It's more like he doesn't want to know. He just doesn't want to get his hands dirty, that's what it is. I'm not the engineer, I'm just another...

Question seven

Teacher 1: Well it's a pretty amazing package, isn't it? I mean, I haven't come across one which would allow you to interact the way it does. You can even check your pronunciation against a native speaker. I wonder where this is going to leave us. If things keep developing at this rate then we won't be needed in ten years' time. Nobody will want language teachers any more.

Teacher 2: Don't worry about it, it might never happen.

Teacher 1: You can say that, but I'm not so sure...

Question eight.

Student 1: So I've got another one.

Student 2: Oh yeah.

Student 1: What do you erm say to someone with a degree, in erm, philosophy?

Student 2: A burger and fries, please...

Student 1: What you've heard it?

Student 2: You told it to me before, not an hour ago... Good grief, don't you remember? You and your jokes!

Language Focus Index